Church, Faith and Culture in the Medieval West

General Editors
Brenda Bolton, Anne J. Duggan, and
Damian J. Smith

About the series

The series *Church, Faith and Culture in the Medieval West* reflects the central concerns necessary for any in-depth study of the medieval Church – greater cultural awareness and interdisciplinarity. Including both monographs and edited collections, this new series draws on the most innovative work from established and younger scholars alike, offering a balance of interests, vertically though the period from c.400 to c.1500 or horizontally across Latin Christendom. Topics covered range from cultural history, the monastic life, relations between Church and State to law and ritual, palaeography and textual transmission. All authors, from a wide range of disciplinary backgrounds, share a commitment to innovation, analysis and historical accuracy.

About the volume

St Paul's Cathedral stood at the centre of religious life in medieval London. It was the mother church of the diocese, a principal landowner in the capital and surrounding countryside, and a theatre for the enactment of events of national importance. The cathedral was also a powerhouse of commemoration and intercession, where prayers and requiem masses were offered on a massive scale for the salvation of the living and the dead. This spiritual role of St Paul's Cathedral was carried out essentially by the numerous chantry priests working and living in its precinct. Chantries were pious foundations, through which donors, clerks or lay, male or female, endowed priests to celebrate intercessory masses for the benefit of their souls. At St Paul's Cathedral, they were first established in the late twelfth century and, until they were dissolved in 1548, they contributed greatly to the daily life of the cathedral. They enhanced the liturgical services offered by the cathedral, increased the number of the clerical members associated with it, and intensified relations between the cathedral and the city of London.

Using the large body of material from the cathedral archives, this book investigates the chantries and their impacts on the life, services and clerical community of the cathedral, from their foundation in the early thirteenth century to the dissolution. It demonstrates the flexibility and adaptability of these pious foundations and the various contributions they made to medieval society; and sheds light on the men who played a role which, until the abolition of the chantries in 1548, was seen to be crucial to the spiritual well-being of medieval London.

T0358897

*To my grand-mothers Simone Ouellet Rousseau
and Yvette Goulet Rousseau*

T0361836

MAKERS
—— OF THE ——
MEDIA MIND

Journalism Educators and Their Ideas

COMMUNICATION TEXTBOOK SERIES
Jennings Bryant—Editor

Journalism
Maxwell McCombs—Advisor

BERNER • Writing Literary
Features

FENSCH • The Sports Writing
Handbook

TITCHENER • Reviewing
the Arts

FENSCH • Writing Solutions:
Beginnings, Middles,
and Endings

SHOEMAKER • Communication
Campaigns about Drugs:
Government, Media,
and the Public

STEPP • Editing for Today's
Newsroom

BOGART • Press and Public: Who
Reads What, When, Where,
and Why in American
Newspapers, Second Edition

FENSCH • Associated Press Coverage
of a Major Disaster: The
Crash of Delta Flight 1141

GARRISON • Professional
Feature Writing

FENSCH • Best Magazine
Articles: 1988

DAVIDSON • A Guide
for Newspaper Stringers

GARRISON • Professional
News Writing

SLOAN • Makers of the
Media Mind: Journalism Educators
and Their Ideas

MAKERS

—— OF THE ——

MEDIA MIND

Journalism Educators and Their Ideas

Wm. David Sloan, Editor

Routledge
Taylor & Francis Group
New York   London

First published 1990 by Lawrence Erlbaum Associates, Inc.

This edition published 2013 by Routledge
711 Third Avenue, New York, NY 10017
2 Park Square, Milton Park, Abingdon, Oxon, OX14 4RN

Routledge is an imprint of the Taylor & Francis Group, an informa business

Library of Congress Cataloging-in-Publication Data

Makers of the media mind : journalism educators and their ideas /
   edited by Wm. David Sloan.
        p.   cm.
   Includes bibliographical references and index.
   ISBN 0-8058-0698-9 (cloth).—ISBN 0-8058-0699-7 (paper)
   1. Journalism—United States—Study and teaching (Higher)
2. Journalism teachers—United States—Biography.   I. Sloan. W.
David (William David), 1947–
PN4788.M35   1990
070'.071'173—dc20   90-39192
                                                        CIP

To Guy and Fay Sloan,

Who Encouraged Their Children To Learn

Editor

Wm. David Sloan
University of Alabama

Contributors

"The Practitioners"
James G. Stovall
University of Alabama

"The Philosophers"
Gary L. Whitby and Lynn K. Whitby
Central Missouri State University

"The Legists"
Charles Marler
Abilene Christian University

"The Theorists"
James W. Tankard, Jr.
University of Texas

"The Methodologists"
Donald R. Avery
University of Southern Mississippi

CONTENTS

Contributors vi
Acknowledgments ix
Preface xi

IN SEARCH OF ITSELF:
A History of Journalism Education 1

1   THE PRACTITIONERS 23
     by James G. Stovall

 Curtis D. MacDougall, Reactionary Liberal 29
 Chilton Bush, Journalism Professional as Scholar 36
 Hillier Krieghbaum, Combination Journalist/Educator 41
 Roland Wolseley, Educator on General Assignment 47
 Edmund C. Arnold, Guru of Modern Newspaper Design 53

2   THE HISTORIANS 59
     by Wm. David Sloan

 James Melvin Lee and Professional Progress 68
 Willard Bleyer and Propriety 76
 Alfred McClung Lee and Institutional Evolution 83
 Frank Luther Mott and Devotion to the Press 91
 Sidney Kobre and Sociological History 99
 Edwin Emery and Ideological History 106

3 THE PHILOSOPHERS   117
         by Gary L. Whitby and Lynn K. Whitby

         Lawrence W. Murphy and Journalism as a Liberal Art   126
         Ralph Casey and Propaganda Analysis   134
         John Drewry and Social Progress   142
         Jay Jensen and Neo-Liberal Thought   149
         John Merrill and Existential Journalism   159
         James Carey and the Cultural Approach   167

4 THE LEGISTS   177
         by Charles Marler

         Fredrick Siebert and the Legal Method   187
         Harold L. Cross and the Right to Know   195
         Frank B. Thayer and Economic Influences   201
         William F. Swindler and the Constitution   207
         J. Edward Gerald and the Political Method   214
         Harold L. Nelson and Historical Continuity   220

5 THE THEORISTS   227
         by James W. Tankard, Jr.

         Wilbur Schramm, Definer of a Field   239
         Malcolm MacLean and "the Iowa Experiment"   249
         Donohue, Olien, and Tichenor
                  and the Structural Approach   258
         Steven Chaffee and Jack McLeod:
                  The Wisconsin Collaborators   268
         Maxwell McCombs, Donald Shaw, and Agenda-Setting   278

6 THE METHODOLOGISTS   287
         by Donald R. Avery

         Ralph Nafziger and the Methods Schism   296
         William Stephenson and Q-Methodology   302
         Bruce Westley, Eclectic Scholar   307
         Guido Stempel and Newspaper Readership   313
         Percy Tannenbaum and the Social Psychology
                  of Communication   319
         Wayne Danielson and Computer-Assisted Research   325

         Glossary of Terms   331
         Index   343

Acknowledgments

The editor and contributors appreciate the help numerous people offered in the preparation of this book.

We should mention first Prof. Roland Wolseley, who suggested the original idea from which the book grew and provided material that he had collected over the years.

Along with Dr. Wolseley, several of the outstanding educators who are the subjects of these essays were kind in their response to the idea and generous in the assistance they gave. We especially appreciate the help given by the late Wilbur Schramm and Professors Edmund Arnold, Steven H. Chaffee, George A. Donohue, Edwin Emery, Sidney Kobre, Hillier Kreighbaum, Alfred McClung Lee, Maxwell E. McCombs, Jack M. McLeod, Clarice N. Olien, Donald L. Shaw, and Phillip J. Tichenor.

For personal insights and assistance in gathering information from various archives and files, we wish to acknowledge the contributions of many former students of the "Makers of the Media Mind," researchers, and organizations, including W.J. "Jack" Bell (East Texas State University, retired), Beverly Bethune (University of Georgia), Del Brinkman (University of Kansas), Donald F. Brod (Northern Illinois University), David C. Coulson (University of Nevada-Reno), Everett E. Dennis (Gannett Center for Media Studies), Hazel Dicken-Garcia (University of Minnesota), Diane Fuller (University of Missouri), Richard B. Kielbowicz (University of Washington), C. Richard King (University of Texas, retired), Marvin D. Koenigsberg (Brooklyn College of the City University of New York), Karen List (University of Massachusetts), Gilbert O. Maienknecht (Central Michigan University, retired), Luigi Manca, Harold L. Miller (State Historical Society of Wisconsin), Cynthia K. Moran (Drew University), Raymond B. Nixon (University of Minnesota, retired), Paul V. Peterson (Ohio State University, retired), Daniel W. Pfaff (Pennsylvania State University), Tom Reilly (California State University-Northridge), O.W. Riegel, Nancy L. Roberts (University of Minnesota), Earl M. Rogers (University of Iowa), Keith P. Sanders (University of Missouri), Ted C. Smythe (California State University-Fullerton), Marcia H. Stout (William C. Brown Publishers), Mary Swartz (College of William and Mary), William

Taft (University of Missouri, retired), Hiley Ward (Temple University), Cleveland Wilhoit (Indiana University), Linda L. Wilson (University of Minnesota), and the Freedom of Information Center at the University of Missouri.

Providing advice of immeasurable value was Dr. Edward Mullins of the University of Alabama, who read the entire manuscript and made suggestions throughout.

We also would like to thank Cecilia Hammond, Cheryl Parker, Li Jun, and the support staff of the Communication Research Center of the University of Alabama for their help with the production of the manuscript; Dr. Charles Self for assistance with the "glossary of terms"; Dr. Jennings Bryant and Dr. Maxwell McCombs, consulting editors for Lawrence Erlbaum Associates, for their support of the project; and the people at LEA for their encouragement.

Preface

Is there any task more likely to meet with disagreement than making a list of the "10 greatest" of anything? In writing this book, making a decision about which journalism educators to include and which to leave out was the most difficult part.

We began by deciding to make this book a collection of analytical essays focusing primarily on the ideas contributed to the field of mass communication, rather than a biographical encyclopedia including every notable educator, for surely the volume would be immensely heavy if every prominent person in the field were included. Thus, our first criterion for selection was the importance and originality of the contribution an individual has made to the intellectual vitality of the field.

Second, because we envisioned this book itself as a contribution to the knowledge of journalism education, we made a decision in the beginning that to be included an individual must have served as a journalism teacher at the university level. The reader thus will not find biographies of a number of individuals who wrote important works on journalism but never graced a classroom with their eloquence.

Then, we divided the field into the most prominent areas of specialized knowledge (practical skills, history, philosophy, law, theory, and methodology) and arbitrarily decided that from five to seven individuals should be included in each area.

We also accepted the fact from the beginning that probably no one else would agree with us fully in the selection of the 38 most important educators the field of journalism has possessed during the last 80 years or so. Each reader will, we presume, believe that several of his or her choices should have been included or that some individuals we have included should have been omitted. We will not be offended by the disagreement but instead are resigned to it.

The most evident omission is female educators. To justify our oversight (except for Clarice Olien), we point to the fact that for most of its history males dominated journalism education. It was not until the last 20 or so years that women became numerous. Although they now make up a growing segment of the field, their entry into it has been recent, and time has not allowed their contributions yet to join the handful of truly exceptional ones. The reader will note that except for a few the educators included in this book are either retired from teaching or are nearing retirement age. Youth is the enemy of fame. We have no doubt that if a book similar to this one is written in 20 years women will comprise a substantial portion of it.

Our hope is that this book will accomplish two purposes. The first is to acquaint readers with the lives of the preeminent figures our field has had. The second is to provide concise discussions and evaluations of the most important ideas in the field. It is only in the intertwining of those two approaches that we can come to a full understanding of the field of journalism scholarship. Too frequently, journalism students and professors as well have thought of ideas as some type of entity unconnected to any human mind, almost as if they materialized spontaneously out of the nebulous region from which concepts spontaneously materialize. Ideas, however, cannot be appreciated fully without an understanding of their creators, for ideas are creations and therefore must bear some of the characteristics of their creators. We offer this book in the hope that students and professors will find it useful in explaining and assessing the most critical ideas in our field, that they will find enjoyment and useful knowledge in getting to know the giants of their field—who, we think most will agree, have been overlooked for too long—and, finally, that many professors will meet old friends.

Journalism education for much of its history has been little more than the handmaiden of the journalism profession. We believe that these biographical essays will demonstrate that in many instances it has been critical in making the media mind.

IN SEARCH OF ITSELF:

A History of Journalism Education

Wm. David Sloan
University of Alabama

In Search of Itself:
A History of Journalism Education

Robert E. Lee received a number of job offers at the end of the Civil War. He accepted one to become president of Washington College, now Washington and Lee University. Believing an intelligent press played an instrumental role in contributing to an informed, responsible citizenry, in 1868 he proposed to the college's trustees that they establish 50 scholarships "for young men proposing to make printing and journalism their life work and profession."[1]

The trustees responded favorably, and in August of the following year the college distributed a circular announcing the scholarships for boys of unimpeachable character above the age of 15. The plan allowed the students to pay their tuition by working in a printing shop. Major John J. Lafferty, editor of the *Virginia Gazette*, offered his newspaper's shop for instruction, and Washington College appointed him to the position of Superintendent of Instruction in Typography and Stenography. Emphasizing printing as an adjunct to a curriculum in the classics, the program then commenced, with six students enrolling the first year, and remained in the catalogue until 1878. Response to the program, however, was unenthusiastic; and newspapers, according to a contemporary, "became facetious over a programme which was inherently absurd . . . [for] practical journalists, who had worked their own way upward by diligent application, knew the impossibility of learning the lessons of Journalism within the walls of a collegiate institution."[2]

Thus began journalism education in the United States. In the years since Lee proposed college training for journalists, it has gone through various alterations and now has become a staple in the curriculum of hundreds of universities, both public and private. The earliest training was technical, primarily in printing.

---

[1]The terms of the scholarship were stated in a circular letter from the faculty of Washington College that was issued August 19, 1869.

[2]Augustus Maverick summarized journalists' reaction in his biography *Henry J. Raymond and the New York Press* (Hartford, CT: A.S. Hale, 1870), p. 356.

The first 4-year programs in the early years of the 20th century emphasized journalism education in conjunction with the liberal arts, particularly the social sciences, a curriculum intended to prepare students to help journalism achieve its full potential in serving society and democracy. By the 1920s, and with increasing force in the 1930s, training in occupational skills had become the heart of the program. In most schools, it still occupies that spot. Beginning in the 1940s, theoretical research was added to the traditional research in such areas as law and history. It took on growing importance in graduate study, even though it still accounts for only a small part of the undergraduate curriculum. Each stage in journalism education brought new approaches and combined them with what had gone before. Today, virtually all journalism curricula emphasize professional training, and many combine them with the concepts of liberal arts, social sciences, and theory.

The importance of professional training can be seen from the fact that journalism departments today supply most of the work force for the nation's news media. Along with that role, journalism education has successfully carved out for itself a niche in academia. One might even say that it has been a casualty of its own success. As it expanded into other fields, such as advertising, public relations, and broadcasting, it frequently adopted a new name, "mass communication" or simply "communication." At some universities, this hybrid has become one of the areas with the largest student enrollment, and it bears little resemblance to the parent that gave it birth.

Despite the growth, journalism education still confronts some of the same, most basic questions and issues it has always faced. Some professional journalists still consider college training unnecessary, if not useless in some of its forms, and scholars in other academic areas continue to question its legitimacy. As new programs for journalism education slowly started and then multiplied in the early part of the 20th century, the opposition's and journalism educators' response created a tension. The result has been one of the most evident, peculiar features of journalism education. One might say it is schizophrenic. It has not known which way to go: Should it become primarily professional, or should it be a traditional academic discipline? Possessing a sense of inferiority to both professional journalism and academia, it has tried to prove itself to both. One inferiority complex is difficult enough to overcome, but two create a severe problem. Criticized from two directions, journalism education has attempted to take divergent paths at the same time. Traveling in two directions, it has never decided on, much less obtained, its destination. Its history therefore has been marked by the question of what the role of journalism education is. Is it to be professional training, or is it to be academic study? If it serves as a trade school for the press, how can it obtain legitimacy as an academic discipline? The consistent thread tying together the whole historic fabric of journalism education has been the discipline's search for itself.

Nevertheless, it would be unfair to say that journalism education has not played a role of considerable importance. At its most elementary level, it has provided many educated individuals to fill positions with the news media. In its job of improving the media, however, it usually has been just the tail wagged by the dog. The new ideas and practices it has contributed to professional journalism have been rare and infrequent. Yet, even if journalism education has made few prominent improvements in the media, it is not difficult to imagine that the media would be operated with less responsibility and competence today were it not for the influx of journalism graduates into the ranks of reporters and editors. Journalism education also has worked a pervasive, though less obvious, influence through the ideas that hundreds of professors have imparted everyday to thousands of students. Most of those ideas have been in accord with the ideas of professional journalism, and thus journalism education has served to reinforce the concepts and attitudes of the field. Education therefore primarily has contributed to the status quo, including its problems, rather than to changing or elevating the practices of journalism.

In influencing other academicians, journalism education has been less successful. Although others recognize the importance of mass communication in today's world, rarely have they turned to journalism educators for explanations. For their part, journalism professors have done little to persuade others of the validity or consequence of their scholarship. Trained as generalists and still tied to the notions of superficial knowledge they found perfectly acceptable during their careers as working journalists, most of them never have acquired the marks of serious scholars. As a consequence, much of their research is based on a paucity of sources and a narrowness of ideas. It does not measure up to the standards of scholarship expected of serious scholars, and their faculty colleagues still think of professors in the journalism and communication programs as mere teachers of a trade and novice researchers.

In defense of journalism educators, it is only fair to point out that they have a task that few of their colleagues face. Although English professors have been able to concentrate their entire careers on Shakespearean scholarship and biology professors have done the same with research on microbes, journalism educators are part of that minority who spent their early career in a profession and then were expected to become scholars. They have had to teach not only practical skills courses but conceptual ones as well. The fact that so many have done both jobs well testifies to their versatility and talent. The number of educators in other fields who, if required, could satisfy a professional constituency while meeting their obligations as scholars surely must be small.

Never, in fact, has the role of the journalism educator been a comfortable one. Professional journalists responded to the earliest ideas of education in journalism with outright ridicule. Their opposition was ardent in the early years and did not diminish for decades. Even today, one sees remnants of that original opposition, with some journalists still believing that the classroom can do little to prepare students for the real world of journalism. Even E. L. Godkin, the intellectual editor of the *Nation*, considered it absurd to establish "a special chair or a special class of journalism in colleges," for the ability to gather and write news was "a gift."[3] Most journalists' arguments in the late 1800s emphasized one theme: Newspaper offices, not college classrooms, were the only place where an aspiring journalist could learn the trade. Henry Watterson, who as editor of the Louisville *Courier-Journal* would soon join the small circle of the nation's preeminent journalists, argued the point in words echoing those of other editors. "There is but one school of journalism," he observed, "and that is a well conducted newspaper office."[4]

Whitelaw Reid of the New York *Tribune* was one of the handful of journalists who advocated education for the field. In a lecture entitled "The School of Journalism," which he delivered April 4, 1872, at New York University,[5] he proposed a model curriculum aimed at providing a well-rounded education for aspiring journalists. It included political history, American and world history, politics, law, literature, modern languages, philosophy, and economics, combined with professional instruction. Reid's ideas typified the early suggestions for a college curriculum, emphasizing liberal arts over practical training. Many of the programs founded in the next half century would use that approach.

Reid's proposal did not materialize at NYU, but officials at two other schools, Cornell University and the University of Pennsylvania, slowly began to move on the idea of education for journalism. In 1875, 3 years after Reid had offered his suggestions, the president of Cornell offered a similar proposal for a Certificate in Journalism. "I have long wished," Andrew D. White said, "to establish general and special courses in our colleges and universities with reference to those contemplating journalism as their profession in life."[6] The plan was to combine education in the

---

[3]*The Nation*, June 26, 1879.

[4]Quoted in Charles F. Wingate, *Views and Interviews on Journalism* (New York: F.B. Patterson, 1875), p. 15.

[5]Quoted in James Melvin Lee, *Instruction in Journalism in Institutions of Higher Learning*, Bulletin No. 21 (U.S. Department of the Interior, Bureau of Education, 1918), p. 8.

[6]Quoted in Barnett Fine, "First Journalism Schools Scorned: University of Hard Knocks Was Only One Recognized by Editors When General Lee Founded First Courses — Now 171 Schools Offer Instruction — Editors Cooperate," *Editor and Publisher* (July 21, 1934): 160. For several items of material in the early part of this narrative, I've relied on Fine's article. Although brief, it provides a readable and detailed summary of the first half century of journalism education, told from the point of view of the positive progress of education toward professional training.

liberal arts with training in the university's print shop. As with Reid's suggestions, President White's came to naught. In 1888, however, Cornell, under a new president, Charles K. Adams, began to offer journalism under the instruction of Prof. Brainard Smith of the English department. The courses remained in the catalogue only briefly, though, being dropped just 2 years after they first were offered.

Shortly thereafter, Eugene Camp, a member of the editorial staff of the Philadelphia *Times*, began to urge the creation of a journalism curriculum at the University of Pennsylvania. In an address to school alumni entitled "Journalists: Born or Made?" he argued that the conditions of the newsroom made it impossible for a newcomer to obtain proper training there. The university in 1893 took up his challenge and began to offer courses in the fall semester under the supervision of Joseph French Johnson, formerly a member of the staffs of the Chicago *Tribune*, the *Republican* in Springfield, Massachusetts, and the *Ohio Tribune*. He believed that the university should "not expect to graduate editors" and therefore emphasized a liberal education for his students.

These early attempts at journalism programs planted the seed for two efforts that began in the 1890s, one initiated by Joseph Pulitzer and another by the state press association of Missouri. Along with a program at the University of Wisconsin established by Willard Bleyer, those two shortly would come to serve as the models for most later programs. In 1892 Pulitzer offered to underwrite a journalism school at Columbia College in New York City. Columbia rejected the offer. Pulitzer persevered. Motivated by a belief in the power of the press and its key role in a democratic society, in 1903 he offered Columbia another gift to start a school, this time $2,000,000. A main culprit in the excesses of yellow journalism a few years earlier, Pulitzer nevertheless believed that journalism needed to be elevated and enlightened. One of his motivations may have been to clear his conscience for the part he had played in yellow journalism. It is clear, whatever his motivation, that he earnestly wanted to raise journalism above the practices that yellow journalism had made notorious. He wanted the journalist to be more than a mere tradesman, and he believed journalism education could make the field a profession and give it responsibility, enlightenment, and prestige.

Columbia had turned down Pulitzer's first offer. It did not jump at his second. President Nicholas Butler and college trustees doubted whether journalism was a legitimate academic subject and feared for how offering it might affect Columbia's academic reputation. They also were reluctant to do anything that might give the impression that Pulitzer or his newspaper, the New York *World*, had an influence on the school—despite the fact that Pulitzer's proposal included a statement to the effect that once he had given the money, he would keep his hands off the program. Pulitzer was so eloquent and persuasive in arguing the case of college journalism education that eventually the trustees accepted. As they had expected, the editor did attempt to influence the implementation of the program, and their wrangling ended only after he acquiesced in their demand that the college have full control. For their part, Butler and the trustees failed to abide fully by the terms of the agreement; and it was not until 1912, a year after Pulitzer's death, that Columbia finally began construction of the building to house the journalism school. It opened the following year.

During the debate over starting the school, Pulitzer wrote one of the most notable arguments for college journalism education ever made. Horace White, the editor of the Chicago *Tribune*, writing in the January 1904 issue of *North American Review*, stated that college journalism education served no purpose. In the May issue of the same magazine, Pulitzer responded that those journalists who placed their faith in the newsroom for training were in error.[7] "What is the actual practice of the office?" he asked. "It is not intentional but only accidental training; it is not apprenticeship—it is work, in which every participant is supposed to know his business." No person in the newsroom, he declared, "has the time or the inclination to teach a raw reporter the things he ought to know before taking up even the humblest work of the journalist." He followed that argument with a second. If journalism ever were to become a profession, it could only do so through college training. With education, journalism would "grow in the respect of the community as other professions far less important to the public interests have grown."

Those two practical arguments completed, he followed them with a final one of more consequence. It was only through education, he declared, that journalism could properly perform its role in a democracy. He believed that education would offer occupational training for future journalists; but that goal, he said, never had been his ultimate one. From the time he began his planning for a school, his "chief end . . . was the welfare of the Republic. It will be the object of the college to make better journalists, who will make better newspapers, which will better serve the public."

Even though the earliest efforts to establish journalism education had occurred in the east, it was left to several schools in the midwest to provide the lead in its development. At the 1896 state convention of the Missouri Press Association, the publisher of the Columbia *Herald*, E. W. Stephens, gave an address on the need of the state and the nation for journalism schools. Perhaps by no coincidence, the University of Missouri was situated in Stephens' hometown. Following his urging, the convention unanimously adopted a resolution proposing a "plan to devote a chair in our state university to journalism, and [to have] the president . . . appoint a committee of three to press the subject upon the attention of the curators of that institution." The curators needed

---

[7]*North American Review* 50 (May 1904): 641-680.

urging, but in February 1898, "[i]n response to a request from the executive committee of the Missouri Press Association," voted to establish a "Chair of Journalism" at the University of Missouri. Beginning that fall, the course catalogue listed a department of journalism and included a curriculum, but for several years they existed in name only. Walter Williams, however, a printer and confirmed newspaperman with a high school education,[8] persisted in insisting that the university institute the program. Finally, in 1908, the state legislature voted funds to begin the first school of journalism in the nation. Williams was named dean. Later, he served as president of the university.

Whereas Pulitzer's goal at Columbia was to improve society through improving journalism, Missouri's purpose was to train journalists for the profession. In 1909 Williams reported to the Missouri Press Association that the curriculum included courses in "history and principles of journalism, ethics of journalism, newspaper administration, news gathering, reporting, editorial writing, correspondence, newspaper jurisprudence, the law of libel, illustrative art, comparative journalism, and newspaper making, which includes all branches of newspaper work." Many schools later adopted curricula similar to Missouri's, with substantial emphasis on courses in professional skills. The year following Williams' presentation to his state press, he stated his philosophy of what he called "the new education for journalism." It "differs from the old," he said, "in its recognition of journalism as a profession, as law and medicine are professions. It does not make less insistence upon the broad, general, cultural education nor does it set aside the training which only practical experience can give. The new education for journalism seeks to supplement these with specific instruction, correlating with professional courses and certain carefully chosen academic courses."[9] Williams' assertive pronouncement indicated that advocates of journalism education now were ready to take their place in academia and alongside their fellows in professional journalism. For several decades afterward, Missouri occupied a position as the premier school of journalism education, and even today it remains one of the better programs for the professional education of journalists.

Even though Missouri holds the distinction of having the first journalism school, other midwestern universities already had offered well-developed programs before Missouri. In 1904 the University of Illinois, following 3 years of offering a series of journalism courses, combined them into a cohesive 4-year curriculum, the first such program in the nation. At the University of Wisconsin, Willard Bleyer taught the first journalism courses in

---

[8]Frank W. Rucker, a member of the Missouri faculty, provides a favorable biography of this education pioneer in *Walter Williams* (Columbia, MO: University of Missouri Press, 1964).

[9]*Editor and Publisher* 10 (Dec. 24, 1910): 20.

1906 as part of a 2-year program. The offerings steadily increased, and in 1912 the university created a department of journalism.

Bleyer held firmly to the view of Progressive reformers of the period that society needed to be improved and that one means to accomplish the improvement was through professionalization of occupations. In those views he agreed with Joseph Pulitzer. "[T]he function of most of the courses in journalism," he reasoned, "is to teach students how to think straight about what is going on in the world at large and how to apply what they have learned to understanding and interpreting the day's news. . . . [I would] be willing to pit the average journalism graduate against the average liberal arts graduate, not on the basis of his fitness to enter upon a journalistic career, but on the basis of his ability to think straight and to apply what he has learned to present day social, political, and economic problems. That, after all, is the final test of the value of a college education, and that is the test that I believe the average school of journalism graduate is ready to meet."[10] The program at Wisconsin, therefore, did not emphasize journalism skills solely for the sake of providing a trained labor force for the newspaper business. Bleyer built a curriculum aimed at helping students understand how the press worked in a democratic society. They learned practical skills also, but Bleyer hoped that his graduates would do more than get jobs on newspapers. He wanted them to help make conditions in both the press and society better. Although his views resembled those of Pulitzer, Bleyer imagined the ideal journalist as a scholar also.

With these schools having laid the groundwork, journalism education fairly exploded. A look at the numbers for the two decades following the founding of Missouri's school will indicate the growth in a nutshell. In 1912, the year in which the American Association of Teachers of Journalism (now the Association for Education in Journalism and Mass Communication) was founded, 33 colleges offered instruction in journalism. By 1918 that number had increased to 91; in 1920, to 131. The following year, the number had jumped to 171. In 1928, approximately 300 colleges offered journalism courses, and 56 of them had separate schools or departments.

All of these programs were designed around either the Missouri concept of professional skills or the Pulitzer-Bleyer concept of studying the press in society, or a combination of the two. The predominant approach was to emphasize broad education with some specialized training in journalism in order to assure that journalism fulfilled its obligations to society. Educators expressed their views in a set of "Principles and Standards of Education for Journalism" adopted in 1924 by the American Association of Teachers of Journalism (AATJ) and the American Associ-

---

[10]Bleyer, "What Schools of Journalism Are Trying to Do," *Journalism Quarterly* 8 (1931): 35-44.

ation of Schools and Departments of Journalism. The statement read in part that journalism education "must be sufficiently broad in scope to familiarize the future journalist with the important fields of knowledge, and sufficiently practical to show the application of the knowledge to the practice of journalism." It should not be, however, primarily professional training. Ideally, the statement said, "a four-year course of study . . . [should include] such subjects as history, economics, government and politics, sociology, literature and language, natural science, psychology, and philosophy. . . . [The] aims and methods of instruction should not be those of trade schools, but should be of the same standard as those of other professional schools and colleges."[11]

The 1930s, the decade of the Great Depression, wrought a change in the direction of journalism education. Many Americans blamed big business for the depression. They lumped newspapers in with other businesses, for American journalism truly had become a business. No longer dominant were the 19th-century ideas of appealing to the popular interests, solving social problems, and supporting political causes. In the modern century, newspaper owners had become businessmen, and they recognized the great potential for their properties to make profits. They became conservative. Amidst the conditions of the depression, critics blamed newspapers for contributing to the problems. Owners, they claimed, consistently opposed government programs and supported political policy and candidates whose main purpose was to protect the wealthy. Newspaper owners themselves, liberal critics such as Oswald Villard and Harold Ickes argued, were more interested in making money than in helping alleviate the severe problems facing the nation and most of its people. Fundamental changes, they proposed, were needed to get newspapers performing responsibly.

One might have expected that journalism education, in such an environment of criticism, would change to help meet the needs. Following Pulitzer and Bleyer's model, journalism education should have become even more concerned with educating students so that they could help bring a new social conscience to the press. Indeed, some teachers in the 1930s joined in the criticism of the press and advocated emphasizing broad ideas of responsibility and democracy in journalism education. In his 1934 presidential address to the American Association of Teachers of Journalism, Kenneth Olson condemned the press for its opposition to New Deal reforms and its failure to be "a champion of [people's] rights." The problem, he argued, was that owners were more concerned about making money than serving the public. The newspaper "has become the voice of an institution representing stockholders' interest in profits. More and more, as it has demonstrated its effectiveness as an advertising medium, the

---

[11]AATJ and AASDJ, Council on Education, "Principles and Standards of Education for Journalism," *Journalism Bulletin* 1, 4 (1924): 30-31.

newspaper has become an aide of business until today it is one of the foremost agencies in our American scheme of distribution. . . . I cannot avoid realizing the social significance of this development. As the newspaper has become more dependent upon advertising it has become less dependent upon its readers and less concerned with their welfare."[12] In the AATJ presidential address 4 years later, Edward Doan, although less ardent in condemning the press, argued for a broader view of journalism education than mere training for a trade. Schools, he proposed, needed to teach professional ideals, tolerance for divergent ideas, and dedication to making the American democracy work.[13]

Just the opposite happened. Rather than increasing its role as critic of the press, journalism education became its defender. Rather than helping to improve journalism, it contributed to the status quo. Rather than studying the press in its broad social context, it increased its emphasis on teaching professional skills. At the peak of public criticism of the press, the AATJ adopted a resolution at its 1935 convention, only 1 year after Olson's address, condemning "those self-appointed critics of the American press who through ignorance, prejudice or self-interest question the fidelity or the integrity of the great majority of the press of the United States in fulfilling its function."[14] Even though a number of journalism educators individually had criticized the performance of the press in failing to address the problems of the depression, the AATJ represented the majority view.

Why such a change took place can be explained by the efforts of the press itself. Despite the fact that college journalism programs had multiplied so quickly in the two decades before the depression, newspaper editors and owners still considered them largely unnecessary. With the onset of criticism created by the depression, the attitude began to change. Even the Missouri proposal, which had received the state press association's backing, had been the butt of ridicule early on. "I remember very well," said the editor of the *County Appeal* in Monroe, Missouri, "when the idea of a school of journalism was first advanced. . . . I recall with some degree of amusement the annual resolution W. W. Stephens would lay before the Missouri Press Association on its behalf. I could not forget the fervor with which Walter Williams always moved its adoption. Just to humor these popular members, all of us would vote for the resolution, then go behind the barn for a hearty chorus of laughter at the idea of training for journalism

---

[12]The text of Olson's address is reprinted under the title "The Newspaper in Times of Social Change" in *Journalism Quarterly* 12 (1935): 9-19.

[13]The text of Doan's address is reprinted under the title "The Job of the Journalism Educator" in *Journalism Quarterly* 16 (1939): 38-46.

[14]"Proceedings of the American Association of Teachers of Journalism," *Journalism Quarterly* 13 (1936): 69.

anywhere except in the office of a country newspaper."[15]

That view had begun to change as early as the 1920s. A number of newspapers and professional organizations recognized that colleges could provide a training ground for reporters and editors. Several encouraged colleges to establish journalism programs based on Missouri's model. In 1921 Joseph Medill Patterson and Robert McCormick, owners of the Chicago *Tribune*, provided the backing for the founding of the Medill School of Journalism at Northwestern University. The efforts of the New Jersey Press Association led to the establishment of a journalism department at Rutgers in 1925. The Southern Newspaper Publishers Association provided financial support for the reestablishment of a journalism program at Washington and Lee. In 1927 the New Orleans *Times-Picayune* funded a chair of journalism at Tulane.

Many professors not only welcomed but sought such professional sponsorship. At a time when some of their faculty colleagues in other departments questioned whether education should be tied closely to professional preparation, a growing proportion of journalism professors embraced the idea. John Drewry, chair of the journalism program at the University of Georgia, which had been founded in 1921, was one who worked energetically to tie education and the profession together. "[A]s editors become acquainted with what the schools are doing," he declared, "their opposition disappears. Education in journalism, once . . . not wholly necessary in the eyes of all newspapermen, today seems . . . to have the goodwill of the active members of the fourth estate."[16]

The growing cooperation worked a change in the academic curriculum. As educators and the press courted one another, coursework became increasingly practical. Providing professional training, rather than preparing students to improve journalism in order to improve society, became the primary focus of education. Practical skills—reporting, copy editing, typography, writing advertising copy—became the heart of the curriculum.

Although universities wished to retain high academic credentials for faculty members, the press wanted instructors whose qualifications primarily were professional experience. Since most instructors already had professional experience, they sided with the press. Among university presidents and faculty outside journalism, there was growing concern about the trade-orientation of journalism professors, their tendency to defend anything and everything that the press might do, and their lack of attention to the press' societal obligations. Some university administrators reacted by urging that, among other things, journalism professors be required to hold PhD degrees. In response, the AATJ adopted a statement at its 1935 convention condemning "as un-

---

[15]Quoted in Fine: 200.

[16]Drewry's views on journalism education are detailed in the essay "John Drewry and Social Progress" in this book.

sound and short sighted any policy that emphasizes the PhD at the expense of adequate professional experience and actual writing pertinent to journalism as a qualification" for journalism teachers.[17]

Such changes placed education within the domain of professional journalism and distanced it from the traditional intellectual realm of university education. Such changes in journalism education were not, however, unique within the university. They were part of a trend. Whereas college education through the 19th century had attempted to provide students with the critical understanding of and ability to participate in their culture, land grant colleges founded beginning in the latter part of the century were practical and professional in their orientation. By the middle of the 20th century, enrollment in professional areas had burgeoned, and a large proportion of the undergraduate population was specializing in career education.

As newspaper owners came under the fire of critics in the early 1930s, they responded by increasing their support of journalism education in an attempt to improve their public image. Journalism educators were more than happy to accept the support. The growing cooperation was evident in the resolution adopted by a joint committee representing four professional organizations and two of the young education organizations, including the American Newspaper Publishers Association and the American Association of Schools and Departments of Journalism. It stated: "We recognize the increasing demand of newspaper organizations for college trained workers. We believe it the proper mission and obligation of schools of journalism to supply the demand. . . . [W]e recommend to the organizations which the joint committee represents that they advance, by word and act, in every proper manner, a greater degree of cooperation between schools of journalism and the press."[18] The cooperation that the resolution promised served the purposes of both. It offered educators official respect from professional journalists. It offered the press a trained workforce steeped in the values and attitudes of the profession, at the same time giving owners, now on record as supporting education, an aura of social responsibility.

Surveying the field in 1934, Barnett Fine of Columbia University noted the change with satisfaction. "Increasingly, during the past decade," he wrote in the trade journal *Editor and Publisher*, "have the press . . . and the schools drawn closer together. . . . No longer is there any conflict between newspapermen and schools of journalism. In fact, editors everywhere have cooperated with these professional schools, drawing upon journalism graduates for the most important positions." Sounding as if he believed journalism education had achieved its most important objective,

---

[17]"Proceedings of the American Association of Teachers of Journalism," *Journalism Quarterly* 13 (1936): 69.

[18]Quoted in Fine: 204.

Fine concluded that "journalism schools are no longer subjected to ridicule and scorn" from the press.[19]

Undergraduate journalism education has remained essentially the same ever since. Some additions and minor adjustments have been made, primarily on the graduate level, but the curriculum remains at heart a nuts-and-bolts training course. Although some of the concepts from graduate education have filtered down to the undergraduate level, professional preparation continues to be the focus of most programs. The ties between education and the profession have strengthened, and a large body of professors consider themselves primarily partners with journalists rather than independent teachers and scholars. They view their role in the narrower sense of providers and advocates for the press rather than in a broader societal and intellectual concept of educators as scholars, thinkers, and critics. As a result, they perform as defenders of the press, as if they were Miladies fighting for their knight's honor. They have acted as promoters of the press rather than as independent authorities ready to critique it when necessary. Their primary goal frequently has been to serve the press rather than the greater society in which it operates. Stated in a historical sense, schools have adopted the Missouri model of education, rather than the Pulitzer-Bleyer philosophy. Yet, many professors do hold to the latter, and some take seriously their role of educating students to understand the media and how they work in society, of helping improve the practices and performance of the media, and serving as critics of the media to assure that the media better serve society. The differences such a philosophy presents to the professional model provides considerable dynamic and healthy tension.

Since the 1940s,[20] the most evident changes in journalism education have come at the graduate level. Attention to communication theory has been the most obvious addition, while the requirement that professors have a PhD has become widely accepted. Those two trends are not unrelated, and both have had an effect on undergraduate teaching and on journalism. Although fundamentally undergraduate education has changed little, graduate education normally takes the lead in providing concepts; and it can be argued that ideas engendered at the graduate level eventually will influence teaching on the undergraduate level. The obvious effects that theoretical research has had on undergraduate teaching, however, and on the practice of journalism are

---

[19]Fine: 206.

[20]For suggestions on how best to explain the history of journalism education after 1940, I appreciate the contributions of a number of my colleagues. Especially helpful were the observations of Prof. Edward Mullins, chairman of the Accrediting Committee of the Accrediting Council for Education in Journalism and Mass Communication. I have taken many of their ideas, but the essence of the narrative is mine. Should, therefore, any explanations be faulty, the blame is also solely mine.

few. Such concepts as gatekeeping and agenda-setting, which came out of communication theory, are unusual in that professional journalists generally are aware of them. Teachers, for the most part, however, have been unsuccessful in applying other theoretical ideas directly to undergraduate instruction in skills. The main influence has been subtler, but perhaps more pervasive, as ideas, theories, and research studied in graduate school have influenced future professors. Although they may rarely mention theory to undergraduate students, they carry the perspectives gained from theory and research into class every day.

Studies on persuasion and propaganda during World War II gave the impetus for theoretical research. Researchers involved in the American war effort were especially interested in the effects of communication, how Axis propaganda could be neutralized, and how Allied propaganda could work its greatest effect. Working in government programs were a number of researchers who had served on university faculties prior to the war. That research would receive increased emphasis in journalism programs was suggested in 1944 when the University of Minnesota's school of journalism established a research division, the first of many that would follow at other large schools. (The fact that it was *large* schools, usually those with doctoral programs, that devoted increasing attention to research should be emphasized, for most schools having no or only small master's programs remained almost totally oriented toward teaching practical skills.) Researchers into communication theory were interested in areas other than professional journalism. They were curious about the effects of communication, the process by which it takes place, and related topics. These concerns took them away from the daily practices of journalists and their skills.

Such research carried educators into studies that offered intellectual challenges that were, for many, more rewarding than teaching professional skills. It also offered a way for journalism programs to gain academic respectability. By focusing on theoretical issues, it helped purge journalism education of the criticism that it was primarily concerned with teaching a trade. It offered individual teacher-researchers a means of raising their prestige in the academe—and along with it, we might add, their professorial rank and salary. Journalism professors who were productive researchers finally began to gain some respect from colleagues in other departments. For the most part, they still were not considered scholars of the first rank, but neither were they viewed as second-class citizens.

Research required, however, specialized training beyond the master's level. Whereas instructors with newspaper experience could teach occupational skills to undergraduate students, more and more schools began to expect their faculty members to conduct and publish research. The PhD degree became a primary consideration in hiring faculty members. As the need for faculty members with doctoral degrees increased, schools recognized the need to offer doctoral training. The first doctoral programs were instituted in the late 1940s.[21] With the universities of Missouri, Wisconsin, Illinois, Iowa, and Minnesota taking the lead, the number of schools offering programs increased slowly at first, to only 8 in 1966. In the next decade, however, the number multiplied quickly so that 20 programs existed in 1975. The number reached 31 in 1988.

In conjunction with the increased emphasis on the PhD, the requirements for professional journalism experience diminished. Whereas a minimum of 5 years' experience had been considered the standard since the AATJ resolution of 1935, by 1960 schools were lowering their expectations. Professional journalists greeted these changes with suspicion, arguing that, as a writer in the trade magazine *Editor and Publisher* said, neither "a Ph. D. [n]or M. A. necessarily has any value to a teacher of journalism." Schools required advanced degrees, the writer argued, "because the academicians hold the upper hand on the campus." The emphasis on the PhD had taken place despite the fact that journalists knew that "[i]t takes an experienced newspaperman to teach newspapering competently." Students, he declared, "get something from contact with a man or woman still panting from covering the latest story. Such a person sparks them in a way the regular classroom teacher can't."[22] Despite the objections of professional journalists, the doctoral degree was becoming as much a necessity as professional experience. Some journalists argued, however, that if doctoral degrees were necessary for academic status, then journalism teachers should not be concerned about prestige. Professional expertise, they believed, should be its basis. "I don't know that they [should] want to become more respected members of the academic community," wrote one journalist. "Many schools are looking for Ph.D.s on the faculty; so that tends to get them away from experienced newspaper types. If they become more accepted, they won't necessarily be doing a better job."[23]

As with the PhD, professional journalists reacted to the increased emphasis on research with disdain. They believed that

---

[21]In 1934 the School of Journalism at the University of Missouri conferred its first PhD degree on Robert Housman. During the next decade and a half, however, it awarded only four other doctoral degrees, all in 1940. In 1949 the program resumed and has operated without interruption since. Erika J. Fischer and Heinz-D. Fischer, compilers, *50 Years of Communication Research: A Bibliography of M.A. theses and Ph.D. dissertations from The School of Journalism, University of Missouri-Columbia, 1921-1971* (Columbia: University of Missouri, 1972).

[22]Dwight Bentel, "Want a Teaching Job? Line Forms on Right," *Editor and Publisher* (Jan. 5, 1957): 46.

[23]Loren Ghiglione of the Southbridge, Mass., *News*, quoted in "1990 — Journalism Education in the Next Decade. 19 Big Questions and a Host of Answers," 1982 report of the Journalism Education Committee of the Associated Press Managing Editors Association: 22.

research that did not have practical application to the needs of newspapers was useless. One participant in a conference of members of the Associated Press Managing Editors Association expressed the attitude of many journalists when he observed that most research conducted by educators had no value. "I look," he said, "at the quarterlies that these scholarly people put out. But I find very little of practical value that comes out of these journalism research publications. They are normally written in a way that hardly represents anything that I would expect from people coming from a journalism school. They don't seem to have much practical orientation. They certainly aren't like the kinds of material that I see coming from newspaper research departments or research consultants. . . . [B]y and large, I have not been very impressed by the journalism research that I've seen, as a source of practical application and assistance for newspapers."[24]

Researchers responded to such criticism by pointing out that research does not have to be applied research to be valuable. One role of research is to expand understanding and intellectual horizons. Its practical benefit may not be immediately recognizable, but it contributes to the vast field of knowledge and in the long run may improve how people think and act. Others responded that it was not the role of a university to conduct research primarily for the benefit of an industry. If newspapers wanted particular research done, they argued, newspapers should hire researchers. Furthermore, they pointed out, journalists never have shown much interest in research and have made little attempt to understand or use that which has been accomplished.

In their criticism, however, that much of the research done by educators was arcane, journalists found many professors who agreed. "Do you read *Journalism Quarterly?*" one journalist asked rhetorically. "Well, they have these charts that X equals Y minus 9 and all that crap. I've given up. I've spent more time trying to figure that out, and I finally found that it was totally worthless.... I went to [a] journalism educators' convention. . . . And I went around to these different sessions, and I never heard so much crap in my life. Research papers on little known facts. . . . And some guy gets his Ph. D. on this strength."[25] Educators surely would not use such language publicly, but many could be found arguing just as strongly that research was not addressing broad or important topics. Too much of it dealt with trivialities. The reasons were numerous, but many researchers simply had limited perspectives from which they viewed the problems to be addressed. There was wide agreement among faculty critics that one cause of the problem was the "publish-or-perish" syndrome, requiring that young faculty members publish reports of their research in order to retain their jobs. That led researchers to examine situations that could be conveniently studied rather than issues that

[24]Larry Fuller of the Sioux Falls *Argus Leader*, quoted in ibid.: 24.
[25]Richard Leonard of the Milwaukee *Journal*, quoted in ibid.: 23.

possessed importance.

For various reasons, student enrollment in journalism programs steadily increased beginning in the 1960s. Although journalists criticized the nature of research being conducted in the schools, newspapers obtained greater and greater numbers of their staff members from the schools. In 1960, approximately 11,000 students were enrolled in journalism and mass communication programs. In 1973 the number had increased to 48,000. By 1988 it had jumped again to approximately 140,000.[26] It is true that among the more recent figures were large numbers of students majoring in fields other than journalism, especially advertising and public relations. Still, journalism programs provided a growing percentage of reporters and editors. In 1987, despite the claims of many editors that they preferred staff members with degrees in fields other than journalism, journalism graduates accounted for 85% of all new employees hired by daily newspapers. On campuses, the large enrollments also aided mass communication programs in a pragmatic way. University administrators could not ignore their largest programs, and increased funding often followed the recognition. Rarely, however, did departments consider the funding adequate to keep up with the increased needs, and many found themselves fighting for funds to which better established departments had staked their claims years earlier.

Surveying the half-century of journalism education since the University of Missouri had started its program, a writer in *Journalism Educator* in 1958 gave a reasonably accurate assessment of its progress. It had grown, he wrote, "from the fumblings of infancy and the uncertainties of childhood into an adolescence marked by a surprised recognition of increasing power." Attempting to predict its future course, he observed that it was "entering a period of maturity, a maturity notable, thus far, for introspective self-criticism and self-conscious striving toward improvement." The writer was unreasonably favorable in his judgment that journalism education had won a place with both professional journalists and academicians, but he nevertheless accurately observed that journalism education had made considerable contributions by turning out graduates to work in professional journalism and by conducting research and criticism.[27]

Nevertheless, today, three decades after that assessment, many journalists continue to question the value of journalism study. In 1983, a survey of editors (almost half of whom had majored in journalism in college) found that a substantial proportion believed that the study of liberal arts would be more valuable

---

[26]The enrollment figures are taken from the annual reports published in *Journalism Educator*. Paul Peterson wrote each one until 1988, when Lee Becker assumed the task.

[27]Simon Hochberger, "Fifty Years of Journalism Education," *Journalism Educator* 35 (1958): 2-5, 24.

for future journalists than the practical techniques learned in journalism schools. Epitomizing that view, Bill Hosokawa, editor of the editorial page of the Denver *Post*, declared that his years of experience made it apparent that "the nuts-and-bolts journalism courses were valuable in getting a running start in newspapering, but the liberal arts parts of my education (English, history, political science, sociology, philosophy, etc.) were much more important in handling my job."[28] Such views, which have been common since the beginning of journalism education, suggest an irony: While educators were attempting to professionalize their programs in order to serve the press, there was a widespread belief among professional journalists that such training had questionable value. Education was the lover scorned.

Journalists' ideas about education, on the other hand, have not always been thought through fully. Although claiming they would prefer students with a liberal arts education, many of those same journalists have criticized schools for not training students adequately in journalism techniques. Their principle of argument has been this: When they have new reporters with journalism degrees who understand techniques, they would prefer to have reporters with a broad education; when the new reporters have a broad education, their employers complain that schools have failed to teach them the principles of journalistic techniques. Newspaper size can explain some of the paradox. Bigger papers have preferred reporters and editors well-educated in humanities and social sciences. Smaller ones have been interested primarily in beginning reporters who possess basic skills, who can take on assignments and hit the ground running, and who additionally bring the prestige of a college degree to a small staff.

Part of the explanation for the inadequacy of graduates has been the decline in intellectual ability as larger and larger proportions of the American populace have gone to college. Students of average ability have tended to shy away from intellectually challenging disciplines such as history or philosophy and to be attracted to professional areas. Such areas emphasize skills more than the rigorous thinking required in some of the traditional scholarly disciplines, and they offer occupational training and the direct path to a job, which for most students is the goal of education. Journalism schools have had more than their share of such students. The average level of ability of graduates has declined, not only in journalism but throughout the university, meaning that more journalism students with unexceptional talent have entered the workforce. The low salaries newspapers pay have exacerbated the problem of mediocre students. With average beginning yearly salaries around $15,000 on newspapers, many of the best students, especially males, have found fields such as economics, engineering, marketing, science, law, business, and

---

[28]Quoted in James Johnson, "The value of a J-school degree," *Editor and Publisher* (Feb. 12, 1983): 44.

medicine more appealing. Only a small percentage of students who select journalism have mastered both basic journalistic techniques and the broad fields of liberal arts by graduation time. Such students are the ideal ones whom editors want to find, but they have become as rare as good newspapers.

Part of the reason for journalists' complaints is a continuing difference in their beliefs and those of universities about the role of journalism education. Journalists believe the curriculum should combine liberal arts with training in journalistic techniques with the primary purpose of preparing students for newspaper work. Most teachers share that view, considering it adequate to teach little more than basic skills in journalism courses. Many others, however, are unconvinced that the primary function of education is to teach occupational skills or that the role of university is simply to provide workers for an industry. They believe education must help students to understand a complex world and to develop intellectually. The extreme effect that those differences can produce was illustrated in the program the Allied Daily Newspapers organization instituted in 1986. This group of 55 newspapers in the Pacific Northwest and Alaska created a system of evaluating the 14 college journalism programs in the region. The newspapers were concerned that some schools were giving too much attention to theory and not enough to basic skills. They also hoped to induce professors to work more closely with the press. Most schools in the region agreed to participate in the program. The faculty, however, of the most prestigious one, the University of Washington, voted unanimously not to do so. In explaining the faculty reasoning, the chair of the journalism school wrote Allied that its "proposal seeks to prescribe such matters as specific courses, faculty activities, and criteria for staffing, the authority for which has traditionally and by legislation rested with the University. . . . It is incumbent upon us to exercise this authority with due consideration for the interest not only of daily newspapers but of all the constituencies in this State. These include students, other prospective employers, and the public interest that demands a balancing of competing claims."[29] The president of Allied responded that the Washington faculty members were "paranoi[d]." Rather than dealing with the school, he said, he would give his "energy and financial resources to those schools of journalism/commmunications . . . which have the same goals and interests as I do. . . . Your program will not be evaluated and therefore will not be recommended."[30] At its 1987 national convention, the Association for Education in Journalism and Mass Communication adopted a resolution supporting the faculty's position.

---

[29]Letter, Dr. Kurt Lang, director of the School of Communications, University of Washington, to Ted Natt, editor and publisher, Longview (Wash.) *Daily News*, June 8, 1987.

[30]Letter, Ted M. Natt to Kurt Lang, June 12, 1987.

Such an attempt by a group of newspapers reveals that thinking about journalism education remains limited. Despite more than a century of experience, members of the press frequently think of education as little more than a source of skilled employees. Many, if not most, journalism teachers likewise have no broader view of their role than to train students in journalistic practices and to serve as advocates of the press. A distinct minority have established themselves as serious scholars.

Still, it is undeniable that journalism education has exercised a pervasive influence. That influence has been felt primarily through education's ability to produce thousands upon thousands of graduates trained in the skills of journalism and steeped in the traditions and value systems of the press. Also of importance have been the ideas and innovations produced by a number of individual educators. Along with the thousands of their less famous colleagues, they have served as a major force in American journalism in the 20th century, as makers of the media mind.

1

The Practitioners

James G. Stovall
University of Alabama

The Practitioners

The need to teach journalistic skills has been both a boon and a burden to journalism educators. It was especially so to the educators in the 1920s through the 1940s, as they dealt with four major challenges facing them and their programs.

1. They had to establish programs in journalism education that were both practical enough for the profession they were trying to serve and scholarly enough to reside in academia.
2. They had to recruit into their ranks people who were skilled and experienced in the profession but were also committed to teaching and to the concept of journalism education.
3. They had to develop a curriculum that would go beyond the teaching of basic reporting, writing, and editing courses.
4. They had to produce a literature of journalism education—a body of material from which journalism teachers could choose course material and upon which the discipline of journalism education could build.

First and foremost, they had to establish the legitimacy of journalism education and particularly the teaching of journalistic skills on campus. Within academia, they sought to make journalism programs full-fledged units of the scholarly community, trying to take them beyond the technical school reputation they had acquired. At the same time, they had to maintain contact with the journalism profession and cultivate the goodwill and support of professionals by offering courses that taught students the practice of journalism. They also had a duty to their students to assure that they received the training they needed to make a good start in their first jobs.

Journalism education's search for legitimacy was necessitated by critics in both the profession and in other areas of academia who could offer many reasons why journalism programs should not exist. Professionals often complained that journalism courses could not give students the training in journalistic skills they *really* needed in order to survive in the profession. Consequently, they maintained, colleges and universities should turn out broadly educated liberal arts students and leave the training of journalists to the journalists. Academic critics, on the other hand, argued that as long as journalism programs had to concentrate on teaching skills, rather than on the role of journalism and communication in society, they would continue to be second-class academic citizens.

Journalism educators tried to satisfy both sets of critics. On the one hand, they had to prove their worth to the profession by taking their programs beyond the teaching of basic skills, making sure journalism students were more than liberal arts students who had taken a few skills courses. They sought to integrate the liberal arts curriculum into the developing journalism curriculum in such a way as to put their particular stamp on the students and to make sure that students had, indeed, a broad base of liberal arts courses. The emphasis that journalism education put (and still puts) on the liberal arts, even in its own skills courses, led many journalism educators to believe that journalism students were even more exposed to the liberal arts than liberal arts majors.

Another part of the struggle to establish journalism education programs, of course, was the need to recruit good people to become educators. Even today few people decide early in life that they want to be journalism teachers. In the first half of the 20th century, a career as a college journalism teacher was almost unknown. It was not a job to which many people naturally aspired, and the paths to it were many and varied. For the most part, faculty members were recruited from the ranks of the profession, but why they chose the classroom over the newsroom is often unclear. In looking at how each of the "practitioners" examined in the following pages entered the field of journalism education, one is struck by the lack of a "Damascus road experience" on the part of any of them. Asked what made him turn from a reasonably successful career as a journalist in Washington and elsewhere to a journalism teaching job in Manhattan, Kansas, Hillier Krieghbaum could identify no single reason or experience. Likewise, Roland Wolseley writes about his entry into the teaching profession: "Three years at the [newspapers where he was then working] were enough for me, and the taste of part-time teaching at the university level was pleasing. Full time, I thought, could be still more so. And it was."[1] Edmund Arnold, as an employee of Mergenthaler, had spent much of his time leading seminars and workshops, and the switch to a journalism faculty represented little change to him. Suffice it to say that those who entered journalism education during the period of its formation were those committed to an idea that journalism was a legitimate classroom subject.

They often were faced with the question: after reporting, writing, and editing, what? The journalism education curriculum was by no means standard, and the early educators found themselves

---

[1] Roland Wolseley, *Still in Print* (Elgin, IL: David C. Cook, 1985), p. 62.

groping about, creating courses where personal inclination or professional necessity led them. Courses in specialized reporting often depended on a faculty member with a special interest in the area. What about editorial writing—was that something that could or should be taught to aspiring journalism students? (Didn't journalism teachers have enough trouble getting the concept of objective reporting across to their students without encouraging them to write editorial opinion? And how soon could a student reasonably expect to become an editorial writer?)

Gradually journalism educators realized that their curricula, with some exceptions, had to be tied to the basic skills of reporting, writing, and editing. They needed to establish courses that further developed students in these areas and that gave them some deeper understanding of the problems and challenges they would encounter as professionals. Chilton Bush's course in "Reporting of Public Affairs" (discussed more fully in the following biography) was a good example of how journalism educators sought to marry the skills curriculum with the liberal arts basis that they felt journalism students needed. Here was a way of putting the journalism education imprint on a liberal arts subject and further legitimizing the worth of the journalism program. Curriculum development, however, was no simple matter with simple answers. Deciding what should be taught, in addition to *how* it should be taught, is a matter of continuing debate, and journalism educators have never found the answers easy.

The final challenge of early journalism education—and perhaps one of its most formidable—was developing a body of literature, especially textbooks, that could be used in the classroom. To say that in the 1920s, 1930s, and 1940s there was a scarcity of textbooks in journalism is to make a vast understatement. The reasons for this scarcity are simple and obvious. The field was new, and the curriculum offerings were unstable. More often than not, journalism instructors were faced with gathering their own material to use in a course. A few of the more ambitious ones continued to develop this material and found publishers. A few, but not many.

Even in the 1990s, publishers describe journalism and mass communication as an "underpublished" field. Journalism instructors find that textbooks for courses as basic as "advanced reporting" are not in abundance, and they are forced to do what their predecessors did—gather their own material and teach without a text. Some of the books that are available have been on the market for years and exist with periodic though not extensive updates.

Why has this happened—particularly in a field devoted to writing and blessed with many good writers? Were the early books written by the pioneers of journalism education so good that they limited the literature in the field from expanding? Although some of those books were very good, they also had their critics. Curtis MacDougall's *Interpretative Reporting*,[2] possibly the most widely used book in the professional skills area, has faced continuing criticism. It serves as an illustration of what has happened in this area.

From the beginning of journalism education, there has been some general agreement on what should be taught in the areas of basic skills and on a general approach to basic journalism training. Students should learn how to gather facts; they should have some knowledge of how to interview people and how to look things up. Students should be skilled in writing—putting those facts into the forms of writing that are acceptable to news organizations. Students should also have some knowledge of how to present their information to the public; they should know the rudiments of editing in the broadest sense of the term. There has been little disagreement about any of this and practically no new approaches to the teaching of journalistic skills. Even when Mac-Dougall offered a slightly different approach with his title, *Interpretative Reporting*, a close reading of the book found that there was little that was new or even different about what he had to say.

Consequently, innovation has not been a characteristic of the teaching of journalistic skills. Yet innovation is not the only criterion by which this area of journalism education should be measured. Those "makers of the media mind" selected for inclusion in this section were leaders because they were challenging teachers and because they directed their efforts and talents to the creation of a literature for the practice of journalism. They helped establish journalism education as a full-fledged member of academia while at the same time maintaining the connections necessary with the journalism profession. Their work helped mold the skills courses that are a part of every journalism program; and even though none is any longer active in the classroom, all continue to exercise great influence on journalism education.

---

[2]*Interpretative Reporting* was first published in 1938 and is currently in its 9th edition. The latest edition (New York: Macmillan, 1987) was co-authored by Robert Reid.

Curtis D. MacDougall, Reactionary Liberal

Many adjectives could be used to describe Curtis MacDougall (1903-1986): acerbic, liberal, prolific, narrow-minded, insightful, kind-hearted, irritating. He was all of these things and more. For more than 40 years, he was one of journalism education's "characters," a many-faceted man with strong opinions, a quick mind, and a seemingly unlimited capacity for work.

The most accurate long-term adjective for MacDougall, however, might be "influential." His basic reporting text, *Interpretative Reporting*,[1] has been in print for more than 50 years and has been used at one time or another by almost every journalism education program in the country. His students number in the thousands, and his admirers are legion. His many books, articles, and speeches helped set the tone and added to the debate surrounding journalism education for a half century. It is unlikely that his death in 1986 will remove the long shadow that he cast over his profession and his discipline.

MacDougall was born in 1903 in Fon du Lac, Wisconsin, the son of a doctor and a schoolteacher. His father wanted him to follow in his own footsteps and become a physician; his mother hoped he would go into the ministry. By the time he was 15, he had made his own choice—newspapers. He was working as a part-time reporter for the Fon du Lac *Commonwealth Reporter*. He began earning $1 a week and continued with the paper for 5 years until he was earning $7.50 for a 6-day week.[2]

He received a bachelor's degree from Ripon College in 1923, a master's degree in journalism from Northwestern University in 1926, and a doctorate in sociology from the University of Wisconsin in 1933. (Three decades later, in 1965, he received a LittD from Columbia College.) During this time MacDougall took on reporting jobs for the Two Rivers (Wis.) *Chronicle*, the Chicago

---

[1] Curtis MacDougall, *Interpretative Reporting* (9 eds.) (New York: Macmillan, 1938-1987). The 9th edition is co-authored by Robert Reid.

[2] Edward H. Eulenberg, "Blacklisted in 1984?" *North Shore* (December, 1984): 50-51.

Bureau of United Press (where he covered the last hanging in Illinois), and the St. Louis *Star-Times*. He was editor of the Evanston (Ill.) *News-Index* from 1934 to 1937, during which time the paper won the grand award from the National Editorial Association. From 1939 to 1941, he was the state supervisor of the Illinois Writers' Project and oversaw the work of Saul Bellow, Nelson Algren, and Studs Terkel among others. He also served briefly as an editorial writer for the Chicago *Sun* in 1942.

His first foray into journalism education came in 1927 when he was head of the journalism courses at Lehigh University. There he published the *Brown and White Style Book*, in 1928, the early forerunner of his famous reporting text. In 1932, while he was a graduate assistant in the school of journalism at the University of Wisconsin, an expanded version of this small book, retitled *A College Course for Beginning Reporting*, was brought out by Macmillan and Company. Finally, in 1938, the book appeared as *Interpretative Reporting* and has been a staple of the journalism education literature ever since. The original 1938 title had been *Beginning Reporting*, but MacDougall changed it to emphasize the responsibilities that a reporter had. (He later said that he chose "interpretative" over "interpretive" because that was the preferred spelling in his dictionary at the time; with that choice, MacDougall has managed to raise eyebrows ever since.)[3]

An underlying theme of the book—one that is reflected in the title and that remained constant through the nine editions of the work—was that of reporter responsibility. MacDougall felt that many of the most important decisions made on the newspaper were made by reporters. They made the initial decisions about what to select for their stories and what to leave out. (MacDougall paid little attention to the role of the editor; ideally, he believed, an editor should play a supporting role for a reporter.) MacDougall favored giving more power and responsibility to the reporters, allowing them to make a larger share of the judgments about what news is and how it should be handled.

An example of this attitude can be found in the preface to the fifth edition, published in 1972. MacDougall discussed the then-current trend toward "new journalism," something many editors and educators viewed with alarm. He sympathized with those journalists who wanted to break out of the restrictions that many news organizations had applied. Discontent among young journalists, he pointed out, was not only a product of the times but was "almost entirely in opposition to what is considered excessive conservatism in news and editorial policies."[4]

Although he did not say so directly, MacDougall probably agreed with the young journalists of the day who felt that the journalistic profession, rather than being too liberal as Spiro Agnew had charged, was too conservative, timid, and reactionary.

---

[3]Ibid., p. 52.

[4]*Interpretative Reporting* (5th ed.), p. vi.

He wrote:

> These young idealists want more investigations, not merely to uncover political and governmental crookedness but also to ferret out weaknesses in the social and economic environment as well. They believe that the communications media should crusade more and should be interpretative to explain why bad situations exist. They cite the examples of Rachel Carson, who sounded the first important warnings against pollution in *Silent Spring* a decade or more before the press took up the cause; of the veteran iconoclast Vance Packard with *The Hidden Persuaders* and many other exposes; of Ralph Nader, who began pleading the consumer's cause in *Unsafe at Any Speed* and who continues to report on unsavory conditions which newspapers in the past have ignored. The young liberals recall Lincoln Steffens and other journalistic muckrakers of the early part of the century and want to know why the communications media have abandoned the crusading role to others today.[5]

Undoubtedly, MacDougall wanted to know that as well. Yet, he showed his conservative side too. On the very same page as these words appeared, he argued that this New Journalism, if it were to have a lasting impact, would have to be "built on the same rules that have dominated news gathering and writing for a long, long time. . . . The author remains convinced that the first step upward in journalism is through mastery of the fundamentals of thorough, objective reporting."[6]

MacDougall argued that an interpretative approach to reporting demanded that students not only be thoroughly trained in reporting methods but that they also be equipped to understand what they were reporting, that they realize that events are part of a continuum, and have causes and effects, and that the journalists themselves should be free of the prejudices that would hinder their understanding of these events.

One of the criticisms leveled at *Interpretative Reporting* when it was first published in 1938 and continued through most of its editions was that it did not do what its name implied. As good a basic reporting text as it was, it did not teach or adequately explain the art of interpretation and how a reporter should apply it. One sympathetic critic was Chilton Bush, long-time professor at Stanford University, who reviewed the 1938 edition for *Public Opinion Quarterly.* "In no respect does it supply—as the title suggests—an explanation of a separate and, perhaps, higher technique, viz., interpretative writing. It does not even analyze the method of *Time*, although it cites that magazine's success and points to it as 'an indication that the public is not satisfied with

---

[5]Ibid., pp. vi-vii.
[6]Ibid., pp. viii.

the mere objective reporting of the news.'"[7]

The ninth edition (published in 1987 and co-authored by Robert Reid) is still having difficulties in those regards. It devotes only two pages to the "interpretative viewpoint," much of which is a description of the development of fuller reporting than was the case before World War I. An analysis of what "interpretative reporting" is and a systematic means of applying that concept to reportorial situations are still absent from the book.

Yet this deficiency should not obscure the book's worth as a beginning reporting text, and nothing can argue against its long-lived usefulness to journalism teachers. It has provided them with an excellent tool for introducing the world of reporting to students. Each edition has been full of current examples that provide small case histories of the author's points. The book has remained a vital influence in journalism education, in part through the sheer will power and hard work of the author. MacDougall never let a new edition come out without some substantial revision. (This practice brought some friendly criticism from fellow journalism professors who did not like what they considered MacDougall's "wholesale changes" from edition to edition.) He tried to keep pace with current trends in both society and journalism, including chapters on environmental coverage and the nuclear age when those issues presented themselves. Whatever its faults, *Interpretative Reporting* has remained a textbook that many teachers have refused to abandon, despite many temptations to do so.

MacDougall joined the journalism faculty at Northwestern University in 1942 and remained there until his retirement in 1971. One estimate has the number of students who came under his tutelage at more than 5,000, and there is little doubt that his influence stretched across a broad expanse of the journalistic profession. One former student said of him, "I never had a teacher I respected more, worked harder for or was challenged more by than a man named Curtis MacDougall. . . . He was known as a stimulating lecturer who'd work students beyond exhaustion while teaching them more than they thought they'd ever know."[8] MacDougall developed a reputation for hardrock integrity and for demanding that students think. His own views were often extreme, and he welcomed students who would challenge him. He also cared deeply about his students and their personal welfare; more than once, he brought students into his own home to live when they did not have the means to live elsewhere.

He was a force both on and off campus. A political liberal he came under the scrutiny of the Federal Bureau of Investigation; in fact, the bureau kept tabs on him for 30 years, and long after his retirement, when he finally got access to his file, it contained nearly 300 pages. He was never shy about expressing his views. In

---

[7]*Public Opinion Quarterly* 2 (1938): 511-512.
[8]Eulenberg, p. 54.

1948, in the midst of the Cold War, he spoke before a group of editors and journalism students at the University of Colorado and blasted the American press for "aiding and abetting the anti-democratic hysteria." It was a speech to which many of the editors did not take kindly, but it was typical of MacDougall—saying what he thought to those he thought should hear it.[9]

MacDougall ran for Congress in 1944 as a Democrat and then joined the Progressive Party under Henry Wallace in 1948. He became the party's nominee for the U.S. Senate seat from Illinois, withdrew from the race and then rejoined the race. Northwestern University officials, though never taking any overt action, had put pressure on him to withdraw. MacDougall had little chance of winning, but he campaigned anyway on a platform that called for ending the draft, extending of Social Security, and enacting of national health insurance and civil rights protection for all citizens. Some 22 years later, in 1970, he again ran for Congress only to lose in the Democratic primary.

MacDougall's academic interests ranged beyond teaching reporting. He was vitally concerned with the state of American journalism and the role that it played in the formation of public opinion. He produced a number of books on these subjects, including *Newsroom Problems and Policies* (1941), *Covering the Courts* (1946), *Understanding Public Opinion* (1952), *Greater Dead Than Alive* (1963), *Gideon's Army* (1966), and *Principles of Editorial Writing* (1973). All the while, of course, he was updating and bringing out new editions of *Interpretative Reporting*. Each of these books was widely reviewed and sparked both positive and negative comments. MacDougall was in his writing like he was in person—a man who could generate discussion and even controversy.

Possibly his most ambitious work was *Understanding Public Opinion*. He wrote the book with a simple purpose in mind: knowledge of public opinion and how it was formed would make the editor "better prepared to conduct a successful editorial campaign" and the reporter "able to report and write with greater understanding." The subject matter, of course, was not so simple. MacDougall began his nearly 700-page analysis with a highly prescriptive set of points for the reader to keep in mind. They included the thoughts that social phenomena do not just happen but have a cause and an effect; that tolerance of a point of view does not mean approval; that the majority is not always right; that the popularity of an idea and its rightness or wrongness are not related; and that "the proper concern of the student of public opinion should be its 'why.'"[10]

Reviewers' comments were mixed. W. Phillip Davidson, writ-

[9]J. Harley Murray, "MacDougall Lashes Press on War Hysteria," *Editor and Publisher* 81 (May 8, 1948): 68.

[10]Curtis MacDougall, *Understanding Public Opinion* (New York: Macmillan, 1952), pp. v-x.

ing for *Public Opinion Quarterly*, pointed out many of the book's flaws from the viewpoint of a public opinion specialist, but he concluded, "While by no means the perfect text, this book contributes much that would be stimulating and useful to many courses on public opinion and communications. And in a field where such texts are comparatively few this is something to be grateful for."[11] Many of the non-journalism reviewers were impressed with MacDougall's witty and lively writing style. The fact that he stated his opinions so succinctly—always a MacDougall trait—was noted by one reviewer who took pains to quote one of the book's subheads in the chapter about American education: "American schools tend to turn out conservatives and conformists and to discourage heresy in all fields."[12] If nothing else, such writing was a refreshing change for most academicians.

MacDougall wrote the book at a time when the formation and manipulation of public opinion was a subject that touched, and often disturbed, him deeply. His liberal politics had led him to speak out repeatedly against Red scares and Communist baiting, but the times were against him. He wanted his students to understand the many facets of public opinion so that they could adequately deal with it when they went to work in journalism. For him, at least unconsciously, the book was a massive attempt to give meaning and substance to his advocacy of "interpretative reporting." Journalists who wrote about public opinion had to understand what it was about, and this book was his attempt to help them do so.

MacDougall carried a concern about the integrity of newspapers throughout his career as a journalist and an educator. In particular, he wanted a newspaper to present information that it could verify, that it could assure readers was true. He was offended by the prevalence of astrology columns and reports of UFOs, Big Foots, and Loch Ness monsters. Two books, published more than 40 years apart, demonstrate that concern. In *Hoaxes* (1940), MacDougall described many large and small hoaxes that have caught on with the public. He sought to explain them in terms of principles that are the basis of human gullibility: indifference, ignorance, superstition, suggestion, and so forth. In *Superstition and the Press* (1983), he took newspapers to task for their extensive coverage of cults, fortune telling, psychic healing, and the like. "The space given scientists and other iconoclasts is meager by comparison with that devoted to the views and acts of the ignorant, superstitious and gullible," he wrote.[13] One reviewer of the book said that MacDougall "clings touchingly to the notion that newspapers have an obligation to tell the truth."[14] That, of course, was exactly what MacDougall had in mind. Although others

---

[11] *Public Opinion Quarterly* 16 (1952): 292-295.
[12] *Understanding Public Opinion*, p. 529.
[13] Quoted in *The Humanist* 44 (July 1984): 40.
[14] *The Humanist* 44 (July 1984): 40.

dismissed these stories as harmless, MacDougall always carried the feeling that they chipped irrevocably away at a newspaper's credibility.

MacDougall retired from full-time teaching at Northwestern in 1972, but he continued writing and speaking until his death. One of his last great battles was over the shape of journalism education. As a journalist, MacDougall had been a staunch defender, particularly against editors who blithely suggested that future journalists would be better off with liberal arts degrees than journalism degrees. In a speech to the National Conference of Editorial Writers in 1960, MacDougall said that the typical journalism school student was better trained in the liberal arts than the typical liberal arts student. "As teachers of journalism we have to spend fully half our time teaching or reteaching these liberal arts illiterates the background they should have mastered long before coming to us....Most of the faults that journalistic employers find in our products are faults of their liberal arts training which we just didn't have time to correct."[15]

His view of journalism education turned out to be a disappointingly narrow one, however. In the 1960s he alienated many of his colleagues by his criticism of the trend of journalism programs to broaden into communication studies. He scoffed at what he called the "communicologists," the people whose qualification for teaching was a PhD and not professional experience. He felt that the training of reporters and editors would inevitably suffer if the classrooms were staffed by people without sufficient professional backgrounds. He never accepted the idea that journalism itself and the expanding field of mass communication were acceptable fields of study by scholars and researchers and that this study could exist within a professional training program.

MacDougall died in November 1986. He was still writing and speaking, working as usual on a number of projects. One was the ninth edition of *Interpretative Reporting*, which was published posthumously. Another was finding a publisher for *Spilling the Beans*, a chronicle of attempts by universities—including his own—to muzzle liberal professors during the McCarthy era.[16]

He held many opinions, and he had a tight grip on all of them. His position as a giant in journalism was due in part to his longevity and that of *Interpretative Reporting* (which his hard work assured) and in part to the large volume of work that he produced. His enormous energy was matched by an able and lively intellect. He was first and last an interpretative reporter of his time and profession—the kind that he continually urged his students to become.

---

[15]Quoted in Curtis MacDougall, *The Press and Its Problems* (Dubuque, IA: W.C. Brown, 1964), p. 504.

[16]Eulenberg, p. 55.

Chilton Bush,
Journalism Professional as Scholar

During the formation of modern journalism education in the 1920s, 1930s, and 1940s, journalism teachers walked a difficult path between the profession from which most had come and the world of academia in which they were attempting to reside. To go too far into one would mean disassociation and even alienation from the other. Journalism education needed people who were comfortable in both worlds—those who could combine credible professional experience with quality scholarship and those who could build bridges between the two areas. Chilton Bush (1894-1972) was such a man.

Bush was a scholar of the first order. He understood scholarship—and particularly social science research—to the extent that he was at ease working and writing in the scholarly community. He used public opinion research in seeking answers to questions in the communications field, and he did so in a way that brought him respect from both professionals and academicians. He was a specialist in measurement of media audiences and newspaper reading behavior. His professional background gave him a clear vision of what journalism education ought to be, and his talent for writing helped him use that vision to formulate a concept of journalism education that took it beyond the liberal arts.

Bush was born in 1894 and took to newspapering early in his career. He worked as a reporter in Memphis and New York and received his bachelor's, master's, and PhD degrees from the University of Wisconsin. In 1925 he joined the University of Wisconsin faculty and taught there for 9 years. Then he moved to Stanford University to head the Department of Communication and Journalism. In 1955 he established the Institute for Communication Research, later headed by Wilbur Schramm. Bush received much recognition for his work, including Sigma Delta Chi's award for distinguished journalistic teaching; and upon his retirement in 1961, the University of Wisconsin cited him for "distinguished service in journalism."

Bush remained active after his retirement, doing research and consulting for a number of California newspapers. He helped the American Newspaper Publishers Association establish a News Research Center, which he headed for a number of years. The Center issued regular bulletins about research into newspapers, and these bulletins were later compiled by Bush into five volumes en-titled *News Research for Better Newspapers*. The bulletins and volumes contain information not only based on public opinion surveys but also on surveys of editors and reporters about their attitudes and the content of their newspapers.

During the more than 40 years that Bush actively published his research, he showed himself to be sensitive to the needs of his professional constituents but also a scholar who could maintain high standards of research. His special research interest—partic-ularly late in his career—was newspaper readership, and he did yeoman work in trying to answer some of the very practical ques-tions that editors and publishers had about their readers. He was at home with newspaper people, and he wrote so that they could understand the data that he produced and the analysis that he formulated. Bush died of cancer in 1972. His obituary in the New York *Times* called him "a pioneer in communications research and opinion polling . . . [who] had trained hundreds of young men and women for journalism."

In 1929 Bush published the first of two books that were to dis-tinguish him as a journalism educator and help give distinction to journalism education itself. *Newspaper Reporting of Public Af-fairs*[1] went beyond the writing and reporting texts of the time. The book is important because it attempts to combine what the journalism students might learn in social science or liberal arts courses with the specialty skills that they will need when on the job.

Then as now, journalism education was under attack by some in the professional world as being unnecessary. Broadly trained liberal arts students were the people who were needed to staff newsrooms, many editors argued. "Give them to us," they said in effect, "and we'll teach them about journalism." Educators were under pressure to prove that the students they turned out were bet-ter trained than liberal arts students and that their training could be useful. To do these things, journalism educators had to take students beyond training in writing and editing and beyond the information they would receive in a liberal arts course. Com-bining journalism and liberal arts subject matter was the under-lying purpose of *Newspaper Reporting of Public Affairs* and *Edi-torial Thinking and Writing*,[2] published three years later.

In *Newspaper Reporting of Public Affairs* Bush introduced various aspects of local government to journalism students, but he did so with a different focus from the one they would receive in a political science course. Bush began a course at Wisconsin enti-tled "Reporting of Public Affairs" in 1927 and found little in the journalism education literature that he could use. As with most

---

[1]Chilton Bush, *Newspaper Reporting of Public Affairs* (New York: Appleton, 1929).

[2]Chilton Bush, *Editorial Thinking and Writing* (New York: Appleton, 1932).

journalism instructors, he began to gather his own material, and he soon realized that he had enough material for a book—one which would be of help not only to him but to other journalism teachers. In the book, he described how reporters would work in covering the courts, city hall, local politics, and corporations. He paid particular attention to sources of information, such as court calendars and police blotters. He discussed the advantages and disadvantages to the journalist of working "with" public officials, particularly with police in their investigations. He also included some information that he found students would need but were not receiving in other courses, such as the work of the federal government on the local level.

Bush described the various kinds of stories that usually arise from covering government and public affairs and presented numerous examples for the student to examine. In a later edition, he included an expanded discussion of the "fair trial-free press" conflict that reporters must deal with. He also dealt with the "public" nature of private enterprise—the way in which corporations worked and kept their books, how local banks operated, the structure of labor union operations, and so on.

In the preface, Bush claimed two purposes for the book other than presenting material about municipal government: to point out the imperfections of local government so that the reporter can deal with them and possibly help in reform efforts and to give students "a professional and realistic" attitude about the role of the newspaper as a leader in public affairs. (In the first editions of the book, Bush spent little time with the journalistic aspects of writing and reporting. In a revised edition published in 1965 he included much more in these areas, making it a book that could be used for two courses instead of just one.)

Bush's efforts in *Newspaper Reporting of Public Affairs* were well received. A reviewer for *Social Service Quarterly Review* wrote:

> Too much cannot be said in praise of nine-tenths of the contents of this useful and informing book. It should be used as a textbook in all schools of journalism and should be read and reread by younger—or older—students in or out of college who contemplate the espousing of journalism as their life-work. It is in the main accurate, clear, adequate, and well balanced.[3]

The reviewer's only quibble was that the book was "too academic" and the view of journalism too idealized. The reviewer called upon the author to acknowledge that many reporters and newspapers were not committed to accuracy and fairness. "Why not point out that a great deal of the sloppiness, carelessness, superficiality, and irritating inefficiency of the papers is deliberate and

---

[3]Victor C. Yarros, "A Review of Newspaper Reporting of Public Affairs," *Social Science Quarterly Review* 3 (1929): 328-329.

intentional?" he asked. Probably neither of these criticisms disturbed Bush or his colleagues. In seeking academic legitimacy for their field, journalism educators could easily forgive themselves for being called "too academic" by other academicians. And they did not dwell on the faults of newspapers because of the general attitude that in a journalism training class, criticism of the profession was not the best teaching method.

Bush developed an approach to editorial writing similar to the one he had developed for reporting public affairs, but it went even further in combining the disciplines of journalism and the liberal arts. In *Editorial Thinking and Writing,* Bush went beyond the writing and teaching of his day in trying to demonstrate that journalism education is built upon the liberal arts offerings. In observing others' habits of thinking, Bush wrote, "I have been left with the conviction that one thinks better if he becomes conscious of his method of thinking."[4] Bush pointed out in his preface that although some students, such as those in medicine and engineering, acquire a method along with their major field of study,

> The student of journalism often learns the techniques of presenting his thoughts in writing and acquires a considerable amount of information about the social sciences without going deep enough into any subject to acquire a habit of disciplined thinking. This book, therefore—although it discusses the editorial as a literary form, the editor's relation to his readers, and a few other matters of importance to the editorial writer—tries mainly to provide the student of journalism with an explanation of the thinking process in terms of modern social problems, together with a considerable amount of practice material.[5]

Bush did not claim that his book, or a course taught with it, was a substitute for a course in logic. "A good course in logic succeeds in teaching the student an approach to moral evaluation and provides him with a truer sense of ethical values and with some knowledge of speculative science. This book, although it does not entirely ignore the aims of the course in logic, has only a practical purpose."[6] Assigning and demonstrating that practical purpose was where journalism education could distinguish itself as an academic discipline.

Bush's approach to editorial writing provided something of a formula for editorial analysis and method, something that could be used as a teaching tool in the classroom. It also provided students with the opportunity to practice using the formula by analyzing the editorials of others and writing editorials of their own.

---

[4]*Editorial Thinking and Writing,* p. vii.
[5]Ibid.
[6]Ibid., p. x.

The book discussed causal and functional relationships, analysis, analogy, values, and refutation. It suggested that editorials should provide geographical and historical settings, identify and classify forces involved in conflicting issues, and suggest resolutions to those issues. Bush drew heavily not only on the thinking and methods of logic but also on rhetorical theory to teach students about the formation of a good editorial. Bush told his readers that editorial writing involves 10% writing and 90% analysis. "Effective editorials, it is true, are in great measure the result of skillful and apt expression, but even in greater measure they are the product of intelligent analysis."[7]

This art of "intelligent analysis" was what Bush sought to instill in those who read and used his books. In a larger sense, it was deeply ingrained in his vision of how journalism education could work in not only training students to perform in the field but in giving them something extra with which to begin their careers.

---

[7]Ibid., p. 14.

Hillier Krieghbaum, Combination Journalist/Educator

The good journalism professor is the person who has the professional ability to wear the green eyeshade and the intellectual acumen to look beyond it. Ideally, the journalism professor should have enough quality experience working in the profession to enable him or her to understand the challenges and rewards of the work and to gain credibility with students and other professionals. He or she should also exhibit just as much skill in the classroom with an ability to inform, excite, and inspire students who are on the threshold of their careers. Finally, the best journalism professor should have a farsighted view of the role of journalism in society, an ability to ask the pointed and troubling questions about that role, and a willingness to suggest information and solutions to those questions.

Few people fit the above description of "journalism professor" as well as Hillier Krieghbaum (1902-).

He is a man who stood at the forefront of journalism education during its formative years, regarding it as not just a training ground for future reporters and editors but as a means of bettering the profession and the individuals who inhabit it. His two basic axioms for journalism education are these:

> First, train future journalists to know enough to ask intelligent questions, to understand the answers from news sources, and then to present the material so that the general public can understand it. . . . Second, communication teachers should pay attention to training, not only for operating a VDT, but where the graduate will probably be in 25 years.[1]

One of Krieghbaum's great abilities—and one that led to much of his contribution to journalism education—is the gift of clear sight and straight talk. In his 11 books and numerous articles about journalism and journalism education, he has been able to describe clearly and succinctly the customs of the practice of

---

[1]Krieghbaum to the author, November 25, 1986.

journalism and the problems that arise from it. He has been a friend and critic of journalism education itself, willing to admit its faults and face up to its shortcomings and yet always the staunch defender of its ultimate worth. As such, Krieghbaum's voice has been widely heard and respected during his 25 years as a journalism educator and his long career as a journalist.

Krieghbaum was born on November 2, 1902, in South Bend, Indiana. His start in journalism came when he began working on a magazine in high school. He graduated from the University of Wisconsin in 1926 with a bachelor of arts degree in journalism. As an undergraduate, he worked summers on the South Bend *News-Times*, and for several months after graduation he worked for the Reading (Pa.) *Times*. Early in 1927 he joined the United Press news service as a correspondent in New York City. The next year he became UP's bureau manager in Philadelphia and was transferred to St. Paul to serve in the same capacity in 1930.

Harrison Salisbury—later foreign correspondent for the New York *Times*—credits Krieghbaum with saving his job with the United Press. Salisbury was working in the Minneapolis bureau under Krieghbaum when he was assigned to do an in-depth piece on the effects of the Depression. The assignment was an important one because, in Salisbury's words, "The Depression was clamping down on a nation that didn't know what was happening to it. UP was beginning to run stories exploring the situation, and I was assigned to do one about Minneapolis. We didn't then know that the story was the same everywhere, only the details were different. I found that the city was dead; nothing was moving; each day more haunted men lost their jobs." Salisbury interviewed many of these people, as well as civic, business, labor, and social leaders. He put the story together, and it was sent out and received instant congratulations. Following these almost as quickly, however, were complaints from the editors of the Minneapolis *Journal*, who felt that their city had been maligned. They demanded Salisbury's firing. Krieghbaum stood up for Salisbury with the the UP brass and the *Journal* editors. "Somehow Krieghbaum smoothed it all down," he wrote. "He mollified the *Journal*."[2]

In 1933 Krieghbaum began working on a master's degree at the Medill School of Journalism at Northwestern University while also working in the UP bureau in Chicago. His studies were interrupted when he was transferred to the Washington, D.C., bureau of UP, where he was a science writer and late night editor. His interest in science writing remained with him for the rest of his career and led to some of his important contributions as a journalism educator. In 1938 he became an assistant professor of journalism at Kansas State College (later University) in Manhattan, Kansas, and in 1939 he completed his master's degree at Northwestern

---

[2]Harrison E. Salisbury, *A Journey for Our Times* (New York: Harper & Row, 1983), pp. 92-94.

University.

Just after the bombing of Pearl Harbor in December 1941, he returned to Washington, where he headed the UP bureau covering the War Production Board, the Office of Price Administration, the Office of War Information, and other civilian war agencies. Nine months later he left this job to join the U.S. Navy and served during World War II, attaining the rank of lieutenant commander. After the war, he worked for the Veterans Administration as a public information specialist for the department of medicine and survey, and in 1947 he was an information specialist with the World Health Organization Interim Commission, handling public information for a meeting in Geneva, Switzerland.

Many of these experiences contributed to Krieghbaum's interest in science and medical journalism and his more wide-ranging interest in specialized reporting. His books in this area include *American Newspaper Reporting of Science News* (1941); *When Doctors Meet Reporters* (1957); *Science, the News, and the Public* (1958); and *Science and the Mass Media* 1967).[3] (From 1950 to 1960 he was chair of the surveys committee of the National Association of Science Writers and from 1960 to 1964 was secretary treasurer of the Council for the Advancement of Science Writing, Inc. He was a member of the screening committee for the AAAS-Westinghouse Science Writing Awards (1959 to 1968) and a judge in the United States Steel-American Institute of Physics Science Writing Award (1969 and 1970).[4] During the summer of 1960, Krieghbaum was a visiting lecturer at the Japanese Science Journalism Seminars held in Tokyo and Osaka under the auspices of the Asia Foundation and the Japan Newspaper Publishers and Editors Association. In the fall of 1982, he lectured at the First InterAmerican Seminar on Science Journalism at Santiago, Chile. He was project director of New York University's Gould House Seminars for Science Writers sponsored by grants from the National Science Foundation during 1960 to 1962, and for the next 3 years he supervised a study of the National Science Foundation's institutes programs.

Many of Krieghbaum's ideas about the importance of the science writer to the general public are contained in his book *Science and the Mass Media*. There he argues that the "applications of science now underpin our contemporary way of life." He writes:

Despite popular enchantment with the applications of science,

---

[3]Hillier Krieghbaum, *American Newspaper Reporting of Science News* (Manhattan: Kansas State College Bulletin, 1941); *When Doctors Meet Reporters* (New York: New York University Press, 1957); *Science, the News, and the Public* (New York: New York University Press, 1958); *Science and the Mass Media* (New York: New York University Press, 1967).

[4]Information supplied by the New York University News Bureau, May 1970.

many of the more important and complicated problems facing United States citizens today are heavily intertwined with science and technology. They cannot be approached soundly without an appreciation of their scientific implications. Often these require understanding subtle nuances grounded in basic research. To illustrate, think of the background needed to discuss intelligently such topics as population explosion and birth control, uses and abuses of automation, pollution of the natural environment, water conservation and irrigation, uses of insecticides and pesticides, testing of nuclear weapons, peacetime uses of atomic power and the relationship of cigarette smoking and cancer. Before the final decision is made in any democracy, the people should have an opportunity to consider the problems. . . .[5]

More and more of the nation's resources and brainpower are being devoted to science and technology, Krieghbaum says, and the profession of journalism cannot afford to ignore this trend. In this book, Krieghbaum goes on to address many of the problems involved in a marriage of science and journalism—the difficulty of training reporters, the dangers of oversimplification, the distrust of scientists themselves, and so on. He concludes by saying, "Training for science journalism has become too important for a hit-and-miss educational approach."[6]

At the end of World War II, Krieghbaum married Katherine Lancaster, and in 1946 they moved to Eugene, Oregon, where he became an associate professor of journalism at the University of Oregon. He found living conditions there unsuited for his and his family's tastes, and they left after a year. He worked for a time with the World Health Organization when it was in its infancy. "That was not particularly successful," Krieghbaum said later. "Maybe I wasn't cut out to be in public relations."[7] He joined the New York University faculty in 1948 and remained there until his retirement to emeritus status in 1973. He was chairman of the department from 1957 to 1963.

During this time he became a noted writer and commentator on the nation's press. His career as a journalism educator was capped in 1972 with the publication of *Pressures on the Press*,[8] a book that sought to explain the position the nation's news organizations should play in American society. The book was written during a time of increasingly shrill criticism of the press, particularly by officials in the Nixon administration, and the book

---

[5]Krieghbaum, *Science and the Mass Media*, pp. 3-5.

[6]Ibid., p. 231.

[7]Hillier Krieghbaum Oral History, audio tapes, 53706 (August 10-12, 1980), Mass Communication History Center, State Historical Society of Wisconsin (Madison).

[8]Hillier Krieghbaum, *Pressures on the Press* (New York: Thomas Y. Crowell, 1972).

refers to many of the pressures that are exerted on journalists. The book is wide-ranging in its discussion of the roots of criticism of journalism, the role that journalists play in society, the means by which journalists do their work, the rights of the free press and of privacy, and the ways in which journalists can exert control and constructive criticism on themselves.

Although the author offered no startling solutions to the problems facing the press, he did contribute a clear-eyed analysis of the press' shortcomings and the dangers of anyone, even the press itself, in trying to exercise control over its actions. In the end, Krieghbaum proposed the establishment of a system of media review boards at the local, regional, and national levels to act as a forum for those who have complaints against a news organization. He wrote:

> By participating honestly and actively in the review system, the media would gain substantial advantages in the marketplace of public opinion since much of the current resentment against them arises from the frustrated and angry feelings that one's chances of winning a battle with the press are even less than in the proverbial fight with city hall. With some modest successes, the media review boards should damp down such sentiments to a substantial degree.[9]

Writing in the *New York Times Book Review*, Ben Bagdikian called Krieghbaum's book "the best general compendium since Bryce W. Rucker's *The First Freedom* and William Rivers' definitive updating of Wilbur Schramm's survey of the mass media."[10]

Krieghbaum achieved fame in journalism education through publication of his numerous books on science writing, as well as *Facts in Perspective: Editorial Page and News Interpretation* (1956) and *The Student Journalist* (1963), which he co-authored with Edmund Arnold. He served as president of the American Society of Journalism School Administrators in 1960-1961 and was active in the Association for Education in Journalism for many years. That activity culminated in 1972 with his election to the AEJ presidency.

One of his chief concerns as a leader in journalism education was its relationship with the journalistic profession. In the presidential paper for the 1972 AEJ convention, he documented what he called "the shocking separatism between those who teach and those who practice journalism in America today."[11] He did this by surveying the attitudes of journalists working in towns nearest the then 60 accredited schools of journalism. He succinctly

---

[9]Ibid., p. 237.

[10]Quoted in *Book Review Digest* (1972): 738.

[11]Hillier Krieghbaum, "Presidential Paper for the 1972 A.E.J. Convention," delivered at the national convention, Carbondale, IL, 1972, p.1.

outlined what he had found:

> There is a very real communications gap between professors and practitioners. Many of the newsmen had not been on their local campus during the past 12 months and some had not made any other off-campus contacts with their local school's journalism teachers.[12]

Krieghbaum said he felt this gap between educators and professionals was especially unfortunate during a time when criticism of the press was so widespread. "At a time when the mass media are under criticism and attacks as heavy as any in a generation, educators have a responsibility, I believe, to join the professional practitioners in supporting what is good and trying to correct what is wrong."[13] He had spent a good part of his AEJ presidency promoting greater cooperation, and later, reflecting on his tenure as president, he said, "What I felt was that AEJ should work very closely with the profession. In other words, the professors and the professionals have a common goal. They [AEJ officers] should spend a considerable amount of effort in building bridges between the profession and the professors. . . . Maybe we just strung the lines, but I think the bridges are in operation now."[14]

Krieghbaum thus closed his active career as a journalism educator with a plea for more cooperation between the profession and the campus. For him, it was a natural crusade. As one brought up in the environs of reporters and editors, he had devoted much of his career to the training of future journalists. That these two sides of journalism—its present and its future—should be brought closer together was an idea that found no greater advocate than he.

---

[12]Ibid.
[13]Ibid., p. 6.
[14]Hillier Krieghbaum Oral History.

Roland Wolseley,
Educator on General Assignment

Roland Wolseley (1904-) describes himself as a "generalist, seeking through my books . . . and journalistic criticism to portray a whole area, analyze and describe it, and then evaluate or criticize it."[1] A look at his life's work bears out this claim. He has been interested in and informed about many subjects enough to write intelligently about them. As a journalism educator, Wolseley's activities anticipated a number of specialities and trends that were to develop in the discipline, such as mass communication, international communications, religious journalism, the study of ethnic journalism, and the tenuring of professionals on journalism faculties. His career exemplifies the kind of person many journalism educators hope their students will be—one who is able to deal with a variety of subjects with clarity and intelligence.

Wolseley's interests have covered many areas in his long career—magazine journalism, religious journalism, history, travel, criticism. To each he has made substantial contributions. His overriding interest has been in raising the level of journalism education and in advancing the discipline with his work. His scholarship has had a sometimes quiet but often important influence on the shape and scope of the academic field.

Wolseley was born March 9, 1904, in New York City.[2] His father was the son of Eastern European immigrants and worked for the H.J. Heinz Co. When Roland was 9, his father had a business trip that took him and his family to Germany, France, and England and then to Brazil, Uruguay, Argentina, Chile, and Peru. Soon after their return to America, however, his parents separated, and he lived with distant relatives in New Jersey. Early in his life, with no particular push from his relatives, Wolseley developed deep religious convictions. He soon took up the doctrine of pacifism. Ironically, his father enrolled him in a military school in upstate New York. After one day there, the young Wolse-

---

[1] Letter from Roland Wolseley to David Sloan, April 7, 1986.

[2] Most of the information on Wolseley's life is taken from Roland Wolseley, *Still in Print* (Elgin, IL: David C. Cook Foundation, 1985).

ley simply walked out, took a train back to New York City, and called his father, who was living alone in the city. His father was surprisingly sympathetic, and some months later Wolseley was enrolled in Schuylkill Seminary in Reading, Pennsylvania. The seminary was actually a 4-year prep school, 2-year junior college, and theological seminary.

There Wolseley developed an interest in journalism and began writing for the Schuylkill *News* and the Reading *Herald-Telegram*, and he was the out-of-town correspondent for the Philadelphia *North American*. He found the work as a reporter exciting. "I enjoyed learning the news before the general public did," he wrote.[3] He left Reading in 1923 to attend Northwestern University and study journalism, working for the *Daily Northwestern* for more than 3 years. He also wrote reviews for the *Friday Literary Review*, a supplement of the Chicago *Evening Post*.

Immediately after graduating in 1928, Wolseley got a job in the public relations department of the Pennsylvania Railroad, a job he thoroughly disliked but the only one that was available. He returned to Northwestern University to study for his master's degree, supporting himself by teaching journalism classes at a local Catholic women's college and a local adult high school. (His classes at the Catholic school were attended by a nun in full habit acting as chaperone.) The material that he prepared for these first courses helped him in co-authoring (with H.F. Harrington) the textbook *The Copyreader's Workshop*,[4] published in 1934.

Wolseley graduated that same year and went to work for the Evanston *Daily News-Index*, under the editorship of Curtis MacDougall. His positions on the paper included reporter, copy editor, and city editor. Three years later, he received an offer from his alma mater, Northwestern, to join the faculty full-time. In his writing courses, he developed a system of line-by-line criticism and a set of symbols that would identify common errors. His description of his students in the 1930s recalls many of the remarks journalism teachers make about their students a half century later:

> They did not know how to spell correctly, their writing was obscure and involved, and they liked overlong words and sentences. To find that their own students were ill in this manner was especially frustrating to journalism teachers since their pupils were expected to be impeccable in such matters. Various degrees of illiteracy were not so important for engineers, mathematicians, or scientists, but for neophyte writers to be incapable of writing a clear sentence was disgraceful.[5]

[3]*Still in Print*, p. 37.
[4]Roland Wolseley, *The Copyreader's Workshop* (New York: Heath, 1934).
[5]Ibid., pp. 63-64.

Wolseley's most important work of his early career can be found in the text he co-authored with Laurence Campbell, entitled *Exploring Journalism*, published in 1943 by Prentice-Hall. An introductory text for the first journalism courses, it was widely adopted and was revised in 1949. The authors sought to lay out the world of journalism for both the students considering the field for a career and for those simply interested in the subject. It was a forerunner to the mass communication introductory texts of today, with chapters on the various areas of journalism and a discussion of the "business of journalism."

Wolseley and Campbell took the view—not uncommon for the time—that journalism could be fun and exciting as a life's work, but they were also convinced that journalism performed a vital function for society. Journalism, they wrote, was "democracy's weapon: . . . the average man's means of discovering the truth about men and events. And all men must know the truth if they are to survive physically and spiritually."[6]

Another part of the book was devoted to the introduction of the practice of journalism—reporting and writing. The authors discussed the techniques of these activities, but in the main their discussion focused on establishing the context of these activities for students. This approach undoubtedly made the book useful and valuable to journalism educators. Texts on writing and reporting were available (although not in abundance), with Mac-Dougall's *Interpretative Reporting* leading the field, but books that sought to explain journalism in a broader context were harder to find. A *Journalism Quarterly* reviewer (Willis Tucker) wrote of the second edition in 1949: "Textbooks that survey the field of communications must not only draw upon a full reservoir of accumulated fact but must also tap the tributary currents frequently enough to appease the students who regard any superseded fact as an archaic curiosity. Teachers of journalism therefore will welcome this second edition of a textbook that is widely used in survey or introductory courses."[7]

Wolseley followed this second edition with *Newsmen at Work* (1949) and *The Magazine World* (1951).[8] In the latter work, he took much the same approach to magazine journalism that he had taken to the field in general in *Exploring Journalism*. He produced a broad-based work, covering many of the areas of magazine publishing, including circulation and advertising, its history, specialized publications, and so on. Again, journalism teachers, badly in need of such a text, welcomed his work. The *Journalism Quarterly* reviewer (Ted Peterson) praised Wolseley as having "brought together for the professional and general reader

---

[6]Roland Wolseley and Laurence Campbell, *Exploring Journalism* (Englewood Cliffs, NJ: Prentice-Hall, 1943), p. 3.

[7]*Journalism Quarterly* 26 (1949): 221.

[8]Roland Wolseley, *Newsmen at Work* (New York: Houghton, 1949); *The Magazine World* (New York: Prentice-Hall, 1951).

a complete, up-to-date picture of magazine publishing. No other book in print is quite like his. Of how-to-do books, there is no end; but Professor Wolseley emphasizes *what* is being done rather than how to do it."[9]

Another service that Wolseley had been performing for journalism education was the completion of the various editions of *The Journalist's Bookshelf*.[10] First published in 1939 and revised periodically, these bibliographical books sought to keep up with the expanding number of publications related to the field of journalism and journalism education. Despite acknowledgments of their usefulness, many reviewers criticized the editions as being too limited in scope; they felt Wolseley should have expanded his definition of journalism and journalism-related works. In the early editions of the work, Wolseley introduced the book with an essay entitled "On the Literature of Journalism." It was this essay for which he was taken to task by a reviewer for *Public Opinion Quarterly* (Ralph Casey) of the fourth edition:

> It seems strange that the author is so concerned over the failure of journalists to write novels dealing with newspaper life....
>
> Clearly, the main function of the journalist is to write truthfully, objectively, and in clear and concise prose of the happenings of life and to comment intelligently on contemporary developments. These tasks in themselves are demanding and socially-useful responsibilities. But Professor Wolseley gives little credit to the journalist for the skills and achievements required in the newspaper orbit. Newspaper work is pictured as menial. Writing the successful novel is breath-taking![11]

Other reviewers were more sympathetic with what Wolseley was trying to accomplish. Commenting on the sixth edition, a *Journalism Quarterly* reviewer (Charles Higbie) wrote:

> To a great extent, it achieves what Wolseley set out to do when he drew up the first edition for publication in 1939, to provide a list of major titles in American journalistic literature. By his vision and execution he has played a significant part in the crusade to move journalism from an avocation into a self-conscious way-of-life—in other words, a profession.[12]

Wolseley's own career had taken a turn during the time he was producing these early editions of *The Journalist's Bookshelf*. A pacifist and conscientious objector during World War II, Wolseley found himself under increasing pressure from the Northwestern

---

[9]*Journalism Quarterly* 28 (1951): 508.

[10]Roland Wolseley, *The Journalist's Bookshelf* (New York: Burgess, 1939).

[11]*Public Opinion Quarterly* 10 (1946): 394-395.

[12]*Journalism Quarterly* 33 (1956): 96.

University administration because of his lack of a terminal degree. Despite his productive publication record, he was denied promotion and salary increases, and in 1946 his contract was terminated. (Ironically, 5 years later, Northwestern University offered him a job, which he turned down.) He then joined the faculty at Syracuse University. In 1948-1949 he was president of the Association for Education in Journalism, and in 1951 he was selected as a Fulbright Lecturer to Nagpur University in Nagpur, India. He was instrumental in helping that university begin its journalism program.

This adventure helped Wolseley produce two books, one which he wrote, *Face to Face with India,* and another which he edited, *Journalism in Modern India.*[13] The second book was put together because there was little that Indian students could use to study journalism. The book combines information about journalism in India with instructions for students in reporting, writing, and editing. *Face to Face with India* is derived from the notes that Wolseley took on the social and political customs of the Indian people when he was there.

Wolseley also had been developing an interest in religious journalism during this time. His own religious convictions had led him early on to work with churches and various religious organizations and to do some writing for religious publications. But he contends, in his autobiography, that he does not write about religion so much as the relationship of religion to the media of mass communication. This interest led him to produce a number of works: *Interpreting the Church Through Press and Radio* (1951), *Careers in Religious Journalism* (1955), and *Writing for the Religious Market* (editor) (1956).[14] In *Interpreting the Church,* he sought to examine the ways in which religious organizations had explained themselves to the larger public. He found that in many ways, these organizations had been deficient in communicating through secular media, and he called upon religious leaders to pay more attention to the need for effective communication outside their own denominations and congregations. *Careers in Religious Journalism* was aimed at students who were interested in working full-time in religious journalism; the book contains many references to people who were doing just that, and it was this part of the book that reviewers felt was its strongest point. *Writing for the Religious Market* brought together essays from 18 writers (Protestants, Catholics, and Jews) about their experiences in religious journalism. Again, the purpose was to inform students about the work and the opportunities available to

---

[13]Roland Wolseley, *Face to Face with India* (Friendship Press, 1954); *Journalism in Modern India* (Asia Publishing House, 1954).

[14]Roland Wolseley, *Interpreting the Church Through Press and Radio* (Philadelphia: Muhlenberg Press, 1951); *Careers in Religious Journalism* (New York: Association Press, 1955); *Writing for the Religious Market* (New York: Association Press, 1956).

them.

In the 1950s, Wolseley's interest turned to criticism, and again he produced a useful and helpful work to journalism education, *Critical Writing for the Journalist.* In it, he tried to guide the thinking of those who sought to review the arts for newspapers and magazines. "Perhaps attitudes are of more importance than rule to the journalistic critic," he wrote, citing "open-mindedness, not to the point of vacuity but to the extent of avoiding dogmatism" as a trait critics should develop.[15] The book was designed to give journalism teachers a tool to use in the growing number of critical writing courses.

Wolseley collaborated again with Laurence Campbell to produce a reporting text, *How to Report and Write the News,* in 1961, and he wrote yet another book on magazines, *Understanding Magazines,*[16] in 1965. His last major contribution to the literature of journalism education before his retirement in 1972 was a study of the history of black newspapers. This study came to fruition in 1971 with the publication of *The Black Press, U.S.A.*[17] Wolseley's interest in black newspapers stemmed from his time as a reporter and editor in Chicago and his contacts with black journalists there. He was fascinated by the conditions under which they worked, and he began collecting clippings and other information about the whole area (as he did about many subjects that interested him). In 1968 the state of New York urged its colleges and universities to develop courses concerned with black history and society, and a course on the contemporary black press was offered by Syracuse. The book then grew out of the need to have some organized material in this area.

The Black Press, U.S.A. was greeted by excellent reviews on its publication and was hailed as the best study of the black press available. The *Library Journal* described the book as "full of biographical, historical, statistical and sociological information on the subject, facts not readily available elsewhere under one cover. Empathy is evident throughout but objectivity is seldom compromised."[18] The *Negro History Bulletin* said that the book "should be widely read and discussed."[19]

The bulk of the work that Wolseley did in journalism and journalism education gave credence to his self-description as a "generalist." In every area to which he turned his attention, however, he was an influential force in directing the course of his academic field.

---

[15]*Journalism Quarterly* 36 (1959): 232.

[16]Roland Wolseley, *How to Report and Write the News* (New York: Prentice-Hall, 1961); *Understanding Magazines* (Ames: Iowa State University Press, 1965).

[17]Roland Wolseley, *The Black Press, U.S.A.* (Ames: Iowa State University Press, 1972).

[18]*Library Journal* 96 (1972): 3753.

[19]*Negro History Bulletin* 34 (1972): 190.

Edmund C. Arnold,
Guru of Modern Newspaper Design

For three decades, the name Edmund Arnold (1913-) has been synonymous with "newspaper design." No single educator or practitioner has had as much influence on the way the American newspaper looks, and few journalism educators have stayed at the forefront of their specialities, despite rapid and momentous changes, for as long as Arnold. His ideas about typography, design, and layout have continued to influence editors both here and in many foreign countries. His books, *Functional Newspaper Design*[1] and its successor *Modern Newspaper Design*, are as much at home in both the newsroom and the classroom today as when they were first published.

Not that Arnold formulated a set of rules in the 1950s and always adhered rigidly to them. In the introduction to *Modern Newspaper Design*, he wrote:

> I have sometimes changed my mind. Sometimes this has been due to new facts learned from continuing and growing research in this area. Sometimes it has resulted from impeccable logic leveled at me by fellow newspapermen. Sometimes it's been due simply to the highly educative process of growing older. Sometimes it has been because I agree with Emerson, "What's the use of having a mind if you can't change it?"[2]

It has been Arnold's strength that he has recognized changes and tried to guide those changes into line with his basic axioms of presenting information with the printed word. Arnold's first love is newspapers, and he cares deeply about the health of modern journalism. His strength has been in design, but he readily concedes that content along with good design is what allows a newspaper to survive. That attitude is a natural one, because Arnold

---

[1]Edmund Arnold, *Functional Newspaper Design* (New York: Harper & Row, 1956).

[2]Edmund Arnold, *Modern Newspaper Design* (New York: Harper & Row, 1969), p. x.

has not always been a "designer." He "grew up" as a reporter, editor, and publisher, and he still maintains an active interest in these aspects of journalism. Indeed, Arnold's ideas about the way a newspaper should look gain in credibility because of the professional experience that he gathered early in his professional life.

Edmund Clarence Arnold was born June 25, 1913, in Bay City, Michigan.[3] He attended a Lutheran parochial school for 8 years and then public junior high and high school. In junior high, he was invited to write a column for the school paper and later confessed, "When I saw my first by-line, I was hooked." In high school one of his teachers was Mattie Gay Crump, who taught high school journalism for more than 40 years and whose newspapers and yearbooks won many awards. During his senior year, Arnold edited the high school's weekly newspaper, a paper that was completely self-sustaining.

At Bay City Junior College, he edited both the newspaper and the yearbook, and he took any other job he could get to make ends meet. He received an AA degree in 1934; and for most of the next two decades, that was all of the formal education that he had. It was in the midst of the Depression, and Arnold worked at a number of jobs including being advertising manager for two department stores.

In 1939 he went to work for the Frankenmuth News, a weekly newspaper about 15 miles from his hometown. He was hired to sell advertising, but within 2 weeks he was the editor. The paper was running mostly preprinted material when he began, but he started covering events in the community, and the News soon expanded and discarded the preprints. Arnold began applying some of his later famous layout principles to the little paper, and it won awards from the Michigan Press Association and the National Editorial Association. In addition, a number of his editorials appeared in newspapers around the state, and one he wrote the week after Pearl Harbor was distributed nationally.

Arnold joined the Army in 1943, and after training stints in Michigan, Oregon, Missouri, and New Jersey—and working on military publications at almost every stop—his command was sent to Europe. The Battle of the Bulge was underway, and Arnold was in the middle of it. A general in the division saw some copies of Stars and Stripes and asked Arnold to see if he could find some more. The division was about 25 miles from Strasbourg, where the paper was supposedly being published; so Arnold and a fellow corporal drove there to find its offices. They were unsuccessful the first day, but they returned the next and finally found the offices. The city had been occupied by Americans, but they had left, leaving it open for the Germans to return. The Stars and Stripes staff stayed behind, however, and continued to publish. Arnold spent much of the rest of his time in service dividing his time between

---

[3]Much of the information about Arnold's life and career was provided to the author by Arnold in an unpublished set of biographical notes.

working for his division newspaper and for *Stars and Stripes*. He also served as an instructor for the educational network that was being established by the Army for its occupational forces.

When he returned home, the publisher of the Frankenmuth *News* sold the paper to Arnold and another employee. About 2 years later, Arnold accepted an offer to become picture editor of the Saginaw *News* (while still maintaining his connections in Frankenmuth). Saginaw had the typographic facilities to allow Arnold to execute many of his budding ideas about design, and he turned the paper into a bright and pleasing product. He served for a short time on the staff of the Michigan Press Association and then worked as night editor of the Lansing *State Journal*. He took advantage of his night working schedule to attend classes at Michigan State University, and in 1954, more than 20 years after he began college, he graduated summa cum laude with a degree in journalism.

During this time Arnold had been writing a column on newspaper design for *Publisher's Auxiliary*. The subject was one that had not received much attention from trade magazines, but Arnold and the editors discovered that readers had a great deal of interest in it. Arnold found himself in a position to exercise a great deal of influence on the newspaper profession, which was paying more and more attention to appearance. The threat of television taking readers away from newspapers was beginning to emerge, and many editors were seeking ways to improve the look of their product.

Immediately after his graduation from Michigan State, Arnold took a position that was to make him even more influential. The Merganthaler Linotype Co. in Brooklyn, New York, had been looking for someone to replace John Allen, the first man to write systematically about newspaper design. The company asked Arnold to take on the job of editing the prestigious *Linotype News*, a publication that had gained much from Allen's influence.

Allen had written an excellent book about the subject, but it was becoming dated, and both Linotype and Harper Brothers asked Arnold to produce one. *Functional Newspaper Design* was published in 1956 and immediately hailed as an excellent tool to guide the designers of modern newspapers. Arnold's ideas about newspaper design seem obvious today, but that is because of the 30 years of influence that they have had. Arnold argued, as the title of the book suggests, that the appearance of the newspaper was a vital part of the "communication" that the newspaper had with its readers and that all the items on a newspaper page should serve the purpose of promoting that communication. Everything—every line, every piece of type, every box—should have a function. Type faces should be chosen because they are easy to read. Elements should be placed on a page so that they send messages to the reader about the content of the paper.

The idea of "functionalism" was carried on a decade later in another book of Arnold's dealing with the same subject, *Modern*

Newspaper Design. Functionalism, he wrote, asks two questions: does a typographic element do a job? and can this job be done better, quicker, more efficiently, more profitably? Arnold gave as an example the use of the "jim dash" in headlines of the 1930s. The jim dash, rarely used today, is a hairline of type, about one-half inch wide, that separates decks of a headline and ultimately separates the headline from the story. To Arnold, and many other designers, the jim dash served no useful function; it got in the way of a reader who was trying to find his way through a headline and into a story. It was also expensive and time-consuming for the composing room personnel to insert jim dashes into headlines. Arnold's discussion of the jim dash led to a corollary axiom: "Rarely do we find a nonfunctional element; almost invariably the nonfunctional is also the malfunctional."[4]

Arnold's ideas of functionalism were not radical, but they did represent a departure from the way newspapers had been designed. On many papers, little attention was given to the appearance of the paper, either its planning or execution. Most papers had few layout and design rules, and many had continued unchanged for decades. Moving into the 1950s, many newspapers looked much as they had looked in the 1920s. Many of the practices of the composing room went unquestioned for years. Arnold's influence stemmed from an ability to ask questions and ask them in a way that showed he understood the process of producing the newspaper.

Underlying his thoughts on newspaper design were a love for the work of the journalist and the desire to see newspapers survive and flourish. He also subjugated his ideas on appearance to the mission and the content of the newspaper, never losing sight of the fact that the newspaper is an information vehicle and one that is vital for the maintenance of a free society.

He considered the work of the newspaper editor as that of an artist, a manufacturer, and a merchandiser. He knew that many in the profession would not take kindly to any of these descriptions, but he realized that newspaper people had to think in these terms if they were to survive. He helped introduce and legitimize a thinking in the newspaper craft that professionals could be creative with more than their words. Indeed, they had to be creative if they were going to produce a product that people would buy. Editors had to think about their customers and things they needed and wanted. The "manufacturer" in Arnold's editor was the person who wanted to produce a product at its lowest costs. This fell into line with his advocacy of functionalism. Nothing should appear on the page that does not have a purpose.

Functional Newspaper Design won the George Polk Memorial Award and established Arnold as the main advocate of modern newspaper design. Arnold was also "discovered" as a public speaker when he was asked to fill in for a sick friend at a meeting

---

[4]*Modern Newspaper Design,* pp. 7-9.

of the West Virginia Press Association. He found that not only were people willing to read about his ideas, but they were also willing to listen to him talk about them. He began a schedule of public speaking engagements that continued almost non-stop for the next 30 years. As an example, Arnold has appeared at more than 200 American Press Institute seminars, far more than any other single presenter.

Yet another element in Arnold's influence over the appearance of the American newspaper is the fact that he personally had redesigned so many of them. His design consulting began with the Lowell (Mass.) *Sun* and has included papers such as the Kansas City *Star* and *Times*, the Louisville *Courier-Journal* and *Times*, the Toronto *Star*, the Boston *Globe*, and newspapers in practically every state in the nation. Possibly his single most influential piece of design work was with the Louisville papers, which became the first metropolitan newspapers in the country to adopt the six-column format. The fact that the Louisville papers adopted Arnold's ideas on what he called the "op format" forced other editors to rethink their positions on the narrow column of type. Today, the six-column format is probably the most common format newspapers use. Arnold was also responsible for the redesign of the *Christian Science Monitor*, developing a five-column format on a broadsheet. It was a design that perfectly suited the *Monitor's* practice of accepting many small advertisements.

In 1960 Arnold left Linotype and joined the faculty at Syracuse University, where he continued his writing and speaking. His specialty was in newspaper design, but his interests were far broader. While at Linotype, he had been in charge of the company's advertising department, and in 1960 he published *Profitable Newspaper Advertising*,[5] a book aimed at the retailer and small businessman who were considering advertising in the local newspaper. He also took an active interest in high school journalism and wrote a number of books and articles aimed at improving its quality. His interest in newspaper design led to a more specialized interest in typography and to the publication of *Ink on Paper*[6] in 1963 (updated in 1972), which the *Library Journal* called "practical, fundamentally accurate, even witty and always to the point."[7] The book explores the fascinating world of type, both from a historical and a modern, practical point of view.

Arnold remained at Syracuse until 1972 when an old friend, George Crutchfield, invited him to Virginia Commonwealth University, where Crutchfield was chairman of the journalism program. Arnold taught there for 8 years before retiring to continue his active seminar and consulting schedule.

Despite his background and many contacts with professional

---

[5]Edmund Arnold, *Profitable Newspaper Advertising* (New York: Harper & Row, 1960).

[6]Edmund Arnold, *Ink on Paper* (New York: Harper & Row, 1964).

[7]Quoted in *Book Review Digest* (1964): 36.

journalists, Arnold has been a staunch advocate of journalism education and a defender against its professional critics. He has been particularly critical of the lack of support that high school journalism programs have received from local newspapers. "I get exercised when editors criticize J-schools because their graduates can't spell," he wrote:

> I tell them . . . that it's your fault! No one can teach spelling or grammar at college levels. That has to be done in grade school. And you, Mr. Editor, aren't demanding that of your schools. In fact, you don't know what's happening—or isn't happening—in your schools. . . . You ought to alert your community to the real function of your schools—and that isn't winning football games. Then you can criticize J-schools.[8]

Arnold's influence on American journalism and on journalism education has been far-reaching. The sheer volume of his work—including 25 books, 3,000 articles, and innumerable demonstrations, seminars, and consultantships—has assured him a prominent place in the annals of journalism education. By helping to make newspapers more attractive, he not only helped newspapers attract readers but helped the journalism profession recruit young people into its ranks. He showed that newspapers not only could tell exciting stories but could be visually exciting as well. He demonstrated that there is a place in journalism for the literate and visually creative person, and he became a prime example of those very traits himself.

---

[8]Arnold, biographical notes.

2

The Historians

Wm. David Sloan
University of Alabama

The Historians

Among the major areas of study in journalism education, history appears to practitioners the most irrelevant to their profession. Concerned with day-to-day affairs of the present, they feel little urge to learn about journalism history. It seems to have little bearing on what they do each day or how they do it.

What, after all, do colonial printers and penny press editors have to do with getting a story today, on deadline? What could party press editors possibly have to do with freedom of the press? What does journalism history—and, for that matter, journalism historians—have to do with how journalism is practiced today?

The answer is, almost everything.

The present is the most recent moment of history. Everything that exists is the outcome, in some way, of what occurred before. The way every person behaves is the product of earlier influences. For journalists, those influences may include a discussion with an editor earlier in the day, training from college days, or the techniques that the mass media adopted a hundred or more years ago. How contemporary journalists perform, what attitudes they hold, and what outlooks they adopt are influenced to a considerable degree by the lessons of history. But just as important as history to the contemporary journalist is the historian.

How people perceive the past is determined to a large degree by how historians explain it. It is only through the historian that most people ever learn about history. Professional journalists have learned about journalism history primarily through textbooks by journalism educators. What they learned has, for the most part, been just what the professionals wanted to learn. Educators have explained history in a way to reinforce practitioners' belief in the merit of their profession. They have lent friendly bias and moral support. They have provided excellent propaganda.

The history of journalism as told by educators, with some exceptions, is this story: Journalists have always recognized that their primary obligation was to present the news independent of political parties and other special interests. The history of journalism documents the continuing progress toward that ideal. Thus, over three centuries of American journalism one can see developments that advanced news gathering practices, popular appeal, and freedom from politicians' influence. Journalists also have recognized that their duty has been to work for the welfare of the general public. A key to their ability to perform their duties has been freedom of the press. But throughout history, a number of forces continually have opposed the efforts of sincere journalists. One has been government, which, from the time of British colonial authorities to the present, has had among its main goals the suppression of dissenting views, the limitation of the news media's freedom, and the restriction of the public's right to know. Another has been the conservative establishment, including reactionary owners of the news media. They have been more interested in protecting their own position and investments than in allowing the news media to present the news unhampered and to work to solve social and political problems. Such an explanation, whether true or not of either history or of the present, serves the function of assuring journalists that they are performing properly and have a long history to back them up.

Most educator-historians have written from one of two perspectives. The Developmental approach has been the most popular explanation of journalism history, followed by the Progressive approach. The first emphasizes the progress of journalism practices, whereas the second presents an ideological explanation of history. The Developmental interpretation grew out of a change that took place in journalism beginning in 1833. In that year Benjamin Day founded the New York *Sun*, America's first successful general-interest cheap newspaper. The "penny press" created a revolution in journalism and in attitudes about what the nature of newspapers should be. It also provided the foundation for historians' views about journalism history. From this changed perspective emerged the Developmental interpretation. Beginning with the publication in 1873 of Frederic Hudson's *Journalism in the United States, from 1690 to 1872*,[1] it continues today as the most commonly held perspective.

Hudson's was the first survey history of American journalism written after the appearance of the penny press, and in its interpretive basis it provided the approach most later historians used. Hudson had been managing editor of the New York *Herald*, the newspaper which more than any other of its time emphasized news over opinion as the function of newspapers, which prided itself on being uninfluenced by political parties, and which had been the most successful mass newspaper in American history. Assuming that the *Herald's* practices were the appropriate ones for newspapers, he tended to explain earlier journalism in terms of how it performed in accordance with the successful practices of the *Herald* and how those practices had developed in the past.

As journalism began to professionalize in the late 1800s, in-

---

[1] Frederic Hudson, *Journalism in the United States, from 1690 to 1872* (New York: Harper & Row, 1873).

terest in the history of the profession began to grow. Historical studies increased in number, and they largely echoed Hudson's themes. Most historians came out of the news media professions, and in the 20th century many taught in professionally oriented college programs in journalism. Because of their professional perspective, they considered the penny press, with its emphasis on news, mass appeal, and political autonomy, to have been the origin of the "modern journalism" of their own times. They believed the professional standards that had developed over time were the appropriate and proper ones for the news media, and they began to apply even more universally the concept of professional progress in history.

The Developmental interpretation had a pervasive impact on historical assumptions because most textbooks for college courses in journalism history were cast in terms of the professional framework. With early textbooks such as James Melvin Lee's *History of American Journalism*,[2] published in 1917, and Willard G. Bleyer's *Main Currents in the History of American Journalism*,[3] published just 10 years later, the Developmental interpretation became entrenched in historical thinking. Bleyer's was the most widely used of the early textbooks, and its successor in the 1940s, Frank Luther Mott's *American Journalism*,[4] continued the Developmental influence on thinking. Studied by generations of students and future historians and journalism professionals, the textbooks tended to reinforce the explanation that the history of American journalism was the story of how the news media evolved in their professional characteristics. Textbooks and other studies, being generally positive about the journalism profession, also exercised a major influence by providing a favorable view of the news media and reinforcing a pro-journalism outlook among students and professionals.

After World War II, changing conditions in journalism encouraged changing attitudes among a new generation of Developmental historians. Several events contributed to the expansion of the professional concept that the news media ideally should be autonomous from outside authority and independent of other parts of society. Influenced much by the news media's role in such episodes as the civil rights movement of the 1950s and 1960s, the Vietnam war, and the Watergate political scandal, historians sometimes viewed history as a clash between the news media and established institutions such as government, religion, the military, big business, and the white racial majority. Thus, although

---

[2]James Melvin Lee, *History of American Journalism* (Boston: Houghton Mifflin, 1917; rev. 1923).

[3]Willard G. Bleyer, *Main Currents in the History of American Journalism* (Boston: Houghton Mifflin, 1927).

[4]Frank Luther Mott, *American Journalism: A History of Newspapers in the United States Through 250 Years, 1690-1940* (New York: Macmillan, 1941).

some earlier historians had emphasized the news media as a means of working within society to achieve social and political change, Developmental historians tended to emphasize such historical topics as press freedom and media-government relations in which the news media confronted other units of society. Recent Developmental historians often appeared anti-nationalist. The devotion of the press, they suggested, should be to journalistic ideals rather than to a nation. Thus, they showed considerable concern with such issues as the news media's autonomy in the area of national security, press freedom during wartime, and the news media as propaganda agents for governmental activities.

The Progressive concept has exercised, next to the Developmental interpretation, the most influence on textbooks. Beginning in the early 1900s, many reform-oriented journalism historians—influenced by the ideas of such Progressive American historians as Frederick Jackson Turner, Charles A. Beard, Claude Bowers, and Vernon L. Parrington—began to view the past in terms of conflict between social classes. Their interpretation, obviously, was ideological and may be summarized this way. The story of the past is that of a struggle in which editors, reporters, and some publishers were pitted on the side of freedom, liberty, civil reform, democracy, and equality against the powerful and malign forces of wealth, class, and conservatism. The primary purpose of the news media was to crusade for liberal social and economic causes, to fight on the side of the masses of common, working people against the entrenched interests in American business and government. The fulfillment of the American ideal required a struggle against those individuals and groups which had blocked the achievement of a fully democratic system. Progressive historians often placed the conflict in economic terms, with the wealthy class attempting to control the news media for its own use.

Considering history to be an evolutionary progression to better conditions, Progressive historians thought of the news media as an influential force in helping assure a better future. They wrote in such a way as to show the news media as tools for social change, progress, and democracy. They explained the past in cycles of democratic and journalistic advance, the latter considered as having occurred when the news media improved in serving the masses in America. They praised journalists and episodes that had contributed to greater democracy, while criticizing those favoring an elitist society and political system. Their ultimate intent was to use history in a way to influence conditions of their own time and eventually to bring about changes from the conservative status quo.

Works by historians outside education such as Oswald Garrison Villard, George Seldes, and Harold Ickes in the 1920s and 1930s provided some of the harshest attacks that have been made on the conservative media. They claimed, among other things, that newspaper owners' primary interest in making profits prevented their papers from leading much needed crusades, that self-serving owners hoped to destroy the democratic foundation of the American political system, and that owners had made newspapers into private profit-seeking businesses rather than public-spirited agencies. That outlook was evident among a number of works by journalism educators such as Alfred M. Lee's *The Daily Newspaper in America*,[5] published in 1937.

Progressive historians continued such attacks after World War II, but they changed their main target from newspaper owners to conservative forces in general. The greatest threat to the news media and the nation, they argued, came from what they considered to be reactionary government leaders and other members of the "establishment." The main objective of the news media, they believed, had to be opposition to those forces. One senses in these historians' writings a strong belief that the only attitudes that were right were their own and that the news media could function correctly only when journalists held such attitudes. That approach to ideological history is demonstrated well in Edwin Emery's *The Press and America*,[6] an especially important work because it has been the most widely used textbook on journalism history since the early 1970s.

The problem that one readily recognizes in journalism historians' works is their superficiality. The Developmental interpretation suffers from acute present-mindedness. That is, historians have tended to impose the views and standards of their own time on the past. Historians instead should examine the past on its own terms. Otherwise, the ultimate value of the past is simply as a stepping stone in the stream to the present. Developmental history has suffered also from its compulsion to view journalism from only one point of view, that of journalism. Thus, the standards used to evaluate not only journalism but all other parts of society as well have been those peculiar to journalism. Developmental history has therefore presented a simplistic, one-sided picture. It has distorted the complexities of the human condition and of many-faceted issues in the past to the simple formula that everything must be judged by journalism values. The same criticisms may be made of Progressive history. In its ideological simplicity, it reduces the multi-colored mosaic of the past to a black-and-white, two-dimensional photograph. People have been good or evil: good if they shared the historian's values; evil if they did not. When such oversimplification pervades the textbooks from which future journalism professionals learn, the result cannot be good. The view that the press is good may be reassuring to professionals, but one has to wonder whether in-house PR in the long

---

[5]Alfred M. Lee, *The Daily Newspaper in America* (New York: Macmillan, 1937).

[6]Edwin Emery and Henry Ladd Smith, *The Press and America: An Interpretative History of the Mass Media* (Englewood Cliffs, NJ: Prentice-Hall, 1954; rev. 5 times).

run serves the best interest of either the general public or even the media professions. (It should be added that historians who cater to the profession or the Progressive ideology do not wade by themselves in shallow water. Among educators the recent attempts to explain journalism history by a "symbolic meaning"— or "cultural"—theory stand out. Historians who promote this philosophy rely mostly on selective secondary sources and then assert that the sources prove the philosophy. They then declare confidently that their philosophy alone offers the true explanation of history.)

Unfortunately, the result of such oversimplification does more than narrow the perspective of professionals. It has left the study of journalism history adrift in a leaking boat of mediocrity. Media historians have failed to act as the unbiased critics that history demands. And they have been content to do so. They have forsaken their obligation to search for truth, and they have found comfort in their role as propagandists.

As a result, they have had little impact on the thinking of historians outside the field. It is ironic that while studying a subject, the mass media, which is claimed to be central to the American democratic, economic, and social systems, journalism historians have done hardly anything to convince anyone outside the field of the media's importance. When non-journalism historians explain the influences that shaped American politics or economics or the character of the people, they rarely mention the news media. Does the fault lie with them or with the media's historians?

The situation with historical works by journalism educators, however, is worse. Educators should be among the scholars who have given the fullest consideration to their field. But in journalism history, the most provocative ideas, soundest methods, and most illuminating insights have come from neither journalism educators nor even people thought of primarily as journalism historians. They have come from non-journalism historians such as Allan Nevins, Leonard Levy, and Bernard Bailyn and from sociologists who do poor history (such as Alfred McClung Lee, who, although teaching journalism briefly, was foremost a sociologist, and, more recently, Michael Schudson). In considering a list of the leading educator-historians, one finds that the reputations of most are not based on solid historical works but on textbooks. For purposes of comparison, can one imagine the prestige of historians of America's past being judged by the authorship of introductory textbooks for college sophomores?

That judgment and the biographies that follow in this section may seem to the reader unnecessarily harsh. However, the quality of the study of journalism history should be judged by standards expected of good history, not by the standards that have dominated journalism. Most journalism educator-historians have not been trained rigorously in the study of history. Therefore, they often have accepted superficial research and simplistic explanations from other historians. If the historians treated in this section were evaluated by the prevalent standards of journalism history, all would receive good marks. But such evaluation would do little to advance the study of journalism history. It would, instead, damage it by holding up for admiration work that is ordinary as measured by rigorous historical standards.

What needs to be done to improve the field? The most fundamental answer is that historians need to come to a better understanding of the range of methods and approaches, vast as they are, involved in historical study. Then they need to think of themselves primarily as historians who have chosen to study journalism, rather than as journalism educators who happen to have chosen history as one of their interests. Only with these approaches will the study of journalism history achieve the potential vitality that it possesses.

But perhaps a more basic question needs to be asked: Does it matter if the field is improved? If the purpose of history is to make practitioners feel good about what they are doing and satisfied that they are right and all their critics are wrong, then journalism historians have done their job well.

But if a purpose of history is to help us understand the past and, perhaps, to help us improve ourselves and conditions of our own time, then journalism history has a way to go. History that presents journalism as virtually perfect is acceptable only if journalism is. Historians need to recognize that they have a duty to seek honestly for the best, least biased explanations of the past that evidence and mature judgment will allow. They need to recognize their obligation to be concerned but detached critics rather than spokesmen for a profession, an ideology, or a philosophy. They need to recognize that there are more ways to evaluate journalism than by the criteria established by journalism practitioners. Although such forthrightness may not satisfy those practitioners who can see the world only through tinted glasses, it may in the long run help improve the vision of others.

James Melvin Lee
and Professional Progress

James Melvin Lee (1878-1929) wrote the first textbook on the history of American journalism. Not a very good work, it nevertheless incorporated a number of characteristics that became standard items in later textbooks. Lee looked at history from the viewpoint of his own time, explaining the past as the source of the present. Previous events gained their importance, he believed, from the fact that they played a role in determining how the press had reached its present condition. Coming from a background as a journalist and holding a favorable opinion of the press of his own time, Lee therefore believed that journalism history was essentially the story of the professional growth of journalism.

Lee thought of history as objective truth. When combined with his present-mindedness, that outlook resulted in the assumption that history could be explained properly only one way and that the one way was the story of how the past contributed to and compared with the present. The function of the historian, therefore, was to gather and present the "facts" arranged in some coherent order—a series of episodes and items that had contributed to journalistic progress—correcting errors made by earlier historians and providing as complete an account as practicable. Such a concept of historical study left little or no room for the possibility that the historian's views colored the historical account or that the historian's own account might not be the most appropriate in explaining the past.

The result was that Lee's *History of American Journalism*,[1] published in 1917 and revised in 1923, provided an antiquarian collection of details arranged in a loose chronological sequence. It showed the path that the press and its major figures had taken as history moved forward to create the professional characteristics of the press in the early 20th century. The book grew out of the course in press history which Lee taught in the journalism department at New York University.

---

[1]James Melvin Lee, *History of American Journalism* (Boston: Houghton Mifflin, 1917; rev. 1923).

The son of a Methodist minister, James Newell Lee, and his wife, Emma (White), Lee was born May 16, 1878, in Port Crane, New York. Upon graduation from Wesleyan University in Connecticut in 1900, he began more than a decade of work on newspapers and magazines, including positions as circulation manager of the Oneonta (N.Y.) *Star* and *Outing Magazine* (1900-1906), editor of *Bohemian Magazine* (1906), literary editor of *Circle Magazine* (1907-1908), editor of *Leslie's Weekly* (1908-1909), and editor of *Judge* (1900-1912). He later served as literary editor of *Editor and Publisher* (1922-1929). Having taught as a guest lecturer on journalism at New York University beginning in 1909, Lee in 1911 was appointed director of NYU's journalism department. He worked in that capacity until his death in 1929. Devoted to both teaching and the journalism profession, he placed special emphasis on journalism ethics and on thorough training of students for newspaper work. He was noted for his broad-mindedness and sympathetic ear; and his office—which he shared with fellow journalism professors Leon Whipple, a civil libertarian, and the urbane Albert Frederick Wilson—provided an informal meeting place for deans, other professors, campus non-conformists, intellectuals, and prominent visitors from the journalism profession.[2]

In his presentation of journalism history, Lee suffered from present-mindedness, that is, the tendency to view and evaluate the past from the perspective of the historian's own time. In none of his writings did Lee provide a statement of his concepts for studying history; and, even though certain intuitive approaches to historiography are evident in his work, he probably never formulated in his own mind exactly what his approaches were. Not having critically considered what the study of history should be, he thus fell easily into the trap that historians should avoid. To provide as accurate a picture and explanation of the past as possible, historians must divorce themselves—as much as they are humanly able—from the ideas and outlooks of their own age and then consider the past on its own terms. This Lee could not do. He applied to periods, people, and episodes of the past the same principles and standards that he believed existed in 1917. Thus, his thinking on what constituted proper journalism in the 20th century molded the picture and evaluations he presented of historical journalism.

It also resulted in an antiquarian approach to selecting and arranging material. Lee merely collected data and made little effort to decide which topics were important enough to justify elaboration and which so insignificant that they could be summarized or eliminated. His book, although important as the first attempt at a journalism history textbook, wound up as a piecemeal

[2]Beatrice Cole, "Leon Whipple — a Fond Memorial By a Former Secretary-Student," *News Workshop* 16: 1 (Department of Journalism, New York University, November 1964), p. 2.

collection of short narratives of hundreds of pieces of information. Even though such a structure contributes no more than a small understanding of journalism history, it did establish the approach that most later authors of journalism history texts used. Whether such an antiquarian structure is a legacy of Lee's work or not, Lee did set the precedent, and subsequent historians have had difficulty loosing their works from what Lee considered an obligation to include as many names, dates, and episodes as his book's pages would hold.

Lee's present-mindedness had a direct, vital impact on his perspective about journalism history. Lee believed that journalism history consisted essentially of the story of the growth and development of the press. Looking back over two centuries of American newspaper history, he could see it as a stream of progress leading from journalism's rudimentary beginnings, through its early awakening to what proper journalism should be, and to its maturity in the 20th century. Although he perhaps never recognized his perspective as such, he assumed that the past had been predetermined by the present—that the purpose of the stream of history was to lead to the present and that the history of journalism simply paved the route by which journalism of 1917 had worked its way. He thus selected for emphasis those events that seemed to have contributed to the progress of journalism; when he included episodes that had not, he evaluated them according to whether they had conformed with the standards and practices of later professional journalism.

His frequent use of words such as "strange" or "unusual" to describe early practices that did not accord with those of 1917 revealed plainly his inability to escape from a contemporary viewpoint. He called a "strange anomaly,"[3] for instance, the fact that in 1880 many small towns had competing daily newspapers, strange, we see, because in 1917 few small towns had daily competition. Such references provide the most obvious indication of Lee's present-mindedness, but other, more subtle approaches pervaded his history. One example may suffice to illustrate. John Campbell, proprietor of the Boston *News-Letter*, America's first continuously published newspaper, like most early newspaper operators placed much emphasis on foreign news and on continuity and completeness in the presentation of such news, as if the newspaper needed to provide an unbroken historical record of events rather than current news of the day. Although to 20th-century journalistic minds, such an approach may seem odd, to printers and readers in the early 1700s it seemed the natural way to operate. But Lee concluded that in this approach, "Campbell did not show enterprise." On the other hand, "his domestic news service in later issues may be considered a little more up-to-date,"[4] for in it he attempted to gather information promptly, serving as

---

[3]Lee, *History of American Journalism* (rev. ed.) (1923), p. 348.
[4]Ibid., p. 23.

a forerunner of later energetic editors and reporters who placed an emphasis on getting news as quickly as possible.

The two most important concepts in proper journalism for Lee were newspapers' political independence and an emphasis on news. They happened to be important historically because by 1917 they had come to be the two preeminent principles of journalism. Lee did not recognize that neither had been the fundamental purpose of the American press during most of its history. With the approach of the American Revolution, colonial newspapers began to side with the opposing interests. Tory and Patriot printers provided little or no space for contrary arguments. Following the Revolution, Federalist and Republican editors in the first party system devoted their papers wholeheartedly and completely to partisanship, to those ideals which they believed best served the interests of their new nation. Jacksonian Democrats and Whigs did likewise in the next generation. Although penny newspapers in the 1830s broke away from an official alliance with parties, most continued to give consistent support to the Republicans or Democrats. Throughout those eras, printers and editors aligned with political ideas. They believed that newspapers played a crucial role in the political life of the nation and therefore that partisanship was the appropriate function of the press. It was not until 1884, when the New York *World* bolted the Republican party and endorsed Democrat Grover Cleveland for president, that newspapers began to grow truly independent. Even then, most newspapers continued to identify clearly with parties and could be expected to endorse party candidates and stances.

Lee did not conceive of party affiliation and political independence in such a manner. He believed that printers and editors always had recognized or should have recognized that the future, or at least the proper, role of the press was political independence and that by siding with parties they had violated their journalistic mandate. Throughout the party press period, Lee declared, newspapers' alliance with political parties prevented them from being "newspapers in the modern sense of the word,"[5] but in the early 1800s they got their "first push toward the legitimate function of the newspaper" by Charles Hammond, the proprietor of the Cincinnati *Gazette*, who had an "inborn love of truth for its own sake" and who "refused to make his paper simply an organ for a great party leader."[6] Although politicians held editors in subjection through government printing contracts and attempted to prevent them from gaining their independence, a "new journalism" emerged with the penny press, one "opposed to politics and independent in spirit."[7] Although "the evolution of independent journalism" came slowly, through the high-minded efforts of such editors as Henry Raymond of the New York *Times* and

---

[5]Ibid., p. 101.
[6]Ibid., p. 143.
[7]Ibid., p. 205.

Samuel Bowles of the Springfield (Mass.) *Republican*, political independence made appreciable advances after the Civil War, and by 1900 some editors such as E. L. Godkin of the New York *Evening Post* "had a vision of a new type of journalism"[8] which soon would emerge as the dominant characteristic of the American press.

How strongly Lee believed in political independence can be garnered from his treatment of two important subjects, the party press and Horace Greeley. If we consider the party press in terms of its own age, we can see that from the struggles of the Jefferson-Hamilton era through the partisan passion of the Jacksonian period, it played a central role in the American democracy. It served as the communication network of the political system, tying together geographically dispersed groups within the parties, presenting party ideology, and helping to educate the public on political issues and politics. The partisanship resulted in intense debate and frequently abusive language, but those characteristics were not unique to the press; they permeated society. In Lee's outlook, however, based on journalistic concepts of 1917, the press' attachment to politics prevented "journals of the period" from being "newspapers in the modern sense of the term."[9] Press partisanship and calumny, which Lee condemned without reference to conditions in the surrounding culture, resulted in what he termed "the darkest period in the history of American journalism . . . a time truthfully characterized as the 'period of black journalism,' when a greater depth of degradation was reached than was ever touched in the so-called 'yellow' period of recent times."[10] In short, since party press practices violated proper journalistic principles as developed by the early 20th century, Lee considered them inappropriate and dismissed party journalism as an aberration in the historical development of modern journalism.

Most historians have agreed with Lee's condemnation of the party press; so his historical perspective may seem proper. His estimation of Greeley, however, varies so much from the predominant historical judgment that it may reveal more. The prevailing view of Greeley has been of an influential popular editor who, although at times eccentric and changeable in opinions, supported a great variety of major improvements in mid-19th century America. Lee, while conceding Greeley's influence, nevertheless denigrated him for his partisanship; for his "carping criticism" of Lincoln and his "dictatorial attitude" toward Lincoln's administration during the Civil War; for using the New York *Tribune* as a voice of his personal views and as a tool to attack opponents and to preach "the partisan gospel, according to St. Horace"; and for placing himself above his newspaper. Greeley, Lee declared, was "one of the worst offenders" in the practice of "bitter

---

[8]Ibid., p. 351.
[9]Ibid., p. 101.
[10]Ibid., p. 143.

personal journalism," a virulently opinionated writer whom "the people refused to take . . . seriously" even after the Democrats and Liberal Republicans nominated him for U.S. President in 1872.[11]

Greeley and many other editors, Lee believed, failed to live up to their primary journalistic obligation to provide fair, unbiased news. For those who Lee believed did emphasize news, he reserved the preeminent spots in history. From his point of view, the story of the progress in newspapers' coverage of news provided the heart of the history of American journalism. Newspapers gained their importance, he believed, because they could serve the universal desire of mankind for information. Lee traced the development of news from the Stone Age to the 20th century. As early as the colonial period, some papers' treatment of news had a distinctly "modern" approach,[12] but reporting in the truly modern sense began around 1800 through the work of Henry Ingraham Blake, "the Father of American Reporting." A writer and printer for the *New England Palladium,* he specialized in meeting incoming ships before they reached the Boston harbor, getting the European intelligence from captain and crew, and rushing back to the newspaper office to set the news in type, stopping the presses if necessary to assure publication of unusually important items.[13]

It was the penny press in the 1830s, however, that Lee believed revolutionized the American newspaper. By severing journalism's ties with political parties, penny newspapers freed themselves to publish all types of news, not just political fare, to appeal to the mass audience. James Gordon Bennett's New York *Herald* began a number of innovations in news content, and in the 1850s Henry Raymond of the New York *Times* "conceived the idea that the first business of a newspaper was to publish the news rather than to print the political views of its editor."[14] The better newspapers employed various methods to assure that they gathered and printed the news as quickly as possible. Speed soon became the distinguishing characteristic of American newspapers. They hired boats to run the rivers between their offices and major cities, outfitted yachts and steamships to race out to meet ships making the Atlantic crossing, placed correspondents in the nation's and world's news centers, experimented with pigeons to carry dispatches from correspondents, started the pony express between Washington and large newspaper cities, and used expensive telegraph service extensively.

Just as Lee used history to chart how journalism had come to fruition in the early 1900s, he also employed it to promote the newspapers of 1917 and his fellow journalists and to defend them against critics. He characterized professional journalists as energetic and ethical. Fearlessness, resourcefulness, aggressiveness in

---

[11]Ibid., pp. 302, 148, 210, 319-320, and 324.
[12]Ibid., p. 67.
[13]Ibid., pp. 154-155.
[14]Ibid., p. 273.

getting the news—these traits had marked true journalists throughout American history. Even the colonial printer, the first in the family of his nation's newspapermen, "as a usual thing was persistent in his efforts to enlighten his neighbors through the press, and in his attempts to found papers may be found that distinguishing characteristic of American journalism which knows no such thing as defeat."[15] Rarely, Lee declared, had journalists searching for news performed poorly, for "stupidity [was] unusual in newspaper work."[16] Twentieth-century journalism, he believed, was heir to a long legacy of professional practices and principles whose merit historical evidence proved.

Writing at a time, however, during which critics were subjecting the press to intense scrutiny and recommending that changes be made, Lee found it especially important to defend journalists' ethics and to argue the case for the press' overall performance. One of the historic roles of newspapers, he argued, had been to protect the public by providing news and scrutinizing the practices of politicians. Beginning in the late 1800s, that role became even more necessary. Journalists, he argued, never had been concerned primarily about their own interests, and since 1900 their ethical standards not only had been maintained but had risen.

To charges that newspapers sold their news and editorial columns to special interests, suppressed news in fear of powerful advertisers, and sensationalized and distorted news of opponents, Lee replied that the ethics of newspapers surpassed those of any other field. Between 1900 and 1917, he wrote, the "most important change to leave its mark upon . . . journalism . . . was in the ethical advance made in all departments of the newspaper. New standards of ethics were established, not only for the editorial, but also for the advertising and circulation departments."[17] What other profession, he asked, could compare its ethical standards to those of journalism? "In the opinion of this writer," he answered, "the ethics of journalism to-day are higher than those of any other profession. What the press does is known and read by all men. It does not print one edition for one class of subscribers and another for another [as politicians do]. . . . [E]very reader knows exactly where the paper stands. It may be on the wrong side, but it is publicly labeled so that no one is deceived. What other professional can say as much?"[18] Very few, almost none, of the serious charges that critics leveled at newspapers in either 1917 or 1923, Lee declared in the concluding chapter of the second edition of *History of American Journalism*, had any validity. History, the book argued, had shown the steady progress and improvement of the American press, and in 1923 journalism performed better than it ever had before.

---

[15]Ibid., p. 28.
[16]Ibid., p. 366.
[17]Ibid., p. 388.
[18]Ibid., p. 443.

In addition to *History of American Journalism*, Lee wrote two other books on press history, *America's Oldest Daily Newspaper; the New York Globe* (1918) and *James Luby, Journalist* (1930), the latter published after Lee's death. He also authored the section "Men of Journalism" in the *Encyclopedia Britannica*. Most of his writing, however, dealt with other areas of journalism and education, including *Wordless Journalism in America* (1915), a study of newspaper cartoons; *Instruction in Journalism in Institutions of Higher Education* (1918); *Opportunities in the Newspaper Business* (1918); and *Business Writing* (1920).[19]

Washington and Lee University awarded Lee a LittD degree in 1925. He served as president of the American Association of Teachers of Journalism in 1916-1917 and was a member of the International Association of Schools of Journalism and of the Intercollegiate Newspaper Association.

Lee died November 17, 1929, in New York City.

---

[19]James Melvin Lee, *America's Oldest Daily Newspaper; the New York Globe* (1918); *James Luby, Journalist* (Washington: Ransdell, 1930); *Instruction in Journalism in Institutions of Higher Education*, Bulletin No. 21 (U.S. Department of the Interior, Bureau of Education, 1918); *Opportunities in the Newspaper Business* (New York: Harper, 1918); *Business Writing* (Ronald Press, 1920).

Willard Bleyer and Propriety

A pioneer in journalism education, Willard Grosvenor Bleyer (1873-1935) was synonymous with the founding and early development of university training in journalism. He created the program at the University of Wisconsin, served as a national leader in the journalism education movement, and influenced many of the early attitudes about journalism education. "The first 10 years," reminisced Bleyer's fellow professor, Grant Hyde, "were the most fun, for they were pioneering years and everything we did, every new course was 'the first in the world.' We laid out techniques now used in all the schools. . . . We invented terminology now used in newspaper offices."[1]

Bleyer's early attitudes, serving as they did as the basis upon which journalism education was built, continue even today to play a role in the thinking about what a university education in journalism should be. The study of journalism history was only one among many of Bleyer's interests; but among the several textbooks he authored, his historical work, *Main Currents in the History of American Journalism*,[2] published in 1927, is the most notable. It replaced James Melvin Lee's *History of American Journalism* as the dominant text, a position it held until replaced itself by Frank Luther Mott's *American Journalism* in the 1940s.

Although Bleyer wrote little else on journalism history, he brought to his textbook a keen sense of the historian for the imperative of research into primary sources and for the need to explain the past meaningfully. His belief that the press played a critical role in society and American democracy underlay his sense of journalism history. The press, he argued, should operate responsibly and with a proper respect for propriety in order to best fulfill its responsibility to society. Although many of his beliefs—elimination of sensationalism, for example—did not accord with those of working journalists and newspaper owners who wanted to reach a mass audience, he nevertheless exercised a

---

[1] Quoted in "The Editor's Column Write," *Quill* (March 1971): 5.

[2] Willard G. Bleyer, *Main Currents in the History of American Journalism* (Boston: Houghton Mifflin, 1927).

strong voice for responsibility and respectability. He argued that journalism should be a true profession with established standards and that the primary means of attaining proper standards was through university education and training. Occupying a position of leadership among early educators through his offices in national associations and through his textbooks, he served as a leading source of ideas for teachers and, through them, for thousands of students who one day would themselves be working journalists. *Main Currents. . .* reinforced through the lessons of history his ideas of what the proper role and methods of journalism had been and should be.

Bleyer was born August 27, 1873, in Milwaukee, Wisconsin, into a family with a newspaper background. Six of his uncles worked on newspapers; and his father, Albert J. Bleyer, worked in the circulation department of the Milwaukee *Sentinel.* At the age of 19, Willard went into newspaper work. As a freshman studying English at the University of Wisconsin, he helped found the *Daily Cardinal,* the student newspaper, and served as its editor. He later served as editor of the campus' yearbook and literary magazine. After receiving an undergraduate degree in 1896 and a master's in 1898, he taught English in a Milwaukee high school, continuing to do newspaper work on the side. In 1900 he returned to the University of Wisconsin as an English instructor and began work on a PhD degree in English, which he received in 1904. The following year, he taught the university's first journalism course, which was offered through the English curriculum. In 1906 he proposed a course of study in journalism, and in 1908 the university changed his title to assistant professor of journalism. In 1912 the university created a department of journalism, with Bleyer as chair and with one additional instructor. In 1927 the department was renamed a school, with Bleyer as director. Faced with a scarcity of instructional material, he set about writing textbooks for a number of courses: *Newspaper Writing and Editing* (1913; revised 1923), *Types of News Writing* (1916), *The Profession of Journalism* (1918), and *How To Write Special Feature Articles* (1920).[3] Then in 1927 *Main Currents. . . ,* his best and most enduring work, was published.

These pioneering textbooks and his work in promoting journalism education as a legitimate university discipline—which, he believed, should be taught as a profession and a social science rather than merely as a trade—gained him national preeminence. In 1912 he helped found the American Association of Teachers of Journalism and in 1917 the American Association of Schools and Departments of Journalism. His efforts through those organizations resulted in 1939 in the formation of the American

---

[3]Willard G. Bleyer, *Newspaper Writing and Editing* (Boston: Houghton Mifflin, 1913; rev. 1923); *Types of News Writing* (1916); *The Profession of Journalism* (Boston: Little, Brown, 1918); *How To Write Special Feature Articles* (Boston: Houghton Mifflin, 1920).

Council on Education and Journalism, a national joint organization of educators and journalists. From 1923 until his death in 1935 he chaired the National Council on Education for Journalism and from 1924 to 1929 the National Council on Research in Journalism. He also contributed to the founding of Sigma Delta Chi (now, Society of Professional Journalists).

Although Bleyer had had a brief experience in professional journalism and even though he argued that journalism should be approached as a profession, he did not bring to his outlook all of the professional views prevailing in the working press. Thus, while arguing for the professionalization of journalism, he also served as critic for some of its practices. He perceived the history of American journalism as the story of the continuing progress and development of proper professional standards in the betterment of society and democracy, even though setbacks, especially during periods of sensationalism, occasionally marred the progress. History thus provided strong evidence of the correctness of his view about what the character of journalism should be.

This view of journalism history grew out of Bleyer's social and democratic outlooks. Bleyer most resembled a classic 19th-century liberal, believing in such ideas as democracy, the ability of the electorate to make responsible decisions when given adequate information, traditional values and morals, temperateness and proper standards of conduct in public affairs, the individual's responsibility to society, and the duty of educated and intelligent public men to foster high standards of tastes and behavior among the larger classes in society. His philosophy mixed a high regard for propriety with a strong sense of an individual's public duty to help improve conditions within society and to help strengthen democracy. He conceived of society as composed of two groups: an intelligent, discriminating class and the "unthinking masses."[4] The masses were ruled by emotions; and the duty of the respectable, enlightened class was to guide the public to a better society based on high standards of intellect, morals, and reform.

In the history of journalism, these tensions resulted in continuing but unsteady progress. Although not a supporter of all features of journalism of his own time, Bleyer nevertheless believed, like most journalism historians, that one major characteristic of American journalism history had been the development and advance of professional standards and practices. The thrust for progress had come, he reasoned, when newspapers had improved their coverage and presentation of news, increased their political independence, and worked to improve social conditions. Setbacks had occurred when newspapers descended to sensationalism and extreme partisanship. Told in terms of the great editors who had dominated journalism, this development then unfolded, in part, as the story of James Gordon Bennett's contributions to news innovations mixed with his pandering to the common

---

[4]*Main Currents...*, p. 2.

tastes of the masses, Horace Greeley's high sense of morals and concern for improving the conditions of mankind, E. L. Godkin's great influence based on his enlightened and elevated conduct of *The Nation* and the New York *Evening Post*, Joseph Pulitzer's contributions—despite his regrettable sensationalism—to greater democracy and social reform, William Randolph Hearst's wallowing in sensationalism, Adolph Ochs' dignified conduct of the New York *Times*, and the 1920s tabloid newspapers' reversion to sensationalism.

These "main currents" gained their significance from the fact that the press worked as a vital force in the social and political life of a nation and possessed a great potential influence for bettering both society and democracy. The critical role the press played provided the basis for all of Bleyer's other perspectives about and assessments of journalism history. He accepted without question the assumption that the press wielded substantial power in shaping and crystallizing public opinion. That influence had been evident from Revolutionary times, when newspapers "played their part in developing a feeling of solidarity among the colonists in the struggle against the mother country,"[5] to Bleyer's own time, when newspapers had helped determine public opinion on issues ranging from government fraud to American participation in World War I. Because of its influence, the press could work as a great instrument for good or evil. It could support corrupt politicians, or it could promote clean, honest government. It could accept abuses in government and society, or it could help bring about reform and justice. It could pander to the masses through emotion and sensationalism, or it could promote intelligent thinking through serious news and political analysis.

Journalists, unfortunately, had not always exercised their duties and great power responsibly. Many owners and editors had been interested primarily in building up large circulations. Mass circulation historically had lain for the most part, Bleyer believed, in "'catering to the tastes of the uninstructed.'"[6] It had its beginning in the methods of Benjamin Day, founder of the New York *Sun*, who "discovered that the secret to popular journalism lay in appealing to the emotions of the masses rather than to their intellects; in amusing, entertaining, and shocking them; in admonishing them against the moral evils of the day."[7] James Gordon Bennett honed Day's methods by "'recording gossip that interested bar-rooms, work-shops, race-courses, and tenement houses, . . . [rather than by] consulting the tastes of drawing-rooms and libraries.'"[8] These newspapers and others that imitated them degraded the role of the press by emphasizing sensationalism to appeal to the baser emotions, pandering to the popu-

---

[5]Ibid., p. 76.
[6]Ibid., p. 209, Bleyer approvingly quoting Godkin.
[7]*Main Currents...*, p. 264.
[8]Ibid., p. 209, quoting Godkin.

lar tastes of the masses, printing vulgarity, and publishing objectionable advertising. All of these practices were calculated to arouse the public, many of whose members could not even read but could be counted on to join in the newspaper-generated gossip. Bleyer's overview of Joseph Pulitzer's unfortunate but temporary descent from responsible civic leadership into sensationalism summarized his outlook on this facet of journalism history. "To reach the masses," Bleyer wrote, "he [Pulitzer] felt that he must give the masses what they wanted in the way of news. Whether the end justified the means may well be questioned. The success of this sensationalism in building up rapidly the largest circulation in this country, led a host of newspapers to imitate the *World's* sensational methods. Thus it exerted an unwholesome influence on the American press."[9]

Instead of appealing to the masses through the emotions, Bleyer argued, newspapers should have been promoting truth, high standards of behavior, good taste, morality, honesty, respectability, wholesomeness, and responsible civic conduct. The outstanding editors in American history, such as Greeley, Godkin, and Ochs, had maintained these lofty ideals of the duty of journalism even though to do so was unpopular and sometimes "unpalatable to many . . . readers."[10] These and the other great editors, such as Samuel Bowles II of the Springfield (Mass.) *Republican*, took seriously their obligation to publish newspapers containing meaningful news, promoting the highest ideals of public duty, and appealing not only to a general readership but to high-minded men and women. Bleyer's concept of the nature of a good newspaper was epitomized in two statements of purpose by Bowles and Godkin, both of whom Bleyer quoted approvingly and frequently. Bowles wrote in 1871 that "the most successful journal [is that] which lays before its readers the highest class of news, most intelligently discriminated and wisely set forth, and which cultivates a taste for such among its readers."[11] Godkin explained his purpose thusly: "I . . . undertook not to produce a paper that would be certain to sell well, but to produce a good paper, one that good and intelligent men would say ought to sell, and whose influence on those who read it, and on the country papers, would be enlightening, elevating, and refining."[12]

Lest Bleyer should be thought an aristocrat unconcerned about the general public, it should be pointed out that he possessed a high ideal of the press as an advocate of democracy and reform. Having lived through the Progressive reform movement of the early 1900s, he fit the historical concept of the Progressive reformer not as a radical but as a moderate, middle-class professional genuinely interested in solving social problems, bettering

---

[9]*Main Currents...*, p. 353.
[10]Ibid., p. 292; see also pp. 238 and 277-278.
[11]Quoted in *Main Currents...*, p. 265.
[12]Quoted in *Main Currents...*, p. 272.

conditions, and enlarging enlightened democracy. He believed the press should serve as an agent in achieving those goals, and he especially commended editors who had fulfilled their social and democratic duties. He praised Greeley for his support of social and political democracy, movements for economic and social betterment, social justice, the rights of labor, and freedom of expression; Bowles for his unequivocal stands against corruption, his support of reform of abuses in politics and business, and his fight for clean, efficient government; Godkin for his advocacy of "true democratic principles in society and government,"[13] civil service reform, progressive improvement in government, and other constructive policies to remedy evils; William Rockhill Nelson of the Kansas City *Star* for his dedication to "'the service of humanity'"[14] by advocating honest elections, democratic government, the abolition of special privilege, civic improvement, wholesome and healthy city conditions, and social and industrial justice; and Pulitzer for his devotion to "'True Democracy, based on equal rights,'"[15] social justice, enlightenment of the masses of readers, progress, and human liberty and for his opposition to a wide array of public evils and abuses.

Combined with his social and democratic outlooks, a final concept influenced Bleyer's view of history. Like James Melvin Lee, the author of the first journalism history textbook, and like most journalism historians to follow, Bleyer believed that the history of American journalism was essentially the story of journalism's progress. Frequent use of words and phrases such as "development of American journalism," "contribution to journalism," "evolution," and "advance"—along with long lists of "firsts" and "innovations"—made Bleyer's perspective evident. It was evident also in his comparison and contrasts of journalistic practices from the past with those of Bleyer's own time. The main streams of progress had been in an increased emphasis by newspapers on news, political independence, and efforts to better society.

To these, Bleyer added formal professionalism. Primarily an academic scholar rather than a professional journalist, he disliked some journalistic practices of the 1920s, especially sensationalism, and believed that changes needed to be made so that the press would better serve society. He shared Progressive reformers' belief that many of society's problems could be solved through professional training and management. The solution to problems in the press, he argued, lay in converting journalism into a true, formally organized profession. That goal could be accomplished through formal university education in journalism, the establishment of educational and professional standards for journalists, the formulation and enforcement of standards of

---

[13]*Main Currents...*, p. 271.
[14]Ibid., p. 320, Bleyer favorably quoting the *Star* upon Nelson's death.
[15]*Main Currents...*, p. 327, Bleyer quoting a New York *Times* editorial.

ethics, and unionization of workers in news-editorial departments. A firm believer in the value of education, he argued that since 1900 "the most important movement for the advancement of the profession"[16] had been the establishment of schools of journalism within universities. In the 1930s, following publication of *Main Currents.* . . , Bleyer became a mild New Deal liberal and argued for formal steps to unionize newsrooms, for professional licensing of journalists, and for legal requirements that owners operate their newspapers in the public interest rather than solely for private gain.[17]

Bleyer underwent surgery in the fall of 1934, resumed teaching, but died October 31, 1935. He left a legacy of the importance of education in journalism, of the historical importance of the press' role in bettering society, and of the need for journalism to operate in accord with the highest standards of propriety, responsibility, and professionalism.

---

[16]*Main Currents...*, p. 352.

[17]See Willard Bleyer, "Journalism in the United States: 1933," *Journalism Quarterly* 10 (1933): 296-301; and "Freedom of the Press and the New Deal," *Journalism Quarterly* 11 (1934): 22-35.

Alfred McClung Lee
and Institutional Evolution

Alfred McClung Lee (1906-) provided a new explanation for why changes had occurred during the history of American journalism. Most earlier historians had structured their narratives around outstanding individuals. Lee, a trained sociologist, challenged that approach. In *The Daily Newspaper in America: The Evolution of a Social Instrument*,[1] published in 1937, he argued that sociological influences, rather than great men, determined the course of history. By applying that concept to the study of journalism history, he brought a new perspective to understanding the past.

Lee also brought to historical study a critical attitude toward the press. An unquestioning admiration of professional journalism had marred James Melvin Lee's study of history. Even though Willard Bleyer was dissatisfied with sensational tendencies in journalism, he still presented a broadly favorable history of the press. Alfred Lee exhibited no such love. He argued that newspapers were owned by conservative businessmen whose main concern was profit. Newspapers therefore tended to serve the selfish interests of their owners rather than the interests of the public and of individual freedom.

That critical approach and the emphasis on sociological explanations made *The Daily Newspaper in America* an important work in journalism history. Yet, it never gained wide acceptance among journalism educators, the reason probably being that educators, who tended to hold a favorable view of professional journalism, disliked Lee's critical approach. As judged by standards of historical study, the book also suffered from methodological flaws and from a simplistic ideological view of history.

Although Lee taught journalism in college for a number of years, he became more prominent in sociology, enjoying an international reputation in the latter field. He was born August 23, 1906, in Oakmont, Pennsylvania, into a family dotted with at-

---

[1]Alfred McClung Lee, *The Daily Newspaper in America: The Evolution of a Social Instrument* (New York: Macmillan, 1937).

torneys, but a number of relatives who were published authors stimulated his interest in writing. Although he worked briefly for the Brownsville (Pa.) *Daily Telegraph* and in other journalistic jobs, he studied mathematics and English composition in his undergraduate coursework at the University of Pittsburgh, where he also worked on the student newspaper and yearbook. He received the BA degree in 1927. He earned a master's degree in sociology at Pittsburgh in 1931 and a PhD in sociology at Yale University in 1933. Both his masters thesis and doctoral dissertation provided study which served as the foundation of *The Daily Newspaper in America.* From 1934 through 1937 he taught journalism at the University of Kansas, chairing a national committee which resulted in the creation of the Sigma Delta Chi Distinguished Service Award in 1935. Lee himself received the research award in 1937 for *The Daily Newspaper in America.* Although he taught occasional courses dealing with journalism, his teaching focused on sociology after leaving Kansas, his career taking him to Yale (1937-1938), New York University (1938-1942), Wayne State University (1942-1949), on leave as visiting professor of journalism at the University of Michigan, (1947-1948), Brooklyn College of the City University of New York (1949-1971), and on leave as visiting graduate professor at NYU (1951-1955). He received a number of national and international awards for service in sociology and co-founded, with his wife, the Society for the Study of Social Problems in 1950 and the Association for Humanist Sociology in 1975. The former is the second largest sociological society in the world.[2]

Lee authored, edited, or collaborated in the publication of 17 books, most dealing with sociology, social problems, or propaganda. An intent to help improve social and human conditions motivated his writing.[3] In describing his purpose, he wrote:

> My books have been efforts to work for greater press freedom, for more popular understanding of communication processes (propaganda), for greater equality of opportunity for all racial and religious groups, for a more accurate understanding of motivation and morality, and for broader acceptance of our humanist heritage. . . . I have looked upon [writing] as a way of helping to make life more livable for more people. As a relative principally of lawyers and clergymen, I learned about human deprivation and suffering rather young and rather vividly. It seemed to me that something was to be done on which I might help.[4]

---

[2]This biographical material is gathered from a number of biographical encyclopedia and a letter and narrative from Lee to the author, June 7, 1986.

[3]Lee to author, June 23, 1986.

[4]Quoted in biographical entry, *Contemporary Authors* (New Revision Series, Vol. 3) (Detroit: Gale Research Co.), p. 329.

Lee made that statement years after he had written *The Daily Newspaper in America* as a young man of 30. Sociological theory and ideological outlooks, rather than humanistic philosophy, provided the framework for his history of newspapers. He attempted to demonstrate that impersonal, automatically acting social forces, rather than great individuals, had determined the historical changes that molded the nature of the newspaper. Journalism historians, he argued, had believed that outstanding individuals were the primary factor in history. But by stressing "the lives and achievements of great men rather than the accumulating and adjusting experience of society," historians clung to a theory "scarcely less naive than the savage's recourse to magical explanation." Great men, Lee said, were simply the products of their time rather than the reasons for historical change. The press had been molded by "the blind forces of society and not appreciably the creative urge of a few Greeleys, Danas, and Hearsts."[5] Although not naming historians, Lee apparently meant to imply such people as Bleyer, James M. Lee, and George Henry Payne, author of *History of Journalism in the United States*, which had been published in 1920.

To explain the historic changes in newspapers, Lee resorted to the biological theory of evolution, which a number of sociologists had attempted to adapt to theories of social change. American newspapers, he said, had gone through an evolutionary growth marked throughout history by a process of invention of or variation from methods, selective elimination of less effective methods, and transmission of the effective methods to other newspapers. Lee summarized the process this way:

> Variations, new folkways [that is, practices], arise to meet new social situations; then, through repeated trial and error and comparison, society [in the instance of newspapers: primarily, owners, employees, and the public] automatically selects the methods which seem to work best. By transmission, folkways pass from individual to individual, group to group, generation to generation. Social instruments like the daily newspaper grow as institutionalized forms in the evolutionary process.[6]

Applied to actual changes in newspaper history, the theory worked this way. A problem or an opportunity presented itself to astute entrepreneurs, who recognized a need for a new practice to address the problem or the value that an invention held. The utility or value of some variations—a new practice or an invention—was so evident that the variations immediately replaced older practices. The utilization of some variations occurred slowly,

---

[5]*The Daily Newspaper in America*, pp. 1 and 2.
[6]Ibid., p. 5.

however, because older practices had become entrenched for various reasons (such as hand compositors' opposition to Linotype machines and newspapers owners' opposition to circulation audits). After their appearance, the variations were tried and compared with older practices. Newspapers then discarded the variations and older practices that did not work well (such as, to use a simplistic example, carrier pigeons as a way of transmitting news reports after the invention of the telegraph). As the variations proved their value, other newspapers adopted them. They then replaced the older practices and became themselves the accepted norm.

A number of social factors accounted for this evolutionary process and the changes that took place. Lee listed some of the most important, not in any particular order of significance, as these: available natural resources, government, character of the population, literacy and reading habits, certain folkways and mores, raw materials and plant equipment, facilities for the transmission of news, and newspaper practices.[7] Among these categories of factors, he included such items as paper-making processes, newspaper production equipment, distribution methods, and labor. The most important, however, were newspaper owners' economic motivation and self-interest. Owners had opposed changes that possessed the potential to damage their investment and profit and had quickly taken up new practices only when to do so directly benefited them. Under their dubious and hypocritical use of the phrase "freedom of the press," for example, they had opposed the struggle of newspaper labor to improve working conditions and salary. Most of the problems with newspapers, their "maladjustments" to variations, Lee implied, could be accounted for by owners' selfish motives and practices.

Despite the innovative approach Lee provided for journalism history, his study suffered because of serious problems in historical method. The essential problem grew from Lee's approach as applied to his purpose. He attempted to explain the past as sociology rather than as history. He purported to write a history of daily newspapers, but he intended to make it a sociological treatise. As a result, he used the methods of the sociologist rather than of the historian. *The Daily Newspaper in America* is interesting as an attempt at a sociological explanation of the press. It does not stand up well as history. The unique methods of sociology are not adequate for the study of history.

The sociologist asks general questions and attempts to test or apply theories. He must rely on statistics gathered from existing communities. Like other social scientists, he tends to be present-minded, interested in constructing models, in establishing regularities he perceives present in the data, in linking together theory and research, and in using the past to substantiate theories offered in explanation of sociological concepts. The historian is

---

[7]Ibid., pp. 10-11.

more interested in the particular and the concrete and places greater emphasis on original sources. The sociologist thinks of his field as a type of "science," which, if properly done, can devise experiments and test them in the social laboratory. The historian, studying events that no longer exist, has no such opportunity. The sociologist/social scientist seeks to explain by developing laws; the historian hopes to generalize also, but his generalizations usually are tentative. The sociologist can measure, but measurement is not always available to the historian. Sociologists use their studies to predict, but historians do not claim that their study allows them to guess the future. Historians study what people have done, thus helping one to understand the past and possibly what people can do, but they do not predict what people will do. The material of history is simply different from that of sociology. It yields a different type of understanding than that which the sociologist seeks. With his approach to *The Daily Newspaper in America* Lee tried to use sociological methods to make history yield a specific social relationship, which the methods cannot do.

The theoretical basis of the study added to the methodological problem. Adopting a model used by various sociologists, Lee believed that Darwin's theory of biological evolution could be used to explain the growth and development of social institutions. The analogy of nature with social forms is specious in itself, but Lee created an additional problem by attempting to apply the theory-of-nature-as-adapted-to-sociology to the study of history. In the late 19th and early 20th centuries, many historians had been enamored with the idea that the evolutionary hypothesis could be used to explain universal change in history. It reached its zenith with Oswald Spengler's *Decline of the West*,[8] published in 1932, which used an evolutionary analogy of biological life to explain the growth, maturity, death, and decay of civilizations. Although such an approach gained a vogue among historians around 1900 who wanted to think of their discipline as a science, it never gained real popularity with professional historians, and it has been discredited since. Lee, however, was writing at a time when such theory was popular in certain circles and did not question the validity of applying evolutionary theory to either sociology or history. He enthusiastically adopted the theory as a sure way to explain sociology and then adapted the biological-sociological hybrid theory to explain history. Finally, he gathered material that fit the theory and used it as "proof" of the theory.

Such use of theory, despite its convolution, still can be simplistic—and can attract by its simplicity—but it is quickly rejected by historians trained to be cautious and to examine grand theories by attention to particulars. Theories and preconceived explanations may suit well the sociologist's approach to discover-

---

[8] Oswald Spengler, *Decline of the West* (2 vols.) (New York: Alfred A. Knopf, 1932).

ing principles of social relationships, but historians are not permitted to know their conclusions before studying the past. Lee's reliance on a biological model perhaps can be excused because it recently had been popular with some historians, but it does not stand the test of time. The historian knows that sociology's quest for "laws" is not the best way to explain the complexities and variety of life in the past.

Ideological simplicity also flawed *The Daily Newspaper in America*. Historians deserve to have and use their particular points of view, but they must recognize that they do indeed possess viewpoints. Otherwise, they assume that their perspective is simply the "truth." An unconsidered belief in one's own rightness can result in exaggeration and over-simplification. Lee believed that he brought no philosophy or "ism" to his explanation of newspaper history.[9] Yet, ideology pervaded the book.[10] He approvingly quoted the sociologist W. G. Sumner's one-dimensional view of history as "only a tiresome repetition of one story. Persons and classes have sought to win possession of the power of the State in order to live luxuriously out of the earning of others."[11] That view marked the classic Progressive interpretation, which viewed American history as the story of a continuing conflict between the elite, wealthy, aristocratic class and the egalitarian, democratic masses. Writing during the Great Depression and New Deal liberalism, Lee thought of newspaper history largely in terms of owners' attempts to control the press for their own selfish ends. "In the struggles of labor unions for more satisfactory hours, wages, and working conditions," he wrote, "in the fights of the publishers to maintain their profits through defending 'freedom of the press,' and in the efforts of legislators and governmental administrators to aid one side or the other, the age old story continues."[12] Such a stark black-white view of history serves the ideologue's cause, but it does a disservice to the understanding of the fullness and complexity of humankind and institutions in history.

The attitude that allowed ideological and theoretical simplicity was demonstrated in another way. A glib acceptance of cause-effect relationships without evidence marked *The Daily Newspaper in America*. In a work intended fundamentally to demonstrate the cause for practices and changes, that habit damaged the foundation. Lee asserted, for example, that newspaper circulation

---

[9]*The Daily Newspaper in America*, p. vii.

[10]The examples of ideology are too numerous to describe here, but typical ones may be found in ibid. on pp. 34, 62, 106-107, 110, 134, 138, 149, 153, 156, 160, 163, 173, 178, 197, 205, 241-250, 329, 408, 504, 567, 571, 596, 605, and 697.

[11]W. G. Sumner, *What Social Classes Owe to Each Other* (New York: Harper & Bros., 1920), p. 30, quoted in *The Daily Newspaper in America*, p. 254.

[12]*The Daily Newspaper in America*, p. 254.

increased rapidly after 1880 because of a growth in "interest in reading" without providing any evidence that such interest had increased and because of "the mechanical improvement of the newspaper industry" without demonstrating how mechanical improvement related to circulation.[13] Similarly, he made such undocumented statements as these: the position of editor emerged in the 1790s because of daily newspapers' larger budgets (rather than because of the need of partisan newspapers to have editors who could write convincingly, as most other historians had suggested); the opposition of religious groups to Sunday newspapers in the 1850s actually "stimulated" their popularity; and in the 1930s J. M. Patterson took certain editorial stands in the New York *Daily News* because he "knew the kind of leadership his masses of readers wanted."[14] Lee did not indicate how Patterson "knew" or even how Lee himself knew the kind of leadership the readers wanted. Lee criticized "'the confident reasoning of a person who is not curious about verifying his result,'"[15] but he did not apply the same standard to his own reasoning.

A number of other methodological problems marred the book. The most serious was its reliance on secondary sources. Good historical study must go to primary or original sources. Lee did not, and a large percentage of his secondary sources were not historical but simply sociological treatises. He frequently used sociologists' theoretical observations to demonstrate the accuracy of his assumptions about history. To prove, for example, that newspaper owners had used the phrase "freedom of the press" simply to protect their own interests, Lee again quoted the sociologist W. G. Sumner. Such catchwords, Sumner claimed, "always reveal the invincible tendency of the masses to mythologize. They are personified and a superhuman energy is attributed to them. . . . They carry a coercion with them and overwhelm people who are not trained to verify assertions and dissect fallacies."[16] Such "appeal to authority" provides no evidence in the study of history.

The Daily Newspaper in America was disappointing as a historical study, but it has exercised considerable importance in the study of journalism history. Even though it never saw widespread use as a text, it did broaden the perspective from which historians would view journalism. In recent years, as historians have looked for approaches other than the professionalized, Developmental perspective, several aspects of Lee's sociological outlook have come into vogue. The assumption that the nature of newspapers is determined by factors in their cultural environment, for

---

[13]Ibid., p. 70.

[14]Ibid., pp. 604, 395, 658.

[15]Ibid., p. 605, Lee approvingly quoting Henshaw Ward, *Builders of Delusions* (Indianapolis: Bobbs-Merrill, 1931), p. 131.

[16]W. G. Sumner, *Folkways: A Study of Sociological Importance of Usages* (Boston: Ginn, 1906), pp. 176-177, quoted in *The Daily Newspaper in America*, p. 409.

example, has held historians' interest in the last decade (even though that observation seems painfully obvious and a poor reward for much scholarly effort). As they have expressed an intensified desire to discover grand theories that explain journalism history, Lee's stature as one of the preeminent historians of the press has grown.

Frank Luther Mott
and Devotion to the Press

Hardly anyone during Frank Luther Mott's lifetime (1886-1964) questioned his rank as the preeminent historian of American journalism. More than a quarter century after his death, he continues to hold that position. He is the only journalism educator to be awarded the Pulitzer Prize for history; and his *American Journalism*,[1] first published in 1941, went through three editions and served as the dominant textbook in journalism history until the 1970s. Even today, in the face of efforts to re-explain journalism history from different perspectives, Mott's ideas cling to the minds of historians.

Yet, Mott's contributions form a paradox. Severe problems plagued his approach. His unquestioning admiration of the press resulted in a superficial explanation of history, and his opinions so tightly gripped his intellect that he failed to recognize the possibility that history could be explained any way other than how he perceived it.

Despite those problems and because of *American Journalism's* wide use, Mott's ideas were passed to thousands of students. They pervaded and to a large degree determined the study of journalism history for more than 30 years. Many historians still look to *American Journalism* as the authority in most matters, as the starting point and the guide for all other studies. As a result, it can be said justifiably that the preeminent historian of American journalism caused more damage than any other person who ever wrote about the field. By imparting a simplistic view of history to generations of students and other historians, he encouraged a superficiality that has handicapped the study of history to a degree unimagined by teachers, students, and other historians. But Mott's ideas extended beyond the field of scholarship. By providing historical "evidence" of the greatness of the press, he

---

[1]Frank Luther Mott, *American Journalism: A History of Newspapers in the United States through 250 Years, 1690-1940* (New York: Macmillan, 1941; rev. 1950, 1962).

helped entrench among working journalists an uncritical devotion to the values of their profession and a one-sided view that the press can do no wrong.

Mott was born April 4, 1886, to David C. and Mary Tipton Mott near the small Iowa community of What Cheer. Two years later his father bought the village's weekly newspaper, *The Patriot*. The son's first memory of newspaper life was that of standing in the *Patriot* office knee-deep in water after a nearby creek had overflowed. The paper provided his early entry into journalism, folding newspapers after school. Thereafter, he worked on various newspapers his father owned, learning at the age of 11 to set type by hand for the Tipton (Iowa) *Advertiser*. That early family newspaper background probably played a key role in Mott's later historical admiration of the press. He attended Simpson College 3 years and then acquired a bachelor's degree from the University of Chicago in 1907. He had gone to Chicago planning to study law, "but in going to my law classes," he wrote, "I had to pass the open windows of the university press, and the smell of printer's ink on damp sheets made me so homesick for printing offices that I gave up the law for journalism."[2] Upon graduation, he worked 11 years on a variety of small newspapers, but then decided to continue his education. He studied English and literature at Columbia University and received a master's degree in 1919.

He taught English at Simpson College and then at the University of Iowa beginning in 1921. Iowa named him professor of journalism and director of its School of Journalism in 1927. In the meantime he began work on a doctorate in English at Columbia, receiving the degree in 1928. He remained at Iowa until 1942, when the School of Journalism at the University of Missouri named him dean, a position he held until retirement in 1951. During his years as a journalism educator, he served as one of the field's national leaders, holding such positions as chairman of the National Council for Research in Journalism, two-term president of the American Association of Schools and Departments of Journalism, editor of *Journalism Quarterly*, and two-term president of Kappa Tau Alpha, the national journalism honor society. Simpson College and Boston, Temple, and Marquette universities awarded him honorary doctorates.

Few journalism educators have been more prolific than Mott. He authored, edited, or co-authored 33 books, along with numerous journal articles and short stories. Most prestigious was the monumental, five-volume *A History of American Magazines*.[3] For volumes two and three, covering the years 1850 to 1885, he received the 1939 Pulitzer Prize for History and for volume four the 1958 Bancroft Prize. Twice, in 1938 and 1957, he received the na-

[2]Stanley Kunitz, ed., *Twentieth Century Authors* (1st Supplement) (New York: Wilson, 1955), p. 695.

[3]Frank Luther Mott, *A History of American Magazines* (5 vols.) (New York: D. Appleton; Cambridge: Harvard University Press, 1930-1968).

tional distinguished service award for research from Sigma Delta Chi, the professional journalism society. He helped institute Kappa Tau Alpha's National Research Award and received it himself in 1958. KTA renamed it the Frank Luther Mott Research Award in 1960. Despite the respect accorded his magazine history, Mott is best known in journalism education for *American Journalism: A History of Newspapers in the United States through 250 Years* (first published in 1941 and updated in 1950 and 1962). Indicating its popularity, the first edition alone went through seven reprintings. Other well-known books included *Interpretations of Journalism* (1936; co-edited with Ralph D. Casey), *Jefferson and the Press* (1943), *Golden Multitudes: The Story of Best Sellers in the United States* (1947), *The News in America* (1952), and his autobiography, *Time Enough* (1962).[4]

In all those works, Mott displayed an admiration of journalism only most rarely tempered by criticism. *American Journalism* resembled an in-house narrative using history as a means of praising the press. It cast a soft light to hide blemishes. But as a spokesman for journalism, Mott at least was honest, noting in the book's preface that he held a "sympathetic admiration for American journalism."[5] Aware of his prejudice, however, he did little to keep it in check. Consequently, *American Journalism* explained all issues from a pro-journalism point of view and usually blamed outside factors for any problems. One example, Mott's discussion of relations between United States presidents and the press, may serve to illustrate.

Woodrow Wilson, Mott explained, got along poorly with the press because of his unusual sensitivity. Warren G. Harding worked amicably with journalists early in his administration, but he restricted his press conferences "after he had blundered in reply to an important question on foreign affairs." Calvin Coolidge took advantage of the press by issuing trial balloons and then, when the public did not accept them, denying that he had made the statements reported by newspapers. Despite such misbehavior, the Washington press corps still treated Cooldige "most generously." From the beginning of Herbert Hoover's term, he placed rigid restrictions on press coverage; and as the difficulties of his administration multiplied, he clamped down so tightly on

---

[4]Frank Luther Mott and Ralph D. Casey, eds., *Interpretations of Journalism* (Crofts, 1936); Mott, *Jefferson and the Press* (Baton Rouge: Louisiana State University Press, 1943); Mott, *Golden Multitudes: The Story of Best Sellers in the United States* (New York: Macmillan, 1947); Mott, *The News in America* (Cambridge: Harvard University Press, 1952); Mott, *Time Enough: Essays in Autobiography* (Chapel Hill: University of North Carolina, 1962).

[5]Mott, *American Journalism* (1941), p. vii. Because the second and third editions of *American Journalism* simply added material at the end of the previous edition, the page numbers throughout the three editions are identical. Thus, the page references used here and in the following notes apply to all three editions.

coverage that "there was no free flow of information." Franklin Roosevelt's relationship with the press started auspiciously, but after a "surprisingly long" honeymoon of 2 years, relations became strained because of "the repudiation of a statement that most of the men [journalists] had reported in good faith, growing doubts about the New Deal and the man behind it, and an occasional stinging rebuke given a correspondent." After Harry Truman's first year in office, during which he worked reasonably well with the press, he grew "more noncommittal and his conferences more infrequent." Mott attributed the change to the fact that in a news conference Truman made "a slip" on a political issue.[6] All relations between presidents and the press had not been so unfortunate, but the problems overshadowed the felicitous situations. Although placing the blame for deteriorating relations on the presidents may seem proper to the professional journalist or to the educator trained in journalism, doing so demonstrates a narrow perspective. Rarely in human affairs or in history can situations be explained as so starkly black and white.

Why did Mott have such a strong pro-journalism outlook? The most obvious answer is that he had grown up with a newspaper background, had worked for newspapers, and had taught journalism. He was likely to take up the values and attitudes of journalism. He looked at history from the journalist's perspective and could not imagine there existed any other way to look at it. But on a more complex level, he believed in the press as a vital component of a democracy. In a 1959 address to the Press Congress of the World, he outlined the reasons why journalism education was needed. They rested on the press' democratic role. The "basic axiom of democracy," he said, was that people had to be informed in order to make wise decisions and that they "must depend upon great mass communication media" to provide the information.[7] That outlook had been fully molded by the totalitarian threats of World War II, when Mott wrote not only *American Journalism* but *Jefferson and the Press* as well and edited *Journalism in Wartime*[8] (both published in 1943). All three books demonstrated his conviction that a free press played a key role in any system of popular or democratic government.

But Mott's admiration of journalism applied only to modern journalism, or to historic journalism which adhered to the principles and practices of modern journalism. Six essential factors characterized what Mott thought proper journalism to be: an emphasis on news as the press' first duty, broad freedom of the press, political independence, mass circulation and popularity, support of the interest of the common people, and the practice of journal-

---

[6]Ibid., pp. 721-723 and 768-769.

[7]"The Edifice of Education for Journalism," Columbia, MO, March 3, 1959, reprinted in *Journalism Quarterly* 36 (1959): 410.

[8]Frank Luther Mott, ed., *Journalism in Wartime* (Washington, DC: American Council on Public Affairs, 1943).

ism as a profession. By these standards he measured and evaluated all journalism history. He departed from his admiration of journalism only when the press failed to perform according to those standards. Those perspectives account, for example, for his devoted defense of Thomas Jefferson as a libertarian advocate of press freedom and his criticism of the party press era as the "'Dark Ages' of American journalism."[9] When he believed that earlier journalists had not abided by modern standards, he condemned them without sympathy for the fact that they could not have known what "modern" standards one day would be. Mott seems to have given little consideration to earlier journalists' inability to predict the future.

Considering modern journalism the apex of history, Mott visualized journalism history primarily in terms of development. History became simply the story of the progress of journalism in light of his six factors of proper journalism. The past was less important for itself than for how it had contributed to the development of what journalism was to become. This view exhibited the fallacy of historical present-mindedness in the extreme. Such an outlook made Mott's outline of journalism history predictable.

His narrative went this way:

The colonial press, treated in an opening session entitled "The Beginners, 1690-1765," provided the genesis of American journalism and the origin of many later practices. During the colonial period could be found the patterns upon which later publications were based, forerunners of the newspaper, early episodes involving freedom of the press, and numerous journalistic "firsts." Mott explained various aspects of the colonial press such as newsgathering methods with an implicit comparison to later practices. In general, he evaluated the colonial press as being relatively crude by 20th-century standards but providing a solid foundation for journalistic practices and achievements that were to come later. Although he found much lacking in the attitudes and performance of many early printers, he believed some had recognized what journalism was supposed to be and had made worthy contributions to the quality and development of the American press.

The revolutionary press of the following period helped promote the cause of independence. After the Revolution, the press became strictly partisan and sank into darkness. It emphasized political opinion rather than news, it appealed to a small group rather than to a mass audience, it subverted journalism's duty to provide reasoned information and replaced it with partisan scurrility.

Despite the darkness, Mott could see that the soul of journalism was marching on, soon to be greeted by "Sunrise," a fortuitous turn of phrase for the arrival of the penny press with the appearance of the New York *Sun*. Of the years following 1833, Mott

---

[9]*American Journalism*, p. 169.

wrote, "The spectacular phenomenon of the period . . . was the advent of the penny paper, with its addition of a new economic level of the population to the newspaper audience. Related to this great event in the history of journalism was the introduction of new facets of the news concept; and these developments . . . produced nothing less than a revolution in news."[10] Modern journalism had, in effect, arrived. For the years intervening until the mid-1900s, all that remained of the historical narrative was to fill in the details of the people and episodes that polished the techniques, and to chronicle how newspapers improved their news coverage and increased their circulation. Prominent in the story were such features as leaders of the stature of James Gordon Bennett, Horace Greeley, Charles Dana, Joseph Pulitzer, and E. W. Scripps, the development of production mechanics and communication technologies, improvements in reporting, the victories for freedom of the press, professionalization with all its attendant advances, and the growth in the size of newspaper operations with the resulting economic stability. By 1940 the story of how journalism had progressed from its crude beginnings to maturity was complete.

The story clearly suited educator/historians and the students they were training to become professional journalists. But what should Mott's proper rank as a historian be?

The answer is not simple. Clearly Mott enjoys a reputation among journalism educators as the historian of first rank. "Mr. Journalism," some called him. Many still consider *American Journalism* the definitive work in the field. Based on extensive research into primary sources, it and Mott's history of magazines established for him a reputation as an indefatiguable historian with an inexhaustible store of information. He also was one of the rare journalism professors to publish research that gained the general respect of non-journalism scholars.

Despite Mott's reputation, a number of flaws in his work, especially in *American Journalism*, prevent his being considered a great historian. Despite winning the Pulitzer and Bancroft prizes, he would not be considered, for example, among the pre-eminent scholars of American history, even if the number of historians accorded that rank were made very large. Some critics argued that even with his magnus opus, *A History of American Magazines*, he showed himself a mere chronicler rather than a thoughtful historian. The vast scope of that work, however, perhaps speaks for itself. Problems are more serious with *American Journalism*, and it is that book that provides the primary basis for Mott's reputation in journalism history. It suffers from its addiction to collections of details, but its scholarly gashes go even deeper.

Most serious was Mott's superficial pro-journalism, Developmental point of view. Immersed in journalism, he could not see

---

[10]Ibid., p. 215.

that newspaper history could be studied from any perspective other than simply the press' professional progress. History therefore became a simplistic detailing of how practices had advanced in order that journalism could become as meritorious as Mott perceived it to be in his own time. Such a view was not only superficial but immensely conceited. It measured, for example, the performance of journalists from generations past as if their entire reason for existing had been simply to contribute to what journalism would be one golden day in the future; and it condemned those who, such as party editors, had not performed satisfactorily according to the standards of "proper" journalism as they existed at the time of Mott's study. Such extreme present-mindedness implied that the journalists of 1800 should have known what proper practices would be a century and a half later and based all their work on modern principles.

Had Mott recognized the intellectual failure of his perspective, perhaps he could have reduced the shortcomings of his approach. But Mott was not one to question his own opinions. Students and colleagues noted that modesty and open-mindedness were not his best characteristics.[11] His limited perspective was all too evident in his scholarship. He believed so strongly in the correctness of his opinion about history that he believed his was not opinion at all. It was, plainly and simply, the only way that history could be. In a review of Louis Filler's *The Muckrakers: Crusaders for American Liberalism*, for example, he chastised the author for letting his "point of view" interfere "with his function as a historian,"[12] the implication being that Mott believed historians could tell history without having a point of view—and, further, that Mott had achieved such perfection. Such confined thinking indicated a limited historical mind, and it restricted the value of the contribution that Mott might have made to the study of journalism history.

Such limitations, however, perhaps say more about the state of sophistication among journalism historians than about Mott. The fact that a historian with such weaknesses as Mott possessed could be recognized as journalism's preeminent historian—and that his reputation would be based, no less, on a textbook—indicates something about the distance the study of journalism history must progress before it can be taken very seriously. Journalism educators, students, and professionals may have considered Mott's ideas valid enough to convince them that history demonstrates the goodness and greatness of the press, but because of the fundamental faults in Mott's thinking he contributed little other than minutely detailed chronologies. He provided no significant or insightful understanding of either history or contemporary

---

[11]Dr. C. Richard King, a student of Mott, to author, May 27, 1986; and William H. Taft to author, June 8 and July 7, 1986. The history course he taught was, observed Prof. King, "in Mott by Mott for Mott."

[12]*Journalism Quarterly* 17 (1940): 52.

journalism.

As Mott's work recedes into the past, we gradually are becoming able to make some detached historical judgments about it. Through the telescope of time, despite the volume of his work—for which he should be justly admired—the legacy of journalism's preeminent historian now appears to be primarily narrow perspective.

Sidney Kobre
and Sociological History

Sidney Kobre (1907-) did more than anyone else to promote the study of journalism history from a sociological perspective. In a series of books covering history by major periods and in a survey textbook, he attempted to show that the development of the press could be understood only through its interrelationship with American society. He applied his concept more fully than any other journalism historian, using his sociological approach as the scheme for five books. He thus sounded a persistent call for broadening the perspective from which journalism historians looked at the press. He also has been one of few historians to produce books covering entire historical periods. His works on the colonial, antebellum, Gilded Age, and 20th-century press stand with only a handful of others providing period overviews. He published more words—some 2,100 pages full—aimed at constructing a complete narrative of the history of American journalism than any other historian.

Despite all his words and his efforts to build a system to explain history, Kobre never attained the stature of less productive historians. Willard Bleyer, author of only one book on history, and Frank Luther Mott and, later, Edwin Emery, who wrote far less on journalism history than Kobre did, became the mentors of generations of history students. Yet none did as much conscious effort to construct an explanation of journalism history as he. Mott and Emery, especially, provided virtually no new understanding of history. Yet, it was their textbooks rather than Kobre's that teachers across the nation adopted. The reason may have been as simple as differences in graphic design or the marketing strategies of the publishers, or it may have been that Kobre's sociological explanation departed too obviously from the prevailing view of simple journalistic progress—even though Kobre clearly shared the traditional Developmental view of history.

The reasons for the limited commercial success of Kobre's works were superficial. Their problems with historical study went deeper. Like so many other journalism historians, Kobre did not comprehend historical method; and, like Alfred Lee, he substituted sociological method for it. The resultant errors were in many ways the same. Compounding the problem, he did an incomplete job at what he most ardently claimed to do. He wanted to provide a sociological explanation of journalism history, but he failed to integrate the media with their sociological environment. Rather than painting a multidimensional picture of the media in society, he drew two pictures: one, in the foreground, of the press and, on a separate background canvass, the other of society.

Born September 7, 1907, in Winston-Salem, North Carolina, Kobre was the son of Max and Sadie Harris Kobre. The family moved successively to Danville and Richmond, Virginia, and then to Baltimore, Maryland. He attended Johns Hopkins University, receiving an undergraduate degree in English in 1927. He worked as a reporter and business editor for the Newark (N. J.) *Star Eagle* from 1928 to 1931 and then joined the staff of the Newark *Ledger* as a reporter and editorial writer. There he developed an interest in journalism history and the background of the American newspaper. To satisfy his interest, he enrolled in evening courses in sociology at Columbia University, receiving a master's degree in 1934. He continued to work for the *Ledger* until 1938, when he joined the Baltimore *Home News* as managing editor. His other newspaper work included positions as managing editor of the chain of *Guide Publications* in Baltimore (1939-1941 and 1946-1949) and owner/publisher of the *Suburban Times* of Baltimore (1941-1942).

In his courses at Columbia, he found that researchers had focused on family, government, and religion as social institutions but had given little attention to the press. He enrolled in the doctoral program in sociology at Columbia and wrote his dissertation on the sociological history of American journalism. He received the PhD in 1944. Returning to newspaper work, he continued to do research into history and the interrelationship of newspapers with society. Study of the latter resulted in a number of journal articles and books about reporting, including *Backgrounding the News* (1939), *Psychology and the News*, with Juanita Parks (1955), *News Behind the Headlines* (1955), *Behind the Shocking Crime Headlines* (1957), *The Press and Contemporary Affairs* (1957), and *Reporting News in Depth* (1982).[1] He attempted with those books to link journalism and social science. In 1949 he joined the journalism faculty at Florida State University and served as director of the Bureau of Media Research from

---

[1]Sidney Kobre, *Backgrounding the News* (Twentieth Century Press, 1939); Kobre and Juanita Parks, *Psychology and the News* (Tallahassee: Florida State University, Bureau of Media Research, 1955); Kobre, *News Behind the Headlines* (Tallahassee: Florida State University, Bureau of Media Research, 1955); Kobre, *Behind the Shocking Crime Headlines* (Tallahassee: Florida State University, Bureau of Media Research, 1957); Kobre, *The Press and Contemporary Affairs* (Tallahassee: Florida State University, Bureau of Media Research, 1957); Kobre, *Reporting News in Depth* (Washington, DC: University Press of America, 1982).

1950 until 1964. He then taught at the Community College of Baltimore until retirement.

In his history books, Kobre attempted to provide an unbroken historical narrative of the American press. His first book, *The Development of the Colonial Newspaper*[2] (1944), grew out of his doctoral dissertation and covered the period from 1690 to 1783. It was a pioneering effort to study the early American press from a sociological perspective and remains the only book treating the entire colonial period of press history. Devoted to individual accounts of colonial papers, it detailed various features of their origins and operation. Kobre based the research, however, only on the newspapers themselves and on secondary sources. He failed to examine such material as private writings and business records of the printers, and he therefore could provide little more than a picture from one perspective. He did a less adequate job of weaving the newspapers into their social environment. Basing his knowledge on secondary sources, he related essentially well-known facts and used them for most of his background. He never succeeded at integrating newspapers and society and therefore failed to achieve his primary goal—explaining the history of the colonial press as a social instrument molded by its times.

Kobre took essentially the same approach to his other books, focusing on the themes of how social, political, cultural, and economic forces contributed to the development of American newspapers. *Foundations of American Journalism*[3] (1958) traced the history of communication from ancient Egypt through 18th-century England and then chronicled the history of the American press from 1783 through the Civil War. It told the story of how newspapers, beginning as small, weak sheets in colonial times, had developed into powerful metropolitan publications by the Civil War. *The Yellow Press and Gilded Age Journalism*[4] (1964) carried the story through 1900, relating how, in the post-Civil War period, newspapers had to adjust to an urban industrial environment. *Modern American Journalism*[5] (1959) completed the narrative. Emphasizing the development of the modern press in terms of press interaction with its environment, Kobre argued that "gigantic forces" including population changes and growth, industrialization, labor organization, and a spirit of social reform transformed America in the first half of the 20th century and thus drastically altered the nation's press. As newspapers mirrored the changes in economics and society, they changed to

---

[2]Sidney Kobre, *The Development of the Colonial Newspaper* (Pittsburgh: Colonial Press, 1944).

[3]Sidney Kobre, *Foundations of American Journalism* (Tallahassee: Florida State University, Bureau of Media Research, 1958).

[4]Sidney Kobre, *The Yellow Press and Gilded Age Journalism* (Tallahassee: Florida State University, Bureau of Media Research, 1964).

[5]Sidney Kobre, *Modern American Journalism* (Tallahassee: Florida State University, Bureau of Media Research, 1959).

conform to new conditions. Thus, there developed a greater emphasis on interpretive journalism and column writing to explain a complex society to readers. Journalism schools and associations of journalists grew in importance as the profession grew more sophisticated. Technological developments in radio and television altered traditional journalistic practices. Because of rising costs of labor and newsprint, publishers employed newspaper consolidations and chain ownership to save money and to buy production material on a large scale, mirroring similar developments in such other businesses as grocery store chains. In 1969 Kobre condensed the material from his four books into a survey textbook, *Development of American Journalism*.[6]

Alfred Lee had provided a sociological explanation of journalism history before Kobre. Both believed that outside factors influenced the press, but there the similarities ended. Lee placed primary emphasis on internal forces and embraced a rigid theoretical view of institutional evolution through impersonal forces and a critical evaluation of the press. Although Kobre agreed that sociological influences shaped the press, he did not hold to such a narrow evolutionary view. Rather than creating an elaborate model of how social forces molded the press, he presented them more generally as influences working on it. He also departed from Lee in the importance placed on the role of individuals. Lee assumed that institutional forces determined how journalists responded. Kobre believed that individuals played key roles, working out and contributing innovations to the development of journalism. Not so devoted as Lee to a theory, he thus presented an explanation more capable of considering a broad range of dynamic factors. He also shared the favorable view of journalism held by Developmental historians. Whereas other Developmental historians such as Mott had believed, however, that progress resulted from journalists' innate knowledge of what proper journalism should be, Kobre argued that sociological factors also had to be considered.

Kobre believed the method used by most other historians was inadequate, and he made a concerted effort to replace it with his sociological approach. He explained his view thusly:

> From my study of other social institutions, such as the family, religion, education, and government, I believed that the newspaper could be treated in the same or similar sociological fashion, and that this approach would yield a better, deeper understanding of journalistic developments. I wanted a sound framework to put together and hold the thousands of facts about journalism history. The sociological approach seemed to be the answer.
>
> As a social institution, the press began because it fitted a need

---

[6]Sidney Kobre, *Development of American Journalism* (Dubuque, IA: Wm. C. Brown, 1969).

or want of the people in the community. The newspaper changed as they did. Each era of journalism . . . was the result of alterations in American life at the time. The population changed; and so did the economic, political, cultural, social, and psychological conditions. And all of these influenced the character and content of the newspapers. The press, in turn, affected and influenced these conditions.

Individual parts of the press (such as the news, headlines, editorials, features, and photographs) and sections (such as the sports, business, fashions) developed in the first place because of certain wants or needs of segments of the public, and grew and changed when that reading public changed. Or when new reading markets appeared and were appealed to by publishers.

Similarly, the traditions and methods of journalism went through cycles. They determined how news was selected and written. They determined how formats of presenting news, features, and photographs were developed. Each era worked out its journalistic methods and traditions and passed these on as a journalistic heritage to the next period.

Social institutions, moreover, while appearing to be mechanical and impersonal, were operated through human personnel. The newspaper, thus, was affected by the background, education, and viewpoint of the publishers, editors, reporters, and other staff members.

The newspaper also was dependent on technological facilities for gathering the news, transmitting it from event to newspaper office, and printing and distributing the finished journals. The press had a business side, depending on subscriptions and advertising for support; hence it was closely related to the economic changes in the United States.

Thus, my interest was in more than placing the media generally in their American social context—not just painting in the historical backgrounds of the press periods. I wanted to discover specifically the interaction of the press with the basic social factors which caused the press to develop from the Colonial Era to the Twentieth Century. The focus was on the fundamental processes and cycles which occurred in the news communication industry.[7]

Kobre believed his sociological approach explained journalism history better than antiquarian (or what he mistakenly termed "historical") methods did. Traditional methods, he thought, only scratched the surface. He argued:

---

[7]Kobre to author, May 7, 1986. In addition to his correspondence to the author, he explained his perspective in detail in "The Sociological Approach in Research in Newspaper History," *Journalism Quarterly* 22 (1945): 12-22, and "A Conversation with Sidney Kobre," *Journalism History* 8 (1981): 18-24. Many of his remarks in the latter work mirror those he made to this author.

The sociological method . . . gave a true, more accurate, more comprehensive view of what happened in the past...and what was happening today. The approach provided a more valuable grasp of (1) the environmental factors shaping the media and (2) the impact of the media on the environment—the public. It showed the external pressures affecting the press and the internal pressures, too.

In emphasizing causes, the sociological method explained how and why the changes occurred in the past and the reasons for the journalistic traditions. It threw light on the birth, growth, and persistence of journalistic methods in the present. It revealed to what extent the media were ahead of the economic, intellectual, social, and scientific institutions, and how far the media lagged behind. What were the long-time, repeating processes and cycles of birth, growth, and decay patterns in journalism? The sociological view sought to answer these questions.

Kobre also believed that the press, although influenced by sociological factors, affected society. By "promotion, opposition, suppression, and omission," he argued, "the press helped or hindered the growth or the decline of various movements or activities."

Even though Kobre produced a large volume of work attempting to recast journalism history in sociological terms, he failed to produce convincing scholarship. The essential reason was that he never mastered historical methods. He confused historical method with mere chronology. Not recognizing Mott's underlying historical assumptions, for example, he believed that Mott did nothing more than present facts in chronological order. He assumed that such a chronological approach—"the straight historical approach"—is what historical method is.[8] Misunderstanding historical method—and therefore not realizing the full dimensions for rigorous study, thorough research, and thoughtful explanation—he therefore never mastered some of the fundamentals of historical study. Some of his work failed on elementary levels. Critics pointed out, for example, such problems as the inadequacy of his background research, resulting in a cursory explanation of the historical background for journalism and in factual errors and misunderstandings. Basing his knowledge of the historical background on secondary accounts, he confined himself to well-known facts and failed to provide original insight.

Other problems marred his works. Among the most apparent was his failure to integrate the media and their sociological background. In view of his primary intent to do so, that failure was most striking. Although claiming that the media were closely related to their background, he rarely provided hard evidence of the

---

[8]Kobre to author; and "A Conversation with Sidney Kobre," ibid.

relationship. Similarly, he frequently claimed that broad cause-effect relationships existed between the media and social forces, but he presented little evidence on which to base the claims.

Finally, like most other journalism historians, Kobre suffered from present-mindedness. Taking the typical pro-journalism view and the Developmental perspective, he told essentially the same story of history as Mott and his predecessors did. He believed that journalism history was primarily the story of journalistic progress. He simply included more sociological, economic, political, and cultural background. He also added one more dimension. He believed that history presented a series of repeating cycles of birth, growth, and decay. He shared that view with some earlier non-journalism historians who believed that the biological evolutionary theory might be used to explain history. The concept of cycles, however, as some historians have pointed out, is more appropriate for explaining the lives of animals than the history of social institutions.

Along with his research, Kobre took a vibrant interest in the teaching of journalism history. He helped found the history division of the Association for Education in Journalism and in 1955, serving as its secretary, started the *Journal of Journalism History*, the first American periodical devoted to scholarly research in journalism history. In the same year he published *Journalism History Guidebook*, a collection of ideas for the teaching of journalism. He also conducted a number of national surveys of teaching methods. In 1981 the newly formed American Journalism Historians Association elected him to its first Board of Directors. In 1985 the AJHA named him recipient of its first award for contributions to the study of journalism history. The award subsequently was renamed the Sidney Kobre Award.

Kobre's books did not sell large numbers of copies, and sales figures may not necessarily indicate a book's quality as historical scholarship. In journalism history, however, where the stature and influence of historians have been based largely on textbooks, sales figures have meaning. Compared to Edwin Emery's *The Press and America*, for example, which has sold about 135,000 copies, Kobre's *The Development of American Journalism* sold only 2,900. The difference provides evidence of how educators and journalism historians responded.

Despite the small sales, Kobre influenced historical thinking. He did more than any other historian to promote a sociological approach to studying journalism history. In recent years, when a "cultural" perspective has become popular, the voluminous contribution that Kobre made to that approach has become more apparent.

Edwin Emery
and Ideological History

Edwin Emery (1914-) succeeded Frank Luther Mott as the most prominent historian of American journalism. He never gained the stature of Mott; but like his predecessor, he gained his reputation primarily through a textbook. In the decade following Mott's death, revised editions of Emery's *The Press and America*[1] slowly replaced Mott's *American Journalism* as the dominant text for students of journalism history. Owing to the peculiar nature of journalism historiography, in which historians' prominence frequently has been based on textbooks, Emery gained visibility and, thus, preeminence.

His prominence attracted a number of students to the doctoral program in journalism at the University of Minnesota. Several of them since have established solid reputations in history and thus added a second dimension to Emery's eminence. Many attest to the encouragement and support he gave and to his importance in their success as historians. No journalism educator has served as mentor to as large a group of good historians as he has. Thus, the influence on the field exercised by his textbook has been augmented by the diffusion of the works of his former students, their relationships with other historians, and their influence on their own students. Although some of Emery's students have questioned his concepts and his scholarship, most hold him in high esteem. They thus have added to his reputation as both a historian and a teacher.

Emery's conception of history was neither complex nor novel. He viewed history from the simple Progressive perspective of good liberals versus bad conservatives. History appeared to him to be the story of how the press supported the rights of the common people against the powerful and wealthy. With this Progressive view, he combined a staunch defense and advocacy of a journal-

---

[1] Edwin Emery and Henry Ladd Smith, *The Press and America: An Interpretative History of the Mass Media* (Englewood Cliffs, NJ: Prentice-Hall, 1954). Revised 5 times; later editions are co-authored by Michael Emery, son of Edwin.

ism that challenged the "establishment" or that challenged the mainstream attitudes of the general public when the public agreed with the establishment. The last third of *The Press and America*, for example, reads more like an essay on the need of the press to defend its rights against attacks from government and from conservative groups than a thoughtful history of journalism. Emery's view is marked by a belief that a liberal press always is right, even when the values and beliefs of the public weigh heavily against it.

Emery was born May 14, 1914, in Chino, California, the son of William E. (a rancher) and Laura A. (Miller) Emery. He received a BA degree in history from the University of California, Berkeley, in 1935. In the same year he joined the staff of the San Francisco *Examiner* as a reporter and married Mary McNevin. In his later academic career, she played an active role in assisting him with various tasks involved in publishing and in working with his students. "One of Ed's greatest assets," recalled one of his students, "is his wife, Mary. She was always at his side helping him, and helping Ed meant also helping his students. I'm sure all of us remember Mary equally with Ed."[2] The following year, he began working as assistant editor, then managing editor, of the *California Monthly* magazine. He then began work on a graduate degree in history at the University of California, receiving the PhD in 1943. He joined United Press that year as a staff correspondent and worked for 2 years in various positions in its San Francisco bureau, including Pacific War news desk editor and bureau chief. Following the end of World War II, the University of Minnesota School of Journalism hired him as a lecturer. In 1946 he was promoted to assistant professor, in 1950 to associate professor, and in 1954 to professor. He served as director of graduate study from 1973 to 1979.

During his academic career, Emery received a number of awards. Sigma Delta Chi/Society of Professional Journalists twice honored him with its journalism research award, in 1950 for his book *History of the American Newspaper Publishers Association*[3] and in 1954 for the first edition of *The Press and America*, which he co-authored with Henry Ladd Smith, who wrote the chapters covering the pre-colonial period through the Civil War. The AEJMC in 1986 presented him with its Eleanor Blum Distinguished Service to Research Award. He also received a Guggenheim Fellowship (1959-1960) and a Social Science Research Council Award (1980) and was named a Distinguished Scholar by the National Academy of Social Sciences (1985). In 1980 SDX/SPJ selected him as national journalism teacher of the year. He also served as national president of the AEJMC in 1974-1975 and as associate editor (1952-1962), managing editor (1963-

---

[2]Beverly Bethune to author, July 6, 1986.

[3]Edwin Emery, *History of the American Newspaper Publishers Association* (Minneapolis: University of Minnesota Press, 1950).

1964), and editor (1965-1973) of *Journalism Quarterly*.

Emery clearly has had a major impact through both his scholarship and his leadership in the profession of journalism education. Just as important has been his influence on his students. Many have gone from their graduate studies into journalism education, and some of the best historians today acknowledge Emery's importance to their own development. Robert Hudson's dedication of a recent book to him typifies their warm regard. Hudson wrote that Emery "remains unchallenged as the leading contemporary historian of mass media."[4]

Students particularly noted Emery's concern for them and his support of their historical study. Ted C. Smythe, an accomplished historian himself, spoke for many of Emery's students when he said, "What marks Emery as a really important figure . . . is his humanity. He was willing to help . . . students, not to take advantage of them. He never softened requirements or anything, but you had the feeling he was for you rather than against you. There was no artificial 'scholarly' rigmarole. He laid it out, and you did it. So far as I could tell, he never had a 'hidden agenda' which was for his benefit. . . . I have always felt that he should be my model in treating students because of the way he so generously treated me."[5]

Emery coupled his interest in students with efforts to encourage them in their own work. Although a Progressive himself, he did not try to force his views on his students,[6] but instead attempted to inspire them to produce work which stood on the merit of its own ideas. Nancy Roberts, a historian who is a graduate of the doctoral program at the University of Minnesota and now a member of its faculty, attributed her early accomplishments in journalism history to Emery. He was, she said, "one of the most encouraging teachers I've ever met. His door was always open for students to come in and discuss ideas." He thus "nurtured much scholarship. The large number of conference papers, journal articles, and books produced over the years by Emery students says something. . . . Many of these efforts were committed to paper because of Ed's enthusiastic support when the ideas were timidly broached by students in his classes and seminars. Ed always exhorted students to publish their work and got them involved in the professional associations."[7] Likewise, Richard Kielbowicz, a student of Emery and now a faculty member at the University of Washington, emphasized Emery's contributions to his students' professional development. "Unofficially," Kielbowicz, himself now an established historian, said, "Emery was director of moral

[4]Robert V. Hudson, *Mass Media: A Chronological Encyclopedia of Television, Radio, Motion Pictures, Magazines, Newspapers, and Books in the United States* (New York: Garland, 1987), p. xv.

[5]Ted C. Smythe to author, March 19, 1987.

[6]Ibid.; Bethune to author; Richard B. Kielbowicz to author, August 23, 1986.

[7]Nancy L. Roberts to author, May 29, 1986.

support or morale for graduate students. . . . Officially, he was director of graduate studies. . . . For me, and, I suspect, other Minnesota graduate students, Emery's help outside the classroom was as valuable as his guidance inside. He encouraged us to attend AEJ History Division regional meetings as well as the annual convention. He would often drive with a vanload of students to the regionals. In this and other ways, he helped socialize us to the profession—underscoring the importance of presenting and publishing papers and participating in scholarly associations. Emery's vigor and industry . . . set an example for all of us planning university careers. In other words, Emery showed us what it took to succeed in an academic institution, not just perform as students."[8]

Although Emery was a key figure in the education of many of the best historians writing today, his most evident impact came from his books. He authored, co-authored, or edited 11 of them. In addition to *The Press and America* and his history of the ANPA, they include *Highlights in the History of the American Press: A Book of Readings* (1954; edited with Edwin Ford), *Reporting the News* (1959; with Phillip Ault), *Introduction to Mass Communication* (8 editions, 1960-1985; with Ault and Warren Agee), *The Publishers' Auxiliary 100th Anniversary Historical Series* (1965; editor), *The Story of America as Reported by Its Newspapers 1690-1965* (1965; editor), *America's Front Page News 1690-1970* (1971; edited with his son, Michael Emery, and R. Smith Schuneman), *Perspectives in Mass Communications* (1982; with Agee and Ault), *Reporting and Writing the News* (1983; with Agee and Ault), and *Main Currents in Mass Communication* (1985; with Agee and Ault).[9]

History of the American Newspaper Publishers Association stands up as the most solid historical work that Emery did, but his influence on historical thinking came from *The Press and America,* which has been widely used as the primary textbook in

---

[8]Kielbowicz to author.

[9]Edwin Ford and Edwin Emery, eds., *Highlights in the History of the American Press: A Book of Readings* (Minneapolis: University of Minnesota Press, 1954); Emery and Phillip Ault, *Reporting the News* (New York: Dodd, Mead & Co., 1959); Emery, Ault, and Warren Agee, *Introduction to Mass Communication* (8 editions) (New York: Dodd, Mead & Co., 1960, 1965, 1970, 1972; and Harper & Row, 1976, 1979, 1982, 1985); Emery, ed., *The Publishers' Auxiliary 100th Anniversary Historical Series* (Washington, DC: Publishers' Auxiliary, 1965); Emery, ed., *The Story of America as Reported by Its Newspapers 1690-1965* (New York: Simon and Schuster, 1965); Edwin Emery, Michael Emery, and R. Smith Schuneman, eds., *America's Front Page News 1690-1970* (New York: Doubleday, 1971); Emery, Agee, and Ault, *Perspectives in Mass Communications* (New York: Harper & Row, 1982); Emery, Agee, and Ault, *Reporting and Writing the News* (New York: Harper & Row, 1983); Emery, Agee, and Ault, *Main Currents in Mass Communication* (New York: Harper & Row, 1985).

courses in mass communication history, and *Introduction to Mass Communication*, which has been used as the textbook in many introductory journalism courses for freshmen and sophomores. For the latter, Emery wrote the several summary chapters on journalism history. Since many students studying journalism in the last 25 years have gained their knowledge of history from those two books, it is not unreasonable to assume that Emery's ideas have played a significant role in fashioning their concepts on the press. The picture that he has given students is one of the press fighting on the side of good, of liberalism, and of freedom against the malign forces of power, wealth, and reactionism.

Emery is a Progressive historian in the classic mold, and the Progressive concept of history fit him like an old, favorite suit. His education was in the ideas of the Progressive historians, but he believed his mentors' views were too moderate. "Studying history at Berkeley from 1931 to 1943," he wrote, "I obviously was under Progressive influence. But my professors were a cautious group with only mild interests in the extremes of Progressive thought offered by Vernon Parrington, Charles Beard, and later [Frederick Jackson] Turner theory disciples....[My professors'] books, like nearly all American history textbooks then and since, reflected a mild-toned Progressive theme."[10] In introducing his own students to historians, Emery remedied what he considered a shortcoming of his own education, stressing precisely those historians his professors had found too extreme, Parrington, Beard, and Turner.[11] His historical ideas showed up in his politics, as he got involved in Democratic-Farmer-Labor Party politics in Minnesota and adhered to New Deal-style Democratic principles. He became acquainted with politicians such as Hubert Humphrey and Walter Mondale and acquired a collection of photographs of him standing with them and other Democratic luminaries.

Emery's own writings, however, came at a time when the Progressive interpretation was falling into disfavor. While other historians were revealing the superficiality of the Progressive interpretation of history and the shortcomings of Progressive historians' research methods, Emery defended the Progressive interpretation against the charge that it consisted simply of a "description of the triumphs of good (liberals) over evil (conservatives)."[12] In his history lectures, a former student observed, "Emery usually painted history in terms of liberalism vs. conservatism, with the former eventually triumphant."[13] Another described him as "an old-fashioned Progressive historian; there were the 'good guys' (us) and the 'bad guys' (everybody else), and in the end the good guys always triumphed as we made

---

[10]"A Conversation with Edwin Emery," *Journalism History* 7 (1980): 23.

[11]Donald F. Brod to author, May 29, 1986.

[12]"A Conversation with Edwin Emery," p. 23.

[13]Kielbowicz to author.

progress toward a better world."[14]

In a journal article evaluating William Randolph Hearst, Emery revealed as much about his own perspective as he did about the subject. He wrote, "The great newspapers . . . are those which are aroused whenever basic principles of human liberty and progress are at stake . . . and which are constantly on guard against intolerance and unfairness. . . . [T]hey do their best to be the kind of progressive community leaders America expects."[15] That statement capsulizes Emery's approach to explaining journalism history. The struggle between liberalism and conservatism, good and evil, permeated his work. *The Press and America*[16] gave, for instance, these versions of history:

—Since the time of Jefferson and Hamilton, America had witnessed a "struggle between big business and workers and farmers" and a "battle for the rights of labor and for a more equitable distribution of wealth."

—In the early 1900s, the two major political parties acted slowly in the "quest for social justice," leaving the Socialist party and the labor movement to seek solutions to America's problems.

—In the 1920s Adolph Ochs of the New York *Times* "exhibited solid capitalistic preferences and an unreasonable fear of any form of radicalism," and the *Times*, like other newspapers, "failed dismally to defend the civil liberties" of people accused of being Communists.

—In the 1950s mainstream newspapers said little "about damage to the environment, abuses by law-enforcement officials, or the need for greater consumer protection. . . . Yet those problems existed while the powerful business and industrial community consolidated its hold on the nation's political, economic and social life."

—The 1960s were marked by "laws discriminating against minorities and women and . . . imperialistic adventures that depleted the nation's treasure."

—In the 1970s the mainstream press failed to investigate adequately such stories as "the role of major oil companies during energy crises, white-collar crime in general, the backgrounds of persons appointed to public office or regulatory commissions on all levels....and other subjects involving power and money."

—President Ronald Reagan's attempts in the 1980s to point out the nobility of America's efforts in the Vietnam war were "ridiculed" (by whom, Emery does not say).

—Recent thinking among Americans on conflicts involving

---

[14]Bethune to author.

[15]"William Randolph Hearst: A Tentative Appraisal," *Journalism Quarterly* 28 (1951): 432.

[16]The fifth edition of *The Press and America* is used for references here. Except for additions of material on recent events, the texts of the various revisions remain essentially the same as the text of the first edition.

Marxists and right-wing forces (as in Nicaragua and El Salvador in the 1970s and 1980s) was shallow, invariably viewing "dissenting intellectuals, churchmen, and peasants . . . as a 'left' tainted with 'Marxist' thinking and Cuban-Soviet support."

—Reagan had an "unfavorable" press conference record, seemed to lose control of events after 1981, had a "disregard for...the public's right to learn about its government," and used anti-Communist rhetoric that was "a throwback to the 1950s."

Such views can be multiplied *ad infinitum* as found in *The Press and America,* and they show up elsewhere. The "good guys-bad guys" division forms the basis of Emery's explanation of the value of freedom of the press found in the basic textbook *Introduction to Mass Communications.* He wrote:

A society possessing and using these freedoms [of press, speech, assembly, etc.] will advance and change as it exercises democratic processes. Very naturally, then, these freedoms will come under attack from those opposed to any change that might diminish their own power or position in society. . . . The press, occupying a key role in the battle for these basic freedoms, is a particular target. To the closed mind, the press has been a dangerous weapon to be kept as far as possible under the control of adherents of the status quo; to the inquiring mind, it has been a means of arousing interest and emotion among the public in order to effect change.[17]

This black-white view of history accounted for another basic aspect of Emery's work. He admired liberal, anti-establishment features of journalism and assumed that they were the ordained ones. When, therefore, he could find the press behaving as he thought it should behave, he served as its zealous protector. When others criticized it, he attacked them. In response to Vice President Spiro Agnew's criticism in the 1970s, for example, he asserted that it "was indisputably true that never before had such a high federal official made such direct attacks on those reporting and commenting on the news,"[18] apparently overlooking the many instances in which Federalist, Republican, Whig, and Jacksonian presidents and vice-presidents had made similar attacks on editors in the 1800s. Of the 1983 documentary "Vietnam: A Television History" televised by the Public Broadcasting Service, he wrote, "Critics hailed it as a stunning achievement...,"[19] ignoring the widely expressed criticism that the series presented a one-sided view. Of public attitudes toward the news media in the

---

[17]Emery, Ault, and Agee, *Introduction to Mass Communications* (7th ed.), p. 26.

[18]*The Press and America* (5th ed.), p. 596.

[19]Ibid., p. 614.

1980s, he asserted that the media fared well,[20] despite the fact that various polls showed that among major American institutions both newspapers and television ranked low in public esteem. As with the ideological colorations of history, Emery scattered such questionable evidence and assumptions about press performance throughout *The Press and America*. The result therefore came closer to advocacy for a particular concept of a liberal press than to good history.

Any historian, however, is entitled to bring values and judgments to the study of history. Indeed, meaningful history requires that the historian have a point of view. Otherwise, a historical account might consist of little more than collections of data with no recognizable coherence or importance. Historians have, however, an obligation to be fair in dealing with historical material, with points of view held by their subjects, and with various perspectives on history. Their goal must be first a search for truth about people and events of the past, rather than ideological dogmatism. They should not set out with a viewpoint and then simply marshal facts to fit it. As facts are gathered to find the truth, they may lead to a viewpoint, but viewpoint never should be used to determine facts. When, on the other hand, a historian selects and interprets facts to fit his philosophy, the result is, at best, didactic history. It offers little benefit except to those historians who have a particular view to propound. Historians should gather all the relevant facts and then ask what conclusions may be drawn from them. They should eschew simplistic explanations and theories of history. They should desire instead to know how and why particular people acted in particular situations in the past.

Attached too warmly to the Progressive view of history, and—after his son, Michael Emery, joined him as co-author with the fourth edition of *The Press and America*—to a mild New Left perspective, Emery too lightly dismissed explanations that conflicted with his own and ignored historical evidence that did not support his opinions. The Consensus interpretation has been the most important since World War II in providing new insight into American history. It argues that, contrary to the Progressive explanation of conflict as the primary ingredient of American history, basic agreement on fundamental principles such as democracy, property rights, and individual freedom marked America's past. Aware of the Consensus interpretation, Emery nevertheless in 1980 asserted that it "is now largely abandoned as a viable major school of historiography."[21] He suggested that the New Left approach had arisen as a more pertinent explanation of American history—despite the fact that only a decided minority of historians consider it more than peripheral to explaining America's past.

---

[20]Ibid., p. 624.

[21]"A Conversation with Edwin Emery," p. 22.

Along with the historian's perspective, research material plays a critical role in historical study. For *The Press and America*, Emery relied mainly on secondary rather than primary sources. Instead of basing his history on a study of his subjects (newspaper pages, for example), as historians such as Bleyer and Mott had done, he drew heavily on other historians' studies. He made rare use of the materials that historians normally consider to be evidence. One might argue that in a work as broad-ranging as a survey textbook, an author would find it impossible to study all the primary sources. That granted, one still must wonder about Emery's selection of secondary sources. He tended toward sources that supported his point of view and ignored or played down those that did not. Revised editions of *The Press and America* took little account of several highly regarded historical studies published in the interim. The reason may have been the amount of work required for rewriting to incorporate new knowledge and explanations.

One suspects, however, that the main reason was that the findings of many of the new studies did not accord with Emery's explanations of history. The explanation, for example, that the American Revolution was to a large extent a "class struggle"[22] appears in every edition of *The Press and America*, despite a number of important works that since 1954 (the year of the first edition) have shown otherwise, including Bernard Bailyn's work on one type of mass medium, *Pamphlets of the American Revolution, 1750-1776*[23] (1965), and *The Ideological Origins of the American Revolution*[24] (1967). The latter argued that the Revolution was above all else an ideological, constitutional, and political struggle. Despite the fact that it won for Bailyn both the Bancroft and Pulitzer prizes for history, Emery included only a bibliographical reference to it. Similarly, he discounted Peter Braestrup's book *Big Story*, the most solidly documented of any historical work on the press and the Vietnam war, with this statement: "...Braestrup's thesis...was angrily refuted by [reporters] Laurence and Arnett."[25] Braestrup had argued that poor reporting and an anti-government attitude held by many journalists had misinformed the American public and helped lead to Vietcong victory. While brushing aside such substantial works that refuted his opinion, Emery on the other hand occasionally emphasized minor works that supported it. In criticizing the Consensus explanation of American socialism, for example, he summarized an obscure article in the infant journal *Kansas*

---

[22]*The Press and America* (5th ed.), p. 62.

[23]Bernard Bailyn, ed., *Pamphlets of the American Revolution, 1750-1776* (Cambridge, MA: Harvard University Press, 1965).

[24]Bernard Bailyn, *The Ideological Origins of the American Revolution* (Cambridge, MA: Harvard University Press, 1967).

[25]Ibid., p. 614.

History.[26]

Despite such problems, *The Press and America* became in the 1970s the most widely used textbook in journalism history—and therefore exercised the potential for helping shape students' and professional journalists' views on the press in the past and in the present. Its primary strength lay in the fact that its perspective may have accorded with the views of many teachers of history (who, it should be remembered, came out of a journalism profession that believed strongly in its own rightness), that it provided much non-journalism American history background, that it was readable, and that its later editions had a strong graphic appeal. On the other hand, many teachers complained that it provided voluminous numbers of names and other details in an encyclopedic style, and that in the last third of its pages it lacked a coherent chronology and became more a contemporary essay than a historical narrative or exposition. More fundamentally, however, it was based on simplistic ideology, and it failed to keep up with recent historical scholarship. In those shortcomings, though, it mirrored much of the historical study done in journalism. In a field in which work is subjected to little critical evaluation, Emery's contributions have fared well.

The problems in *The Press and America* perhaps indicate more about the weaknesses in the field of journalism history than Emery's abilities as a historian. Without doubt, he has been the most infuential educator-historian of the last quarter century. In assessing his career, one of his students wrote of his "enormous influence on our field, through his many publications and through generations of history students he's taught and encouraged."[27] Emery, another student summarized, "put his stamp on a discipline through his scholarly publications and through the students he educated and inspired over four decades."[28] His career testifies to the effect that an energetic researcher and concerned teacher can have on an entire field.

---

[26]Ibid., p. 366.

[27]Roberts to author.

[28]Brod to author. In addition to Emery's students noted previously in this essay, a number of others provided the author with helpful assessments. They include Tom Reilly, Hiley Ward, Paul Peterson, and David Coulson, all historians and professors themselves.

3

The Philosophers

Gary L. Whitby
Lynn K. Whitby
Central Missouri State University

The Philosophers

Although some regard the field of mass communication as a new area of philosophy, its contours as the intellectual upshot of American journalism have hardly been mapped. This has led to certain clear problems in journalism education during its relatively brief history. One of the more definite of these has been whether to teach journalism as an art, a science, or a mere nuts-and-bolts practice. The fact that the field has, in many cases, transcended the last category suggests an ongoing concern for establishing journalism education squarely in some kind of philosophical tradition, whatever it may be. With the development of PhD programs in mass communication throughout the country, this challenge has become something of a mandate.

So long as the system of communication in the United States remained based in a world view that was even partially theological, it could be assumed that journalism, like business, had a vaguely cosmological foundation and telos. From the earliest days of the country, journalism had been regarded largely as a form of business but one tied closely with government and religion-as-government. With the advent of utilitarian philosophy in the late 18th and early 19th centuries, it became possible to regard journalism and business in metaphysical terms: as forms of laissez-faire, in which a providential creator had set in motion certain inalienable laws of human trade that inevitably provided for social progress so long as government did not interfere with the system.

One thinks here, for example, of the period following the American Revolution until the Civil War, in which journalism functioned as a species of laissez-faire underwritten by the residue of a Puritan cosmology (with variants) in the North and an Episcopalian/fundamentalist one (with variants) in the South. Laissez-faire, of course, included the well-known ideas of Adam Smith, who in his book *The Wealth of Nations* (1776) claimed an "invisible hand" to be at work in the affairs of men, which resulted in mutual social benefit that accrued from a discretely owned and operated system of production.[1] In addition, journalism *qua* business possessed not only all the rights of other businesses but was the only form of big business (big by the middle 1800s) to have been specifically underwritten by the First Amendment.

By the middle of the 19th century, however, it was seen that journalism possessed not only revolutionary and laissez-faire dimensions but also a socially formative one, apart from trade or attachment to specific political parties. This dimension was made obvious by the clear equation between political power and forms of journalism operative in the immense social upheaval over slavery. It was William Lloyd Garrison who first sensed this power when he wrote in his *Liberator* that the battle over slavery would have to be fought in the minds and hearts of the Northern people before it could be pursued in the South.[2] And it was Robert E. Lee who, having seen that formidable power incarnate on the battlefield, sought to begin to command it following the war by suggesting the first college courses in journalism.

Besides demonstrating the power of the journalistic word, the period of the Civil War had also, however, brought to an end any potentiality for the philosophical underwriting of journalism by metaphysics. This had been presaged by the rise of materialistic philosophy immediately prior to the war and by the claims of Darwin in 1859. By the early 1840s, Marxian arguments (many of them published in Horace Greeley's New York *Tribune*) for a materialistically rewoven social fabric had indicted *a priori* metaphysics and its attendant religiosity as a popular narcotic. Darwin then gave materialism a biological edge by contending for an animalistic human origin.

Added to this was the unreflecting rise to power of the huge industrial monopolies of the late 19th century, which (given the incipient monopolizing of the press during this period by capital interests) deflected for years the operation of the newspaper along the lines of social concern laid down for it by Horace Greeley.

The renaissance of a social-philosophical concern for the role of the American press came toward the end of the 19th century with the development of the "Chicago School" of pragmatist philosophers. These men—inheritors by then of an American version of pantheistic and material socialism put in motion by a combination of Marxian ideology, New England Transcendentalism, and the social utopianism of such figures as Charles Fourier and Horace Greeley—began to forge a materialistic metaphysics for the press as the instrument of communication in the large city. Such men as Robert Park, John Dewey, Charles Horton Cooley, and George Herbert Mead, among others, argued for the role of the American newspaper as a reunifying communicative force in

---

[1] Adam Smith, *The Wealth of Nations* (Edwin Cannan, Ed.) (New York: Modern Library, 1937), p. 423.

[2] *Liberator* (Boston), Jan. 1, 1831.

a society whose sensibilities had been fragmented by industrialism and urbanism. The newspaper, they felt, would restore the face-to-face system of communication, which had been possible in the small town but which had been lost with the movement of millions to the big city and the consequent advent of social alienation.

To these men, most of whom were futurists to one degree or another, but none of whom was a thoroughgoing materialist in the Marxian or Democritean sense of the word, communication was still something of a mystical wonder whose origins did not admit entirely of intellection, but whose processes and broad beneficial effects could be charted and described. Using Chicago as a laboratory, they set out to divest material determinism of its power by insisting on the force of thought and its "instrumentation" (a term coined by Dewey) in the real world by way of the processes of communication. This idea—which meant, in effect, applying to newly evolved patterns of social/industrial organization consciously wrought systems of communication, in order to humanize them—would lead, they felt, to truth in an industrial society and establish new forms of those cultural certitudes lost in the demise of traditional agrarian society.

That their ideas did not address journalism as a species of economic production and establishment has left them open to a withering Marxian critique, for they were idealistic about the role journalism could play in reconstituting society when journalism itself was such a part of the economic establishment as to blind it to its own exploitation of and by that establishment. Nonetheless, Park, Dewey, Cooley, Mead, and William James have taught us much about the nature of communication, and their ideas are still resonant today.

In the 20th century the press has fallen heir to a pragmatic functionalism. Following Darwin, the parts and functions of organisms could be arranged in nomenclatures so as to indicate the overall role and function of the organism in evolving to a higher form. The adaptation of the organism to its environment is dwelt on in this process, and the viability of the organism as a unit in the evolutionary process is delineated. In the history of journalism, this approach has joined hands with the idea of progress. In journalistic philosophy it has led, in the enlivening presence of technology, to the development and toleration of a variety of types of journalism—everything from muckraking to public relations—and to the viewing of these as functioning parts of a whole represented by the modern school of journalism. Pragmatism is the philosophic glue that holds this model together: in this case a species of pluralism underwritten by the demands and encouragements of a pluralistic/technological news establishment closely tied, in many cases *too* closely, to the academy.

Given the connection between technology and the journalistic establishment in the United States and, indeed, throughout the world, technology itself has not been questioned nearly enough.

Its role as the alter ego of science is so well established and powerful as to admit philosophers little way of thinking around it. Few,
for example, have seriously suggested that any of our questionable technology be "disinvented," for to do so would constitute ret-
rograde thinking. When the philosophy of progress implicit in
the rise of technology is laid bare, however, one can see the relationship between new modes of production and the rise of social
alienation and angst attendant upon economic transformation
and resultant unemployment. This is patently obvious in the
mass innovation of computers in the production of journalism,
beginning in the early 1970s.

If the philosophical underpinnings of journalistic technology
have gone largely unquestioned in the 20th century, the philosophy of positivism in science has been heavily criticized. Werner
Heisenberg's "Uncertainty Principle," which simply points out
that scientists cannot be positive about the motion of atoms,
given that scientists can see only where the atoms have *been* and
not where they are, is by now common knowledge.[3] Likewise,
Thomas Kuhn, a scientist himself, has effectively demonstrated
that scientists do not give up hypotheses when they are proven
wrong but continue to adduce data, and that the certainty of one
scientific generation gives way whenever a major paradigm is
given over for a new one.[4]

These developments have strongly affected philosophers in
mass communication. Early on, operating under a positivistic
"powerful effects" theory of communication, Harold Lasswell developed what would be called the "hypodermic needle theory" of
effects, arguing that mass communication could have a direct,
powerful effect on an audience. Given a changing climate in the
philosophy of science, Lasswell's theories were modified by such
researchers as Carl Hovland, Leon Festinger, and, more recently,
Elizabeth Noelle-Neumann—from a limited effects theory to a
neopowerful effects theory, which considers the weight and abundance of information and which discards a purely behavioral
framework of investigation in favor of a cognitive one.[5]

These and other changes in the philosophy of science have led
to a broader discussion among communication philosophers:
whether, for example, truth exists as quantity or quality.
Although this likely appears as a specious question, one must
nonetheless recognize its presence in departments of sociology as

---

[3]See Werner Heisenberg, *The Physicist's Conception of Nature* (Arnold
J. Pomerans, trans.) (New York: Harcourt, World, Brace, 1955), pp. 12-16,
28-29, 33-41.

[4]See Thomas S. Kuhn, "Revolutions as Changes of World View" in his
The Structure of Scientific Revolutions (Chicago: University of Chicago
Press, 1962), pp. 111-135.

[5]For a good general discussion of this area of the history of journalism
research, see Warren Agee, Phillip H. Ault, and Edwin Emery,
Introduction to Mass Communications (New York: Harper & Row, 1985),
pp. 27-38.

well as in schools of journalism and attendant scholarly organizations, which now contain "qualitative approaches" and "quantitative approaches." This dichotomy amounts to a great divide in the methodology of mass communication research, and it is a problem area of argument that seems to admit of little solution among communication philosophers.

In addition, it has raised in more than one quarter the compelling question of whether journalism education should go forward wearing the intellectual accoutrement of art or science. Interestingly, philosophers on either side of the argument have opted for a materialistic Weltanschauung and have rejected ideal, metaphysics, and noumenon for matter, physics, and phenomenon. The consequence of this has been more emphasis on scientific method and functionalism, on the "science" side of the argument; and, more recently, structuralism, deconstructionism, semiotics, and phenomenology on the "qualitative" side. In a word, mass communication as an area of American pragmatic philosophy, like 20th-century philosophy in general, still has no metaphysical base.

This has led to characteristic problems in journalistic ethos and teleology. On the one hand journalists are faced with a professional and pragmatic journalistic mandate to get the story at any cost; on the other they are confronted with a journalistic code clearly the residue of a tradition of religious allegiance from an earlier age. Confused by way of their obligations to a pragmatically based profession bearing remnants of a code, present-day American journalists have developed a characteristic solipsism—in which the world of real values has been narcissistically internalized. This is readily evident in the stream-of-consciousness writing of the new journalists and in the 1981 fabrication of a Pulitzer-Prize winning story (later withdrawn) by a Washington *Post* reporter.

There are currently three discernible major "approaches" to the problem of functionalism in the philosophy of mass communication: (a) a residue of scientific positivism which has managed to survive from Lasswell to Noelle-Neumann by transforming itself in emphasizing human cognition and the probability of its method as primary virtues; (b) the critical theory of the Frankfurt School of German philosophers, including such names as Theodor Adorno and Jurgen Habermas; and (c) the cultural studies approach espoused and popularized by James Carey and others at the University of Illinois.

In the first of these categories, the emphasis is still on a philosophical objectivity; however, at some institutions, the "R" research method has given way over the last 20 years to the "Q" methodology of William Stephenson—which, by way of the philosophy of Michael Polanyi, admits to the subjectivity implicit in social science and seeks to exploit it.

In the second category, critical studies, the emphasis is on viewing mass communication in classical Marxian and neo-

Marxian terms. The philosophical critique is primarily economic and posits a base-superstructure materialist model of reality in which the economic base produces a culture, including the journalistic establishment, which is darkly colored by economic exploitation. The critique, after Marx, assumes certain clear "syntheses" of tendencies (crises) in the journalistic establishment and points out the economic rationale of these in historical terms.

In the third category, cultural studies, the emphasis is on selectively searching the culture for successful models of communication. This category relies heavily on the Chicago School philosophers and, although it applies the economic critique, does not presume economic determinism but, instead, seeks the structuring ideas of earlier successful cultural-communicative norms and applies these, as received philosophical constructs, to the history of communication as well as to modern communication problems. This category would seem to be one of an idealist pragmatism.

In addition to these, one should not omit the more "creative" approaches of Marshall McLuhan and Harold Innis. Here the point of view is historical-economic, literary, even poetic; and the media are viewed and judged metaphorically. This method would seem to owe a good deal to the methods of literary criticism and possesses the virtues and vices of that criticism: an often ingenious insightfulness whose subjective data do not permit replication or verification. Still, insights of, say, a McLuhan are provocative, even prophetic; and his writings have prompted much thought about media and their role in society.

The dominant problem of communication philosophy in our time remains the anxiety-ridden absence of even a relatively uniform code of belief. With the shift from traditionalism to futurism by the latter half of the 19th century, many important social values were lost. Science, on which so much of 20th-century life is staked, has not been able to recapture those values but has, instead, reigned supreme in its ivory tower in an age that has witnessed the decline of the family; the degrading influence of corporate giantism, including multi-national corporations; the growth and social infiltration of pornography; the rampant increase in the 1980s of sex and violence as aids in advertising; and the advent of solipsism and narcissism in reporting news. Indeed, some would indict science and technology for their seeming complicity in these matters: for practicing an "objective" or value-free methodology whose upshot is nonetheless a clearly radical transformation of traditional social values.

Critical theory, which posits an economic and revolutionary solution to a seemingly universal angst and alienation, and which traces these problems to a society's communication system as constituted by economic practices, is almost entirely negative. In its drive to expose and dismantle particular exploitative systems, it almost blindly accepts industrialism and technology;

and in its idealistic drive to eradicate social dominance, it would appear to ignore such dominance as a characteristic blemish on human nature itself, one apparently built—ineradicably, perhaps—into the very language. Like science, then, at its most basic level of investigation, critical theory cannot thoroughly detect and control the atoms of its materialistic presumptions, words.

The third major area of mass communication philosophy, cultural studies, is made difficult by the vagueness of its epistemology, which, like literary studies, is often productive of findings hardly verifiable. However, a more definite weakness here is that this area of media philosophy admits of less of a telos than critical theory does, which at least has at its center an enduring utopian vision. On the other hand, the cultural studies approach has the advantage of seeing communication, and explicating and judging it, not in strictly economic terms alone but as a cultural whole. In this drive toward a "reassociation" of the modern sensibility lies the potential for great insight into relationships between communication and everyday life.

The following essays do not align themselves neatly in terms of the foregoing description. This is owing to the fact that the "philosophers" of mass communication are all too often not identified as such and, therefore, overlap from one area of mass communication to another. One thus finds philosophers of scientific behaviorism sometimes identified as "theorists" and philosophers of historical method classed as "historians." What the following arrangement of thinkers intends to do is therefore twofold: to identify (a) those who have had the greatest impact on the overall practical philosophical orientation in journalism education at the undergraduate and professional master's level; and (b) those who have made significant contributions to the philosophy of communication as it has been applied to journalism research and education at the graduate level.

In the former category are those early heads of programs who set the course of journalism education squarely in social scientific traditions. In the latter category are thinkers who have written extensively and explicitly about the philosophy of communication and have attempted to apply it to communication research.

Lawrence W. Murphy
and Journalism as a Liberal Art

Lawrence W. Murphy (1895-1969) began his career as a journalism educator in the 1920s, a time when schools of journalism found it necessary to defend their existence both to professional journalism and to the academy. As a humanist, he addressed the formation of journalism education curricula, seeking to prepare future journalists to understand and analyze the world they were to report. As a pragmatist, he saw, at one level, the need to prepare students to be the kind of journalists the newspapers expected to hire and, at a higher level, the need to equip future journalists with skills that would allow them to move the profession of journalism forward.

Lawrence William Murphy was born October 18, 1895, in Madison, Wisconsin, to Lawrence Bartholomew and Lillian (Nicodemus) Murphy. He began his career as a newspaperman, working as a reporter for the Madison *Democrat* and for a number of other papers in Wisconsin, Minnesota, North Dakota, and Illinois between 1916 and 1924. He did both undergraduate and graduate work at the University of Wisconsin, earning his bachelor's degree in 1921. He also did graduate work at the University of North Dakota, taking a master's degree in 1923; pursued graduate studies at the University of Illinois from 1925 to 1929; and completed a LittD degree at Marquette University in 1933. He taught at the University of North Dakota from 1921 to 1924, organizing the school's first journalism courses when he arrived, and setting up and chairing a separate department of journalism before leaving in 1924 to accept the directorship of the School of Journalism at the University of Illinois. He served as director there until 1940, when he stepped down to devote his time to teaching and research, and then as a lecturer at the Medill School of Journalism at Northwestern University (1957) and at Miami University (1960).

Murphy was the founder and first editor of *Journalism Quarterly* in 1924 (then called *Journalism Bulletin*) and later served as a member of the publication's advisory editorial board. Active in professional organizations, he served as president of the American Association of Teachers of Journalism (1930-1931), as president of the American Association of Schools and Departments of Journalism (1936-1937), and as chairman of the National Council on Education for Journalism (1935-1940). He was also a member of the Public Relations Council on Education, the educational advisory council of the Public Relations Society of America, Sigma Delta Chi, and Kappa Tau Alpha. He was the first national president of KTA. He served as a lieutenant in the AEF of the U.S. Army in World War I (1916-1918) and was a member of the American Legion.

When Murphy began teaching in 1921, the nature of journalism education was primarily "nuts-and-bolts" practice, patterned on the newsroom apprenticeship system. This approach is apparent in his two journalism textbooks, *Sport Writing of Today and Selections from the Best Sport Stories* (1925) and *An Introduction to Journalism: Authoritative Views on the Profession* (1930). In the text on sports writing he emphasized that although knowledge of the sport being covered was important, the sports writer needed more:

> The specific qualities desirable in sport writing are much the same as those desirable in other writing of a journalistic nature. . . . In all reporting it is important that there be shown a knowledge of the subject, a knowledge of good English, adequate imagination, planful initiative, ability to observe and record accurately, specially trained judgment, and facility in the use of journalistic technique.[1]

Murphy explained the importance of these qualities in the introductory chapter. The 650 "entries"—stories, columns, and leads—that followed were to be used "as a series of exercises for imitation and analysis" to supplement "other instruction of a practical nature."[2] *An Introduction to Journalism* is also primarily a reader, consisting of speeches and writings by "outstanding reporters, editors, and students of the press." In the foreword, Murphy said that "[d]evelopment of the professional mind is the great aim of professional education," that he wanted students to "become superior to their tools," and that he sought to instill "professional responsibility."[3] He also authored one of the selections of the text, a chapter titled "Ten Tests of a News Story." He called the selection "a guide for readers and cub reporters." Maintaining that a news story cannot be tested by "its nearness in point of time to the happening which it reports" or by "the standards of literature," Murphy offered 10 criteria for judging the merit of a story. These

---

[1]Lawrence W. Murphy, *Sport Writing of Today and Selections from the Best Sport Stories* (Champaign, IL: Service Press, 1925), p. 7.

[2]Ibid., p. 20.

[3]Lawrence W. Murphy, *An Introduction to Journalism: Authoritative Views on the Profession* (New York: Thomas Nelson and Sons, 1930), p. vii.

ranged from examining the content (the story should specifically answer questions the reader would ask) to judging the worth of sources used *in order* to determine if proper emphasis had been given to different parts of the story.[4]

But Murphy wanted to expand journalism education. In a 1930 *Journalism Quarterly* article titled "Cultural Values in the Study of Journalism," he sought to defend the journalism curriculum as more than a series of professional courses and to establish journalism courses as liberal arts courses by examining "some of our concepts of cultural values in relation to the work in journalism." Journalism, he pointed out, "was once a cultural subject in the academic sense"—it was once taught in English departments. Beyond that, cultural values were, he said, found in the core courses taken by all students of journalism. For example, reporting calls for

> handling of subject matter at least comparable to the subject matter of college themes in rhetoric. Here, then, is work that has cultural values at least as great as work in rhetoric—and rhetoric is the only subject in the liberal arts college that all students are required to take. . . . [T]he reporting work is at least equal in cultural value to the one course that all liberal arts colleges agree is cultural.[5]

The reporting course, he argued, gives the student the opportunity to investigate and write about culture—in writing "news stories of university lectures on science, literature, art, music, business, industry, education"; in interviewing "university authorities on the subjects of their specialization"; in "learn[ing] something about human nature by learning to appeal to a large reading public"; and in "learn[ing] to mingle with persons in various walks of life and to converse with them on problems of the day." The same cultural values are available to students of feature writing, editorial writing, and critical writing, said Murphy.[6] Another advantage of studying journalism is gaining "a knowledge of one of the greatest social institutions and social problems the world has ever known." If teachers of political science, economics, and literature find the newspaper worthy of discussion in the classroom and if sociologists consider journalism "one of the great problems of sociology," Murphy argued, surely "[i]t is an error to assume that a cultural program should leave a student ignorant of great problems of civilization."[7]

Murphy compared the cultural values found in journalism courses to those found in other courses, especially liberal arts

---

[4]Ibid., pp. 187-194.

[5]Lawrence W. Murphy, "Cultural Values in the Study of Journalism," *Journalism Quarterly* 7 (1932): 328.

[6]Ibid., pp. 330-331.

[7]Ibid., pp.331-332.

subjects. He concluded that science and foreign language courses contain little, if any, cultural value for the undergraduate student, for the student does not reach deep enough into the subject matter in 2 years to attain that level. History, on the other hand, is where the student finds the greatest cultural benefit, as "history is the basis of the cultural value of much that we learn. Instead of studying philosophy we study the history of philosophy; . . . instead of studying law we study the accumulation of cases—the history of law. . . ." Murphy also noted that history ("yesterday's news") is a good professional course for the student of journalism ("tomorrow's history") because "the study of reporting and current events partakes of the cultural values of the study of history." The close ties between history and journalism, therefore, make a strong argument for considering journalism as a subject of cultural value, he said. Rather than automatically sending students into traditional liberal arts courses, he concluded, journalism educators should examine the cultural content of all types of courses and should direct students to those high in cultural value.[8]

Murphy continued this theme in his 1932 presidential address to the American Association of Teachers of Journalism. In "Professional and Nonprofessional Teaching of Journalism," which appeared in *Journalism Quarterly*, he noted that "[t]here is a notion still extant that certain college courses are liberal and certain courses are not, and first and second year students frequently are barred from courses which have more place in our own culture than the so-called liberal arts courses." Courses such as agriculture, education, engineering, law and commerce, the arts, and architecture were barred as required courses and not permitted as electives. But Murphy thought all such subjects had cultural value for the journalism student:

> Clearly, the journalism and pre-journalism student should be taught to look with joy on knowledge in every field and to regard it as broadening and interesting. If he cannot get the right start in his early years because of penalties, we must in later years restore subjects that have been ruled out and enrich the student's mind on matters which *we* decide are important. . . . We cannot accept the theory that any courses in any colleges are unrelated to the discipline and body of knowledge that make up journalism.[9]

In that same address Murphy said that journalism, or at least the teaching of journalism, should turn in the direction of the sciences. He saw the "weakness of the cub-reporter system, that which old time editors have a tendency to exalt," as the weak spot

---

[8]Ibid., pp. 334-342.

[9]Lawrence W. Murphy, "Professional and Nonprofessional Teaching of Journalism," *Journalism Quarterly* 9 (1932): 54-55.

in journalism education.[10] He called for a scientific, or experimental, approach in the teaching of reporting and editing: developing courses that would produce more than "a good man [or woman] who serves [an] apprenticeship on a good newspaper. The schools and teachers owe the profession more than the substitution of one system for another. They owe the profession an improvement on the system and an improved product from that improved system." Journalism could learn much from the sciences, Murphy felt, by developing "training in accuracy of observation and accuracy in recording" to be used in reporting courses.[11]

The glance toward the sciences was carried even further in Murphy's 1938 presidential address. In "Schools of Journalism, Past and Future," he maintained that experimentation would lead to better and "improved service to different publics." He warned that experimental courses such as photojournalism might meet skepticism or resistance: "It is unfortunately true that, in more than one university, it is considered bad business to engage in such an exploratory kind of study. It is considered bad enough to be up to date, but to anticipate things—that is unforgivable." But such a course would be doubly valuable, he argued. It would provide valuable information in a new field within the profession and should "prepare students for the top positions in this field and for further experimental work in the industry."[12]

In addition to advocating experimentation as a method for improving instruction, Murphy maintained that journalism has close ties with science. At the end of a lengthy comparison of medical education and journalism education, he wrote, "Schools of journalism, now thirty years of age, have grown up with science and in full sight of a world being remade by science. It is reasonable to expect our schools to be more advanced from the standpoint of science and its applications than was medicine before the turn of the century."[13] Advances in technology would continue to bring about great and beneficial changes in the practice of journalism, and the schools of journalism needed to prepare their students to deal with these changes. To this end he called for more research on the part of faculty members and for released time from administration so that the faculty would have time to do that research. Research and experimentation would lead to advances in scientific and other fields. People "trained in journalism," he wrote, "have more than an even chance to make contributions in the field of social theory and philosophy, as well as in the scientific field." Journalism and journalism education had much to offer the public, and research and graduate programs would produce the information and personnel needed to bring

---

[10]Ibid., p. 57.

[11]Ibid., pp. 52-54.

[12]Lawrence W. Murphy, "Schools of Journalism, Past and Future," *Journalism Quarterly* 15 (1938): 39-40.

[13]Ibid., pp. 36-39.

about these advances.[14]

Although his major publications were textbooks on journalistic writing, Murphy was also recognized as a specialist in journalism history. *The Dawn of Daily Newspaper Journalism in the United States: The First Dailies; The Early Penny Press* was originally given as the 1956 Annual Sigma Delta Chi Lectures at the University of North Dakota. In the introductory comments, he briefly described his methodology and advocated the used of primary sources: "Obviously, the best source is the paper itself, and I have examined the several papers involved. My use of original sources led me to question some conclusions and slants given material by later writers, but the original sources cannot be questioned; they establish the facts." Murphy went on to take exception to several interpretations of press history and concluded, "[A]ll the writers added their prejudices or slants to what the original documents could show. And now, I add mine. But I did not hestitate to read some 843 copies of the *Pennsylvania Magazine* to try to get the record straight."[15] His methodology is consistent in his other historical articles. For example, in "John Dunlap's 'Packet' And Its Competitors," he indicated that his "chief source [was] the files of the several papers at various state university libraries and at library centers in Philadelphia, Washington and other cities."[16]

In examining Murphy's books, articles, lectures, and addresses, we find a curious combination of ideas. In his philosophy, is journalism education primarily "nuts-and-bolts practice," a liberal art because of its cultural values, a social science, or a science? At one time or another Murphy's thinking (at least as evidenced in his publications) pointed in each direction.

The textbooks focused on journalism education as "nuts-and-bolts practice." Murphy's own contribution to *An Introduction to Journalism* is a list of "Ten Tests of a News Story"—advice on how to evaluate a news story, advice that could also be used as a guide in writing a story. For *An Introduction* and for *Sport Writing* he gathered together addresses given and articles written by professional journalists. But a closer look shows that *An Introduction* does present more than "how-to's." For example, a tie to the social sciences is seen in a contribution by Joseph E. Sharkey that called for journalists to recognize their growing influence on the public and to act accordingly—responsibly.[17]

Murphy also mentioned this tie to the social sciences in his

---

[14]Ibid., pp. 40-43.

[15]Lawrence W. Murphy, *The Dawn of Daily Newspaper Journalism in the United States: The First Dailies; The Early Penny Press* (Grand Forks, ND: University of North Dakota Press, 1956), p. 5.

[16]Lawrence W. Murphy, "John Dunlap's 'Packet' and Its Competitors," *Journalism Quarterly* 28 (1951): 58.

[17]See Joseph E. Sharkey, "The Mission of the Press," in Murphy's *An Introduction*, pp. 123-127.

1938 address to the American Association of Schools and Departments of Journalism, when he noted that individuals with journalistic training, especially with advanced training, would have the opportunity "to make contributions in the field of social theory and philosophy, as well as in the scientific field."[18] In this same address he dealt at length with the ties between journalism and science and noted with optimism that journalism education's having "grown up with science and in full sight of a *world being remade by science*" would lead to still more advances in journalism.[19] But just a few years earlier Murphy's description of journalism had looked in a different direction—to the liberal arts. In his 1932 address to the American Association of Teachers of Journalism, citing the need to improve upon the methods of journalism education that had been borrowed from the apprenticeship programs in newsrooms, he called for experimentation in the teaching of journalism. At the same time, he stressed the journalism student's need for courses rich in cultural background, whether they be the traditional liberal arts courses or courses in agriculture, the performing arts, or architecture.[20] In 1930, however, Murphy had seen an even closer relationship to the liberal arts, discussing the "cultural values" content of many journalism courses at length.[21]

Was Murphy inconsistent? Or did his concept of the field of journalism change and develop during the 1930s? A look at his own research and his comments on the research of other scholars may help answer these questions.

Murphy's area of specialization was journalism history. He considered history, as he pointed out in "Cultural Values in the Study of Journalism," most definitely to be in the liberal arts. And his methodology was rooted in the liberal arts as well, using the traditional qualitative approach of the historian. For his lecture on early daily newspapers, he read more than 800 issues. For his article on John Dunlap he also read primary sources. He wrote both these pieces in the 1950s, and his methodology was consistent with his early views and practices.

And for all of his talk about how journalism would benefit from science, Murphy looked askance at quantitative methodology in at least one instance. In 1934, responding to "Measuring the Ethics of American Newspapers," a quantitative study by Susan M. Kingsbury, Hornell Hart, and others of Bryn Mawr College, Murphy criticized nearly every aspect of the investigation:

This research does not measure the ethics [of American newspapers]. It may or may not point a direction for further work and it may or may not advance a method which, with amend-

---

[18]"Schools of Journalism, Past and Future," p. 41.
[19]Ibid., pp. 36-38.
[20]See "Professional and Nonprofessional Teaching of Journalism."
[21]See "Cultural Values in the Study of Journalism."

ments, will prove useful, but the current report does not shed a clear light upon the ethical performance of the press. . . . It amasses much data; it gives some notion of the proportion of space devoted to subjects; it labors with the tedious work of clipping, measuring, appraising, computing. But its chief purpose is lost in a maze of work in faulty assumptions and presumptions.

Murphy felt that the sample used in the content analysis study was not representative, that the indexes for classifying stories were faulty, and that the researchers did not define the terms such as "anti-social" well. Their study did not go far enough: "We must have regard in measurements for other things than extent; we must see duration and intensity, too, and we must see them (in an ethics study) in terms of right and wrong, wise or unwise, as determined by social or public welfare. . . ." But the bottom line, he said, was that the study was "at variance with the seasoned and expert judgment of great newspapermen . . . who have judged more stories and more headlines from an ethical point of view than all of the Bryn Mawr researchers combined" and that he preferred opinions of major newspapers to those expressed in the study. "In mathematics," he wrote, "any method is a correct method which gives the correct answer. But the method here pursued does not give the correct answer when it rates the Washington *Post* above the papers I have named (Portland *Oregonian*, Milwaukee *Journal*, St. Louis *Globe-Democrat*, New York *Evening Post*, and others) and when it indicates unsatisfactory ethical scores for them." Increasing the numbers and types of measurements in such a study, he said, would "guarantee that the mathematics are correct" but would not remedy faulty assumptions. He concluded, "There will always be a measure at the end of the work, it is true, but it will be a measure of the wrong thing. This is what we have in the Bryn Mawr research, in my judgment. A measure of something, indeed, perhaps of something that has no name; but not a measure of the ethics of American newspapers."[22]

Perhaps Murphy was inconsistent. Perhaps he spoke of journalism education and the profession of journalism in whatever terms his audience would accept. Or perhaps he was able to see that journalism did not fit conveniently into a single niche—that the teaching of journalism and the journalist's use of a growing technology would benefit from scientific experimentation, that the mission of the journalist was based in the social sciences, and that the content of journalism courses and journalistic writing was and ought to be based in the liberal arts, a direction journalism has returned to in the works and thinking of such men as Jay Jensen and James Carey.

---

[22]Lawrence W. Murphy, "Notes on the Kingsbury-Hart Study," *Journalism Quarterly* 11 (1934): 382-391.

Ralph Casey
and Propaganda Analysis

Among early philosophers in mass communication, Ralph Casey (1890-1962) stands out for his work in the area of propaganda analysis and for his influence in building the University of Minnesota School of Journalism's graduate programs along the lines of social science. Although the focus of Casey's work was not specifically philosophical in the sense of, for example, that of John Merrill, the impact of his thought, writings, and actions has had a decided effect on the philosophy of journalism education.

Ralph Droz Casey was born to James and Linda (Droz) Casey in Aspen, Colorado, May 8, 1890. He was educated at the University of Washington, taking the AB in 1913, and at the University of Wisconsin, where he received the AM degree and, in 1929, the PhD in social science with a minor in journalism. Prior to this, he had worked for a number of newspapers—including the Seattle *Post-Intelligencer* and the New York *Herald*—and had taught journalism at the Universities of Washington, Montana, and Oregon.

At Wisconsin Casey was influenced by the press historian Willard Bleyer, to whom journalism was a form of applied social science. Casey later described Bleyer's influence on him as being "direct" and wrote:

> Dr. Bleyer's award to me of a teaching assistantship enabled me to seek the Wisconsin degree during my first year of residency at Madison. In the second year the department of political science awarded me its fellowship, with no teaching required. My Ph.D. major was political science; my minor in journalism, with two advisors, Prof. Harris in political science; Bleyer in journalism.
>
> I was the first candidate to be awarded a doctorate at Wisconsin under the joint journalism-social science program that Dr. Bleyer had evolved at the Madison institution.[1]

---

[1]Letter from Ralph D. Nafziger, 2 December 1968, cited in "Ralph Casey, Journalist, Educator, Social Scientist," by William R. Lindley, *Journalism*

Given the influence on Casey of Bleyer's social science perspective, it was natural that Casey should implement this point of view when it later fell to him to develop the curriculum in journalism at Minnesota. As Ralph Nafziger has pointed out, Minnesota's curriculum was already "to a considerable extent an adaptation of Wisconsin or Bleyer's ideas. Note the string of department or school heads at Minnesota following World War I: R. R. Barlow, E. Marion Johnson, Bruce McCoy. . . ."[2] All of these men were, Nafziger noted, either students of Bleyer or heavily influenced by his thought. They had, however, used the social sciences mainly as a backdrop for studies in journalism without employing them directly into the curriculum. Casey went beyond this and "explained to the American Association of Schools and Departments of Journalism (AASDJ) in his 1931 presidential address that Minnesota had set up its own courses in contemporary political, social and economic affairs. 'Under such a progressive plan,' he said, 'we can point to the teaching of journalism as an applied social science. . . .'"[3]

The first master's degree in journalism at the University of Minnesota was granted in 1931, and a minor in journalism was implemented for "qualified students who seek the doctor of philosophy degree in one of the social sciences."[4] In 1941, the Minnesota program in journalism was converted into a School of Journalism, and in 1944 Ralph Nafziger was named director of a new Division of Research. According to William Lindley, the press attacked Casey for turning the new school in the direction of research instead of emphasizing professionalism. In a 1955 article in *Journalism Quarterly*, Casey responded to this criticism, declaring:

> Journalism instruction can no longer depend alone on the intuitive guesses of former journalism craftsmen, who upon entering teaching ranks rely too heavily on past personal experiences in the use of technical tools and skills. It is good sense to recognize that the instructor has an obligation to plow back into his teaching some synthesis of the important findings developed in the past decade from systematic and disciplined communications investigations. . . .
>
> Psychologists, sociologists, statisticians, area study specialists in economics, foreign affairs and government, and their kinsmen have given us a wealth of insights into the problems that face the communicator and his audience, and the effects of

---

Educator 33 (October 1978): 20-ff.

[2]Ibid., p. 22

[3]Ibid., quoted from Ralph D. Casey, "Journalism, Technical Training and the Social Sciences," *Journalism Quarterly* 9 (1932): 44, taken from the address delivered 28 December 1931.

[4]Lindley, p. 23.

the communicated symbols on attitude and behavior.

It is fair to emphasize that the best work of trained journalism school investigators will now stand comparison with the
output in communications research of those specializing in the
behaviorial sciences. . . .[5]

A constant rise in graduate enrollment in the Minnesota
School of Journalism led to the establishing of a PhD program in
1951. Five areas of study comprised the program: communication
theory and public opinion, headed by Casey; specialized research
and methodology, headed by Robert L. Jones; history of mass
communication, later headed by Edwin Emery; communications
agencies as social institutions and communications law (one
field); and international communication and foreign journalism.
When Casey stepped down as director in 1958, he had behind him
almost 30 years of constant influence on the philosophical orientation of the study of journalism at Minnesota. When the name of
the School of Journalism was changed in 1966 to "School of
Journalism and Mass Communication," there was no significant
revision of Casey's curriculum.[6]

The impact of Casey's philosophical stance as a journalism
educator becomes clear when one looks at alternatives. The PhD
program at Minnesota might have developed along the lines of
professional journalism, with advanced course offerings in such
areas as editing, news writing, magazine writing, and so forth; or,
it might have developed with more of an affinity with literary
studies. In the first instance, there was apparently heavy pressure
on Casey to develop a graduate curriculum along professional
lines; in the second instance, journalism programs throughout
the country had begun, for the most part, in English departments.
Casey was not insensitive to either alternative, maintaining a
strong professionally oriented undergraduate program and
adding a course in 1931 titled "Literary Aspects of Journalism,"
which was described as a "study of journalistic writing—American, British, and Continental."[7] He clearly felt, however, that it
was the social sciences that offered the student of journalism the
best techniques for understanding and explaining the many phenomena of mass communication.

Casey's work as a scholar also bears the imprint of his social
science convictions. Most of it is discursively philosophical and
speculative rather than applied. Given that his career spanned
two world wars, Casey was much concerned with propaganda and
its influence on the free world. Preoccupied early on with public
opinion and the nature of its formation, Casey published in 1926,
with Glenn C. Quiett, a book titled *Principles of Publicity*. He

---

[5]Ibid., p. 24, taken from Ralph D. Casey, "The Challenge of Journalism
Education," *Journalism Quarterly* 32 (1955): 40-41.

[6]Lindley, p. 24.

[7]Ibid., p. 22.

wrote, "Publicity is the specialized effort of presenting to the public particularistic news and views in an effort to influence opinion and conduct." Such publicity had to be "honest, responsible and above board," he said:

> Current, truthful, and interesting information, written from the point of view of one who desires others to become informed, has a definite news value. And the business of a publicity man, who is writing for the press, is to disseminate to the newspapers such information, or to make it possible for the newspapers themselves to obtain it.[8]

Principles of Publicity, some of whose insights seemed to echo those of Walter Lippmann in *Public Opinion,* dealt with publicity in areas ranging from business to church to newspaper to university public relations divisions. Running throughout the book was the idea that communication should be subjected to a laissez-faire competition and that, as argued by Milton in 1644 (but in a religious context), the truth would emerge when embattled with falsehood. Casey apparently felt this would happen only if the in formation were "honest" and if agencies of information were free to compete. In a 1930 article published in *Journalism Quarterly* dealing with the position of the Scripps-Howard newspapers in the 1928 presidential campaign, Casey praised Scripps-Howard for permitting Heywood Broun to debate in his column the editorial writers for the same paper on the issue of the fitness of the candidates and the worth of their ideas. It was, Casey said, "to the great credit of the group of dailies that they permitted such various expressions of opinion in an election which stirred men so deeply and roused such heated partisanships."[9] In a subsequent *JQ* article, he argued that the columnist could assist in the competition of truth with falsehood by using French verse forms as vehicles of humor and satire in order to make the "column a salutary weapon against the pretense and bunkum of certain aspects of American life." Columnists, he said, could "deflate and reform in cases where a solemn editorial preachment had failed."[10]

In the early 1940s, Casey published three articles in *Public Opinion Quarterly* dealing with censorship and propaganda. In the first of these, he argued that American political parties did not subject to adequate analysis the voting constituency of the country prior to opening the propaganda campaign for a presidential election year. Farmers in particular, he argued, were overlooked even though they constituted one of the most important

---

[8]Ralph Casey, *Principles of Publicity* (New York: D. Appleton and Co., 1926), p. 2.

[9]Ralph Casey, "Scripps-Howard Newspapers in the 1928 Presidential Campaign," *Journalism Quarterly* 7 (1930): 231.

[10]Ralph Casey, "Newspaper Columnists and French Verse Forms," *Journalism Quarterly* 9 (1932): 339.

political groups in the nation. Little or no attention had been given, Casey said, to the average farmer's attitude toward the news stories and features he received during a campaign. Therefore, the effects of opinion-forming political information could hardly be formulated.[11] In a subsequent essay in the spring of 1942 dealing with wartime censorship, Casey argued that "the public should be taken into the government's confidence," that sources of propaganda should not be subject to censorship, and that there should not be any censoring of non-military news, because "[w]hen the legitimate news [that has been] suppressed does leak out, confidence in the government is impaired."[12]

Finally, in the third of this series of *POQ* articles, Casey argued that Americans had a good deal to learn from the British in the art of forming public opinion. Whereas British politicians continued their propaganda efforts throughout the year, the Americans operated on a seasonal basis, closing down all but a residue of their headquarters once a campaign was over. It would be more effective, Casey argued, if there were a constant effort to maintain opinion between elections rather than to reform or recapture it for a subsequent election. He pointed out the role of the journalist in British politics, which was that of a liaison between the press and a given political party, oftentimes giving up his job as journalist to become a public relations specialist for the party. "It seems to this writer," Casey said,

> that there is something to be learned from observation of the propaganda methods of the British political parties. Within the limits of American traditions, election laws, voter psychology, and traditional organization procedures, the intelligent party chairman and national committee could advance their party's welfare by gingerly experimenting with a few of the successful procedures of our British confreres.[13]

In a 1937 book coedited with Frank Luther Mott, titled *Interpretations of Journalism*, Casey argued that propaganda had grown as a factor in American life because of (a) the growth of democracy, (b) the growth of the functions of government, and (c) the rise of industrial productivity. All of these he viewed as the natural upshot of the American political and economic system. The press became, he wrote, "the sounding board for this conflicting volume of appeals." Involved in it was the process of what Casey called "myth-making," which was, he wrote,

---

[11]Ralph Casey, "The Republican Rural Press Campaign," *Public Opinion Quarterly* (1941): 130-32.

[12]Ralph Casey, "The Limits of Censorship, A Symposium," *Public Opinion Quarterly* 6 (1942): 21-24.

[13]Ralph Casey, "British Politics—Some Lessons in Campaign Propaganda," *Public Opinion Quarterly* 8 (1944): 83.

one of the most potent forms of propaganda, and a great political contest is certain to provide us with examples of it. The "myth" is effective because the average citizen is unaware of the process by which it is created and "he is under the illusion that what looms up before him is a disclosure of something hitherto hidden rather than a new creation brought about by the propagandist and practical politician."[14]

It was inevitable that this "myth-making" function of the information process should become a part of the news and that it should have a stereotyping effect on mass audiences. Although Casey felt that audiences should be able to discern the myth from the reality, he was not really critical of propaganda when used by Americans to sell products or ideas to other Americans. Indeed, he wrote, "Moderns have found publicity to be the effective means of motivating individual and mass action."[15]

By 1942 Casey's opinions about the benefits of propaganda had begun to change. Writing in *The Press in the Contemporary Scene*, a collection of articles published under the auspices of the annals of the American Academy of Political and Social Science, he said:

Every journalist now recognizes that he is confronted with a problem of the first magnitude in the unthinking failure of sections of the public to distinguish between propaganda, which is the deliberate and conscious effort to fix an attitude or modify an opinion as it relates to a doctrine or program, and, on the other hand, the conscientious effort of the agencies of communication to disseminate in a spirit of objectivity and honesty.

The "overt acts of belligerent nations" had not been given sufficient weight by propagandists in the United States, Casey wrote. Four "checks" could be imposed on propaganda: (a) able, well-informed men who possessed the courage to rebut propaganda; (b) careful editing and evaluation of the news; (c) a refusal to print sourceless news; and (d) a stronger insistence on the part of the press that its own reporters discover the news. The nature of the press was such that it was required to present both sides of a controversy; however, what was needed to deal effectively with foreign propaganda was what Casey called "counter-propaganda." The American press should, he wrote, "cooperate fully and wholeheartedly with the program of the Government to maintain the morale of the Nation in time of war." However, sound morale was achieved "when citizens of a democratic state are not cut off from the news. Citizens of a democratic nation can be trusted to

---

[14]Ralph Casey and Frank Luther Mott, *Interpretations of Journalism* (New York: F.S. Crofts, 1937), p. 409.
[15]Ibid., p. 412.

accept the bad tidings as well as the good."[16]

Never particularly critical of the American news establishment, Casey became a staunch supporter of the status quo in the years following World War II. In an essay in *Propaganda, Communication, and Public Opinion*, edited by Casey, Bruce Smith, and Harold Lasswell, Casey defended chain journalism and the allied propaganda system that had helped to win the war, and viewed optimistically the expansion of American dominance in the field of international media, particularly book publishing. In the introduction to his book *The Press in Perspective*, he suggested that the best means for improving the press was through "self-analysis, self-criticism, and self-improvement." "We have a feeling," he wrote, "that journalists would find disenchanting the creation of a press council, citizens' council, or board of review. In the end, the influence that public opinion brings to bear on the mass media, and the professional standards those in the craft evolve would appear to be the prevailing determinants that will continue to govern press performance. . . ."[17]

The difficulty with Casey's thought about the role of information in society is simply that it was too optimistic. One senses that he began to feel this himself in the period following World War II, by which time the full negative potential of propaganda had been demonstrated in Nazi Germany and Fascist Italy. Yet he still maintained the view that only the press should be allowed to reform the press, and he continued to feel that propaganda was a necessary ingredient in industrial society. He was not at all critical of such a society *per se* but accepted its manners and mandates unquestioningly.

His optimism regarding the role of public relations in mass communication seems naive to a modern mind critical of publicity processes. Following the fiascoes of Watergate and Three Mile Island—not to mention Chernoble and Beijing—it seems absurd to think that public relations has any truly "public" function at all. Is it not, the modern critic asks, simply a means whereby modern industry and business either excuse their shortcomings to the public or justify their windfall profits? Casey, however, thought it was, or could be, much more than this: that it could indeed be the source of genuine news. It is, of course, both.

Casey's optimism must be judged in light of the feeling of his own time. He was a young man during the first world war, a war fought to make the world safe for democracy. He saw the American dream go down in the depression and saw it emerge victorious

---

[16]Ralph D. Casey and Malcolm M. Willey (eds.), *The Press in the Contemporary Scene* (Philadelphia: American Academy of Political and Social Science, 1942), pp. 66-75.

[17]Bruce Lannes Smith, Harold D. Lasswell, and Ralph D. Casey, *Propaganda, Communication, and Public Opinion* (Princeton, NJ: Princeton University Press, 1946), pp. 23-30; and Casey (Ed.), *The Press in Perspective* (Baton Rouge: Louisiana State University Press, 1963), pp. xvi-xvii.

from World War II. Indeed, it was in the heady aftermath of the second great war that much of his optimism emerged. His was not the heyday of television but of radio and the newspaper, not of pornography and the new morality but of social conservatism and traditionalism, not of the transistor and the computer but of vastly slower means of communication storage and transfer. Considering the exponential increase in information from the end of World War II to the present day, Casey seems almost to have come out of another century—as if the 20th century were two centuries, his and ours.

His philosophical contributions to the building of the program in journalism at the University of Minnesota were significant. The School of Journalism was born during his directorship, as was the master's program. He was responsible, as one of a rather long line of directors who came from the University of Wisconsin, for planting the J-School firmly in social science traditions. If one is a social scientist, this is fine; if not, one may see it as problematic. The criticisms of social science methodology that have been mounted over the last 15 years or so have been applied to such research in mass communication to, perhaps, the extreme. In the process, R-methodology has given way to Q-methodology, which, in turn, has given way to ethnomethodology, social-interactionism, critical theory, and cultural studies. The positivism afoot during Casey's young manhood is nowhere to be seen, making him, again, seem to belong to another century.

One wonders what would have happened to research in mass communication if Casey's philosophy had been of, say, a more literary turn. What sorts of courses might he have developed besides the "Literary Aspects of Journalism"? Might the rapidly developing programs in creative writing, which by now throng the academic countryside, have become a part of the journalism curriculum? And might the present curious estrangement between schools of journalism and departments of English never have occurred?

In any case, the central shortcoming of Casey's ideas of journalism education—an egregious optimism—seems to be, by now, something of an American tradition in both the American press itself as well as in American academic journalism. From the aspirations of the Revolutionary press to the banalities of modern corporate journalism, there is a discrepancy between dream and reality. Likewise, from the positivistic social science philosophy of an earlier day to modern-day probability theory or participant observation, there is a clear retreat from optimism and innocence toward pessimism and awareness of limitations—and thence to a new optimism. How logical then that journalism education should be inhabited by so little of the critical mind and by so few critical traditions.

John Drewry and Social Progress

John Drewry's career as a newspaperman, professor of journalism, university administrator, and author began at a time when journalism education was still finding its place in the academic community. Drewry (1902-1983) made a concerted effort to help it find that place. His philosophy was eclectic, drawn from many journalism educators. He recognized some of the problems in his field and suggested ways to solve them. He was confident that journalism education could be improved, that improved journalism education would lead to improvements in the profession of journalism, and that improved professional journalism would improve the society in which it operated.

John Eldridge Drewry was born to Judson Ellis and Verdi May (Harrell) Drewry in Griffin, Georgia, on June 4, 1902. He was educated at the University of Georgia, where he received a bachelor of arts degree in 1921, a bachelor of journalism degree in 1922, and a master of arts degree in 1925. He did postgraduate work at Columbia University in the summers of 1924 and 1925. He worked as a reporter and news editor for the Athens (Ga.) *Banner-Herald* from 1921 to 1923 and as a book reviewer in 1923. He also reviewed books for the Atlanta *Journal* (1921-1939) and the Atlanta *Constitution* (from 1939) and wrote as a correspondent for the *Christian Science Monitor* (1927-1940). He began teaching as an instructor in the Henry W. Grady School of Journalism at the University of Georgia in 1922. By 1930 he had been promoted to full professor. He was director and dean of the school of journalism from 1940 to 1969. While at Georgia he edited a number of university publications and authored, co-authored, or edited many books and journal articles. He also organized the press bureau, served as publicity director, and created the George Foster Peabody Radio and Television Awards, administered by the school.

Drewry was active in professional organizations and honorary societies, including the American Association of Teachers of Journalism (serving as its president in 1930), the American Council on Education in Journalism, the Georgia Education Association, Phi Beta Kappa (president of the University of Georgia chapter, 1948-1949), Phi Kappa Phi, Sigma Delta Kappa,

Digamma Kappa, and Phi Eta Sigma. He received a number of awards, including a Gold Key Award from the Columbia Scholastic Press Association in 1954 and several distinguished service awards from the University of Georgia Alumni Society, the Georgia Press Association, and the Georgia Association of Broadcasters.

Drewry saw the connections between journalism and literature and, because of the "cultural" content of many journalism courses, he agreed with and quoted Lawrence W. Murphy in categorizing journalism as a liberal art. Writing of the so-called "chasm" between literature and journalism, Drewry said, "An excellent indication of the real relationship between journalism and literature is the fact that many of those who produce what ultimately bears the label of literature are men and women with newspaper experience."[1] Journalism education, he noted, had begun in English departments. In 1929 he called for the separation of the two, for the "utilitarian ends" of journalistic training were better taught by someone with professional journalistic experience—"though, of course, graduate work in English, when supplemented by practical newspaper work, did become an asset." The real problem, he thought, was the general "lack of sympathetic understanding by the English teachers" and the "step-child" status of journalism when taught in the English department. In spite of his desire to establish journalism as a separate department, he thought that the English department had much to offer the journalism student, including "thorough and effective courses in grammar, rhetoric, and composition in the freshman year." He suggested that the English department might cooperate by offering "literature courses which would include: first, survey courses arranged to correlate with the history of journalism courses; and, second, courses in contemporary literature, with special attention given to the journalistic careers of the authors." He also suggested that appropriate graduate-level courses in English could become part of the curricula in graduate programs in journalism.[2] Drewry believed that certain kinds of knowledge—including history, English, political science, literature, economics, sociology, government, modern languages, psychology, and science—were essential to the journalist (and so to the journalism student). Consequently, he called for the journalism student to receive a liberal arts education along with professional courses in journalism.[3] Others Drewry quoted to support his view that journalism and the liberal arts are closely related were Thomas

---

[1]John E. Drewry, *Concerning the Fourth Estate* (2nd ed.) (Athens, GA: University of Georgia Press, 1942), pp. 7, 82. See also the preceding chapter on Lawrence W. Murphy.

[2]John E. Drewry, "Journalism and the English Department," *Journalism Quarterly* 6 (1929): 22-24.

[3]See John E. Drewry, "Is Journalism a Profession?" *Sewanee Review* 38 (1930): 197; and *The Fourth Estate*, pp. 68-91.

B. Wells, Allen Sinclair Will, R.L. Lyman, H.L. Mencken, and Willard G. Bleyer. Eventually, when journalism education more closely fit his standards, Drewry wrote:

> The journalism curriculum in some respects is a better liberal education than the classical bachelor of arts course, especially since the work in journalism vitalizes and interprets the cultural subjects which in so many instances seem sterile and meaningless to the student.[4]

This liberal arts education was necessary if journalism was ever to become a true profession. In an article published in *The Sewanee Review* in 1930, Drewry asked, "Is Journalism a Profession?" He answered his own question with a resounding "no." There were too many "'Marty' Bulls" (after the novel *Splendor* by Ben Ames Williams) working for newspapers, too many "strong-armed, dogmatic, over-bearing braggadoccio[s]." Even the more mild-mannered reporter made too many errors "through . . . lack of information and incompetency." And, he added, "[m]any of the inaccurate and absurd headlines in our newspapers can be traced to copy readers with no educational backround."[5] He saw problems in other areas of journalism as well. In an article titled "American Magazines To-Day," he noted the numbers of magazines being published and asked if readers "have any real reason for reading the magazines of their choice, or do they continue to buy them because of some vague notion that they contain the kind of stories they like? This subject should be one of interest to the intelligent person who would be informed better regarding the present state of affairs in the American republic of letters, and of journalism." The article included a brief history of American magazines and a system of classifying magazines into nine categories. He praised a number of magazines in the "Journals of Opinion" and "Literary Magazines" categories, but of one category he wrote:

> It is unfortunate that such magazines as the Purely Fictional, including the Confessional Group, exist to be enumerated, because obviously their intrinsic merit is *nihil*. But by far the larger number of American periodicals, excluding professional and trade journals which concern themselves with particular vocations, are of this purely fictional kind. Their content is of the most worthless kind of stories, which can have no appeal except to those with the literary tastes of a moron. Some of these periodicals with their photographs of nude women and salacious stories reach the very depths of depravity in writing.[6]

---

[4]*The Fourth Estate*, pp. 82-88.

[5]"Is Journalism a Profession?" pp. 191-194.

[6]John E. Drewry, "American Magazines To-day," *Sewanee Review* 36 (1928): 342-354.

But even if such samples of bad writing or questionable subject matter were discounted, journalism was still not a profession, Drewry said, because "a profession presupposes four things: (1) a body of professional knowlege; (2) a code of ethics; (3) a license to practice; and (4) accountability." Journalism, he said, lacked a system of licensing and a means of holding journalists accountable. So he called for continued improvement in journalism education, with an emphasis on a broad background and on sound professional courses. "Whereas at the turn of the century there were few books and no schools for the training of journalists," he wrote in 1930, "today there are many good books and a number of schools of journalism. There are all sorts of codes of ethics, and soon, I hope there will be machinery for their enforcement."[7]

A decade later Drewry was calling journalism a profession, and it was a profession with a mission: "Journalism, properly conceived and faithfully practised, is a great social science with a two-fold mission: (1) to reflect the activities of society, and (2) to shape the moods and progress of society." The content of the newspaper, he said, should reflect the community or society it represents: the newspaper was a "super-mirror, in which the reader may see reflected a day-by-day picture of the civilization of which he is a part. If the mirror be true, it will give a proportionate view of what is happening in the world. It will not exaggerate the daily manifestations of an anti-social nature, nor will it omit them."[8]

According to Drewry, newspapers, in accomplishing their social mission, had both direct and indirect influence on society. The indirect influence was on "the interests, tastes, language, standards of living, and sense of values of their readers." The direct influence he classed as "civic or community services" and "educational services." His 20-page list of examples of such activities included exposing German spies and quack dentists and doctors; drawing attention to drug addiction and other health-threatening practices; helping to establish hospitals; promoting building of public works systems; organizing amateur athletic associations; promoting civic pride in attractive and well-kept public and private properties; establishing scholarship funds for students of many subjects, not just journalism; and exposing unnecessarily high food prices, resulting in lower prices.[9]

For Drewry, the mission of journalism was not limited to print journalism. In *New Horizons in Journalism* he wrote, "*journalism* in the broad sense, includes all agencies of communications . . . ."[10] Two years later he gave the title *Journalism IS*

---

[7]"Is Journalism a Profession?" pp. 196-197.

[8]*The Fourth Estate*, p. 4.

[9]Ibid., pp. 13-34.

[10]John E. Drewry (Ed.), *New Horizons in Journalism* (Bulletin of the University of Georgia, 1951-52) (Athens, GA: University of Georgia, 1952),

Communications to the *Bulletin* of the University of Georgia and wrote in his introduction, "*Communications* is the new word for *journalism.*"[11] In the 1956 *Bulletin,* he said, "*Communication* in the singular is generally understood to mean the act of transmitting ideas or fact. . . . *Communications* in the plural has come to mean all the mass media. . . ."[12] One year later he wrote on the omnipresence of communications:

> The words *communication* or *journalism* to most people mean headlines, newscasts, comic strips. Actually, there is, of course, much more: the whole democratic process; the relationship of the individual to his job, to his employer, to society; the undeclared never-ending international war of ideologies; the difference among races and religions; the conflict of capital and labor; the legislative and ballot-box conflict of Democrats and Republicans—indeed, communications *is* the *key* to *so much.*[13]

For Drewry, journalism was the answer to many of society's questions and problems. In 1966 he wrote, "With the growing abundance and complexity of knowledge, the relationship between communications and effectiveness becomes increasingly apparent. And the absence of such a relationship is the highway to ignorance, confusion, and chaos."[14]

Drewry's philosophy of journalism education was not unlike that of Lawrence W. Murphy, whom he often quoted. To both, journalism and literature were related; the study of journalism was a cultural study. Drewry consistently called for journalism students to be exposed to a broad range of subjects so that they would be ready and able to cover events and ideas in the world about them. Early on he was critical of the practice of journalism, at one time refusing to call it a profession. But he must have felt the momentum as journalism education "took off" in academe, as the "profession," as he eventually called it, evidenced the social mission he called for. But the momentum evidently never slowed for him, for he had an almost unbridled optimism, a faith in progress.

This optimism is apparent in the titles and introductions to

---

p. vii.

[11]John E. Drewry (Ed.), *Journalism IS Communications* (Bulletin of the University of Georgia, v. 55, no. 1) (Athens, GA: University of Georgia Press, 1954), p. vii.

[12]John E. Drewry (Ed.), *Communications Problems and Progress* (Bulletin of the University of Georgia, v. 57, no. 2) (Athens, GA: University of Georgia Press, 1956), p. vii.

[13]John E. Drewry (Ed.), *Communications: Key to So Much* (Bulletin of the University of Georgia, v. 58, no. 1) (Athens, GA: University of Georgia Press, 1957), p. vii.

[14]John E. Drewry (Ed.), *Greater Communications Effectiveness* (Bulletin of the University of Georgia, v. 67, no. 3) (Athens, GA: University of Georgia Press, 1966), p. vii.

the editions of the *Bulletin* of the University of Georgia which he edited. Among the titles are *Communications Problems and Progress* (1956), *Communications: Key to So Much* (1957), *Onward and Upward with Communications* (1961), *Better Journalism For a Better Tomorrow* (1963), *Higher Ground for Journalism* (1965), *A Forward Look for Communications* (1967), and *Journalism Escalation* (1968).[15] These editions of the *Bulletin*, along with the others he edited, were collections of addresses on journalistic subjects delivered at conferences and conventions sponsored by the University of Georgia's Henry W. Grady School of Journalism, of which Drewry was dean. The addresses themselves, though, were not always so optimistic. Drewry wrote an introduction for each bulletin, and here again we see his undaunted, optimistic point of view. In 1952 he wrote that "the scope and potentialities of journalism are horizon-like in their extensiveness . . . ."[16] He considered journalism to be the "key" to many of society's problems (1957), and in 1960 he tied improvements in journalism to "the upward movement in larger areas." Of the addresses in the 1963 edition, *Better Journalism For a Better Tomorrow*, he wrote, "This volume . . . may be regarded as a road map to higher ground in journalism, and those responsible for its content may be thought of as a very special kind of cartographers of social progress."[17] Of *Higher Ground for Journalism* (1965) Drewry wrote, "The key words in the title this year, 'higher ground,' are in keeping with 'better,' 'advancing,' 'new horizons,' 'attaining goals,' and 'onward and upward' in other titles in this series—all deliberately chosen to make it clear that the emphasis at the Grady School is on new heights both for journalism and for the society which it serves."[18] Similar observations are found in the introduction to *Journalistic Escalation* (1968): ". . . the [Grady] School of Journalism is aware of its service obligation of accelerated progress and improvement by mass media—of *escalation*—both for their own welfare and for the good of the society they serve."[19]

Early in his career Drewry recognized problems in journalism education and in the profession of journalism and sought

---

[15]John E. Drewry (Ed.), *Communications Problems and Progress*; *Communications: Key to So Much*; *Onward and Upward with Communications* (Bulletin of the University of Georgia, v. 62, no. 1), Athens GA: University of Georgia Press, 1961; *Better Journalism For a Better Tomorrow* (Bulletin of the University of Georgia, v. 64, no. 6), Athens GA: University of Georgia Press, 1963; *Higher Ground for Journalism* (Bulletin of the University of Georgia, v. 66, no. 3), Athens GA: University of Georgia Press, 1965; *A Forward Look for Communications* (Bulletin of the University of Georgia, v. 68, no. 8), Athens GA: University of Georgia Press, 1967; and *Journalism Escalation* (Bulletin of the University of Georgia, v. 69, no. 1), Athens GA: University of Georgia Press, 1968.

[16]Drewry, *New Horizons in Journalism*, p. vii.

[17]Drewry, *Better Journalism For a Better Tomorrow*, p. vii.

[18]Drewry, *Higher Ground for Journalism*, p. vii.

[19]Drewry, *Journalistic Escalation*, p. vii.

ways to solve those problems. His philosophy of journalism education called for a broad background of coursework. Early on he suggested that journalism be licensed, providing for the enforcement of ethics and accountability. Evidently convinced that his early criticisms of journalism and journalism education would lead to reform (and, as a journalism educator he was in a position to bring about some of those reforms), he came to believe in a social mission of journalism and took note of ways in which journalists were carrying out their mission. By 1965 he was describing journalists as "cartographers of social progress." Although continuing to recognize the journalism profession's social responsibilities, he expressed no systematic critical theory of either the media or society in these later years—no criticism of problems in the media, only optimism of what lay ahead.

Jay Jensen
and Neo-Liberal Thought

By the end of World War II, the awesome power of the press in international affairs had become apparent. The German press under Adolph Hitler had been bent to his mad purposes, and the Italian press under Mussolini had been similarly subverted for fascist purposes. The Hutchins Commission, whose 1947 publication, *A Free and Responsible Press*,[1] marked the advent of the "social responsibility" theory of the press, was appointed to deal with the role of the press in a changed and changing society. That it redefined the philosophy of press freedom is by now common knowledge; however, to media philosophers of the day, these changes were unfamiliar and portentous. Jay Jensen (1917-) was one of the first to attend to their philosophical-historical backgrounds and to ponder their implications for mass society and mass communication.

Jay Walbourne Jensen was born in Sheffield, Illinois, on June 13, 1917, to Theodore Carl and Gertrude (Walbourne) Jensen. From 1936 to 1939, he was a reporter for, and later editor of, the Sheffield *Times*. In 1939 he moved to Woodland, California, to become editor of the Woodland *Record*. The next year he became editor of the Flodin Publishing company and a publicist for the Conron Association. During the war, he served as an Army major in military intelligence and as a staff officer in an infantry division, and he was also a writer-editor for General Douglas MacArthur's staff in the Pacific Theater.

In 1938 he was graduated from Emory University with an AB in the history of ideas. In 1948 he received the MS in journalism and in 1959 the PhD in communications from the University of Illinois. From 1957 until 1977, he was chairman of the Department of Journalism at the University of Illinois. At various times he has been a Ford Foundation Fellow and a consultant for the National Committee on Violence. He also is a member of Phi Beta Kappa and Kappa Tau Alpha.

---

[1]Commission on Freedom of the Press, *A Free and Responsible Press* (Chicago: University of Chicago Press, 1947).

Most of Jensen's philosophy can be found in *Liberalism, Democracy and the Mass Media,* a book based on his PhD thesis. Here Jensen described the history of ideas affecting the rise to prominence of Western media. Beginning with the rise of liberalism as a *Weltanschauung,* Jensen traced liberal thought from its Greek origins, through Catholic religion (the sanctity of the individual soul) and the scholasticism of Aquinas, and thence into the 17th, 18th, and 19th centuries. Throughout, he emphasized liberalism as an idea only partly determined by the economic circumstances of the Industrial Revolution:

> But what is necessary for one to understand the meaning of Liberalism from the standpoint of this essay is an account which not only identifies Modern Liberalism as a myth-complex of the present industrial epoch, but recognizes the existence of an earlier tradition of Liberal thought and acknowledges the indebtedness of Modern Liberalism to both Greek and Christian philosophy.[2]

Focusing on the role of ideas as a determining factor in the rise of Western media means, for Jensen, the downplaying of economic determinism: "But, although the Liberal *Weltanschauung* was nurtured by the sociological conditions of modern capitalists and the psychology of capitalist enterprise, it was already heavily indebted to a precedent Historic Liberalism that was anything but bourgeois in content and style."[2] Economic factors, therefore, only *contributed* to the rise of liberalism; they did not spawn it. Here one finds Jensen at odds with Marxist philosophers who view the rise of liberalism strictly in terms of an economic determinism.

Jensen locates the individualism so characteristic of classical liberal thought in "the remote headwaters of Greek atomism." By way of scholasticism and the "Liberal conception of the autonomous Self, derived from the Renaissance rediscovery of the ego and the image of 'masterless man,'" individualism eventuates in "an atomic conception of society, organized upon and subject to the claims of individual wills," despite the fact that the individual goodness of man and the doctrine of natural rights were alien to classicism as well as to Christianity. According to Jensen, classical liberalism contained three basic beliefs about the nature of man: (1) "a belief in the absolute value of the human person and the spiritual equality of all individuals; (2) a belief in the autonomy of the individual will; and (3) a belief in the essential rationality and goodness of man."[3]

This view led to accompanying views on the nature of society:

---

[2]Jay W. Jensen, *Liberalism, Democracy and the Mass Media* (Ann Arbor, MI: University Microfilms, 1958), p. 42.

[2]Ibid., p. 50.

[3]Ibid., pp. 53-59.

1. [Classical liberals] believed that the state came into existence by mutual consent of autonomous individuals and for the sole purpose of preserving and protecting the inalienable rights of those individuals.

2. They believed that the natural and proper relationship between the State and the individual is a contractual one, and that when the terms of the contract are violated the consenting individual has not only the right but the responsibility to rebel and establish a new government.

3. They believed that "the government which governs least governs best," government being conceived as having primarily the negative functions of protecting the individual in his rights and liberties in order that he may be free to follow the dictates of conscience and the laws of nature.

4. They believed that social control is best secured not by command of a sovereign, but by the impersonal rule of law which is at once the product of individual wills and the embodiment of Reason.[4]

The upshot of these views for press freedom is familiar history to students of mass communication. The press should be unfettered in dealing with a controversy of ideas true and false; by so being, it will ensure the more obvious disclosing of truth. In Miltonic terms, here one has a responsibility to truth rather than to any individual man's benighted estate: "In our concern for the fool, must we deny the wise man knowledge of evil?" and "For God sure esteems the growth and compleating of one virtuous person, more than the restraint of ten virtuous."[5]

Jenson argues that the system of classical liberalism, which had triumphed as a *Weltanschauung* by the middle of the 18th century in America and some years earlier in England, came under attack even as it was at the zenith of its prominence. The attack came by way of the destruction of the idea of natural law by the Scottish philosopher David Hume and by way of the romantic revolt against reason, led by Rousseau and others. By arguing that there is only an empirical correlation between cause and effect, Hume dealt the death blow to the idea of necessary causation in natural law, arguing instead that what seems rational is really the product of training and institutions. Romanticism, by way of its reliance on the emotions instead of on reason, also undercut classical liberalism. Instead of claiming right reason as its foundation for a view of human nature and instead of assuming a dispersion throughout human society of the ability of arriving at truth, the romantics assumed the presence in certain *individuals* of truthful insight, thereby undercutting the idea of natural law

---

[4]Ibid., pp. 60-61.
[5]John Milton, *Complete Poetry and Selected Prose of John Milton* (New York: Modern Library, 1948), p. 34, cited in Jensen, p. 83.

in favor of the laws of the individual imagination. "Viewed from this angle," writes Jensen, "the liberal Weltanschauung was utterly transformed. The static and mechanical conceptions which had sprung from the genius of Newton and Locke gave way to the evolutionary and dynamic conceptions of Burke and Hegel."[6]

This has led to what Jensen calls a "Neo-Liberalism," a "revolution in modern thought [which] has transformed the Liberal theory of the press from a negative and individualistic theory into [a] positive and collectivistic theory . . . ." In this change the rise of the mass media has "transformed the press system from an exposition of individual will, i.e., of the autonomous Self, into a reflection of collective will, i.e., of the cultural order; and . . . the development of the institutional order of public communication has affected the character and role of the Self in contemporary mass society." "What John Stuart Mill feared most of all," writes Jensen, "—the tyranny of society, of custom, of tradition, of majority opinion; and the stifling of individualism—is perhaps not so far from becoming *le fait accompli.*"[7]

In the face of this "tyranny," what Jensen fears for the press is that it will become, like the Self, a "creature of the cultural order" which will function "primarily as a form of social control" in which behavior will be "routinized in terms of the values and prescriptions" of the cultural heritage of the mass media. This, he argues, amounts to what Joseph Klapper has called the "engineering of consent," in which the media are "exquisitely fitted to turn the status quo into social law."[8] The position of the Self in such a society is submerged with regard to the values of the group, which itself is subject to being persuaded by "higher" group values, that is, those of the church or government. According to Jensen, this change of emphasis from Self, in classical liberalism, to an emphasis on mass man in new-liberalism is less than desirable:

Thus, we see that the Self, the "individual," the *sine qua non* of any Liberal philosophy worthy of its historic tradition, has suffered the meanest degradation—at the hands not only of the revolution in modern thought, but of the mass media as the institutional order of public communication. Everywhere the forms of the new media absorb the Self within themselves, leaving little or nothing to the individual will. And Reason, far from acting to free the mind and will of the Self, is more and more employed in manipulating and subjugating the masses. The objective of public communication is no longer (as described in normative Liberal theory) mainly to facilitate by expression of individual wills the self-righting process inherent in a free and open marketplace of ideas and opinions, and therby to enable men to govern themselves according to the dic-

---

[6]Jensen, pp. 116-26.
[7]Ibid., pp. 306, 315.
[8]Cited in ibid, pp. 310-20.

tates of "right reason" and individual conscience. Rather, the objective function, as understood in positivistic Neo-Liberal theory, is to mask the realities of the political, social and economic order with the symbols of conformism, and by propaganda and diversion to guarantee the loyalty of the masses to the cultural order.[9]

To this problem Jensen poses the answer that what is needed in order to rediscover the lost Self of modernity is a new metaphysics. This, he says, cannot be accomplished by going backward, for classical liberalism was founded on a Newtonian cosmology and an attendant "mechanistic world-hypotheses." This and "its peculiar image of the atomistic Self is in hapless ruin." It must, instead, be founded on a modernist view of the Self as inviolable. This entails either a powerful system of philosophy or a powerful system of religious belief entailing Selfhood, or a combination of both. "What the Liberal faith awaits, perhaps," says Jensen, "is not only an appropriate arrangement of sociological conditions, but a twentieth-century Aquinas." What Jensen apparently has in mind is a neo-scholasticism in which the disparate powers of philosophy and religion would be united in some neo-Thomist way. Jensen sees the philosophy of Alfred North Whitehead as supplying the philosopher's part of the formula, for Whitehead contends for the Self on the basis of "self-causation of actual entities": "[In] all actual entities there is manifest the characteristic of autonomous self-creation." Jensen closes his dissertation with the following:

Therefore, it is to be ardently hoped that the future Weltanschauung of Western culture will postulate, as does the philosophy of Whitehead, an image of the Self as an autonomous entity, somehow apart from, or independent of, the mundane cultural order and having its meaning and reality in reference to a realm of eternal objects, i.e., an immanent or transcendent order of values. For only thus can a new metaphysics of Liberalism restore a respect for the individual and for Reason, and be grounded in enduring principles that will ensure the freedom of the Self, of the press, and of public opinion.[10]

In 1965 Jensen, along with Theodore Peterson of the University of Illinois and William L. Rivers of Stanford University, published *The Mass Media and Modern Society*. Jensen wrote chapters two, six, and seven, and contributed to other chapters as well. Here one finds a good deal of the philosophy in *Liberalism, Democracy and the Mass Media* reiterated and expanded. In Chapter Two, citing Walter Lippmann, Jensen discussed "Man as Symbol Maker" and concluded that "[it] is precisely this symbol-

---

[9]Jensen, pp. 319-320.
[10]Ibid., pp. 322-334.

making function that makes human communication and the social process possible." He viewed the mass media not only as ad-
juncts of other institutions but also as "a form of power with interests and a will of its own." In Chapter Seven he developed this
idea into what he called "The Objective Theory of the Press":

> The so-called objective theory of the press is quite different in
> perspective and intent [from other "prescriptive" theories]. The
> term here, as in its use with other social theories, has a dual
> meaning. First, it refers to a concern with objects outside of
> one's self. Thus, the media are looked upon as having, in some
> sense, an existence of their own apart from the motives and in-
> tentions of men. Like other institutional orders, they are specif-
> ically human inventions. But they tend to develop "objective"
> functions as contrasted with the "subjective" functions assigned
> to them by their creators. Sometimes these objective functions
> are neither intended nor regarded as desirable. Therefore, they
> are not recognized, much less acknowledged, by normative the-
> orists. Nevertheless, they do exist, and it is with their analysis
> and description that objective theory is chiefly concerned.
>
> Second, the term "objective" refers to an impartial, disinter-
> ested way of looking at things. The media are considered with-
> out benefit of ideology, since the avowed aim of objective theory
> is to determine what they actually do, not what they ought to do.
> For what the media actually do may be quite different from, or
> something other than, what men might wish them to do. This
> does not mean that the descriptions or prescriptions of norma-
> tive theory are rejected out of hand. Objective theory recognizes
> that the prescriptions of normative theory may have an impor-
> tant, even decisive, influence on the character and operation of
> the media. Then, too, objective theory accepts much of the de-
> scription of the media in normative theory as valid. But it tries
> to describe the characteristics and functions of the media that
> normative theory ignores.[11]

Objective theory differs from other theories of the press, then,
in that it is descriptive and not prescriptive. "Its analysis and description proceed from an attitude of noncommitment to any
form of ideology (except that of scholarship)." Here the media are
viewed "as a mode of social interaction" which is accomplished by
way of the "symbolic transfer of meanings, values, and beliefs."
"Characteristically, they purvey the ethos of the social order in
which they operate. Yet they also provide the means for response
and for potential challenge to that order." According to Jensen,
the media tell man "who he is, what he wants to be, and how he
can appear to be that way to others." Given this, and sounding the

---

[11]Theodore Peterson, Jay W. Jensen, and William L. Rivers, *The Mass
Media and Modern Society* (New York: Holt, Rinehart and Winston, 1965),
pp. 19, 119.

same warning stated earlier in his dissertation. Jensen wrote: "Therefore, as man depends more and more on the media for knowledge and guidance, he becomes more and more vulnerable to manipulation and exploitation by the dominant orders of society." Logically, then, "[o]bjective theory . . . regards the media generally as comprising an institutional order whose policy and behavior are determined by the dominant orders of society."[12]

One of the objective functions of the press, according to Jensen's 1969 report to the National Commission on the Causes and Prevention of Violence, involves its "traditional right of free expression" having been "converted from a natural right into a property right, one that can be exercised only by those affluent enough to own or have access to the media but denied all others." The contours of this "right" means that "freedom of the press [is] a moral right, not . . . a natural right." Here the media have an obligation to inform, and the citizen has an "obligation to become informed." At the end of this report, Jensen sounded some of his old disappointment at the change from classical liberalism to Neo-Liberalism, but the tone was not so dark as in *Liberalism, Democracy and the Mass Media:* "From a faith that the marketplace of ideas would best be served by a free play of individual rights against a natural harmony of interests, the tradition has moved to a joining of freedom with responsibility, of rights with obligations, enforceable not by law but by moral persuasion and social pressure."[13]

In the spring 1960 issue of *Journalism Quarterly*, Jensen discussed, as part of a forum on the teaching of journalism in colleges and universities, the implications of his philosophy for journalism education. He listed three mandates for the would-be critic of mass communication. Criticism must be conducted "(1) in an objective manner; (2) with due regard for the influence of political, social and cultural forces in their historical development; and (3) with due regard for the contextual relationships of the media with their environment— with the demands, the values, the aspirations and life interests of the society in which they exist." What is evident is Jensen's concern that media criticism, as a form of journalism education, go forward in a non-prescriptive and detached manner. He agreed with C. Wright Mills that "primary experience" was quickly being replaced by "secondary experience." Given this fact, the mandate for media critics is to approach the media not so much in terms of what they intend to do but in terms of what they actually do. Jensen posed here, again, his "objective theory" of the press and aimed an oblique dart at Marxist critics as well as other ideologues:

---

[12]Ibid., pp. 118-122.

[13]Jay W. Jensen and Theodore Peterson, *Historical Development of the Media in American Life, a Report for the National Commission on the Causes and Prevention of Violence* (1969), Vol. IV, pp. 8-13.

It should be clear enough by now, I think, that—from the stand-point of an institutional perspective and the philosophy of method previously expounded—there is a great disparity be-tween the kind of criticism I've been espousing and the ideologi-cal kind one finds in the bulk of contemporary literature. And it seems to me that, while ideological criticism is always to some extent related to reality, it usually is to a considerable de-gree myopic in its description of reality. Further, while ideolog-ical criticism may, by means of its prescriptions, help to give direction and substance to man's existence, he can never really understand the nature and significance of the media until he lifts the veil of ideology and looks upon the realities behind it.[14]

In many respects Jensen is the most significant philosopher of mass media in our time. He is one of the relatively few who have taken into account the fact that the way the press functions in any period is connected to the social, religious, economic, and scientific ideas of that period. In other words, the *Weltanschau-ung* of a period will normally command its press system in both ethos and eidos. This is a distinctly non-materialistic position. That is, it assumes ideas, not matter, as being primary and power-ful in the creation of cultural realities. As such, it obviates eco-nomic determinism in favor of an ideational optimism.

To parody what has been said of William Shakespeare, it may be said of Jensen that he has seen media and seen them whole. That is, his philosophical view of media has not been one of dis-parateness and fragmentation. His command of press history alone is powerful enough to warrant him a place as a serious his-torian of press ideas. But his gifts to the field do not stop there. He has seen classical liberalism go down before the onslaught of 20th-century capitalism and, instead of mouthing the shibbo-leths of social responsibility, has questioned the very premises of it with regard to the new definitions of mass Selfhood. He there-fore belongs to an endangered species of press philosopher: those who, old enough to remember the contours of individual cultural beauty, freedom, and thought, refuse to relinquish them for what-ever reason.

In his search for a new metaphysics with which to structure a definition of individual freedom, Jensen has put his finger on the great emptiness not only of the modern press in particular but of 20th-century humankind. This metaphysical vacuum manifests itself as a problem of belief, a problem as old, surely, as the hu-man race. And, yet, it would seem that our century is really the first to be absent a cogent metaphysics. Such as it is, the one we have is one of relativism, evolution, and the contextual—eventu-ating into a characteristic social anomie whose sole faith appears to be in a vague scientism and an even vaguer definition of

---

[14]Jay Jensen, "A Method and a Perspective for Criticism of the Mass Media," *Journalism Quarterly* 37 (1960): 261-266.

progress. The influence of the mass media in this is paradoxical. In a time when there appears to be a metaphysical vacuum, there are more images and information than we ever have had before. Indeed, there seems to be an inverse relationship operative here: As metaphysics and social belief decline, the supply of information increases—but information for what purpose?

Jensen's faith in what he views as the possibility for creating a new metaphysics on a rational basis—by way of Whitehead's idealist philosophy—reveals both his rationalist turn of mind as well as his stance as a classical liberal. He is canny enough to know, however, that philosophy alone is not enough: thus his call for "a twentieth-century Aquinas." This is to say that a *Weltanschauung* is not quite something that can be manufactured. It rests on structures of feeling and frames of social belief that may themselves admit of little intellection and may be, instead, quite irrational. Certainly this has been the character of most religious faith, despite the efforts of scholasticism to "prove" deity. And if, as Jensen argues, the headwaters of classical liberalism spring from the remote mystical quarters of Christendom, as well as from early Greek thought, it should not seem curious to say that perhaps the single greatest problem facing the press today is one of belief—and not just religious belief (although this is indeed a problem, given the animosity of the press toward religion) but "social belief" as well. Can one exist without the other?

Jensen can be criticized for not dealing at all with the economic factors swirling around and through the American press system. Indeed, if there is one shortcoming that characterizes too many press philosophers today, it is that they have looked unshaken on the storm of economic exploitation of and by the media. In particular, they have accepted the rise of media technology as some kind of normative process, if not progress. Only quite recently has there been any sociology of media technology. Even the Marxists may be indicted here, for, although they see clearly the element of economic exploitation present in the ownership patterns of technology, they have largely failed to criticize any social dominance in the engineering of technology itself. Surely this has led to an impasse in any philosophical critique of the press, for, if the means of press production (the inventions) are themselves sacrosanct from any suggestion of implicit dominance, then the history of technology can be excused or banished to oblivion as being pointless.

Jensen's primary shortcoming as a media philosopher, however, is more mundane than this: He did not write enough. His dissertation did not foreshadow this fault; for it was, indeed, both lengthy and provocative, a quite unusual combination in dissertation writing. Although his great promise as a scholar and philosopher certainly did not go entirely unfulfilled, it may nonetheless have been attenuated by his 20-year tenure as chair of journalism at Illinois. The key to the clear virtue of his work lies in his having been educated in the history of ideas at an excellent university. His grasp of press history and philosophy was no doubt the greater for his having grappled, early on, with the imposing ideas out of which our modern press system emerged and in which it still largely lives.

John Merrill
and Existential Journalism

John Merrill (1924-) is one of the few trained philosophers working in academic journalism. His books *The Imperative of Freedom, Existential Journalism*, and *Philosophy of Journalism* have had a strong impact on the field; and he has emerged as one of the most prominent philosophers in mass communication, itself a relatively new area of philosophical thought and inquiry.

John Calhoun Merrill was born January 9, 1924, in Yazoo, Mississippi, to J.C. and Irene Merrill. He was educated at Delta State University, where he took a BA in 1949, having married Dorothy Jefferson, a college assistant dean, the year before. In 1949 he began studies at Louisiana State University, taking the MA in journalism there in 1950. He earned the PhD in mass communication in 1961 at the University of Iowa and the MA in philosophy at the University of Missouri in 1976.

Merrill has extensive experience both as a professional journalist and university professor. He worked for a number of newspapers in Mississippi before becoming an assistant professor of journalism at Northwestern State College of Louisiana in 1951, teaching there until 1962, when he went to Texas A & M as an associate professor. He taught at A & M for 2 years, before moving to the University of Missouri, where he stayed till 1979. Since then he has been a professor of journalism at Louisiana State University in Baton Rouge. He has also been a special correspondent for the *Corriere della Sera* (1963-1968) and the *Neue Zuercher Zeitung* (1965-1970). In addition, he has worked for the U.S. Information Agency as a lecturer abroad and as a consultant to the Central News Agency in Taiwan.

In 1960 Merrill, along with S. Jack Odell of the University of Missouri Department of Philosophy, published *Philosophy and Journalism*, a book which contained many of the seeds of Merrill's mature ideas on the subject. According to its authors' introduction, this was the first book that "attempted to deal systemically with journalistic philosophy." Divided into two "Parts," the book dealt first with basic concepts of philosophy, such as deductive and inductive reasoning, conceptual analysis, ethics, and the

159

theory of knowledge, "illustrating these in journalistic contexts." Merrill's part of the book dealt with an in-depth application of these categories to journalism and an explication of the myriad connections between journalism and philosophy.[1]

Merrill and Odell argued that "Philosophy should, in our view, be the foundation of modern journalism."[2] The journalist was, they said, faced with various problems, questions, and issues:

> These are extremely complex and most of them cannot be resolved by recourse to common sense, personal biases, or even to insights and information gleaned from such fields as economics, political science, sociology, and psychology. It is not certain, of course, that even philosophy can give all the answers desired, but sooner or later the questioning and concerned journalist must put his mind to philosophizing.[3]

It seemed to the authors of *Philosophy and Journalism* that "a kind of Machiavellianism" was dominating the philosophical thought of journalists, a "kind of hardheaded pragmatism," which often resulted in questionable ethics on the part of both novice and seasoned journalist:

> Youthful optimism and idealism in journalism turn sour with the passing years, and a tough journalistic realism—often a camouflage for cynicism—takes root and often turns a person with a healthy ideology into an ideologue. The journalistic ideologue is quite common today in journalism even in the ranks of the self-styled liberals and progressives who claim to have open minds.[4]

Merrill, using Odell's basics and relating these to journalism, applied them to the areas of journalism education, journalistic codes, social responsibility, and objectivity. In Chapter 5, titled "Axiology: Journalism and Values," he mentioned the "existential concept of authenticity related to value," later writing that "the Journalist who values his authenticity and his integrity has one dedication: to selfhood."[5]

Such individualism was to become a prime motif in Merrill's most mature philosophical statement, *Existential Journalism*. Here he explicated, 17 years after *Philosophy and Journalism*, the basic ideas of existentialism and applied them to the journalistic practice of the mid-1970s. He described existential journal-

---

[1] See John C. Merrill and S. Jack Odell, *Philosophy and Journalism* (New York and London: Longman, 1960), pp. ix-xii.

[2] Ibid., p. ix.

[3] Ibid., p. x.

[4] Ibid.

[5] Ibid., pp. 108, 125.

ism as "a frame of mind—an attitude—which is thrust by individual journalists into their journalism, imbuing it with a vitality, a depth, a commitment, a character of flux, a creativity and originality which is almost universally lacking in modern 'corporate' journalism."[6] It was, indeed, this "corporate" journalism which sought to "purge journalists of the personal, of the ego," and it was against the corporate mind, as applied to journalism, which the existential journalist strove and struck out. "We have enough emphasis on the freedom and responsibility of the journalistic *system* and on the *mass media* themselves," Merrill wrote. "What we need is more emphasis on the individual journalist and on *his* freedom and *his* responsibility."[7]

The existential journalist rebelled against the corporate mind, Merrill said:

> He has an attitude of commitment, of rebellion, of individuality, of creativity, of freedom. He commits himself to himself and his own standards, not to the often asinine rules and practices of the organization. He pushes, straining constantly against the encompassing institutional restrictions which are closing in on him. He cares little about strict professionalism or institutionalism; more important to him is a sense of self-esteem and self-reliance. He takes stands; he chooses; and he is willing to take the consequences of these choices. This is often quite painful.
>
> He suffers; he often stands alone; at times he is penalized—he is not promoted, he does not get the raise, he is put off over in some "corner" of the operation where he is "safe" and at times he loses his job. But he truly exists; he lives. He is no simple thing fitting snugly into the "system," functioning in cooperation with all the others for the production of some standard, unstimulating product. Or—if he does—he does it fighting all the way. The existential journalist's lot is a difficult one in today's journalism, to be sure. Only occasionally will he be appreciated and rewarded by those in authority. But, of course, he always has his reward—the reward of existence, of truly living, itself. He wills, he chooses, he acts, he commits himself, he progresses: in effect, he makes himself daily. He is the existential journalist.[8]

Juxtaposed to this kind of journalist is the "corporate" one. His qualities and actions are quite different from those of the existential journalist: "His number is legion. He conforms. He makes the usual marks; he interviews with the 'normal' questions; he writes the regular '5-W' lead, and works his story into the

---

[6]John Merrill, *Existential Journalism* (New York: Hastings House, 1977), p. 16.

[7]Ibid., p. 17.

[8]Ibid., p. 19.

standard 'inverted pyramid' form. He submits his work to an editor who 'corrects' it—modifying it in many ways, from subtle distortion to denuding it of its basic and original significance and meaning (if it had any)." The corporate writer does all this without protesting. He continues to write his predictable pieces with "machinelike efficiency." He is, along with his editors, living in an "inauthentic" world, one which denies his humanity and "enthrones routine and efficiency."[9]

The upshot of Merrill's ideas, of course, posits a staunch individualism. In 1974, 3 years before *Existential Journalism* and 14 years after *Philosophy and Journalism*, Merrill wrote *The Imperative of Freedom, A Philosophy of Journalistic Autonomy.* Here one finds much the same founding idea to be stated later in *Existential Journalism*: The journalist must strip off the influence of the corporation and return to the principles of the journalism of an earlier day, to basic principles of individualism and press libertarianism. "[T]his will not be considered 'progressive,'" Merrill wrote,"—and progressivism has 'liberal' overtones. Actually, one could just as logically argue that it is really 'progress' to recapture as much of the pure essence of libertarianism as possible." The sort of progress being argued here is individual, not collective. "Society is for the person," Merrill wrote, "not the person for the society. Man is valuable, important, sacred if you like, *qua* man, and he should salvage as much of the essence of personhood from the encroaching embrace of modern society as he can."[10]

In *Existential Journalism* Merrill developed dichotomous categories for the individualistic existential journalist and the coporate hack. One of these is the "involved"/"aloof" category. The existential journalist does not stand apart from his materials or from the people from whom he gets stories: "He does not believe in neutrality. . . . [H]e thinks it desirable that he bring his own ideological beliefs, preferences and biases to bear on his journalism. He is the person many refer to as the 'activist' journalist. . . ." By contrast, the "aloof" journalist believes in objectivity and that the reader should not be encumbered with the reporter's biases, feelings, prejudices, and opinions.

Another such category is what Merrill calls the "Dionysian"/"Apollonian" one. Here the dichotomy is between Dionysus—the god of emotion, intuition, and irrationality—and Apollo, the god of beauty, reason, order, wisdom, and light. The existential journalist follows Dionysus; the corporate journalist, Apollo. The same essential dichotomy is present in what Merrill calls the "poetic"/"prosaic" stances. Here the accent is on style. The existential journalist is "poetic," possessed of "a kind of 'open' or flexible style"; the "prosaic" journalist, on the other hand, "a kind of 'closed' or mechanistic style." Finally, two other cate-

---

[9]Ibid., p. 21.

[10]John Merrill, *The Imperative of Freedom* (New York: Hastings House, 1974), pp. 15, 16.

gories are "personalist"/"factualist" and "existential"/"rational."
These juxtapose the essential contraries found in the other pairs:
an emphasis on personal involvement versus distance and objectivity, and an emphasis on emotions as opposed to pure intellection.[11]

Although compelling, Merrill's ideas are inhabited by a number of problems. The basic one is that Merrill posits for journalism a futuristic philosophy based on quite traditional libertarian
principles. In recapturing "as much of the pure essence of libertarianism as possible," there is an implicit return, a backward
glance, to an earlier, pristine time when the press was relatively
unfettered. One thinks here of the 19th century and of such editors as Benjamin Day, James Gordon Bennett, Horace Greeley,
and, to a lesser degree, Henry Raymond. Such men were indeed
free, as editors, to do with their papers as they liked. One wonders,
however, how free were the men and women who worked for
them.

Whereas this laissez-faire, libertarian spirit of journalism is
to be restored, it is to be based, according to Merrill, not on deistic, romantic, or utilitarian principles but on a broad and futuris-
tically oriented solipsism in which the inner voice of the journalist is to be his or her guide.[12] Although this is essentially a late
romantic idea, as well as one that came, under the name of
"oversoul," to structure much of New England Transcendentalist
thought, it is not referred to as such by Merrill. A number of the
existential philosophers on whom Merrill relies, including
Sartre and Camus, do not accept anything but a quite materialistic version of this inner voice, whereas several of the deistic, romantic, and utilitarian philosophers thought of it in essentialist
terms. There is then, at the heart of Merrill's philosophy, an implicit conflict between the forward glance and the backward
glance, between what he proclaims as existential and what he
largely defines as essentialism.

This central problem leads to some related ones. First, there
is no definition of society in Merrill's philosophy. The well
known position of Adam Smith, as a utilitarian philosopher, was
that there was an "invisible hand" (the economic version of Puritan providence or, later, the transcendentalists' oversoul) at work
in the affairs of men so that what was produced by one benefited
all others. There is no such system of mutual benefit among Merrill's existential journalists. And unless Merrill's philosophy is
to be taken as being entirely descriptive and not *pre*scriptive, this
poses a social anomie that journalists are helpless to relieve precisely because they are the producers of it. What then of the social
responsibility of the journalists? "Their only responsibility to
themselves and to society," says Merrill, "is the responsibilty of

---

[11]*Existential Journalism*, pp. 37-42.
[12]"[A]uthenticity for the existential journalist comes from within." Ibid.,
p. 137.

breaking ranks and remaining free."[13]

Second, Merrill calls on the reporter to revolt from the chains of corporate journalism. He does not call for a change in the corporate structure itself. Indeed, Merrill seems obliquely concerned for the welfare of this system:

> But, I can hear myriads of cautious organization-persons crying: Is there not a danger that existential journalists would pose problems for the viability and stability of the newspapers and other media? Wouldn't existential journalists go too far with this individualistic, creative urge? Wouldn't they go overboard and hurt the collective, corporate effort we're making?
>
> My answer: Some of them well might. And, in many cases, it would be good if they did. We need a lot of fresh air blowing into most journalistic media. But, actually there is nothing for the media managers and the conformist journalists to fear, for there is no serious danger from these existential journalists. They will simply not be numerous enough to pose any real danger to the ever-growing corporate structure of journalism.[14]

If corporate structure is a central problem for modern-day journalism and if existential journalists are going to be too scarce to unman it, then why call them to the battle? It would seem that there is beneath the surface of Merrill's existentialist stance a strain of conservatism, which says to the establishment, "Look boys, this may sound like pretty wild stuff, but it really isn't so dangerous after all."

Furthermore, it is easy to *say*, as Merrill does, that the existential journalist ". . . suffers . . . stands alone . . . is penalized . . . is not promoted . . . does not get the raise . . . is put off over in some 'corner' of the operation where he is 'safe' and at times . . . loses his job. But he truly exists; he lives." But maybe he or she doesn't live; maybe he or she dies of physical or spiritual-intellectual starvation. One exaggerates here to make a point: Merrill's existentialism focuses almost entirely on what is wrong with the individual, not on what is wrong with the system; and, given that "there is nothing for the media managers and the conformist journalists to fear" from "these existentialist journalists," the system will supposedly remain unaffected by those most qualified to redress it.

How then is the existential journalist to survive, and what good can he or she do? To parody St. Paul, shall one suffer that angst may abound? Is one's work to be relegated always to a characteristic negativism, and is protracted suffering to be one's characteristic—and pyhrric, *ironically* pyhrric—affirmation? Is this not at once too timid and too heroic? Why not change the system if it is (as, indeed, it is) so bad?

---

[13] *The Imperative of Freedom*, p. 4.
[14] *Existential Journalism*, pp. 66-67.

The third problem related to Merrill's mix of traditionalist and futurist philosophies is that there is no telos for the existential journalist. He or she has nowhere to go because (a) he/she has no specified beliefs about what society should be like and because (b) his/her approach is, therefore, almost entirely negative. What is the purpose then of one's journalistic practice? The answer is "... to live every minute of every day in such a way as to maximize his own freedom and autonomy. He can thus create small 'islands of decreasing entropy,' as Norbert Wiener has put it." Not everyone can be a journalist, and not every journalist can be an existential journalist (at least, as noted, Merrill assures us that this will not be the case). Therefore, we are to have a condition in which there is a great deal of freedom for a few and a great deal of apparent drudgery for others. Is this not a species of pessimism? Again, the question comes: Why not change the system?

The fourth problem with existential journalism is that, given the absence of a social theory and teleology, the existential journalist can have little, if any, ethos on which to found his or her actions. "Existentialism," admits Merrill, "is not very clear on the matter of ethics."[15] Indeed it is not. As a late species of romantic materialism, it is naturally tempered with a pragmatic axiology in which each act is absent any metaphysical principle of direction. What is a right act for one reporter, therefore, may be a wrong one for another. And we quickly land in a solipsistic bog where values are relative and where, given the powers of self-interest and self-pleasure, narcissism abounds. The meaning of ethics—the discipline dealing with what is good and bad and with moral duty and obligation—is thus put askew. The difficulty here is that, as Merrill notes, "Intrinsic in existentialism is the rebellion against firm rules and collectivized standards. The *person* is enthroned, not the group." This "personhood" is the touchpoint of existential "authenticity." Authenticity occurs when the individual follows his or her own lights and not those of the group. "Only when the person stops listening to the voice of 'they' can he truly hear the call of conscience, and become truly authentic."[16]

This is more than a little hopeful. In the first place, not every journalist appears to be possessed of a conscience. What, for example, of the German journalists who acquiesced to Hitler's takeover of the German press and his subsequent slaughter of millions of Jews? Where was the existential conscience then? Surely there were a few Germans who objected, among them Thomas Mann and Karl Barth. But no one much remembers any *journalist* who did so. Mann was a novelist, and Barth a theologian. In the second place, even if we could be assured that our existential journalist possessed a conscience, how would we know he would use it for our benefit? "As ethics comes into play in existentialism at all," writes Merrill, "it is an individualistic ethics, a

---

[15]Ibid., p. 132.
[16]Ibid., pp. 132, 37.

very personal thing."[17] Given the deploring of social codes and group values by the existential journalist, it is quite possible that his actions as a journalist might not be at all socially acceptable but, instead, socially deplorable. Merrill would seem to suggest that there is a degree of interconnectedness among existential journalists who rebel against the system and that this might give them a unity of thought and value. Given the materialistic foundations of much of existential thought, this is not likely to be any sort of spiritual interconnectedness but instead, perhaps, a psychic one involving common and deep psychological structures. We should say at this point that Merrill nowhere states this, but it seems implicit in much that he does say. It too seems unduly hopeful and, at best, speculative. It is also quite mystical. If codes are indeed "straitjackets," as Merrill insists at one point (and he is right), the assumption of the availability of psychic "deep structures" for the existential journalist as a safeguard in the absence of codification seems something of a nimbus cloud.

Despite these problems in Merrill's philosophy, he remains one of the most thoughtful and intelligent minds on the subject of the philosophy of mass communication in society. His insistence on authenticity and genuine individuality, despite the absence in his thought of some way of ensuring the nurturing of these, rings true. Although the weight of his ideology seems mostly romantic, his indictment of the corporate journalist is accurate and to the point. The problem of corporate structure itself must, of course, eventually be addressed and solved before there can be much press freedom. Merrill is probably right when he assures the corporate managers of news that they have nothing to worry about because the number of existential journalists will always be small. The great news automatons seem not to be in much danger.

There will always be a place for rebels in any system, no matter how fair or unjust that system may be. Witness Lucifer's war with heaven. A problem that is more pressing than encouraging rebels, however, would seem to be the problem of how to word the thoughts and feelings of those too timid or afraid, because of the structure of the news system, to speak out. They were created equal with the rest of us. They exist too.

---

[17]Ibid., p. 132.

James Carey
and the Cultural Approach

The name of James W. Carey (1934-) has been at the forefront during the last decade or so of mass communication theory, history, and research. His wide-ranging mind has touched not only on these areas but also on those of ethics, advertising, international communication, popular culture, political journalism, press economics, press criticism, and literary journalism. His "cultural approach" to communication has, indeed, been applied to most, if not all, of these areas and has become something of a byword not only among his students and fellow scholars who look to him for intellectual guidance but also among those who, although perhaps disagreeing with him vehemently, have found many of his ideas stimulating and useful in their own research. Along with John Merrill, Carey is easily the most provocative philosophical mind in the field.

James William Carey was born in Providence, Rhode Island, on September 7, 1934, to Cyril Joseph and Rita Miriam (Lyons) Carey. He was educated at the University of Rhode Island, graduating in 1957, finished a master's degree at the University of Illinois in 1959, and remained at Illinois for the PhD in mass communication, finished in 1963. Immediately following his graduation, he was named to the faculty at the University of Illinois, where he taught until 1967, when he was named director of the Institute of Communications Research, a post he held until 1976. From 1976 until 1979, he was the George Gallup Distinguished Scholar at the University of Iowa School of Journalism. Since 1979, he has been Dean of the College of Communications at the University of Illinois.

In addition, Carey has taught at Pennsylvania State University and University College, Dublin; has held a National Endowment for the Humanities Fellowship in Science, Technology, and Human Values; was an Associate Member of the Center for Advanced Study in 1975; was the president of the Association for Education in Journalism and Mass Communication during 1977-1978; served on the national accrediting council in journalism and mass communication for 5 years; was distinguished scholar in residence at the Gannett Center for Media Studies in New York; has published more than 60 essays, monographs, and reviews on popular culture, the history of the mass media, and communication theory; is editor of the international journal *Communication*; and is on the editorial board of eight other journals. An impressive speaker on a number of topics, he has lectured at more than 25 universities in the United States and Europe.

Most of Carey's philosophy has been, according to him, shaped by two men, the Canadian economist and historian Harold Adams Innis and John Dewey.[1] Drawing on Innis' *The Bias of Communication* and *Empire and Communications*,[2] Carey poses two of Innis' fundamental questions as questions for the philosopher in mass communication: (a) "What are the underlying causes of change in social organization, defined broadly to include both culture and social institutions?" and (b) "What are the conditions which promote stability in any society?"[3] These two questions become the fabric of a general unweaving of Innis' ideas, as Carey adumbrates their implications for communications. Innis' central idea, that there is a "bias of communication" posited by way of whether media are "space-binding" or "time-binding," is taken by Carey as implying in the case of the former, "the growth of empire . . . a concern with expansion and with the present and . . . the hegemony of secular political authority." In the case of the latter, Innis' idea implies the "concern with history and tradition . . . [and] little capacity for expansion of secular authority. . . ." which "[favors] the growth of religion, of hierarchical organization, and of contractionist institutions."[4] Oral/aural cultures are time-binding, emphasizing the past, with its array of ritual and tradition; visual/print cultures are space-binding and tend to emphasize the present and the future and to be destructive of tradition. An appropriately balanced society exists when the time-binding social unit exists in equilibrium with the space-binding one: a conjunction between, say, religion and the state where both are equally empowered but in different ways; or, similarly, between the moral and the technical elements in a society. Classical Greece was, according to Innis, such a moment in history.[5]

The bias of communication in the West, according to Carey's reading of Innis, has been the bias of print. Print not only drove

---

[1]Much of my summation of Carey's philosophy is taken from two key essays: "Harold Adams Innis and Marshall McLuhan," published in the *Antioch Review* 27:1 (1967); and "A Cultural Approach to Communication," published in *Communication* 2:1 (1975).

[2]Harold Adams Innis, *The Bias of Communication* (Toronto: University of Toronto Press, 1971); *Empire and Communications* (Oxford: Clarendon Press, 1950).

[3]Ibid., *Antioch Review*, p. 6.

[4]Ibid., p. 9.

[5]Ibid., p. 13.

out the Western oral tradition but forced its major exponents—morals, values, metaphysics—to become fugitive. In Innis' eyes, this has led Western civilization "to the brink of nihilism" and has resulted in the transformation of religious and linguistic concerns from "the theological and sacred to the political and secular." Carey takes these broad principles and applies them as a critique to the theories of Marshall McLuhan, arguing, with Innis, that the effects of media have less to do with the senses than with social organization: "My argument is simply that the most visible effects of communications technology are on social organization and not on sensory organization."[6]

Carey's epistemological method, therefore, becomes broadly cultural/historical, dwelling on those moments when the time-binding characteristics of culture have given, or are giving, way to space-binding ones. His 1975 article "A Cultural Approach to Communication" contains not only a brief paean to John Dewey as an important influence on his thought but also puts to philosophic labor the insights gleaned from Innis. Carey here employs Dewey's statement that "Society exists not only *by* transmission, *by* communication, but it may fairly be said to exist *in* transmission, *in* communication" to argue the presence of two alternative conceptions of communication in American culture since the 19th century: a *transmission* view and, suggesting Innis, a *ritual* view. The former sees communication in linear terms and develops models to explain it as such, dwelling on questions of effects. The latter exists in terms of ceremony, and its function is the "maintenance of society in time."[7] The ritual view, says Carey,

> . . . will focus on a different range of problems in examining a newspaper. It will, for example, view reading a newspaper less as sending or gaining information and more like attending a mass: a situation in which nothing new is learned but in which a particular view of the world is portrayed and confirmed. . . . The model here is not that of information acquisition, though such acquisition occurs, but of dramatic action in which the reader joins a world of contending forces as an observer at a play. We do not encounter questions about the effect or functions of messages as such but the role of presentation and involvement in the structuring of the reader's life and time. . . .[8]

The cultural approach to communication consists, then, at the simplest level, in viewing media less in terms of their *effects* on the cultures than in terms of their structural and creative dimensions. News becomes less informational than dramatic; the newspaper becomes less a bundle of potential effects than a literary text for explication. The transmission view of communica-

---

[6]Ibid, p. 26.
[7]"A Cultural Approach to Communication," p. 6.
[8]Ibid., p. 8.

tion has, according to Carey, "dominated American thought since the 1920s":

> When I first came into this field I felt that this view of communication, expressed in behavioral and functional terms, was exhausted. It had become academic: a repetition of past achievement, a demonstration of the indubitable. While it led to solid achievement, it could no longer go forward without disastrous intellectual and social consequences. I felt it was necessary to reopen the analysis, to invigorate it with the tension found in Dewey's work and, above all, to go elsewhere into biology, theology, anthropology, and literature for some intellectual material with which we might escape the treadmill we were running.[9]

In all of this, it is the language itself that is the primary epistemological unit:

> I want to suggest, to play on the Gospel of St. John, that in the beginning was the word; that words are not the names for things but that, to steal a line from Kenneth Burke, things are the signs of words. Reality is not given, not humanly existent, independent of language and towards which language stands as a pale refraction. Rather, reality is brought into existence, is produced, by communication, that is, by the construction, apprehension, and utilization of symbolic forms. Reality, while not a mere function of symbolic forms, is produced by terministic systems—or by humans who produce such systems—that focus its existence in specific terms.[10]

Given this primally creative and vatic power of language, "Our models of communication . . . create what we disingenuously pretend they merely describe. As a result our science is, to use a term of Alvin Gouldner's, a reflexive one. We not only describe behavior; we create a particular corner of culture: culture that determines, in part, the kind of communicative world we inhabit."[11] Because of the transmission view of communication—a view which has spread, according to Carey, to our political and communal systems—our models of communication are "deranged"; and we are forced by them to view social organization in terms of "power, administration, decision, and control," a political order, or as "relations of property, production, and trade," an economic order. Carey counterposes against this what he calls "a ritual order," or the "sharing of aesthetic experience, religious ideas, personal values and sentiments, and intellectual notions." "The object, then," writes Carey, "of recasting our studies of communi-

---

[9]Ibid., p. 10.
[10]Ibid., p. 19.
[11]Ibid.

cation in terms of a ritual model is not only to more firmly grasp the essence of this 'wonderful' process, but to give us a way in which to rebuild a model of and for communication of some restorative value in reshaping our common culture."[12]

Having been accused of not specifying his "cultural approach" but, instead, of leaving it in the land of generalization, Carey published a short essay in the *Journal of Communication* in the summer of 1983 titled "The Origins of the Radical Discourse on Cultural Studies in the United States." Although brief, the essay contains a long closing statement, which is perhaps the clearest word to date on just what the "cultural approach" to communication means. It goes as follows:

Cultural studies attempts to think about the mass media not in relation to this or that isolated problem (violence, pornography, children) or institution (politics, economy, family) or practice (film production, conversation, advertising), but as elements, in Raymond Williams' phrase, "in a whole way of life." Societies, in this view, are complex, differentiated, contradictory, interacting wholes. They are threaded throughout, held in this complex unity, by culture: by the production and re-production of systems of symbols and messages.

The mass media are but one important site of study. They, in turn, must be considered in their relationship to everything else. As that is a tall order, the more modest task is to formulate a vocabulary through which it is possible *in principle* to think of the mass media in relation to everything else: to develop a vocabulary that does not artificially constrain one from thinking of the mass media in their widest possible context. Early on, a model of how this could be done within a limited domain was provided by Thomas Kuhn's *The Structure of Scientific Revolutions*, which was a cultural study of science within a pragmatic philosophy of science. With that book, the artificial walls placed around theory and method by positive science came tumbling down.

Despite Kuhn's example, there has been a frequent and telling criticism that cultural studies in the United States, undercut as it is by the cheery optimism of pragmatism, inescapably fails to consider power, dominance, subordination, and ideology as central issues. Power and its verbal coordinates were central issues with C. Wright Mills and Harold Innis, among others. The ferment surrounding American cultural studies concerns its ability to retain enough of the origins, insights, and tone of pragmatism while it squarely faces the fact that societies are structured not only in and by communications but also by relations of power and dominance.[13]

---

[12]Ibid., pp. 20-21.
[13]*Journal of Communication* 33 (Summer 1983): 313.

Carey's thought, then, may be summarized as follows:

1. Because of the development of a print/visual society with the advent of movable type in the 15th century, our civilization has become increasingly a space-binding one. That is, having conquered distance, we have come to exist in a world whose borders are increasingly continuous. Having conquered distance, however, we have simultaneously shattered time and have consequently lost sight of the culture-bearing traditions and rituals that sustained us in an earlier era. Much of this is owing to the uncontrolled development of technology, which imposes upon us its own set of dominance-laden industrial rituals containing little or none of the aesthetic or meaning of traditional ones.

2. Because of the nature of the power structure in technology and its preoccupation with the present and future (it was Henry Ford who said "History is bunk"), the dominant view of communication naturally developed along similar lines, prompting a "transmission" view of communication little different from the subject-object transactional model of science, technology, and business. The "transmission" view of communication accounts for our preoccupation with studies of the "effects" of mass communication. It is outmoded and suggestive of the "dead hand of the past."

3. What we need to recapture includes the rituals of our culture, those symbols of communication that give our lives depth and meaning. In this less objectified version of social interaction, we will, at the same time, recapture as a people our traditions and the temporal sense out of which they have fallen.

The effect all of this might have on society would be to restore what Carey views as the lost public. We now have audiences, he claims; with a ritual view of communication, we might once again have true publics, in which real debate, social participation in politics, and social intellection might once again occur. What this means for journalism education, says Carey, is a restoration of the university tradition and an uprooting of the undue influence of professionalism on the academy. It would also mean, he claims, the resultant development in the academy of more of a concentration on journalism as an intellectual and ethical sphere of activity. At the graduate level, Carey calls for an abandonment of the "school of thought" approach, which organizes itself in terms of narrow questions and appropriate methods for answering them. As a result of this, he writes, "we have cultivated in our students an occupational psychosis: a narrowed and inflexible vision that comes from being philosophically unaware of the root problems of the field and an inability to engage in genuine argument across intellectual divides." What must be done is to abandon the old questions and, instead, "open the field to the most far ranging and acute philosophical reflection possible."[14]

Although these are the bare bones of Carey's argument, they are representative of the core of his thought. As he freely admits, there is great influence here from the Chicago School of pragmatic philosophy, especially from Dewey and Robert Park, as well as a commanding influence from Innis and, to a lesser degree, the English Marxian literary historian Raymond Williams. Despite these claimed and obvious influences, however, there is a good deal in Carey's thought that is original. The very application to mass communication of these ideas, in a specific and rhetorically convincing way, is original. Dewey, in his *The Public and Its Problems*, and Park, in his essay "News as a Form of Knowledge," did little more than touch on what Carey has developed in a number of essays and in a number of contexts of communication. Indeed, Carey's finest achievement rests in his synthesis of pragmatic ideas about communication with the ideas of Innis and, more recently, Williams. Here one sees held together such formidably disparate patterns of thought as American pragmatism, British neo-Marxism, and a withering Canadian critique of American technology. If, however, the power of Carey's philosophy derives from its having come from, almost, the four winds, the fourth wind is still missing. This would be, perhaps, a philosophy that would discountenance technology rather than complain about it and advise us to adapt to it.

Carey does not go far enough in this direction, however. In a 1984 essay in *Illinois Issues* titled "High Tech and Higher Ed," he wrote, "Again, this is not, by indirection or innuendo, an argument against high technology. We probably need a good deal more of it than we are getting."[15] It is, however, precisely technology and its modern rarified upshot, "high tech," which have produced the space-binding system of communication that both Innis and Carey complain of. With passive Marxists like Williams, who in his book *The Long Revolution* views the industrial revolution and technology as the naturally evolved products of a materialistic dialectic, Carey sees technology as inevitable, but apparently views its symbiosis with language as being purely fortunate. Although admitting the forward, futurist thrust of technology as a space-bound dimension of culture, Carey nonetheless would see restored to potency the "backward glance" of the ritual view of communication: rite, religion, metaphysics, and a renewed respect for tradition.

One cannot have it both ways. Marxists escape this cosmological contradiction by insisting that technology will cease to be a cultural problem once the patterns of ownership are divided

---

[14]"A Plea for the University Tradition," *Journalism Quarterly* 55 (1978): 851, 853, 855; the AEJMC Presidential Address. "Graduate Education in Mass Communication," *Communication Education* 28 (September 1979): 292.

[15]Vol. 10, March 1984, p. 23.

evenly and once the division of labor is accomplished in a more equitable way. Carey, though willing to employ the Marxist critique on numerous occasions, is not an economic determinist but, instead, looks back to American pragmatist philosophy and its optimistic emphasis on the power of symbolism and the human imagination as primary agents in social transformation. As noted by Carey himself, this view, the primary view of cultural studies, has come under "frequent and telling" criticism because it does not consider power, dominance, subordination, and ideology as central issues. These persist nonetheless, and it would seem that they are much more closely and deterministically tied to language than Carey might want to admit.

Linguistic dominance is, of course, a problem that philosophy has yet to solve. Although Marx took a brief shot at solving it, his definition of language as "disturbances of the layers of the air" is, one wants to say, also a definition of noise. If culture can exist only in the language and if the language not only refracts but creates culture, as Carey would argue, then dominance becomes a matter of language. Carey's implicit mandate that language, not the economy, be used to expunge dominance is therefore stilled by a logical contradiction. Like the pragmatist philosophers, Carey seems overly optimistic about the transforming power of language and hardly pessimistic enough about the economic dimensions of technology and how these have shaped both culture and language.

One can also criticize Carey for arguing a mode of communication and an analytic point of view that are themselves pre-industrial in thrust and contour. His belief that we should revive a "ritual view" of communication is utopian; yet, as noted, he accepts technology and calls for more of it—while, ironically, criticizing Marshall McLuhan for advocating what amounts to a technological utopia. In Carey one certainly finds the utopian philosopher's vision, but it is a vision sustained neither by a return to nature nor by a collective reliance on the opiate of machinery, but instead by the steady vision of the power of language as a creative symbol. Who will do the creating then? Who will have the power? Those who can use the language most effectively? Those who use it most often? Those who own the great channels of communication already? These are questions that Carey suggests, but never directly addresses. Indeed, given Carey's relative silence on the matter of media ownership, he would seem almost to come off as being traditionally conservative on the issue. However, those who know him know that this is not the case.[16]

Carey is clearly calling for a new frame of social belief, a new "structure of feeling" (to use Raymond Williams' term) in which communication is to have the central role. What, then, is to be the mythos that will drive the kind of linguistic transformation of the

---

[16]The author of this essay studied under Carey at the University of Iowa.

world that he envisions?

While criticizing Carey, one should also note three false criticisms: (a) that he is not specific and clear in what he means by a "cultural aproach"; (b) that his work is not scientific and his scholarship cannot, therefore, be verified or reproduced; and (c) that he is not realistic. In the first case, Carey has made every effort to explain his ideas, and some of those who either condemn or disagree with him appear not to have read his work. In the second case, although he is not a systematic philosopher, his work is not intended to be scientific, but, instead, suasive. The third false criticism, that Carey is not realistic, is more to the point but still not telling. Insofar as he has been able to persuade communication scholars and students to his point of view, he has been realistic indeed, and effectively so! There are presently numerous scholars in the field employing Carey's "cultural approach" and doing significant work with it. Given his skirting of economic issues in the media, however, his method would seem to be less realistic than ideal.

Perhaps the central worth of Carey's philosophy is this: He has opened for discourse and development an immense frontier in the philosophy of mass communication. An American academic field that 20 years ago was closed and inbred with a condign scientism is now open to the insights available from anthropology, semiotics, biology, and literature, among other fields. Carey has been a major force in accomplishing this. Moreover, in his drive to reinstate ritual, drama, even religion, as resonant spheres of communicative experience, the way is now perhaps open for a discussion of (dare one say it?) a metaphysics of communication. Finally, Carey, in his drive for symbolism, has even managed to posit something of a communicative telos in the face of a rampant social functionalism—a feat that, given the place and power of funtionalism as a pragmatic American philosophical tenet, is commanding and significant.

4

The Legists

Charles Marler
Abilene Christian University

The Legists

First Amendment studies—because of man's inherent tendency to attempt to control bad news, criticism, and dissent—made the legists—scholars who developed special knowledge in the law—one of the most dynamic journalism educator categories in the 20th century. Perusal of journals, abstracts, and paper presentations reveals an ever increasing fascination for First Amendment studies because of the centrality and need for protection of freedoms of expression in each generation. The legists have produced the literature for a specialized historical study of freedom of expression; they and their students have found First Amendment study inherently interesting—a living history that is critical to the republican form of government of the nation. The role of the legists grew sucessively more crucial between 1925 and the present.

The U.S. Supreme Court in *Gitlow v. New York* (268 U.S. 652, 1925) ruled it could review state statutes that allegedly abridged the freedoms of the First Amendment because these freedoms were synonymous with the guarantees of the Fourteenth Amendment. The latter amendment was written to tether states' tendencies to abridge personal rights. After *Gitlow*, neither Congress nor a state could shorten the breadth of First Amendment freedoms; both the First and the Fourteenth Amendments protected freedom of the press. Until this intersection of legal values, press or journalism law—as it was known—focused primarily on civil tort actions, such as libel, and their common law roots. The Supreme Court in *Gitlow* left ajar the door to the development of two realities about freedom of expression—broader constitutional protection, but new and vexing constitutional issues—in a society that would grow increasingly complex and litigious.

The era of constitutional press law really dawned in 1931 when the Supreme Court used the *Gitlow* precedent to review a state gag law and accept the Blackstone definition of freedom of the press in *Near v. Minnesota* (183 U.S. 697). Prior restraints, the court said, are anathema with rare exceptions. Throughout the 1930s and into the 1940s the Supreme Court engaged in significant constitutional testing of city licensing ordinances, and state-based torts were remodeled by the Supreme Court in the

1950s and 1960s. The catalog of 20th century constitutional testing and boundary setting eventually would include all of the most important legal problems of the mass media: prior restraint, taxation, licensing, contempt, libel, privacy, pre-trial news coverage, pornography, access, reporter privilege, right of reply, commercial speech, broadcasting, obscenity, and copyright.

During the *Gitlow-Near* period, a small group of young, bright journalists and future media law scholars appeared at the nation's fledgling journalism departments and schools. One had been a lawyer since 1911; two would soon earn law degrees; one other would later become a lawyer; and the fifth would specialize in political science. They were Fredrick S. Siebert, Harold L. Cross, Frank B. Thayer, William F. Swindler, and J. Edward Gerald.

—Siebert in 1923 finished his AB in journalism at the University of Wisconsin. While he was a student at the University of Illinois Law School in 1928, he published an article about contempt of court in *Journalism Quarterly* and attracted the attention of Col. Robert R. McCormick of the Chicago *Tribune*. McCormick enlisted Siebert's help in the *Near v. Minnesota* appeal. The young discovery of McCormick earned the JD degree in 1929, joined the journalism faculty of Illinois, and became the polestar of the legists, the articulate spokesman for the history of libertarianism.

—Cross was graduated LLB from Cornell in 1911, and as a young New York lawyer in 1922 he became the counsel of the New York Herald *Tribune*. He began teaching law of journalism at the Columbia University Graduate School of Journalism in 1929 and became in the 1950s the father of right-to-know legislation.

—Thayer earned the M.A in journalism from Wisconsin in 1916, taught and practiced journalism at several places until 1935 when he finished the JD at Loyola, and joined the Wisconsin journalism faculty that year. He was the first of the legists to write a major treatise about press law in the United States, *Legal Control of the Press*.

—Swindler earned the MA in journalism from the University of Missouri in 1936 after bachelor's degrees at Washington University in St. Louis. He became an instructor at Missouri in 1938 and would finish a PhD there in 1942 with a dissertation about international press law. Swindler emerged as the bibliographer of press law and a historian of the Constitution and the U.S. Supreme Court.

—Gerald was graduated in 1927 with a BA in English at West Texas State College and then earned the BJ in journalism at the University of Missouri in 1928. He became a faculty member at Missouri in 1929 and finished his MA in 1932. The leading political-social theorist of the group with a PhD in political science, he published until the early 1980s.

These five legists would not yield any of their preeminence in mass communications law until in the late 1960s when the constitutional emphasis reached the flood stage. Although their foundational work stood above the flood line, other scholars appeared to research and write most of the new interpretations. The foremost of the heirs of the group in post-1960s mass communications law teaching and scholarship was the sixth legist who is profiled in this section:

—Harold L. Nelson was Gerald's first PhD student at Minnesota in 1956, specializing in journalism history and law. He also was a colleague of Thayer and Siebert. Nelson became the bridge from the early scholars to the legists in journalism education in the 1970s and 1980s.

The progenitors of these half-dozen scholars were few, and the history of journalism educators' involvement in mass communications law is relatively young, roughly parallel to the history of the 4-year journalism curriculum. The history of mass communications law education can be divided into four periods: the Traditional (1904-1930), the Transitional (1931-1943), the Developmental (1944-1968), and the Contemporary (1969-present).

Traditional Period (1904-1930): Although Swindler noted that identifiable journalistic law began to emerge in 1888 with Samuel Merrill's *Newspaper Law*,[1] journalism educators' involvement in writing literature for the field did not occur until the appearance of such elemental works as *The Law of the Press*[2] by William G. Hale and Ivan Benson in 1923, *Newspaper Law*[3] by William W. Loomis in 1924, and *The Law of Newspapers*[4] by William R. Arthur and Ralph L. Crosman in 1928. The Hale-Benson and Arthur-Crosman contributions overlapped the Transitional period because their second editions were published in 1933 and 1940. The primary Supreme Court case in the Traditional period was *Gitlow*, which eventually would alter press law's preoccupation with defamation and copyright and shift the pedagogy and research, adding constitutional emphases to the older tort and criminal concerns.

Transitional Period (1931-1943): The beginning of this period was marked by the *Near* decision. Siebert's involvement with Col. McCormick and the *Near* appeal demonstrated the activist role in the development of law that journalism legists could fulfill. Siebert also published in 1934 *The Rights and Privileges of the*

---

[1]William F. Swindler, *A Bibliography of Law on Journalism* (New York: Columbia University Press, 1947), p. 8.

[2]William G. Hale and Ivan Benson, *The Law of the Press* (St. Paul: West. Publishing, 1933).

[3]William W. Loomis, *Newspaper Law* (Salt Lake City, UT: Porte, 1924).

[4]William R. Arthur and Ralph L. Crosman, *The Law of Newspapers* (New York: MacGraw-Hill, 1928).

Press,[5] but its usefulness was still focused on tort law, primarily libel and copyright. The *Near* prior restraint decision; the Supreme Court's resolution of licensing, taxation, and contempt issues; and the regulatory bent of the New Deal in this period accelerated the need for more journalism law scholarship and classroom law in the journalism schools.

Developmental Period (1944-1968): The publication of Thayer's *Legal Control of the Press*[6] in 1944 opened this period. It represented the first comprehensive press law treatise in the United States and would go through four editions, the last in 1964. The Supreme Court, in between the first edition and the appearance of its replacement in 1969, produced successive constitutional landmarks in *Associated Press* (326 U.S. 1, 1944) for anti-trust law, *Roth* (354 U.S. 476, 1957) for obscenity, *Sullivan* (376 U.S. 254, 1964) for libel, *Estes* (381 U.S. 723, 1965) for cameras in courtrooms, *Sheppard* (384 U.S. 333, 1966) for pretrial coverage, *Hill* (385 U.S. 374, 1967) for privacy, and other cases. The legists again in this period helped to create law. Cross, in the activist mold of Siebert, worked for the American Newspaper Publishers Association and influenced the 1966 Freedom of Information Act passed by Congress. Research and publication highlights of the Developmental period were Thayer's treatise, Gerald's *The Press and the Constitution*[7] (1948), Swindler's *Bibliography of Law on Journalism*[8] (1947), Siebert's *Freedom of the Press in England 1476-1776*[9] (1951), Cross' *The People's Right to Know*[10] (1953), and Nelson's *Freedom of the Press from Hamilton to the Warren Court*[11] (1967). Broadcasting's maturation during the 1940s and 1950s introduced new legal problems involving all three branches of the federal government and—coupled with increased advertising regulation—grafted administrative law onto the challenge to the legists. Thayer's fourth edition textbook and Swindler's *Problems of Law in Journalism*[12] (1955) were out of date constitutionally by the end of the Developmental period. Mass communications law had arrived at a new age. New legists

---

[5]Fredrick S. Siebert, *The Rights and Privileges of the Press* (New York: D. Appleton Century, 1934).

[6]Frank B. Thayer, *Legal Control of the Press* (Chicago: Foundation Press, 1944).

[7]J. Edward Gerald, *The Press and the Constitution* (Minneapolis: University of Minnesota Press, 1948).

[8]William F. Swindler, *A Bibliography of Law on Journalism* (New York: Columbia University Press, 1947).

[9]Fredrick S. Siebert, *Freedom of the Press in England 1476-1776* (Urbana: University of Illinois Press, 1952).

[10]Harold L. Cross, *The People's Right to Know* (New York: Columbia University Press, 1953).

[11]Harold L. Nelson, *Freedom of the Press from Hamilton to the Warren Court* (Indianapolis: Bobbs-Merrill, 1966).

[12]William F. Swindler, *Problems of Law in Journalism* (New York: Macmillan, 1955).

appreciated the growing body of literature and the pedagogical example of the developers, but they faced the new challenge of making sense out of the rapidly evolving law of mass communications. The alternative was to succumb to legal future shock.

Contemporary Period (1969-present): With a mass of new consitutional law in hand, and more to come, the new legists' assigned themselves the research, writing, and tutorial burden to prepare media practitioners and their own successors to interpret and use properly the new dimensions of media law. The Thayer treatise mantle was passed to Nelson, who with Dwight Teeter Jr. produced *The Law of Mass Communications*[13] (1969, 1973, 1978, 1982, 1986), a new guide for the classroom and the newsroom, and Donald M. Gillmor and Jerome A. Barron published the same year a new case law source, *Mass Communication Law: Cases and Comments*[14] (1969, 1974, 1979, 1984). Other legists began proliferating textbooks and special studies as the enrollments at the nation's journalism schools and departments, coincidentally, grew faster than ever.

Society and the Supreme Court continued to interact with the media at the legal level—applying, fine-tuning, and creating constitutional law. Outcomes were cases such as *Red Lion* (395 U.S. 367, 1969), Fairness Doctrine; *New York Times* (403 U.S. 713, 1971), prior restraint; *Branzburg* (408 U.S. 665, 1972), reporter privilege; *Miller* (413 U.S. 15, 1973), obscenity; *Gertz* (418 U.S. 320, 1974), libel; *Tornillo* (418 U.S. 241, 1974), right of reply; *Cox Broadcasting* (420 U.S. 469, 1975), privacy; *Virginia Pharmacy* (425 U.S. 748, 1976), advertising; *Herbert* (596 F. Supp. 1178, 1979), discovery; and *Richmond Newspapers* (448 U.S. 555, 1980), court access. Most of these cases involved state statutory law and came to the court because of First and Fourteenth Amendment constitutional questions. The conservative Burger court, particularly in *Gertz* and *Miller*, complicated further the legists' job by partially rejecting the federal constitutional standards articulated by the liberal Warren court in *Sullivan* and subsequent interpretations and in *Roth*. In *Gertz* and *Miller* the court gave back to the states some of the policy-making power in libel and obscenity law.

Other contextual trends in the Contemporary period were development of an identifiable media bar and the increase in the size of alleged and awarded damages, factors motivating more suits. Some members of the developing media law bar contributed to the growing body of literature of mass communications law. At the meetings of academic and professional journalists, legal and ethical debate multiplied; the Socratic method flourished; the

---

[13]Harold L. Nelson and Dwight Teeter Jr., *The Law of Mass Communications* (Mineola, NY: Foundation Press, 1969).

[14]Donald M. Gillmor and Jerome A. Barron, *Mass Communication Law: Cases and Comments* (St. Paul, MN: West Publishing, 1969).

journals heralded legal articles; and editors generated new legist periodicals, notably *News Media and the Law* of the Reporters Committee of Freedom of the Press and *Media Law Reporter*, a weekly media law opinion service of the Bureau of National Affairs. Not the least of the period's significant trends was the development in 1974 of the Law Division of the Association for Education in Journalism, which was possible after the reorganization of the AEJ into divisions in 1965. Nelson was chairman of the committee that proposed and brought about the new AEJ structure, and his colleague Teeter organized the Law Division in 1973 and was its first chairman and newsletter editor.[15] Gerald was the first of the new division's invited speakers. The division has acquired a role of agenda-setting among current legists engaged in research, writing, and teaching. Also, the Law Division of AEJ, which became AEJMC, entered into a liasion relationship with the Forum Committee of the American Bar Association and its publication *Communications Lawyer*.

Research directions among legists over the years can be measured by a comparison. In 1941 Siebert called for more "case studies and fewer studies of cases . . . thorough analyses of individual instances rather than digests of a number of instances."[16] The methodological bequest of the six legists of this chapter actually was the symbiotic product of the interrelationship among the philosophy and methods of the journalist, the lawyer, the social scientist, the political scientist, the economist, and the historian. By 1975 Gillmor and Everette E. Dennis were making the case for the use of social science methods, particularly the application of political science methods in media law.[17] Thomas Schwartz of Ohio State University in 1984 also urged legists to apply methods of political science to media law—parallel to the doctrine of Gerald, the best of the sextet of pioneering legists.[18]

A further summarization of the contributions of the six legists—Siebert, Cross, Thayer, Gerald, Swindler, and Nelson—reveals the careers of six libertarians of Miltonian persuasion. All were practicing balancers concerned about governmental encroachment upon liberty but equally concerned about social and ethical dimensions of press performance. All were seminal scholars contributing works worthy of new study and use. Some were activists whose careers extended deeply into legal influences outside of the classroom—particularly Siebert, Cross, and

---

[15]Whitney Mundt, "Headnotes," *Media Law Notes* 14 (Spring 1987): 2.

[16]Fred S. Siebert, "Some Notes on the Course in the Law of the Press," *Journalism Quarterly* 15 (1941): 289-291.

[17]Donald L. Gillmor and Everette E. Dennis, "Legal Research and Judicial Communication" in Stephen H. Chaffee (Ed.), *Political Communication: Issues and Strategies for Research* (Beverly Hills: Sage, 1975), pp. 283-305.

[18]Thomas A. Schwartz, "A Call for Alternative Approaches to Research in Communication Law," *Media Law Notes* 11 (June 1984): 1-3.

Swindler.

Because of these six legists, three university journalism schools exerted unusual influence on the discipline's attempt to keep apace and ahead of mass communications law developments. They were Wisconsin, Minnesota, and Missouri. At Wisconsin, Thayer earned his MA; Siebert received his AB; Thayer taught (1935-1961); Nelson taught (1955-1981); and Nelson's *Mass Communications Law* co-author Teeter earned his PhD under Nelson. Minnesota's effect was enhanced by Gerald—the most brilliant of the legists—who earned his PhD in political science from Minnesota, taught at Minnesota (1945-1974), and trained Nelson at Minnesota. In addition, Gillmor was on the Minnesota faculty. Gerald also was involved in Missouri's effect because he earned the BJ and MA in journalism at Missouri and taught there (1929-1946). Swindler studied for his MA and PhD degrees at Missouri. Finally, Gerald's role further was unique because he tied together the influence of these three universities as he studied at Missouri, taught at Minnesota, and tutored Wisconsin's Nelson.

Other noteworthy legists and their specialized studies from the Contemporary period included Gillmor, *Free Press and Fair Trial* (1966); Clifton O. Lawhorne, Southern Illinois University, *Defamation and Public Officials* (1971); Don R. Pember, University of Washington, and his unique work *Privacy and the Press* (1972)[19] along with *Mass Media Law* (1977, 1981, 1984, 1987);[20] Fred W. Friendly, Columbia University, and his two studies that presumably would meet Siebert's criteria for detailed case explorations, *The Good Guys, the Bad Guys and the First Amendment* (1975)[21] and *Minnesota Rag* (1981);[22] Daniel M. Rohrer, Boston College, and his useful commercial speech study *Mass Media, Freedom of Speech, and Advertising* (1979); John D. Stevens, University of Michigan, and his delightful little book *Shaping the First Amendment* (1982),[23] which is reminiscent of Gerald's *The Press and the Constitution*; the significant libel study by Randall P. Bezanson, Gilbert Cramberg and John Soloski, *Libel Law and the Press: Myth and Reality* (1986);[24] and Richard F. Hixson, *Privacy in a Public Society: Human Rights in Conflict* (1987).[25]

---

[19]Don R. Pember, *Privacy and the Press* (Seattle: University of Washington Press, 1972).

[20]Don R. Pember, *Mass Media Law* (Dubuque, IA: Wm. C. Brown, 1977).

[21]Fred W. Friendly, *The Good Guys, the Bad Guys and the First Amendment* (New York: Random House, 1976).

[22]Fred W. Friendly, *Minnesota Rag* (New York: Random House, 1981).

[23]John D. Stevens, *Shaping the First Amendment* (Beverly Hills: Sage, 1982).

[24]Randall P. Bezanson, Gilbert Cramberg and John Soloski, *Libel Law and the Press: Myth and Reality* (New York: Free Press; London: Collier Macmillan, 1987).

[25]Richard F. Hixson, *Privacy in a Public Society: Human Rights in

Other writers of general mass communications law treatises from the Transitional and Contemporary period include Walter A. Steigleman, State University of Iowa, *The Newspaperman and the Law* (1950);[26] Dwight Teeter; Dale Spencer, University of Missouri, *Law for the Newsman* (1971, 1973, 1975);[27] Kenneth S. Devol, California State-Northridge, ed., *Mass Media and the Supreme Court* (1971, 1976, 1982);[28] William E. Francois, Drake University, *Mass Media Law and Regulation* (1975, 1978, 1982, 1986);[29] Robert Trager, Southern Illinois, co-author with lawyer Marc A. Franklin, *The First Amendment and the Fourth Estates* (1977, 1981);[30] Wayne Overbeck and Rick D. Pullen, California State-Northridge, *Major Principles of Media Law* (1981, 1985);[31] T. Barton Carter of Boston University, Franklin, and Jay B. Wright of Syracuse University, *The First Amendment and the Fifth Estate: Regulation of Electronic Mass Media* (1986); and Ralph L. Holsinger, Indiana University-Bloomington, *Media Law* (1987).

Perhaps as important as any of the legists in this essay are the unnamed legists of journalism classrooms and journals. They are the legists who instilled within new journalists and scholars the importance of preservation in society of the robust exchange of diverse viewpoints in the marketplace of ideas—the preservation of the people's right to know, the preservation of the press' right of access to information, publication, and circulation, and the preservation of the totality of the First and Fourteenth Amendments for society. Without these liberties, journalism would be a muted messenger.

Conflict (New York, NY: Oxford University Press, 1987).

[26]Walter A. Steigleman, *The Newspaperman and the Law* (Dubuque, IA: Wm. C. Brown, 1950).

[27]Dale Spencer, *Law for the Newsman* (Columbia, MO, and Los Angeles: Lucas Brothers, 1971).

[28]Kenneth S. Devol (Ed.), *Mass Media and the Supreme Court* (New York: Hastings House 1971).

[29]William E. Francois, *Mass Media Law and Regulation* (Columbus, OH: Grid, 1975).

[30]Robert Trager and Marc A. Franklin, *The First Amendment and the Fourth Estates* (Mineola, NY: Foundation Press, 1977).

[31]Wayne Overbeck and Rick D. Pullen, *Major Principles of Media Law* (New York: Holt, Rinehart and Winston, 1985).

Fredrick S. Siebert
and the Legal Method

An article titled "Contempt of Court and the Press" in a 1928 issue of *Journalism Quarterly* led young Fredrick S. Siebert (1901-1981) into involvement in *Near v. Minnesota* and secured his pacesetting role among First Amendment law teachers. Twenty-six-year-old Siebert was a University of Illinois law school student, whose credentials were an AB degree in journalism from the University of Wisconsin in 1923, a year as a reporter at the Duluth *Herald* in Minnesota in 1923-1924, a short term on the copy desk of the Chicago *Herald-Examiner* in 1924, and 2 years of teaching at Bradley University. He was born December 13, 1901, on the Mesabi Iron Range in Tower, Minnesota, to Frank F. and Sarah (Paine) Siebert, and reared in the nearby town of Eveleth. Siebert's early Minnesota years and his year on the Duluth newspaper might have alerted him to the existence of the Minnesota Public Nuisance Law and the *Saturday Press* of J. M. Near. Oddly, he had never heard of either.

Siebert wrote in his meticulously documented *Journalism Quarterly* article that tolerance of press misrepresentation of judges "is wisely considered better" than the arbitrary, government abridgement of "the sacred liberty of speech, printed or spoken." Significantly, he identified himself for the first time with libertarianism by quoting the sentiment of Senator James Reed of Missouri: "Liberty of the press and liberty of speech is not the right to expose and defend the right, it is the right to advocate the wrong."[1]

Reactionary publisher-lawyer Col. Robert R. McCormick of the Chicago *Tribune*, fresh from First Amendment clashes with Henry Ford and the city of Chicago, was considering getting involved in J.M. Near's legal battles with authorities in Minnesota when he encountered the Siebert article. He summoned young Siebert to his Chicago office and commissioned him to write a paper about the history of liberty of the press from British com-

---

[1]Fredrick S. Siebert, "Contempt of Court and the Press, " *Journalism Quarterly* 4 (1928): 22-33.

mon law through the developing ideas of Justices Oliver Wendell Holmes Jr. and Louis D. Brandeis of the U.S. Supreme Court. Fred Friendly says Siebert was "obviously flattered that McCormick was soliciting his advice."[2] Siebert attended several later conferences about the Near case with the McCormick law firm—McCormick, Kirkland, Fleming, Martin, Green & Ellis—and the *Tribune* lawyers incorporated Siebert's freedom of the press paper into the newspaper's brief filed with the U.S. Supreme Court, which in 1931 would hand down the landmark opinion prohibiting prior restraints.

The year after the first conference with McCormick, Siebert received the JD degree from the University of Illinois law school and was admitted to the Illinois Bar in 1929—the same year he was named an instructor of journalism at Illinois, where he became an assistant professor in 1937 and taught through 1940. In 1934, with support from the University of Illinois, McCormick, and the American Newspaper Publishers Association, Siebert took his family to England on an 8-month sabbatical. He devoted the time to research about the British background to American liberty of expression—the preliminary investigation that led in 1951 to his best-known work, *Freedom of the Press in England 1476-1776: The Rise and Decline of Government Control.*[3] The book is the definitive work on the subject and was selected for the journalism research award by Kappa Tau Alpha, the national journalism honor society.

Another outgrowth of the initial contact with McCormick and of Siebert's research into origins of legal protections of freedom of expression were memoranda used in filing briefs with the Supreme Court in three other landmark cases—*Associated Press v. United States* (326 U.S. 1), an antitrust case; *Grosjean v. American Press Co.* (297 U.S. 233), a taxation case; and *Hannegan v. Esquire,* an obscenity case. Also during his early days at the University of Illinois, Siebert served as legal counsel to various press associations.

The key influences on his work were Willard Bleyer of Wisconsin and Eric Allen of Oregon—Bleyer, Siebert said, because he established the first school of journalism with a research orientation, and Allen, because of his intelligence and his administration of an excellent journalism program. Siebert had a longstanding correspondence with Allen.[4]

In his own classroom Siebert developed a concern about the textbooks, course content, and methodology of the Law of the

---

[2]Fred Friendly, *Minnesota Rag* (New York: Random House, 1981), p. 77.

[3]Fredrick S. Siebert, *Freedom of the Press in England 1476-1776: The Rise and Decline of Government Control* (Urbana: University of Illinois Press).

[4]Siebert. Interview by Robert V. Hudson, 21 April 1970, interview MCHC 70-65, transcript, AEJMC Collection, State Historical Society of Wisconsin, Madison, WI.

Press course and wrote pioneering articles to provide guidance and encouragement to instructors who were beginning to develop courses and cope with the growing complexity of First Amendment law. In 1928 he first expressed his rationale for the Law of the Press course in a review of *The Law of Newspapers* by William R. Arthur and Ralph Crossman. "The pressure of events," he wrote, "often makes...slight knowledge of the law an indispensible adjunct to the mental equipment of the laymen. In no field of modern enterprise is this more true than in the newspaper business." The Arthur-Crossman combination text-case book was one of only three press law books available at the time, one being a case book, *The Law of the Press* by William G. Hale and Ivan Benson (1923), and the other *Newspaper Law* by William W. Loomis (1924). Siebert criticized the Arthur-Crossman book on two counts: first, its neglect of a discussion of what Siebert considered sacred—the phrase "freedom of the press," and, second, its omission in the cases of the subjects' real names. "What the volume gains in ethics," wrote Siebert, "it seems to lose in vitality and punch,"[5] recognizing the value of the factor that inherently interests journalism students who may be baffled temporarily by the intricacies of the law.

Opposed to the casebook approach and disappointed in the Arthur-Crossman option, Siebert set about to write his text—*The Rights and Privileges of the Press* (1934), an expository approach for the practicing journalist and the student. Swindler commended the book for its "positive approach" from "the standpoint of what a newspaper can do."[6] Absolutists found no encouragement from Siebert. A balancer in his theoretic approach to the First Amendment, he sketched his philosophy in the book thusly:

> The battles for a free Press are a part of the march of democracy. . . . As the people became enfranchised, the Press has been made free. In return it has been the duty of the Press to protect the public by bringing the activities and officials of government to the bar of public opinion through the publication of accurate facts and enlightened comment. On the other hand, the Press as an institution is not superior to the system of government under which it operates but is subject to its laws and regulations.[7]

He, unlike Arthur and Crossman, built the book on an explanation of the roots of the term "freedom of the press." Then he focused on three areas—access to information, defamation, and obscenity—an appropriate approach because he wrote the book on the eve of the later burst of cases in the 1930s and before the de-

---

[5]Fredrick S. Siebert, "The Law of Newspapers," *Journalism Quarterly* 5 (1928): 33-34.

[6]William S. Swindler, *A Bibliography of Law on Journalism* (New York: Columbia University Press, 1947), p. 26.

[7]Fredrick S. Siebert, *Freedom of the Press in England* , pp. vii-viii.

velopment of broadcasting law.

Siebert's bias toward exclusion of much material included today in the press law textbooks and courses was explained, after 10
years of teaching, in his 1939 article titled "Some Notes on the
Course in Law of the Press." He proposed that legal problems of
advertising and business be taught in a Law of Newspaper Management, legal notices in Community Journalism, circulation
law in Newspaper Circulation, photography law in News Photography, constitutional issues in History of Journalism, and court
reporting in Advanced Reporting. "The three-hour one-semester
course, which seems to be the current average, is far too crowded,"
wrote Siebert, "to attempt more than an introduction to the legal
problems of the student in the editorial curriculum." His course
outline included essential units about news gathering rights,
copyright, unfair competition, libel, contempt of court, freedom
of the press, right of privacy, obscenity, and law of photography.
"The purpose of the course," he wrote, "is not to make lawyers or
advocates but to inform the student of the rights and responsibilities of his job." He advocated a classroom methodology of imparting the general principles of law, clarifications of identifiable
trends, and application through hypotheticals to ensure that students learn how to apply the doctrines to specific situations. He
cautioned the teacher against duplication of law school methods
devoted to intricacies of legal reasoning, discussion of vagaries of
the judicial system as in political science, and overemphasis of a
topic in which the teacher has specialized.[8]

Since the appearance of the Siebert pedagogical article, the title of the general First Amendment course typically has been
changed to Communication Law, which still usually is a 3-hour
course; all areas of media law have been more fully developed;
and more textbooks have become available. His insight and influence did little to settle the debates about types of texts, how to
resolve the content problem, and what method in the classroom
is most effective. Remaining constant are only his central points
about the importance of teaching the foundations of freedom of
the press and principles of implementation of the law, plus ensuring that practitioners can use the principles in real situations.

Analysis of Siebert's article reveals, however, that he understood the paradoxical principle that the more change occurs the
more things remain the same. His first and last articles in *Journalism Quarterly* dealt with problems of protecting property
rights in mass media materials initiated by technological developments—in the late 19th century in publishing and in the late
20th in satellite transmission.[9] He was acutely aware of the crit-

<hr>

[8]Fredrick S. Siebert, "Some Notes on the Course in Law of the Press,"
Journalism Quarterly 15 (1939): 289-291.

[9]Fredrick S. Siebert, "Rights in News," *Journalism Quarterly* 4 (1927):
45-54, and "Property Rights in Materials Transmitted by Satellite," *Journalism Quarterly* 38 (1971): 17-25.

ical role of technological determinism as one of the factors in the development of freedom of expression, according to his *JQ* articles and his discussion in *Freedom of the Press in England 1476-1776* about the impact of the printing press on the English monarchy's resolve to stifle dissent. He recognized the stages of the technological phenomenon as these: (a) invention, (b) enhancement of expresion, (c) lack of understanding and protection of the innovation, (d) rise of controls as government senses problems, (e) struggle to preserve the value of a new or improved channel, and (f) establishment of a new balance in society.

Another of Siebert's contributions was an emphasis on international comparative study of freedom of communication. As early as 1931 he advanced this approach to understanding freedom of expression; he read to the Press Congress of the World at Mexico City a paper titled "International Protection of Rights in News." The influence of high-speed presses, telegraph, radio, and television, he observed, had enabled or would enable pirates to send news westward without independent investment to compete with its originator. "The world turns too slowly on its axis," he wrote, "to keep up with journalistic enterprise." He looked at the situation in numerous countries and shuddered at the proposed solution: government-subsidized media. "In a world where government is the servant of the people and responsible to the electorate, a subsidized press has been universally condemned. The results would be disastrous to the republican form of government. It would result in censorship, suppression, and propaganda."[10]

Other works in which Siebert's international comparative work enriched the outcome included his 1927 and 1971 articles about rights in news; *Freedom of the Press in England 1476-1776*; "Contemporary Regulations of the British Press"[11]; and his essays "The Authoritarian Theory" and "The Libertarian Theory" in *Four Theories of the Press* done with Theodore Peterson and Wilbur Schramm (1956).[12]

Siebert authored these other books: *Copyreading: A Collection of Laboratory Exercises* (1930), *The Mass Media in a Free Society* (1956), *A Study of Master's Degree Programs in Journalism* (1963), *Report on Copyrights, Clearances and Rights of Teachers in the New Educational Media* (1963),[13] and two chapters in *Free Press and Fair Trial: Some Dimensions of the Problem* (1970),[14]

---

[10]Fredrick S. Siebert, "International Protection of Rights in News," *Journalism Quarterly* 9 (1932): 290-304.

[11]Fredrick S. Siebert, "Contemporary Regulations of the British Press," *Journalism Quarterly* 8 (1931): 235-256.

[12]Fredrick S. Siebert, Theodore Peterson and Wilbur Schramm, *Four Theories of the Press* (Urbana: University of Illinois Press, 19956).

[13]Fredrick S. Siebert, *Report on Copyrights, Clearances and Rights of Teachers in the New Educational Media* (Washington: American Council on Education, 1964).

[14]Fredrick S. Siebert, Walter Wilcox, George Hough III, and Chilton R.

which was an attempt by Siebert, Walter Wilcox, George Hough III, and Chilton R. Bush to quantify the influence of news coverage on the criminal trial system.

The first contributor—and one of the most prolific of the early writers—of careful constitutional analysis of press cases in *Journalism Quarterly*, Siebert wrote numerous articles for the journal, including others about 17th-century press controls; regulation of corontos; legal research; political advertising, with Edith Dyer; English newspaper taxes; radio news legal problems; and anonymous source protection.[15] He also was a member of the editorial board of *Journalism Quarterly* and wrote articles about public records access for *Editor & Publisher*, "Legal Developments Affecting the Press" for *Annals of the American Academy of Political and Social Science*, and "The Law and Journalism" for *Virginia Law Review*.[16]

After his tenure at the University of Illinois, his teaching and administration career continued as a professor at Northwestern University in 1940-1941, director of the School of Journalism and Communications at the University of Illinois in 1941-1957, director of the Division of Mass Communication and Journalism at Michigan State University in 1957-1960, dean of the College of Communication Arts at Michigan State in 1960-1967, and professor of journalism at Michigan State from 1967 to his retirement in 1973. He was active in the Association for Education in Journalism, serving as its president in 1960; the American Association of Schools and Departments of Journalism, serving as its president; Sigma Delta Chi; Kappa Tau Alpha; and Alpha Delta Sigma.

Various organizations recognized Siebert for his contributions. His most notable awards were the Illinois Press Association Medal in 1938, a University of Missouri School of Journalism Medal, the Distinguished Service to Freedom of Expression award from the Law Division of AEJMC in 1979 for his pioneering work in freedom of expression litigation, and the Kappa Tau Alpha Award for *Freedom of the Press in England 1476-1776*.

Siebert charted three purposes for this latter work: (a) to trace the development of English press control, (b) to present the docu-

---

Bush, *Free Press and Fair Trial: Some Dimensions of the Problem* (Athens: University of Georgia Press, 1970).

[15]Seventeenth-century controls, *Journalism Quarterly* 13 (1936): 381-393; corontos, *Journalism Quarterly* 16 (1939): 151-160; legal research,*Journalism Quarterly* 19 (1942): 69-70; political advertising, *Journalism Quarterly* 20 (1943): 139-143; English newspaper taxes, *Journalism Quarterly* 21 (1944): 12-24; radio news law, *Journalism Quarterly* 23 (1946): 189-192; and professional secrecy and the journalist, *Journalism Quarterly* 36 (1959): 3-11.

[16]Siebert, *Editor & Publisher* 62 (8 March 1930): 11; "Legal Developments Affecting the Press," *Annals of the American Academy of Political and Social Science* 219 (1942): 93-99; and "The Law and Journalism," *Virginia Law Review* 32 (1946): 771-780.

mentation, and (c) to interpret 300 years of observable trends, from the advent of the printing press to the drafting of the U.S. Bill of Rights. He identified three theories that would influence the press in any society: (a) the Tudor-Stuart theory, which is based on the state's justification of control through the assumption that the responsibility for protection of the safety, stability, and welfare of the state is inherent in the state; (b) the Blackstone-Mansfield theory, which is based on the acceptance of the concept of a sovereignty that limits freedom through its understood power; and (c) the Camden-Erskine-Jefferson theory, which limits the sovereign through natural law and creates freedom as a natural right immune from man-made law. He further concluded that philosophical principles played a secondary, but important, role in the development of freedom of expression, and that absolutism is foreign to theories of liberty. The disagreements then arise from the nature and number of limitations. Siebert posited two variables that determined the nature of press freedom in a given society. First, "The extent of government control of the press depends on the nature of the relationship of the government to those subject to the government." Second, "The area of freedom contracts and the enforcement of restraints increases as the stresses on the stability of the government and of the structure of society increase."[17]

In his essays in *Four Theories of the Press*, Siebert expanded upon these propositions and identified four assumptive areas that determine the nature of press freedom in a society: "(1) the nature of man, (2) the nature of society and the state, (3) the relation of man to the state, and (4) the basic philosophical problem, the nature of knowledge and of truth."[18] In these two essays the Stuart-Tudor theory became the Authoritarian Theory—very close to the Soviet Communist Theory—and the Erskine-Camden-Jefferson theory became the Libertarian Theory. Siebert implied that the newest theory—the 1947 Social Responsibility Theory of the Hutchins Commission—nuzzled more closely with the Authoritarian than the Libertarian in its tacit approval of government intervention into perceived failure to inform citizens fully, completely, and accurately. In 1952 Siebert forecast: "How much freedom we shall enjoy will depend on how widespread are the threats and feeling of insecurity and instability."[19]

Siebert's legacy is his role in introducing legal research methods to the community of journalism law scholars, his participation as a lawyer in key 1930s press law judicial appeals, and his definitive *Freedom of the Press in England*. He explored at a critical time the libertarian roots of freedom of the press in the United States and gave to journalism a claim on the research and teach-

---

[17]Siebert, *Freedom of the Press in England*, pp. vi, 5-7, 9-10.

[18]Siebert, "The Authoritarian Theory" and "The Libertarian Theory" in Siebert, Peterson, and Schramm, *Four Theories of the Press*, p. 10.

[19]Siebert, *Freedom of the Press in England*, p. 131.

ing of the law that would shape journalism's practice in the 20th
century and beyond.

Harold L. Cross
and the Right to Know

Harold L. Cross (1890-1959) crusaded for the abatement of the cult of secrecy in government; he aimed his lances at the "You Mustn't Know This" and the "You Can't Print That" statutes. In the short period between 1947 and his death in 1959, he woke up to the acceleration of abuse of the concept of privacy by government; wrote the definitive legal brief for the freedom of information movement—*The People's Right to Know: Legal Access to Public Records and Proceedings*; and through tireless efforts and influence began to open the public's business to its own eyes and ears.

To a lesser attorney-scholar-professor, the task might have been quixotic, but Cross from 1922 to 1937 had learned to succeed and survive on the libel battlefield as general counsel of the New York *Herald Tribune* and sometimes for the New York *Evening Post*. Since 1929 he had taught law of journalism at Columbia University, and in 1947-1948 while pursuing his duties in the Graduate School of Journalism and the new American Press Institute programs for practicing journalists, he became alarmed about government officials' use of gas-light era statutes and precedents to seal off the public's business.[1] He began writing about his concerns for *Editor & Publisher*.

Six causative factors, he believed, fueled the secrecy trend: (a) the international backwash created by totalitarian governments' secrecy and news intervention, (b) the retention of censorship habits from World War II, (c) the burgeoning of the right of privacy doctrine, (d) successful advocacy of confidentiality statutes by the proponents of non-disclosure, including social workers, (e) erosion of faith in publicity as a crime deterrent, and (f) the tendency of the press to let records and meeting closures go unchallenged because of other pressures.[2]

Cross' key ideas included the assertions that without freedom

---

[1] Harold L. Cross, *The People's Right to Know: Legal Access to Public Records and Proceedings* (New York: Columbia University Press, 1953), p. xv.

[2] Ibid., pp. 12-13.

of information "the citizens of a democracy have but changed their kings" and that the resolution of the problem would come from winning the point that "access" is equivalent to "printing" and "circulation" in the guarantees inherent in the First Amendment press clause.[3] When he went before Congressional committees, he argued that the constitutional right to know had its genesis in the provisions of the First, Fifth, Ninth, and Fourteenth Amendments and the natural rights theories. Beginning with the premise that access is the first of the rights implicit to the speech and press guarantees of the First Amendment, he reasoned that the Fifth safeguarded the stipulations of the First, that in the Ninth the sovereign people reserved certain rights to themselves, and that the Fourteenth asssured due process of law in preservation of personal liberties. Natural rights and popular government, Cross would say quoting James Madison, without means of getting access to information "is but a prologue to a farce or tragedy or both."[4]

Because of Cross' reputation as a libel lawyer and lecturer and his interest in the right to know, the American Society of Newspaper Editors in 1950 enlisted him for a token retainer as a collaborator to attempt to turn the secrecy tide. "Enlisted as an adviser, he became our leader," wrote James S. Pope, chairman of the ASNE Committee on Freedom of Information. Cross "caught a vision clearer than ours," said Pope, "and produced a potent manual-of-arms for a battle we had only begun to comprehend."[5] The manual was his report to the ASNE committee published as the book *The People's Right to Know*. Cross "in his thinking . . . was a veritable 20th century Coke," the English chief justice who told James I that not even the throne was above the law, wrote J.R. Wiggins of the Washington *Post*.[6] The Cross-ASNE relationship oftentimes troubled Cross because he had "a client that did not always know its own mind," wrote Wiggins, because media opinion on access issues was varied within and without the ASNE. The attorney-scholar frequently thought that the rank-and-file of the ASNE did not appreciate his work.[7] Thus, Wiggins concluded that Cross's patience and caution with his client were remarkable. His task also was formidable because of the multiple uses of secrecy in a bureaucracy. "The charms of secrecy," he wrote, "like those of

---

[3]Ibid., p. xiii, and Harold L. Cross, "Right to Know," *Freedom of Information Center Publication* No. 26, University of Missouri, Columbia, MO, May 1960.

[4]Cross, statement, Congress, House, Government Information Subcommittee on Government Operations, 16 November 1955.

[5]Cross, *The People's Right to Know*, pp. xi and vii.

[6]J.E. Wiggins, "Harold L. Cross," *American Society of Newspaper Editors Bulletin* (September 1959): 3.

[7]Virginius Dabney, Richmond, VA, to Herbert Brucker, 14 March 1958, in Freedom of Information Center, School of Journalism, University of Missouri, Columbia.

heiresses, inspire different kinds of love."[8]

Cross' love of freedoms under the Constitution inspired his thesis: "Citizens of a self-governing society must have the legal right to examine and investigate the conduct of its affairs, subject only to those limitations imposed by the most urgent public necessity."[9] He realized that the love of liberty, the love of an open society, and policies of disclosure invariably angered, irritated, injured, inconvenienced, or troubled the subjects of the disclosure. But he concluded the cost-benefits balance weighs toward free information flow. "Principle," he observed, "has ever been at odds with pinpricks." He strongly believed in the value of the press' role in a democracy and repetitively defended its vigilance, resourcefulness, and courage in bringing information about the government to the people "speedily, in substantial volume and at bearable cost."[10]

To improve press performance, Cross developed the expository book for the ASNE in which he identified the common and statutory roots of the problem; the contemporary common, statutory, judicial, and regulatory law; and definitional problems for records and meetings law. The book also included a detailed survey of the federal and state right to know scenes. To enforce a legal right to inspect public records or attend public meetings, he said, four questions must be answered properly: "(1) Is the record or proceeding public? (2) If public, is it open to inspection or attendance? (3) If it is open, to whom is the right of inspection or attendance accorded? (4) If public and open to inspection or attendance by the applicant, will the court in the circumstances existing allow that person the necessary legal enforcement process?"[11]

On behalf of the ASNE, Cross repeatedly testified before committees of Congress, laying down the right-to-know case and answering questions with brilliance and imagination. The rights of the First Amendment "are vested in all persons, in each of us," he would argue. "The remedial legislation here suggested is advocated in behalf of the people, not of any news media alone." On another occasion he told a subcommittee that he was concerned about "to put it bluntly, last but far from least, the right of Harold L. Cross to know." He believed that abuses of information policy were more rampant than ever in the mid-1950s; and he stressed repeatedly his conclusion that the state of the law, in the absence of action by Congress, left the people, the press, and Congress without any right to inspect federal non-judicial records. He particularly recoiled at the scenes of journalists reduced to the status of suppliants pleading for the grace of public officials, who by design of the Constitution were to serve the citizens, including journalists, instead of suppressing information. He chaffed at the way

---

[8]Harold L. Cross, "The Ohio Decision," *ASNE Bulletin*, 1 June 1955, 7.

[9]Cross, *The People's Right to Know*, p. xiii.

[10]Cross, *FoI Center Report* No. 26.

[11]Cross, *The People's Right to Know*, p. 19.

suppressers identified the "public interest" criterion with their self interests to generate plausible rationalizations to avoid exposure, criticism, embarrassment, or just being pestered. The time, he would say, was pregnant for a return to the philosophies of Patrick Henry and James Madison. "Congress is the primary source of relief," he preached to the committee. "The power of Congress, if it will but act, is ample to legislate freedom of information for itself, the public and the press."[12]

The former Columbia professor knew that "cults of secrecy never slumber."[13] So he continued to compile and publish in the late 1950s supplements to *The People's Right to Know*; one was published after his death. During his lifetime he saw the amendment by the U.S. Congress of the 1789 housekeeping statute, which was being used by federal officials to suppress information, and the development of new and stronger open records and meetings laws by many state legislatures, under prodding by state press associations with Cross ammunition.[14] He died knowing that the toughest part of the access fight was ahead for the proponents of the FoI Movement, but his spadework was essential to the statutory pinnacle of the movement, the federal Freedom of Information Act (1966) and the Government in the Sunshine Act (1977). He once wrote that he chose "to look upon each successive President as just another politician whose temporary duties as an official cannot override his permanent and fundamental duty as a citizen and debtor to justice'."[15] He undoubtedly smiled when the Supreme Court in the executive privilege case *Nixon v. United States* ruled unanimously that no man is above the law.

Cross—the ultimate resolute FoI advocate, a builder of the Columbia University Graduate Schoool of Journalism, a sometimes apple grower, a sometimes arctic traveler—was born July 8, 1890, in New York City. His parents were Charles Arthur, an auditor, and Jennie Lavinia (Lown) Cross. He was educated at Columbia High School in South Orange, N.J., and Cornell University, where he was graduated LLB in 1911. He was admitted to the New York bar and practiced with two firms in New York City in his first year as a lawyer, becoming a member in 1916 of the second firm, Sackett, Chapman & Stevens. The partners changed the name of the firm in 1920 to Sackett, Chapman, Brown & Cross, and at the time of Cross' death it was Brown, Cross & Hamilton.

Cross became involved with journalism in 1922 when he began to serve as general counsel for the New York *Herald Tribune*

---

[12]Congress, House, Government Information Subcommittee, 26 November 1955, and 8 May 1956.

[13]Cross, *FoI Center Report* No. 26.

[14]5 USC 22.

[15]Cross, Key West, FL., to Virginius Dabney, Herbert Brucker, and J.E. Wiggins, 2 February 1958, in Freedom of Information Center, School of Journalism, University of Missouri, Columbia.

through his firm, which came to deal particularly with newspaper litigation. He developed specialization in libel and copyright laws, became secretary of the newspaper, and was elected vice president of the New York *Herald Tribune* Fresh Air Fund. His academic bent began to emerge in 1929 when Columbia University appointed him as a lecturer in the law of libel. He was appointed an associate professor in journalism in 1931; and he resigned his active law practice after 26 years in 1937 to accept a full-time role as professor of journalism, teaching libel, freedom of the press, and history of journalism. In 1943 he spent a year in Chungking, war-time capital of China, as dean of a Post-Graduate School of Journalism set up by Columbia under the auspices of the Central Political Institute of China. In the mid-1940s he commuted twice a week by rail or air from his Maine farmhouse to teach his classes at Columbia. He served as associate dean of the Columbia Graduate School of Journalism from 1948 to 1950, his last year with the university.

At this point the American Society of Newspaper Editors secured his help in its people's right to know project. He retired from the official ASNE counsel role in 1958 because of health but continued to provide advice when the ASNE Freedom of Information Committee called on him. ASNE FoI chairman Pope evaluated Cross' labors after the attorney's death: "We got not only a brilliant mind. We got a man with the heart and spirit and wisdom of a truly great editor; a man who made us see the scope of our job, who reacted powerfully against tyranny, petty or otherwise."[16]

The People's Right to Know brought to Cross the recognition of Kappa Tau Alpha, the national journalism honor society, which selected the book as the best research work in journalism in 1953. Also the University of Arizona in 1958 presented Cross its John Peter Zenger Award for distinguished service to freedom of the press; the Society of Professional Journalists, then Sigma Delta Chi, honored him as a Distinguished Achievements Fellow; and the University of Maine awarded him an honorary doctor of laws degree. Groups dedicated to the FoI movemeent regard him as their patron saint; these groups included the ASNE FoI Committee and the FoI Center at the University of Missouri. He wrote articles primarily for *Editor & Publisher*, the *ASNE Bulletin*, and the Missouri FoI Center publications. He was a member of the New York State Bar Association, New York County Lawyers Association, American Society of Newspaper Editors, Sigma Delta Chi, Kappa Sigma, Phi Delta Phi, the Cornell Law Association, the Grange, the Rotary Club, Masonic Order, and the Presbyterian Church.[17]

---

[16]Harold L. Cross, *The People's Right to Know* (Second Supplement) (Columbia, MO: Freedom of Information Center, School of Journalism, University of Missouri, 1959), p. i.

[17]New York *Times*, 10 August 1959, and Wiggins, *ASNE Bulletin*,

The life and work of Cross is significant in each of its three professional periods: (a) his legal relationship to the New York *Herald Tribune* at the time that it was probably the best newspaper in the United States, (b) his academic period at the Graduate School of Journalism, which was marked by his introduction of law to a generation of Columbia-educated journalists, and (c) his freedom of information period in partnership with the ASNE. Certainly, his masterpiece was *The People's Right to Know*—the freedom of information movement benchmark.

His right-to-know handiwork, however, does not stand inviolable; his critics in academia, the government, and the public continue to argue against a constitutionally protected right to know on innumerable grounds. Rarely does a session of Congress or a state legislature close without a major attack on right-to-know laws. For instance, for a few days during the summer of 1989, the state of Texas, becauses of a rider on an unrelated bill, closed arrest records in the state on the authority of the legislature and the governor. An embarrassed legislature and governor had to undo the unconstitutional action in a special session. Cross would agree with William F. Buckley, who cheers the upsetting of court rulings and legislative lawmaking "to remind ourselves that we are a self-governing nation."

September 1959.

Frank B. Thayer
and Economic Influences

Frank Barnes Thayer (1890-1965) researched and wrote the first American treatise about journalistic law, and it became a standard textbook in the post-World War II journalism classroom. *Legal Control of the Press* through four editions (1944, 1950, 1956, 1962) bore the effect of Thayer's preparation and experience in reporting, law, journalism education, and newspaper ownership. More than any other of the communication law educators of his era, Thayer interlaced his analysis of legal controls with that of the impact of economic controls of the press. Although Gerald and Swindler, too, were commentators about the business side of journalism controls, Thayer uniquely prepared himself for scholarship in legal and economic management of newspapers.

He earned the BA from Oberlin College in 1912 and the MA in journalism from the University of Wisconsin in 1916. His journalistic interest surfaced early as he worked for the Conneaut *News-Herald* in his Ohio hometown, where he was born August 18, 1890, to Edson Courtwright and Nell Barnes (Ford) Thayer. He was a descendant of Richard Thayer, who settled in Braintree, Massachusetts, from England before 1630.

His second interest—the law—likewise emerged early, and he studied it during the summers of his Oberlin days in the firm of Perry & Hitchcock in Jefferson, Ohio.

Thayer's third interest—teaching—entered the scene when in 1916 with a new master's degree he became an instructor in journalism at the University of Kansas. Subsequently, he served as an instructor at the State University of Iowa in 1917-1919, an associate professor at Washington State College in 1919-1922, and a visiting and assistant professor at Northwestern's Medill School of Journalism in 1922-1925. In Chicago in 1921 he organized and served as the first president of a professional chapter of Sigma Delta Chi, which now is the Society of Professional Journalists, and that chapter eventually became the Headline Club of Chicago. He also helped organize a student chapter at the Medill School of Journalism.

The fourth influence on Thayer's career—newspaper ownership—appeared during his short experiences at the Conneaut *News-Herald*, Springfield (Mass.) *Republican*, Erie (Pa.) *Dispatch*, and Detroit *News*, and the writing of his first book, *Newspaper Management* (1926, 1938). In 1928 Thayer merged two newspapers in Creston, Iowa, to form the daily Creston *News Advertiser* and served as its president until 1932. Then the call to law school beckoned for the 1932-1935 interim, and the year Thayer finished the JD at Loyola he was admitted to the Illinois Bar, became counsel until his death with the Chicago firm of Kaiser, Dodge, Dornbaugh & Sullivan, and joined the University of Wisconsin faculty as teacher of journalism and of press law until his 1961 retirement.

Thayer advanced to professor at Wisconsin by 1941. His early years there were marked by his contributing to *Survey of Journalism* (1937, 1957);[1] becoming adviser to the Wisconsin student chapter of Sigma Delta Chi; beginning 27 years of service in 1937 as adviser to the *Badger* yearbook and 11 years as adviser to the *Daily Cardinal* student newspaper; writing articles about libel, contempt, and news as property for the *Wisconsin Law Review*, *Notre Dame Lawyer*, and *Editor & Publisher*; serving as national vice president of Sigma Delta Chi in 1941-1946; and the writing of his most influential book, *Legal Control of the Press* (1945). Sigma Delta Chi honored him and *Legal Control* with its 1945 award for research in journalism.[2]

Swindler's evaluation of Thayer's *Legal Control* was that he had covered in it the standard topics of press freedom "more exhaustively than any other text" but faulted the work for weakness in the treatment of advertising law and legal notice advertising.[3] Thayer's foresight in filling the textbook void with a comprehensive legal treatise placed him in a preeminent position in communication law education. Not until 10 years later would another competitive textbook appear, Swindler's *Problems of Law in Journalism* (1955). Thayer's own modest estimate of his principal contribution was the blending of the knowledge of an attorney with the knowledge of a newspaper man.[4]

"The function of this treatise," Thayer wrote in the preface to the third edition of *Legal Control*, "is not to serve as a digest of cases but as an interpretation of the general principles governing the solution of problems as they arise." His method included the use of an *Instruction Manual for Law of the Press*, a companion to each edition that included case problems and solutions—marking the introduction of supplements, which is common today in the rapidly evolving field of communication law. He was amused by

---

[1]George Fox Mott, *Survey of Journalism* (New York: Barnes & Noble, 1937).

[2]"June Deadline for Journalist," *Publishers Auxiliary*, 20 May 1961.

[3]William F. Swindler, *A Bibliography of Law on Journalism* (New York: Columbia University Press, 1947), p. 26.

[4]*Publishers Auxiliary*, 20 May 1961.

students who thought they would find all of the answers in his press law course and by journalism instructors who criticized press law textbooks for their failure to show how a particular case ultimately ended. He cautioned both that the emphasis should be on finding the problem and that in many cases the answer has not been judicially decided.[5]

Thayer approached freedom of the press as a non-absolute, qualified right rooted in primordial laws of nature, if not natural law, which he identified as the laws of self-preservation, reproduction, spirituality, reason, and association. "The right of association implies communication of expression," he wrote. Of the options for preservation of free expression—license and accountable liberty—Thayer chose the latter, which necessitates legal controls to "enforce responsibility and to institute effectively regulations for the common good of society." He believed the two critical tests of freedom of the press were: (a) Are government prior- and post-publication restrictions reasonable, and (b) is the press free to cover accurately and to criticize fairly government activities? He also cautioned the media against attempting to resolve every press control effort—particularly on the part of public officials and advertisers—through call for a law. Thayer believed that ethics and business policy should be employed to resolve these kinds of societal control efforts.[6] In a 1951 article he cited the experience of the Georgia press in 1939 and 1949 with a retraction statute as an example of the what-the-lawgiver-gives-the-lawgiver-can-take-away syndrome. In this case public opinion had supported a retraction statute proposed by the press in 1939 to reduce libel damages for newspaper defendants. Ten years later public officials secured its repeal with the help of a public eager to forget the bad news of the Depression and World War II. In the Cold War era the public perceived the retraction law as a means to discriminate against the public in favor of the press. Thayer's exposition of the Georgia experience illustrated the Siebert proposition that freedom shrinks as the stresses on society and government increase. Thayer's formula for meeting the continuing challenge was this: "If freedom of communication is to be preserved, the fundamental concepts of freedom tempered with responsibility must remain as the polestars to guide independent thinking and to aid in the growth of the nation for better living."[7]

Thayer was the first to develop a significant unit about privacy in a journalism law textbook. He defined privacy as "the right of seclusion as to one's person, name, or representation of self. . . . One cannot escape, however, certain obligations by merely claiming immunity therefrom under the cloak of a right

---

[5]Frank B. Thayer, *Legal Control of the Press* (3rd ed.) (Chicago: Foundation Press, 1956), pp. v-viii.

[6]Ibid., pp. vii, 2.

[7]Frank B. Thayer, "Shifting Concepts in Laws Affecting the Press," *Journalism Quarterly* 28 (1951): 24-30.

of privacy." He based his forecast about right to privacy development on the premise that violation of a personality "may be a
breach of the right of liberty of the press."[8] He believed that when
the press injured human rights, a need emerged for protection of
personality and identity.[9]

Although Thayer's *Legal Control* served as a primary text for
the press law field for almost 30 years, organizational weaknesses beset the work. Some of the weaknesses can be understood
because of the undeveloped state of some areas of press law in the
1940s. For instance, he scattered broadcast applications
throughout his book and left development of independent units
about broadcasting law to his successors. Obscenity and blas-
phemy, because of the condition of criminal libel at the time, appeared in the middle of the libel portion of the book. However, the
logic is difficult to grasp as to why in the third edition a right-to-
know section is sandwiched between sections about broadcast
competition and postal privileges rather than under the theoretic
treatment of freedom of the press or access issues. Thayer's struggle with organization in his treatise revealed as much about the
evolutionary potential of press law as about his analytical capacity. He sensed correctly that the decades ahead of him would con-
front the press with new legal problems. "As new situations arise
in publishing," he wrote, "the old principle of ubi jus ibi
remedium, meaning that there is no wrong without a remedy
[technically, no right without a remedy for the violation of a
right], comes to mind."[10] The opportunities for press restrictions,
said Thayer, were legion.[11]

In *Newspaper Business Management* (1954), his next major
book, Thayer advised publishers to retain legal counsel but to
maintain awareness about five categories of law: (a) business law,
including corporation, contract, and tax law, (b) libel law, (c) advertising and trade practices law, (d) labor law, and (e) postal regulation. His philosophy about the relationship of economics and
liberty was summarized in his belief that "the American newspaper is a private enterprise with a public function."[12] Thayer re-
butted the Hutchins Committee Report of 1947 that proposed the
denial of the right to own a printing press. "Clearly," wrote
Thayer, "this reiterated denial is wrong on the basis of Anglo-
American constitutional law." But he worried about the central-
ization of ownership among newspapers—"that they would be
controlled and operated on the basis of capitalistic enterprises
rather than as media of comment and reported facts."[13] He also

---

[8]Thayer, *Legal Control of the Press*, pp. 437, 433.

[9]Ibid., pp. 159-189.

[10]Thayer, "Shifting Concepts in Laws Affecting the Press," p. 27.

[11]Thayer, *Legal Control of the Press*, p. vii.

[12]Frank B. Thayer, *Newspaper Business Management* (New York:
Prentice-Hall, 1954), pp. 11-17, 412.

[13]Thayer, "Shifting Concepts in Laws Affecting the Press," 25-26.

listed invasion of privacy, carelessness in defamation prevention, and trial by newspapers as the three legal problems among the ten weaknesses of the press confronting publishers. To fortify newspapers against intrusive regulation and to correct its weaknesses, Thayer argued that publishers needed to build their philosophies on the premise that press freedom was designed for the protection of the press and the people.[14]

In addition to the testimony of his books, Thayer left an important heritage through the Wisconsin students he advised and taught. When Wisconsin student newspaper editors were trying to absorb the embarrassment of their mistakes, he would lift their spirits with a quip: "Even the New York *Times* makes mistakes." The publisher of the *Wisconsin State Journal*, Don Anderson, said, "Few have taught on this old campus with so much of that great quality, humanity." Anderson added in a tribute to Thayer, "You could not get into this room all the students, past and present, who would rise and say: 'He is my friend.'"[15] Fittingly, Thayer received at a Wisconsin Gridiron Banquet, sponsored by the campus Sigma Delta Chi chapter, the red derby for the outstanding contribution to the event. The red derby harmonized with his love of showmanship and the colorful anecdote, which he used to enliven banquets and classrooms. He was, according to the Wisconsin *Daily Cardinal*, one of the university's most loyal football fans, an honorary Wisconsin special deputy sheriff, and a lover of the circus—the latter to the point of membership in Circus Fans Association of America. His students came to expect anything from fluttering pigeons to female gate crashers at the annual Gridiron Banquet. He freshened his lectures with illustrations from experiences and people he knew, ranging from the court bailiff to the football coach. The capstone honor bestowed upon the bespectacled professor was the establishment of the Frank Thayer Graduate Scholarship Fund at Wisconsin.

Thayer's enthusiasm and service were manifested in three other areas on the Wisconsin campus—Sigma Chi fraternity; Delta Theta Phi, the law fraternity; and the campus humor magazine, the *Wisconsin Octopus*. He was the Sigma Chi national fraternity's grand annotator in 1923-1925, was adviser of the Wisconsin chapter in 1941-1961, was recognized with the rarely awarded Order of Constantine in 1948, and was honored by the dedication in 1964 to Thayer of a new Sigma Chi house. The law fraternity, Delta Theta Phi, was organized with Thayer's help, and he served as its adviser in 1949-1955. His sense of humor had another outlet in his advisership to the *Octopus* in 1945-1959.

He also was a member of the Institute of Newspaper Controllers and Finance Officers, serving on the publication committee; Inland Daily Press Association and its law committee; Newspaper Advertising Executives Association; National Newspaper

[14]Thayer, *Newspaper Business Management*, pp. 419, 416.
[15]"June Deadline for Journalist."

Promotion Association; Association for Education in Journalism; American Bar Association; Chicago Bar Association; the University Club; and the Masonic Order, 32d degree, and Shriners.

He wrote in his fields of law and media management until very near the end of his life, with *Avoiding Libel Liabilities* (1964) published as his last work. Other contributions to the literature of the field were co-editorship of *The Lee Papers* (1947) and authorship of articles in the *American Bar Association Journal*, *Forbes*, *Billboard*, and *Journalism Quarterly*.

Thayer was a scholar-teacher, lawyer-management specialist who infused the field of communication law with an understanding of the interaction of economic and legal variables. He stated this theme effectively in 1950: "Although anyone in the United States has the right to own and operate a printing press, this right does not provide the economic stability to continue such operation or to conduct a publishing business."[16]

---

[16]Thayer, "Shifting Concepts in Laws Affecting the Press," p. 25.

William F. Swindler
and the Constitution

"The Constitution provides no exception" to "abridging the free-dom of speech," wrote William F. Swindler (1913-1984). "Unless and until extreme and necessitous circumstances are shown, our aim should be to keep speech unfettered and to allow the processes of law to be invoked only when the provocateurs among us move from speech to action."[1]

Swindler's theoretic approach to freedom of expression stemmed from his deep, double interests in the roles of the insti-tutions of journalism and law in society. His secondary and un-dergraduate education occurred during the 1930s, a crucial, con-stitutional testing period of the First Amendment; he earned in 1935 AB and BS degrees from Washington University in St. Louis. His career-long relationship with legal historiography began dur-ing his graduate studies at the University of Missouri at Columbia, where he was graduated with the MA in 1936 and the PhD in 1942. There he developed an abiding interest in interna-tional press law through his doctoral dissertation, "Phases of In-ternational Law Affecting the Flow of International News." He would later say in his landmark journalism law bibliography that journalistic law cannot be defined without its international developments, through both historical understanding and the challenges of new technology.[2]

The St. Louis native, born October, 24, 1913, to Merton Clay and Nona Pearl (Traller) Swindler, really pursued two careers— the first, that of the journalism practitioner and educator, 1936-1956, and, the other, that of the attorney and legal historian, 1956-1984. Throughout his graduate studies and journalism-ori-ented career, he worked intermittently in the media while teach-ing at the University of Missouri as an instructor, 1938-1940; at the University of Idaho in Moscow, moving from assistant pro-

---

[1]William F. Swindler, *Problems of Law in Journalism* (New York: Macmillan, 1955), p. 37.

[2]William F. Swindler, *A Bibliography of Law on Journalism* (New York: Columbia University Press, 1957), p. 22.

fessor to professor and head of the Department of Journalism, 1940-1944; and at the School of Journalism in the University of Nebraska at Lincoln, 1946-1956, as a professor and director. His media experience during these 20 years included reporter and editorial writer for St. Louis *Star-Times*, 1936-1938; special correspondent, St. Louis *Post-Dispatch*, 1938-1940; editorial writer, Lincoln *State Journal*, 1946-1950; editorial columnist, Hastings *Tribune*, 1952; special correspondent, Columbia Broadcasting System, 1952; and freelance magazine writer. This background of academic and professional testing of legal and ethical behavior motivated Swindler in 1955 to make a proposal that was novel at the time among journalism law textbooks. He believed that journalism law teachers should expose their students to First Amendment law against the background of constitutional law and Anglo-American political philosophy. His conclusion: "To see the subject as a whole against this background is to make a creditable beginning toward the student's concept of a professional ethic of journalism."[3]

Also, during his academic-professional journalism period, Swindler wrote for *Journalism Quarterly* "Some Recent Legal Developments Relating to the Press," "The Press and Its Relationship to Administrative Law," and "The AP Anti-Trust Case in Historical Perspective"; "Confidence Law" for *National Publisher*; "Wartime News Controls in Canada" for *Public Opinion Quarterly*;[4] founded and edited a series of journalism bulletins for the University of Idaho, 1944-1946, and Nebraska, 1947; prepared his press law bibliography; served on the editorial board of *Journalism Quarterly*, 1945-1958; and wrote *Problems of Law in Journalism*, 1955.

The 1947 annotated bibliography, although now 40 years old, remains an excellent starting place for the communication law scholar with its more than 1,100 entries—books, treatises, journal articles, and special studies—dating back to 1844. Swindler selected them from more than 3,000 English-language works done in the previous 100 years. He launched the bibliography of journalistic law, which he described as "an obvious hybrid," to identify early works of lasting value and to provide "a guide to the selection of current and future material." Swindler's "A Bibliographic Note" is a masterful tour through the Anglo-American roots of press law, which dealt in the main with libel. He found that "a definite concept of journalistic law" began to emerge with

---

[3]Swindler, *Problems of Law in Journalism*, p. xx.

[4]William F. Swindler, "Some Recent Legal Developments Relating to the Press," *Journalism Quarterly* 16 (1939): 161-164; "The Press and Its Relationship to Administrative Law," *Journalism Quarterly* 18 (1941): 256-262; "The AP Anti-Trust Case in Historical Perspective," *Journalism Quarterly* 23 (1946): 40-57; "Confidence Law," *National Publisher* 21 (June 1941): 8; and "Wartime News Controls in Canada," *Public Opinion Quarterly* 6 (1942): 444-449.

James Paterson's *Freedom of Speech, Press and Public Worship* (1880) in England, Samuel Merrill's *Newspaper Libel* (1888) in the United States, Fisher and Strahan's *Law of the Press* (1891) in England, and a noticeably more abundant flow of periodical literature on journalistic subjects in the Yellow Journalism period. He attributed this development to the explosion of newspaper circulation in England and the United States in the last quarter of the 19th century. Swindler dealt very little in the essay with the 20th century textbooks on press law, noting only that the British journalistic law texts compared favorably with the American texts of Arthur and Crossman, Hale and Benson, Siebert, and Thayer.[5]

Swindler's textbook, *Problems of Law in Journalism*, was written after he had taught press law for 15 years, and represented a transition between the Siebert-Thayer textbook era and the books of today. Its scholarly depth demanded able and enthusiastic teachers, wrote Gayle Waldrop.[6] Swindler used a modified case approach to present "a selection of the pros and cons as to the basic principles affecting journalism." He believed "the student needs to trace the development of a judicial line of thought, not only in one case but in successive cases, and not only in the prevailing view of a majority on the bench at a given time but in the dissenting opinions of the minority."[7] To attempt to accomplish this comprehensive view of the issues, Swindler left out many procedural details and structured the presentation of chapters in a proposition-discussion-case order. The propositions were statements of what he deduced to be essential journalistic practices. For instance, under privacy, he asserted, "The right of privacy does not apply to news situations." Then he discussed the 1955 condition of the right of privacy and presented key passages from *Sidis v. F-R Publishing* (113 F. 2d 806, 1940), which protected *New Yorker* magazine's "ruthless disclosure" about a former child prodigy, and other cases.[8]

The foundation on which Swindler built the textbook was his answer to this question: "How shall the public interest in the regulation of private industry be reconciled with the public interest in the free flow of news?" He believed the solution to this dilemma was implicit in the "original constitutional protection of press freedom" but understood that the monopoly trend of business, including newspapers, had brought administrative law into the fray, challenging newspapers as editorial activity and business.[9]

Thus, Swindler presented the material in *Problems of Law in Journalism* in a sequence new to such textbooks—in three sec-

---

[5]Swindler, *A Bibliography of Law on Journalism*, pp. vi, 3-22, 8.

[6]Gayle Waldrop, review of *Problems of Law in Journalism*, by Swindler, in *Journalism Quarterly* 32 (1955): 230-231.

[7]Swindler, *Problems of Law in Journalism*, p. ix.

[8]Ibid., pp. 261-266.

[9]Ibid., p. 11.

tions relating the First Amendment to, first, the news side of newspapers; second, the business side of newspapers; and third, the newest challenge, "law of radio journalism," as Swindler termed it. The broadcast law section was embyronic compared to today's texts. Thayer's third edition of *Legal Control of the Press* (1956), the standard of the day, had included only a chapter about advertising in the non-news area and little discussion of the emerging broadcast law, except as it related to such areas as defamation.

Swindler's first premise was formed as the question, "What are the limits to press freedom?" which he answered through a discussion of the prior restraint cases *Near v. Minnesota* (283 U.S. 697), *Schenck v. United States* (249 U.S. 47), *Abrams v. United States* (250 U.S. 616), *DeJonge v. Oregon* (299 U.S. 353), and *Dennis v. United States* (841 U.S. 494). His solution of the problem is akin to Justice Hugo Black's distinction between speech and action. Swindler put it this way: "The command of the First Amendment is so clear that we should not allow Congress to call a halt to free speech except in the extreme case of peril from the speech itself," which he defined elsewhere as "action." However, he said, "This does not mean . . . that the Nation need hold its hand until it is in such weakened condition that there is not time to protect itself from incitement to revolution."[10]

Then, "what are the limits to public authority in restricting of expression?" Swindler asked in presenting his second principle. He laid out his answer in a discussion of the anti-litter case *Griffin v. Georgia* and its progeny: reasonable use of police power can be used to regulate time, place, and manner of expression, but any such plan is unconstitutional that fails to protect the First Amendment rights of communicators, willing recipients, and unwilling recipients.[11]

Swindler adopted for his textbook organization the now familiar tripartite structure of guarantees implicit in the press clause of the First Amendment: freedom of newsgathering, publication, and circulation. He led the way for later textbooks to present the case more logically than the pioneering works. Leaning on Harold Cross' *The People's Right to Know* (1953)[12] and other access works, Swindler echoed the alarm about officeholders who concluded that "secrecy is demanded by public policy and the public interest—a complete reversal of . . . the essence of democratic government: The people have a general right to examine the records maintained by their public servants."[13]

In another area—tort law—Swindler observed that the general principles of libel were in the most part arrived at by the courts

---

[10]Ibid., p. 37.

[11]Ibid., pp. 38-39.

[12]Harold Cross, *The People's Right to Know* (New York: Columbia University Press, 1953).

[13]Ibid., p. 77.

before World War I, were fundamentally sound, and were elemental to guiding a reporter's practical newsgathering. Swindler, who believed that one obligation of the press law teacher was to help students find the trends in law, did presage implicitly the controversy that would develop in the next decade because of the *New York Times v. Sullivan* (376, U.S. 254, 1964) actual malice doctrine. Comparison of the Swindler generalization about "malice in fact" with the *Saturday Evening Post v. Butts* (388 U.S. 130) "actual malice" definition illustrates the shift that would occur. Swindler wrote, "The law will assume that the failure of the newspaper to verify the particular statement upon which the defamation rests is due to a willful disregard of the rights of the individual generally"; the Supreme Court majority wrote in *Butts* (1967) that actual malice is "extreme departure from the standards of investigation and reporting ordinarily adhered to by responsible publishers."[14]

Swindler treated another tort, right of privacy, less thoroughly than Thayer, and Swindler did not sense the likelihood of the argument that Prosser would make in 1960 that privacy was four torts, not one. For instance, Swindler's generalization that "the right of privacy does not apply to news situations" failed to recognize two developing torts of privacy invasion—false light and public disclosure. However, Swindler alerted media and scholars very early to the dangers of an infliction of emotional distress tort, which emerged in the "intentional infliction" form in the 1980s.[15]

In other areas, Swindler taught that courts tend to interpret shield laws narrowly, reducing their effectiveness, and that in the copyright area Congress, but not the courts, failed in providing protection of news from unfair competition among media. He included only four pages about obscenity and newspapers, disregarding the state of obscenity law in the decades before the *Roth* decision brought in the national community standard rule. Swindler's Problems section about the business side of the newspaper emphasized the constitutional testing of the New Deal attempts to reorder a bankrupt and wartime society, including its news media. Swindler believed that the applications of anti-trust law in *AP v. United States* (1945) to news media "in its historical perspective . . . would seem to be too belated to have achieved more than a theoretical adjustment in American journalism,"[16] a prescient observation given the increased media monopolization pattern of late.

Shortly after the appearance of *Problems of Law in Journalism* and after 20 years as a journalism educator, Swindler was drawn more by the attraction of law than by his commitment to

---

[14]Ibid., p. 149.

[15]Swindler, "Some Recent Legal Developments Relating to the Press," pp. 163-164.

[16]Swindler, "The AP Anti-Trust Case in Historical Perspective," p. 57.

newspapers. He abandoned journalism administration and teaching and in 1958 finished the LLB at the University of Nebraska, was admitted to the Nebraska Bar, and was appointed professor of legal history and director of development at Marshall-Wythe School of Law at the College of William and Mary in Williamsburg, Virginia. In this later stage of his career, even more distinguished than his journalism stage, he served as general counsel to the Virginia Commission on Constitutional Revision, 1968-1969; editor and director for the Research Project on State Constitutions beginning in 1968; chairman of the ad hoc committee on Supreme Court History for the Judicial Conference of the United States, 1972-1974; and member of the publications committee of the Virginia Independence Bicentennial Committee.

Although he no longer wrote extensively about press law at William and Mary, he delved even more deeply into the roots and interpretation of constitutional history. His books included *Common Law in America* (1959), *Magna Carta: Legend and Legacy* (1965), *Magna Carta* (1968), *Government by the People: Theory and Reality in Virginia* (1969), three volumes of *Court and Constitution in the 20th Century* (1969, 1970, 1973), *Justice in the States* (1971), 10 volumes of *Sources and Documents of United States Constitutions* (1972-1974), *The Course of Human Events: The Continental Congress, 1774-1789* (1974), and *Principles of Constitutional Law* (1974).[17] In the field of legal history, he also was a contributor to *Encyclopedia Americana* and wrote frequently for various bar journals.

The journalist-legal historian created a leadership niche for himself among his peers during both of his careers. He served as vice president of the American Association of Journalism Teachers in 1946, a director in 1960 and vice president in 1962-1964 of the American Society for Legal History, and a director of the American Judicature Society beginning in 1972. He was a member of the American Bar Association, British Society of Public Teachers of Law, American Law Institute, National Lawyers Club, District of Columbia Bar Association, Virginia Bar Association, Selden Society, and Phi Delta Phi.

Swindler's impact on the developing field of communication law, had he continued in it until his death in 1984, could have been even more important than the works he did produce. Nevertheless, he did help shape press law education through his transitional textbook with its emphasis on understanding trends of the law, his trailblazing press law bibliography, his model of the

---

[17]William F. Swindler, *Magna Carta: Legend and Legacy* (Indianapolis: Bobbs-Merrill, 1965); *Government by the People: Theory and Reality in Virginia* (Charlottesville: University Press of Virginia, 1969);*Court and Constitution in the 20th Century* (Indianapolis: Bobb-Merrill, 1969); *Sources and Documents of United States Constitutions* (Dobbs Ferry, N.Y.: Oceana Publications, 1982).

modified case method in the classroom, his suggestion that ethics and law are inextricable, and the constitutional books of his later period, which are relevant to the foundational work of today's legists.

J. Edward Gerald
and the Political Method

J. Edward Gerald (1906-), the intellectual giant of this sextuplet of legists, has spent his life in various sections of the Great Plains, learning about what Texas editor Frank Grimes called the "mudsills of human liberty"—the "unalienable rights" of the First Amendment to the Constitution—and societal interaction.[1]

He was born May 6, 1906, in Evant in central Texas, near Waco, to hotelkeeper James Edward and Martha Alice Gerald, who moved to West Texas when he was 11. The first 30 years of his life would expose him, from the vantage point of the Great Plains, to a world war, two droughts, and the Great Depression—impressing upon him the need for improvement of society's institutions. He recalls the 1930s particularly as a time when people were driven "from the carnivals of trade to the temples of the mind in quest of patterns of social and economic justice."[2] His parents generated for him a love of reading. They were permissive with him about religion; his father was an agnostic and his mother a Baptist.[3] He discovered a love of journalism when his high school teachers praised his writing. The first step in his post-secondary education was to earn a bachelor of arts degree in English from West Texas State University in Canyon in 1927. While in college he served as editor of the college newspaper and worked on a weekly newspaper and on a daily in the summers. These times and places colored his later seminal thinking and writing. The West Texas frontier of Gerald's formative years was more aristocratic than democratic—a laboratory in which strength was tested by strength and rugged individualism was tempered only by fundamentalist, Calvinist religion and moral attitudes. The latter influence caused its citizens to adopt personal rules of responsibility that tempered rugged individualism in the interest of

---

[1]Frank Grimes, editorial, Abilene (Tex) *Reporter-News*, 6 August 1945.

[2]J. Edward Gerald, *The Press and the Constitution 1931-1947* (Minneapolis: University of Minnesota Press, 1948), p. 1.

[3]Gerald, interview by author, 11 June 1987.

helping others.[4] The unique West Texas mixture of fiercely held individual freedoms, aristocracy, and social helpfulness shaped the attitudes even of those who rejected the Calvinistic doctrine as Gerald did. This societal mix provided the context of the early development of Gerald's beliefs that media should serve the other social institutions necessary to self-government.

Gerald left Texas for the University of Missouri and earned a bachelor of journalism degree in 1928 and a master of arts in journalism in 1932. In between these two degrees he was a staff correspondent for United Press in Denver in 1928 and editor of the Canyon *News* and manager of Warwick Printing Company in 1929. He first taught journalism at Missouri, as an instructor in 1929-1930, an assistant professor in 1930-1935, an associate professor in 1935-1946, and acting dean in 1941-1942. He took a sabbatical in 1936-1937 to work as a copyreader on the St. Louis *Star-Times* and was manager in 1937-1941 of the Missouri Press Association, Inc. He completed the PhD in political science at the University of Minnesota in 1945 and became a professor of journalism in 1946 at Minnesota, where he served until his retirement in 1974.

Two scholars in the early years of his Missouri-Minnesota period, Gerald believes, most profoundly influenced journalism education and helped shape his ideas: Willard G. Bleyer of Wisconsin and Walter Williams of Missouri, Bleyer because of his doctrine that journalism should be used to improve society and Williams because he was a man of action who invoked "in journalists a sense of effort and idealism." Gerald described Bleyer as a "modest prairie radical" because of his dedication to improving society for others,[5] a role that Gerald himself would come to fulfill.

During his Minnesota years he was a Guggenheim Fellow in Britain in 1953-1954 and an occasional student at the London School of Economics and Political Science in 1953-1956; a consultant with the Governmental Studies Division of The Brookings Institution in Washington, D.C., in 1964-1966; and a visiting professor at the University of Texas-Austin in 1966. He developed in his teaching, research, and writing a triology of interests— freedom of expression, media economics, and social responsibility of the press—and produced significant works in all three areas. Chronologically, his books are *Statutes of the State of Missouri Relating to Notice by Publication*, ed. (1935), *The Press and the Constitution* (1948), *The British Press Under Government Economic Controls* (1956), *The Social Responsibility of the Press* (1963), and *News of Crime* (1983). He also wrote chapters in books:

---

[4]A. C. Green, *A Personal Country* (New York: Alfred A. Knopf, 1969), pp. 120-121.

[5]Gerald, interview by R. Smith Schuneman, 9 July 1971, Minneapolis, manuscript, AEJ Archives in State Historical Society of Wisconsin, Madison.

"The Role of the Press" in *Controlling Human Behavior* (1959), "Freedom in Mass Communication" in *Social Science and Freedom* (1955), three chapters about world opinion and democracy in *Guide to the Study of World Affairs* (1951), and "Cost Comparisons" in *Solutions to Urgent Financial and Accounting Problems of Daily Newspapers* (1951).[6]

He wrote numerous reports, monographs, and journal articles focused on his three primary interests. His most important articles in press freedom were *The Outlook for International Press Freedom* (1947), "Study of Press Freedom Teaches American Heritage," "Abstract of A.V. Miller," "Right to Know, But How Much?" "Truth and Error—Journalism's Tournament of Reason," and "Press-Bar Relationships: Progress Since Sheppard and Reardon."[7]

He served as editor of the *Missouri Press News and Bulletin* of the Missouri Press Association (1937-1941), editor of the foreign bibliography section of *Journalism Quarterly* (1945-1953), vice president (1951) and president (1952) of the Association for Education in Journalism, chairman of the AEJ Committee on Professional Freedom and Responsibility (1951-1953) and member (1953-1967), member of the *Bulletin* Committee and Steering Committee of the Institute of Newspaper Controllers and Finance Officers (1949-1955), member of the Board of Student Publications at Minnesota, consultant for the Program of Information on World Affairs for public schools of the Minneapolis *Star* (1947-1950) and member of its Advisory Committee (1951-1969), president of the Minnesota chapter of the American Association of University Professors (1955-1956), member of American Civil Liberties Union (Minnesota branch), member of American Political Science Association, and a charter member of the Minnesota Press Council. He also received a McMillan Fund grant for study in England (1966), the Sigma Delta Chi national award for distinguished research in 1948 for *The Press and the Constitution, 1931-1947*, the AEJ Theory and Methods Division award, and the Sigma Delta Chi Distinguished Teacher Award in 1974. After his retirement he stayed active as a visiting lecturer at Indiana, Texas-Austin, and Utah.

In the classroom at Minnesota, "Mr. Press and Society," as he

---

[6]J. Edward Gerald, *The British Press Under Government Economic Controls* (Minneapolis: University of Minnesota Press, 1965); *The Social Responsibility of the Press* (Minneapolis: University of Minnesota Press, 1963); *News of Crime* (Westport, Conn.: Greenwood Press, 1983); Daniel Starch, *Controlling Human Behavior* (New York: Macmillan, 1936).

[7]J. Edward Gerald, "Study of Press Freedom Teaches American Heritage," *Journalism Quarterly* 26 (1949): 112-114; "Abstract of A.V. Miller," *Journalism Quarterly* 26 (1949): 77-78; "Right to Know, But How Much?" *International Press Institute Report* (1967); "Truth or Error—Journalism's Tournament of Reason, *Quill* (1969): 12; and "Press-Bar Relationships: Progress Since Sheppard and Reardon," *Journalism Quarterly* 47 (1970): 223-232.

was sometimes known, was unrelenting in his insistence that performance reach the highest of professional standards.[8] Everett E. Dennis of the Gannett Center for Media Studies, a Gerald-trained doctoral product, recalls a case method law course in which the students were required to write analytically about 600 memorized cases. It was "the toughest exam I ever took," says Dennis. "He was a demanding and difficult man, a formidable taskmaster, who pushed his students into productive work and roles."[9] Among other scholars he trained were Harold L. Nelson of Wisconsin, Alex Edelstein of Washington, Donald Gillmor of Minnesota, Richard Gray of Indiana, and Daniel W. Pfaff of Pennsylvania State, plus virtually every other doctoral candidate during his Minnesota tenure. Gerald's disciples hold him in awe as they have developed an almost spiritual relationship with him. His rigorous organization—not great speaking ability—marked his lecture method; a parallel rigor drove the critical, analytical emphasis he gave to his research and writing.

Gerald's rich background of English, journalism, political theory, economics, and sociological inquiry—plus his intellectual brilliance—enabled him to combine the tools of all these disciplines in his methodology. He called upon quantitative data and documentary methods to create scholarship that was "essentially humanistic . . . linked to a penetrating philosophical inquiry."[10] He contributed significantly to the "media as social institutions" movement, building on the foundations laid by Bleyer, Ralph Casey, Fredrick S. Siebert, and others. In the First Amendment area, Dennis believes that "no other media law scholar . . . ever came close to Gerald's intense intellectuality and prowess." His first major legal work is marked by the influence of Zechariah Chaffee (author of *Free Speech in the United States* [1942])[11] and other constitutional scholars more than the pioneers in press law.

The Press and the Constitution, 1931-1947 stands as a landmark in the historiography of First Amendment literature by journalism scholars. Gerald uniquely addressed the issue of press law from the totality of the First Amendment, including the speech, assembly, and religion clauses. Gerald's political science, economic, and sociological approaches provided the scope necessary to divorce his work from the press-centric approach of Fredrick S. Siebert and others.

His purpose in *The Press and the Constitution* was to analyze critically the development of constitutional protection of the

---

[8]SJMC Alumni Newsletter, School of Journalism and Mass Communication, University of Minnesota, May 1974, pp. 1, 6.

[9]Everett E. Dennis, New York, to author, 12 December 1986.

[10]Gerald, *The Press and the Constitution*, p. 3, and "Study of Press Freedom Teaches American Heritage," p. 71.

[11]Zechariah Chaffee, *Free Speech in the United States* (Cambridge: Harvard University Press, 1941).

press between *Near v. Minnesota* and the Wagner Act, and he understood that non-media cases were shaping the press clause as much as explicit press cases. So the reader finds analysis of the implications for the press clause of First Amendment issues in such spheres as labor policy, picketing, freedom of religion, use of streets and parks for assembly and speech, and others.

Gerald was almost alone in arguing that freedom of the press depended on broader issues than "Congress shall make no law abridging . . . freedom of the press." He was helping new communication law scholars to discover that the essence and richness of the First Amendment lie in the protection of expression for everyone in the marketplace of ideas—not just for the press. "Freedom of speech and press," he wrote, "are the same, involving the same legal principles and the same public interests," and he echoed these sentiments in a 1949 article when he described freedom of speech and press the "master matrix of all liberty."

He also astutely analyzed the controversy about whether to leave freedom of the press and the attainment of socially directed goals to the editorial virtue of editors or to government intervention. The Hutchins Commission recommended in 1947 the latter alternative. Gerald concluded that neither approach in the controversy was adequate to the task of changing the press when it needed change, and that "the government by its very nature is an unfit guardian of the welfare of its chief critic."[12] Gerald's proposals in this area of press responsiveness would appear in book form 14 years later in *The Social Responsibility of the Press*.

Also notable in his *Press and the Constitution* was his discussion of the abuse of licensing in the 1930s and 1940s. "Men," he wrote, "had struggled against this type of restraint for long in England and America; this was not the time or the place to revive it." The way in which the U.S. Supreme Court in the licensing cases clarified liberty in the marketplace of ideas for religious sects and the labor movement caused Gerald to conclude that many groups would "benefit from the spread of liberty horizontally among the people." He believed the press would always owe a debt to the Jehovah's Witnesses for their successful battle to clarify personal freedoms.[13]

In *The Social Responsiblity of the Press*, Gerald sought to observe the interactions of major social institutions, including the press, and to explore "ways in which the media may contribute more to the development of institutions that make up our civilization." He identified biased, special-interest institutions as the major counterforce of freedom of speech and press—forces that would subvert the Miltonic tournament of reason. He reiterated his conviction that government should deal only with the worst abuses of the press, that "the press, then, must monitor itself or

---

[12]Gerald, *The Press and the Constitution*, p. 9.
[13]Ibid., p. 140.

deny any responsibility for or loyalty to social norms."[14]

He provided two steps for preservation of an open society and press freedom. First, he would "provide the press with personnel able to understand the intricate problems of the day and competent to make an adequate appraisal." Second, he would "rehabilitate in the community the principles that were in the minds of the founders of the free-enterprise community, those ethical assumptions that led them to believe that a self-righting process exists and that it assures the correction of errors."[15]

The primary technique he proposed for implementation of his two steps was professionalization, including: strengthening of ethics codes; creative solutions to editor-owner rivalry; upgrading of journalism education and employment patterns to a three-level structure for journalists with baccalaureate, master's, and doctoral preparation; development of press councils; and achievement of professional status by the quasi-professional national media associations. "The profession," he wrote, "then would be in a position, for the first time, to deal with public misunderstanding of the media."[16]

He comported with the Siebert premise that freedom tends to erode when society is fearful and under stress, and he wrote that the "political truce represented by the First Amendment" could collapse unless "the majority benefits from the guarantee of freedom of the press."[17] If the First Amendment is weakened, he believed, the collapse of society's confidence in one of its social institutions—the news media—would be the agent that would release the anti-freedom forces of an interventionist state.

Controversial though they be in some journalism quarters, Gerald's ideas about social responsibility, professionalism, press councils, and preservation of freedom of expression were seminal forces in journalism education of the 1950s and 1960s—a major contribution to the development of the study of media as social institutions. As a scholar and teacher, he was a model of the blending of the philosophy and tools of constitutional law, politics, economics, and sociology—of the integration of science and the humanities—of the cross-breeding of individualism and servanthood native to his Great Plains roots. Foremost, he devoted himself to teaching students about personal liberties "so that, in their own time and necessity . . . they shall be willing to go to the personal trouble required to preserve those rights."[18] Gerald's catalytic writings, comparatively the most original of these legists, are worthy of renewed study by the late 20th-century generation of critical theorists.

---

[14]Gerald, *The Social Responsibility of the Press*, pp. 3, 149.

[15]Ibid., p. 149.

[16]Ibid., p. 195.

[17]Ibid., p. 198.

[18]Gerald, "Study of Press Freedom Teaches American Heritage," p. 68.

Harold L. Nelson
and Historical Continuity

Harold L. Nelson (1917-) answered the need of a new generation of mass comunications law teachers and students when the Supreme Court altered so much rudimentary press law in the 8 years between 1957 and 1965 by its decisions in *Yates, Roth, Sullivan, Hill, Sheppard,* and *Estes.* With one of his former doctoral students in history and law, Dwight L. Teeter Jr., he fine-tuned the methods of the historian and the legal scholar to produce a treatise to replace Swindler's *Problems of Law in Journalism* (1955) and Thayer's *Legal Control of the Press* (1962). Nelson had written the chapter about contempt in Thayer's fourth edition, which had led Thayer to ask Nelson if he wanted to write Foundation Press' new textbook.[1] Nelson enlisted Teeter's help, and their ground-breaking textbook was *Law of Mass Communications: Freedom and Control of the Print and Broadcast Media* (1969, 1973, 1978, 1982, 1986)—an analytical, expository presentation aimed at providing historical context to the task of teaching practitioners how to avoid contemporary legal problems.

Nelson, a libertarian in freedom of expression who disclaims absolutism, was educated in his home state of Minnesota. He was born November 28, 1917, in Fergus Falls to Charles and Drusilla Hodgson Nelson, and studied journalism, history, and law at the University of Minnesota, earning the BA in 1941, the MA in 1950, and the PhD in 1956. His research and writing interest developed during those graduate school days, inspired by two key figures in the historiography of press law: his major professor J. Edward Gerald and the history and legal scholar Fredrick S. Siebert. Nelson was the first PhD student of Gerald and the first Minnesota journalism doctoral alumnus; he and Siebert developed close working ties because of their similar research interests.

But Nelson's enthusiasm about the classroom did not emerge until after some professional experience, 5 years of military service during World War II, and his master's work. He worked in public relations for Time Life, Inc. in Minneapolis in 1941; be-

---

[1]Harold L. Nelson, interview by author, 11 June 1987.

came a Naval lieutenant during the war; went back into public relations with the Minneapolis Northwestern National Bank in 1946-1947; and was a reporter and editor with United Press in Minneapolis in 1947-1950.

His entry into an academic career came via an appointment as an assistant professor of journalism at Texas Tech University, Lubbock, in 1950-1951. Then came short periods at State University of Iowa, Iowa City, as an instructor in 1951-1952 and at University of California, Berkeley, as an assistant professor in 1954-1955. He moved to the University of Wisconsin, Madison, in 1955, rose to professor in 1963, and was director of the School of Journalism from 1966 until his retirement from administration in 1975. He was Gonzales Professor of Journalism at the University of South Carolina in 1976 and became professor emeritus at Wisconsin in 1981.

Published fruits of his historical-legal work began to appear in the late 1950s, including "Seditious Libel in Colonial America" in *American Journal of Legal History*,[2] then his first book, a specialized study titled *Libel in News of Congressional Investigating Committees* (1961).[3] His next book, most important alongside *Law of Mass Communications,* was *Freedom of the Press from Hamilton to the Warren Court* (1967).

For this book Nelson gathered and edited documents of 1800-1965—including military orders, court decisions, statutes, speeches, essays, and significant sections from books—to tell the undulating saga of press freedom in the United States. He distilled the nation's struggles with freedom concepts into an introductory essay that enriched the book, which was the second in the American Heritage Series; the first volume was Leonard W. Levy's *Freedom of the Press from Zenger to Jefferson.*[4] Hazel Dicken Garcia selected Nelson's book as an instructive example of an explanatory history that departs from works based on the great man theory and how scholarly synthesis of documents can reveal the past.[5] Levy and Alfred Young wrote in a preface to *Hamilton to the Warren Court* that Nelson "succinctly described and analyzed the evolution of freedom of the press" in a "remarkable compression of . . . its vicissitudes, and its complexities . . . [and] contributed to our understanding of the problems, if not to the solutions."[6]

---

[2] Harold L. Nelson, "Seditious Libel in Colonial America," *American Journal of Legal History* 3 (1959): 160.

[3] Harold L. Nelson, *Libel in News of Congressional Investigating Committees* (Minneapolis: University of Minnesota Press, 1961).

[4] Leonard W. Levy, *Freedom of the Press from Zenger to Jefferso.* (Indianapolis: Bobbs-Merrill, 1966).

[5] Hazel Dicken Garcia, "Journalism and Communication History" in John D. Stevens and Garcia (Eds.), *Communication History* (Beverly Hills: Sage Publications, 1980), p. 24.

[6] Leonard W. Levy and Alfred Young in Harold L. Nelson (Ed.), *Freedom of the Press from Hamilton to Warren* (Indianapolis: Bobbs-Merrill, 1967), p. viii.

Nelson concluded that the United States press of 1960 was freer than it had ever been because of rejection of the "ancient legal restraints of English origin and American adoption." His research led him to the judgment that the American press was freest in the first and last thirds of the 1800s and between 1930 and 1965 with a constricting spasm in the 1950s, in which the government developed a propensity for secrecy. The most restrictive eras in his analysis were 1830-1861, a peacetime period, and 1900-1930, a wartime period. Impressed with the 1930-1965 actions of the U.S. Supreme Court, Nelson placed his faith in the court as "the nation's foremost agency for the furtherance of freedom of the press."[7] He applauded particularly the Warren Court record. In hindsight, one notable omission from Nelson's documentary work was the landmark Warren and Brandeis article "The Right to Privacy" from the 1890 *Harvard Law Review*, from which so much privacy law has been drawn.

When *Law of Mass Communications* appeared in 1969, Sigma Delta Chi, now the Society of Professional Journalists, honored co-authors Nelson and Teeter with its annual award for outstanding research in journalism. Nelson wrote the chapters dealing with the freedom of the press, including its historical and theoretical background; prior restraint; defamation; contempt of court and reporter privilege; access to federal and state meetings and records; and regulation of broadcasting.

Among Nelson's premises was the belief that "the Constitutional imperatives, libertarian in spirit and voice, yet provide certain boundaries to speech and press" in the interest of the individual and society. However, he also observed that in every society some individuals "hate and fear the expression of ideas contrary to their own." Thus, Nelson wrote, "The hand of authority rests light on speech and press at some places and times, heavily at others"[8]—the practical outcome of Siebert's government-society stress and structure theory.

Grafted to Nelson's acceptance of the First Amendment as a libertarian, but not absolute, guarantee, was his appreciation for the U.S. Supreme Court's intervention into individual state abridgement of personal liberties—allowed until *Gitlow v. New York* (1925). The court accepted "a principle long sought by libertarians," said Nelson, by making the Fourteenth Amendment "a barrier to states' depriving citizens of . . . protected liberty of speech and press."[9]

He advocated striking balances under the First and Fourteenth Amendments, and he underscored balancing by encouraging the consideration of competing values in defamation suits: public officials and public figures versus the press, and private

---

[7]Nelson, *Freedom of the Press from Hamilton to Warren*, pp. xlvii-1, xxv, xxi.

[8]Law of Mass Communications, p. 1.

[9]Ibid., p. 40.

individuals versus the press. The "Public Principle," Nelson wrote, goes far back into the law of defamation; it was the principle that in self-governing societies robust debate furthered public good and values. The principle matured to the point the Supreme Court gave First Amendment protection to expression about public officials and figures and protected such material to the point that public plaintiffs could not win compensation for defamation unless they proved actual malice occurred. But the Public Principle and First Amendment protection were not extended to stories about private individuals, and Nelson explained that "society's stake in providing protection against libel to private people is also high, and such people are to be put to a somewhat less stern test than the constitutional barrier of proving actual malice."[10]

Another worrisome balance has been the press and court claims surrounding reporter privilege—the competing attempts to fulfill the public's right to know. The press argues for source confidentiality; the government argues for source disclosure; both argue in the name of the people. Nelson took the position that journalists who asserted that "the First Amendment . . . has protected the craft historically against compelling testimony have not reckoned with the course of court decisions."[11] He described journalists in the pre- and post-*Branzburg* (408 U.S. 665, 1972) era as naive about the history of shield legislation and statements in *Branzburg* that promised protection against "bad faith investigations" and for "legitimate First Amendment interests." Nelson decried, however, the "unlovely fact" that more reporters went to jail in the 1970s, in spite of state shield laws, than for any offense since the 1798-1800 Alien and Sedition Acts. Although some state shield statutes are labeled "absolute," Nelson called absolute protection a chimera. In terms of compromising bona fide shield legislation, the Janet Cooke-Washington *Post* scandal troubled Nelson because Cooke's invented story tended to confirm the arguments of critics who said unethical reporters could use shield laws to conceal dishonest reporting. Nelson's forecast: "These issues and questions run deep. They are not likely to be resolved for all sides soon."

Moving from arguments for confidentiality to arguments for disclosure, Nelson wrote in his section about federal and state open meetings and records an effective sequel to Harold Cross' *The People's Right to Know* and to Cross' idea that freedom of information is integral to the guarantees of the Consitution. Nelson explained the historical FoI role of Cross, the Freedom of Information Center at the University of Missouri, professional journalism organizations, the scientific community, and access advocate Rep. John E. Moss, and presented an exposition of the state and federal access laws rooted in the FoI movement. He concluded that the abuse of executive privilege by the Nixon administration

---

[10]Ibid., p. 137.

[11]Ibid., pp. 357, 361, 371, 380-382, 383.

led to broadened public support for access policies,[12] a phenomenon reversed by the Reagan administration's information policies.

Because broadcasting regulation had matured considerably by the first edition of the treatise in 1969, Nelson also researched and wrote one of the first satisfactorily thorough, narrative treatments of broadcast regulation. In later editions he developed a section about the dual system of protection for broadcast and print media. In discussing *Red Lion*, Nelson observed, "Freedom of expression is a weak freedom as applied to broadcasting" when compared to the strong protection for the "freedom to be unfair" in print; in discoursing about *Miami Herald v. Tornillo*, he wrote that "once again . . . the First Amendment shield proved stronger for printed journalism than for broadcast."[13] His position agreed with the FCC finding that the Fairness Doctrine inhibits constitutional protection of broadcasting. His position also agreed with President Ronald Reagan's 1987 veto of the Congressional bill created to embed the Fairness Doctrine in statutory law. In *The Law of Mass Communications*, Nelson also unfolded an interesting comparison of prior restraint in *Near v. Minnesota* (1931) and *Trinity Methodist Church v. FRC* (62 F. 2d 850, 1932). Minnesota was prohibited from closing a scandalous newspaper; the FRC was permitted to deny a license renewal of a sensationalistic radio station.

With *The Law of Mass Communications*, Nelson helped lead communication law teachers and students into the last quarter of the 20 century. Nelson also liked to teach journalistic writing and editing in addition to the law and history of mass communications. His career carried him into Wisconsin administration and national leadership, particularly with AEJ. He also was a member of the International Association for Mass Communications Research, the American Historical Association, Organization of American Historians, Wisconsin Historical Society, Madison Press Club, Milwaukee Press Club, Madison Literary Club, the national journalism honor society Kappa Tau Alpha, and the Society of Professional Journalists, Sigma Delta Chi. He contributed frequently to journalism and law journals and was a member of the editorial board of *Journalism History*.

His leadership within AEJ included the presidency of the organization in 1967, and he was chairman of the committee that led the reorganization of AEJ in 1965 along specialized, divisional lines, including Divisions of Law and History. At the 1981 convention at East Lansing, Michigan, AEJ honored Nelson with the Paul J. Deutschmann Award, the association's most prestigious award for excellence in research. Wayne Danielson, chairman of the Research Division, said in a hyperbolic presentation: "Nelson's work in law and history has done more to shape the na-

---

[12]Ibid., pp. 393-422.
[13]Ibid., pp. 510, 514.

ture and character of these fields in journalism education than the work of any other contemporary teacher." Others among this sextuplet of legists—especially Gerald and Siebert—could lay claim to this evaluation. Two former Wisconsin Ph.D. students of Nelson in history and law presented papers at the 1981 AEJ convention in his honor: Donald L. Shaw's "At the Crossroads: Change and Continuity in American Press News, 1820-1860," and Teeter's legal treatise "You Can't Think Without Facts." James W. Schwartz summarized Nelson's influence in "HLN—The Character and Career," and the Law Division conducted a symposium in his honor about approaches to the study of media controls titled "The Cutting Edge of the Past."[14]

His legacy in mass communication law is synergistic. He brought to First Amendment freedom research and writing in the 1960s the philosophy and tools of the qualitative historian. He left to media law scholars an appetite for legal history and a greater appreciation for the historical struggle to preserve the liberties guaranteed by the U.S. Constitution.

---

[14]"Nelson receives AEJ award," *AEJ Newsletter*, October 1981, p. 3.

5

The Theorists

James W. Tankard, Jr.
University of Texas

The Theorists

Communication theorists attempt to develop systems or broad principles that will help explain the phenomena of mass communication. Theory can be thought of in a number of ways, but for our purposes we can use a definition from Wilbur Schramm: "By theory here is meant a set of related statements, at a high level of abstraction, from which propositions can be generated that are testable by scientific measurement and on the basis of which predictions can be made about behavior."[1] Communication theory has to be created or constructed by researchers and theorists, and the building of theory is no easy task. It is worth the effort, however, because good theory should add to our understanding of mass communication. It should enable us to make accurate predictions about the outcomes of communication events and situations. And it should enable us to exert more control over the mass communication process.

Much of the first mass communication theory was developed by scholars working in other fields, including sociologist Robert Park, political scientist Harold Lasswell, sociologist Paul Lazarsfeld, and psychologist Carl Hovland. These researchers were contributing to mass communication theory primarily in the period of 1920-1960.

A major push in the direction of research and theory from within the field of journalism education came from Willard G. Bleyer, the founder in 1912 of the journalism program at the University of Wisconsin. Even though Bleyer held a PhD in English, he elected to link journalism education and scholarship with the social sciences rather than the humanities. Bleyer himself taught seminars at Wisconsin in "Press and Society" and "Content Analysis."[2] He issued a call in 1924 for journalism research on accuracy and completeness, the influence of editorials in bringing re-

---

[1]Wilbur Schramm, "The Challenge to Communication Research," in Ralph O. Nafziger and David M. White (Eds.), *Introduction to Mass Communications Research* (Baton Rouge: Louisiana State University Press, 1963), p. 10.

[2]Transcript of interview with Ralph Nafziger, July 8, 1970, AEJ collection, State Historical Society of Wisconsin.

forms, and the effects of competition on news policy.[3] He also created at Wisconsin in the early 1930s a PhD minor in journalism in the doctoral programs in political science and sociology.[4] Many important journalism educators came out of that PhD minor program, including Chilton Bush, Ralph Nafziger, Fred Siebert, Curtis MacDougall, and Ralph Casey. Bleyer's emphasis on a social science approach eventually had a great effect on the entire field of journalism education, with many programs following Bleyer's curriculum.

Wilbur Schramm, who became director of the School of Journalism at the University of Iowa in 1943, also did much to spur journalism researchers to think about mass communication theory. While at Iowa, he proposed a new interdisciplinary doctorate of communication degree. His books—particularly *Mass Communications* and *The Process and Effects of Mass Communication*[5]—were attempts to define the new field of mass communication based on a social science approach.

Research and theory in mass communication took a noteworthy step forward in the 1950s, when the first so-called "rump session" took place at the annual Association for Education in Journalism convention. A number of graduate students and faculty members in the area of communication theory and research methods had begun to complain that the annual AEJ meetings did not include the presentation of research papers, as did annual meetings of associations in sociology, political science, and other fields. Several scholars got together at the 1955 AEJ meeting at Boulder, Colorado, in a post-convention meeting that became the first "rump session." Wilbur Schramm stopped at the rump session on a side trip while driving from the University of Illinois to take his new job at Stanford. Schramm entered the meeting late but apologized, saying, "Sorry I'm late; I sat up all night with a sick factor analysis."[6]

Wayne Danielson, who attended the first rump session as a graduate student from Stanford, recalls that there were 30 or 40 people in the room.[7] Papers presented at the rump session in-

---

[3]Jack M. McLeod and Jay G. Blumler, "The Macrosocial Level of Communication Science," in Charles R. Berger and Steven H. Chaffee (Eds.), *Handbook of Communication Science* (Newbury Park, CA: Sage, 1987), p. 283.

[4]David H. Weaver and Richard G. Gray, *Journalism & Mass Communication Research in the United States: Past, Present & Future* (Bloomington: School of Journalism, Indiana University, 1979), p. 3.

[5]Wilbur Schramm (Ed.), *Mass Communications* (Urbana: University of Illinois Press, 1949); Wilbur Schramm (Ed.), *The Process and Effects of Mass Communication* (Urbana: University of Illinois Press, 1954).

[6]Edwin Emery and Joseph P. McKerns, "AEJMC: 75 Years in the Making. A History of Organizing for Journalism and Mass Communication Education in the United States." *Journalism Monographs* 104 (November, 1987): 39.

[7]Interview with Wayne A. Danielson, Sept. 25, 1989.

cluded one on the measurement of meaning by Charles Osgood and Percy Tannenbaum of Illinois, one on Cloze Procedure by Wilson Taylor of Illinois, and the first presentation of the Westley-MacLean model by Bruce Westley and Malcolm MacLean of Wisconsin.

In a few years, research paper sessions were a regular part of the AEJ convention.[8] The rump group influenced the general convention in another way. The researchers had begun the custom of meeting in December to plan the following year's rump session. These meetings became known as MURUMP, for Midwestern University Rump sessions, because they always met in the midwest. This kind of winter planning session seemed like a good idea to others in the association, and they began to copy it, thus leading to the AEJMC-wide winter meetings still held to plan the upcoming convention.[9]

Much of the early work in mass communication theory was aimed at two goals: investigating the *effects* of mass communication, and attempting to formulate a *model* of mass communication. These two goals were particularly important to theorists working in the 1940s. Effects research became especially popular, with the study of election campaigns by Lazarsfeld and his associates at Columbia University and the study of attitude change by Hovland and his associates at Yale University being prominent examples. The emphasis on effects came to some extent from early attempts to apply scientific method to the study of mass communication, since scientific method is often aimed at determining *causes* and *effects*. The emphasis on effects also came from popular concern about what mass communication might be doing to people—whether that mass communication was children's comic books, children's television, violence on television, massive advertising, or political campaigns in the mass media. Much of Schramm's theorizing, as the title of his book *The Process and Effects of Mass Communication* brings out, was concerned with effects.

The emphasis on trying to develop a good model of mass communication came about because of the great complexity of the mass communication process. It is difficult even to describe the most simple act of communication. A model, by identifying the essential components of the communication process and how they interrelate, can help us to deal with this complexity. Models also seem the logical starting point for research. It is difficult to study a process until one has identified the key components of that process. Schramm presented a half dozen diagrams or models of communication in his essay on "How Communication Works" in the first edition of *The Process and Effects of Mass Communication*.[10] The Westley-MacLean model that was pre-

---

[8]Emery and McKerns, p. 39.

[9]Interview with Danielson.

[10]Wilbur Schramm, "How Communication Works," in Schramm, *The*

sented at the first rump session has been one of the most frequently cited and reprinted.[11]

During the 1960s and early 1970s, mass communication research was preoccupied (some might even say bogged down) with
two topics. The first was attitude change, which grew largely from
Hovland's social psychology research. The second was the effects
of television violence, which reflected a growing concern in society, and received additional impetus because it was supported by
research funding.

Neither of these topics was of primary interest to the journalism educator, whose basic concern was the gathering and transmission of factual information. In response to this concern, in
the 1960s and early 1970s, a new wave of researchers, several of
whom had studied at Stanford with Schramm, began to push the
development of communication theory in journalism programs
in new directions. These researchers, often working as part of research teams, included George A. Donohue, Clarice N. Olien, and
Phillip J. Tichenor at the University of Minnesota; Steven H.
Chaffee and Jack M. McLeod at the University of Wisconsin; and
Maxwell E. McCombs and Donald L. Shaw at the University of
North Carolina. These researchers veered away from the study of
attitude change and the persuasion model of communication that
it implied. They began to investigate variables such as knowledge,
awareness, and cognition, which were more closely related to
journalistic concerns.

In the 1970s and 1980s, communication research and theory
branched out in several other directions.

To some extent in reaction to the large amount of research on
effects, there has developed a research emphasis on the audience
and its uses of mass communication. This *uses and gratifications*
approach attempted to give a more central role to the audience
member in the communication process. Some research on gratifications had been part of the Lazarsfeld mass communication
research program at Columbia in the 1940s; and Schramm, Lyle,
and Parker's *Television in the Lives of Our Children*,[12] published
in 1961, played a major role in refocusing attention on the
audience. Under this new perspective, the audience was seen less
as a passive target and more as an active participant in the mass
communication process.

Another more recent area of mass communication research
and theory has dealt with news values and newsmaking. Scholars
in this area have been concerned with the question of why some
events become news and others do not. Rather than focusing on
the effects of mass communication, this line of research exam-

---

Process and Effects of Mass Communication , pp. 3-26.

[11]Bruce H. Westley and Malcolm S. MacLean, Jr., "A Conceptual Model
for Communication Research," *Journalism Quarterly* 34 (1957): 31-38.

[12]Wilbur Schramm, Jack Lyle, and Edwin B. Parker, *Television in the
Lives of Our Children* (Stanford, CA: Stanford University Press, 1961).

ines the conditions that determine what becomes news. Much of this research has been done by sociologists, including Herbert Gans, Mark Fishman, and Gaye Tuchman.

Another recent line of research has attempted to look at the institutions that produce journalism and mass communication. Theorists in this area are concerned about who owns the media and how patterns of ownership affect the overall messages of the media. These kinds of issues have been of particular interest to *critical theorists*—scholars focusing on the questions of control of the mass media, hegemony, and what ideology is being transmitted through the media.

Researchers also have continued to be interested in the effects of mass communication. It is difficult to ignore effects, and some of the most interesting questions about mass communication basically are questions of effects. This later research and theory dealing with effects are more sophisticated than the earlier effects research. The attempt now is to refine our understanding of effects, to conceptualize effects in more subtle and sophisticated ways, to get away from all-or-nothing conceptualizations of effects, and to specify the conditions under which effects take place.

How good is mass communication theory at this point? If we take as a standard the components of theory discussed, for example, in Jerald Hage's *Techniques and Problems of Theory Construction in Sociology*,[13] theory in the mass communication field probably is still not very good. Hage lists several basic elements of any theory, including concept names, verbal statements, theoretical definitions, operational definitions, theoretical linkages, and operational linkages.[14] Few areas of mass communication theory have spelled out all the elements Hage lists. For that matter, however, the same is probably true of many areas of the social sciences.

Judged in terms of the ability they give us to understand, predict, and control—the three commonly stated goals of science—mass communication theories must also be graded as falling short. Theories in this area seem to come and go with a disturbing quality of faddishness, and not many of them let us predict communication outcomes with much accuracy.

A number of factors have held back the development of theory in the field of mass communication. Some of the best researchers have been lost to the field because they became journalism administrators.[15] Examples include Malcolm MacLean, Bruce Westley, and Wayne Danielson. In other cases, research funding drove the whole field in directions that appeared later to be inap-

---

[13]Jerald Hage, *Techniques and Problems of Theory Construction in Sociology* (New York: John Wiley & Sons, 1972).

[14]Ibid.

[15]Videotaped interview with Steven H. Chaffee, Theory and Methodology Division, AEJMC, 1977.

propriate.[16] The plethora of research on television violence in the late '60s and early '70s is an example.

Another factor slowing the development of theory was a schism in the field between researchers and practitioners. This division, which some have referred to as the "green eye shade-chi square" debate,[17] has existed for years. It may, in fact, be traceable back to Bleyer's early decision to wed journalism education to the social sciences rather than the humanities. A recent survey of journalism and mass communication educators indicates that the schism still exists.[18] This survey divided the field into "four cultures": 40% were *eclectics*, who read both academic and industry media and tend to belong to both types of associations; 30% were *industry isolates*, who read only industry media and belong only to industry associations; 20% were *academic isolates*, who read only academic journals and tend to belong only to academic associations; and 10% were *outliers*, who read no industry or academic media and tend to belong to no traditional associations. The study concluded that "journalism and mass communication faculty are divided into several cultures of intellectual strangers."[19] This division in the field not only means there is a reduced pool of scholars interested in doing research and developing theory; it also drains off energy that could be used in producing more and better scholarship.

The topicality of some journalism research has also limited the development of theory. In some cases, communication research seems to be as tied to current events as news coverage itself. Thus, we see studies of news coverage of Three Mile Island, AIDS, or the last presidential election. Although it may be expected that journalism research would deal with the coverage of news events, this type of research does not lead to the kinds of generalizations that apply across many topics and different times.

Furthermore, the field of mass communication has at times been overly concerned with methodological rigor and orthodoxy. One possible indicator of this "excessive rigor" is the fact that the original McCombs and Shaw paper presenting the agenda-setting hypothesis was turned down for presentation at the annual convention of the Association for Education in Journalism. Apparently the reviewers of the paper found it too unorthodox. One of the problems in the mass communication field is that intensive training in empirical research methods gives researchers an ex-

---

[16]Ibid.

[17]See Jake Highton, "Green Eyeshades vs. Chi-Squares," *Quill* (February, 1967): 10-13. Highton expressed similar views more recently in "'Green Eyeshade' Profs Still Live Uncomfortably with 'Chi-squares,'" *Journalism Educator* 44 (Summer, 1989): 59-61.

[18]David Weaver and G. Cleveland Wilhoit, "A Profile of JMC Educators," *Journalism Educator* 43 (Summer, 1988): 4-41.

[19]Ibid., p. 39.

tremely narrow conceptualization of what is to be considered legitimate research. It was sociologists such as Herbert Gans,[20] using less rigorous methods, who opened up the whole new area of news values and the manufacture of news. Marshall McLuhan wasn't restricted by methodological orthodoxy, and he suggested some intriguing theoretical ideas that in some ways are being treated more seriously now than they were in his lifetime.[21]

Another factor limiting the development of mass communication theory—and this is paradoxical, in light of the factor just discussed—may be the lack of what John Platt has called "strong inference."[22] Strong inference is nothing more than scientific method applied rigorously, but if it is done correctly it allows a field to progress rapidly by logically eliminating alternatives. Platt's approach is similar to the use of *crucial experiments*, which provide support for one explanation while simultaneously ruling out another. Platt argues that this is the kind of thinking that has allowed some fields of science, such as molecular biology, to progress quickly. In the field of mass communication research there is little evidence of *strong inference* at work. In fact, mass communication research is presently showing a trend away from quantitative studies, where strong inference is more likely to be found, and toward qualitative research. There are some very good reasons for this trend. But if Platt is right and strong inference is essential to real progress in a field, qualitative research could be the wrong direction for the field to go.

Progress in theory development also was delayed by a premature embracing of complexity. Studies in mass communication now frequently employ multivariate techniques of analysis such as multiple regression or path analysis. Often these studies involve a kind of "brute force" empiricism, as if the sheer power of the statistical techniques will reveal the mysteries of human communication behavior. If theory is present, it is what we might call "grab bag theory"; that is, the researcher simply suggests that "some of these variables might be related to X." But this rush toward complex studies with large numbers of variables came too soon. There are doubtless many three-variable relationships in the field of mass communication that researchers do not fully understand yet and which need to be studied further.[23]

A final factor limiting theory has been the tendency to rely on

---

[20]Herbert G. Gans, *Deciding What's News* (New York: Vintage Books, 1979).

[21]Some of McLuhan's prophetic ideas are discussed in Elihu Katz, "On Conceptualizing Media Effects," in Thelma McCormack (Ed.), *Studies in Communication* (Vol. 1) (Greenwich, CT: JAI Press, 1980), pp. 119-141.

[22]John R. Platt, "Strong Inference," *Science* (October 16, 1964): 347-353.

[23]James W. Tankard, Jr., "Beyond Hage: Building Communication Theory by Exploring Three-Variable Relationships." Paper presented at the annual meeting of the International Communication Association, Montreal, May 21-25, 1987.

other fields of study to supply the theories. This can be seen in the early stages of mass communication research, when the field was based on the attitude change research of psychologist Carl Hovland, the election campaign research of sociologist Paul Lazarsfeld and others, and the group dynamics research of social psychologist Kurt Lewin. It can be seen later in the influence of social psychologist Ted Newcomb's ABX model on Westley and MacLean's communication model and on Chaffee and McLeod's coorientation model. And it can still be seen today in the research on news values and the manufacture of news, which has been carried out largely by sociologists. Critical theory, with its origins mainly in sociology, also comes from outside the field of mass communication.

Recently, however, the field of mass communication theory may have broken free of the influence of other fields and started developing theory of its own. Examples of this home-grown theory include Chaffee and McLeod's work on family communication patterns and coorientation; Donohue, Olien, and Tichenor's work on the structural approach and the knowledge gap hypothesis; George Gerbner's work on cultivation theory; and McCombs and Shaw's work on the agenda-setting function of the press. Although these ideas have roots in work in other intellectual fields, each has been developed by people largely concerned with mass communication research. And this home-grown theory seems better in some ways than the borrowed theory. For one thing, it seems to address the concerns of the journalist more specifically.

Some of the theoretical ideas just mentioned—agenda-setting and the knowledge gap, in particular—have achieved a rather astonishing success, with hundreds of later studies following up and elaborating on them. What makes some theoretical ideas flourish, while others die on the vine? The "truthfulness" of the theoretical idea is undoubtedly a factor. Ideas such as agenda-setting jibe with our own understanding of the way things are, and furthermore they are usually supported by evidence from empirical studies. Some successful theoretical ideas also have a quality of "jelling" something, perhaps of articulating an idea that many people sense but that no one has quite articulated. Another factor that helps a theoretical idea achieve acceptance is the extent to which its name for a concept or hypothesis makes a good slogan or catch phrase. It is doubtful that McCombs and Shaw's new idea would have become as popular if they had called it "prioritization of issues" instead of "agenda-setting." Likewise, Tichenor, Olien, and Donohue's hypothesis might not have caught on if they had called it "the information differential" instead of "the knowledge gap." Many of Marshall McLuhan's ideas, such as "hot and cool media" or "the medium is the message," also benefitted from being catchy phrases. Wilbur Schramm's metaphors and similes (the "bullet theory" of mass communication effects, the mass media as a "cafeteria," mass media effects accumulating slowly like stalagmites) may have helped to make his ideas memorable in a similar way.

Mass communication research and theory will undoubtedly continue as an ongoing and energetic area of activity. What does the field need in order to develop better mass communication theory?

First, it needs to pay more attention to theory and theory-building. Much research reported in the journals of journalism and mass communication has little or no theory. It is common to see studies that are method-driven, problem-driven, geographical location-driven, and news topic-driven. It is much less common to see studies that are theory-driven. Mass communication research tends to work at the level of hypotheses rather than theories. Even some of the most popular theoretical ideas—agenda-setting or the knowledge gap, for instance—tend to be rather narrow, focusing on a single hypothesis.

Second, the field needs more imaginative theory. Some of the most cited theoretical ideas in the field—the agenda-setting function; the knowledge gap; William McGuire's inoculation theory; and McLuhan's hot and cold media—show the influence of creativity and imagination. They are characterized by use of analogy, metaphor, and other figures of speech, not only in the names of concepts and hypotheses, but even in how the processes work. The field needs more "right brain" vigor to go along with its "left brain" rigor.

Third, the field needs more formally developed theory. There are few areas in mass communication research where an attempt has even been made to spell out a formal theory, with concepts, operational definitions, hypotheses, theoretical rationale, and theoretical and operational linkages. Tichenor, Donohue, and Olien's attempt to define a structural approach to mass communication research[24] and Pamela J. Shoemaker and Elizabeth Kay Mayfield's monograph on building a theory of news content[25] may stand as two of the few examples of this kind of scholarly effort.

Finally, the field should continue to embrace many different methods and approaches to theory-building and testing. The field can use the fruitful ideas of largely non-quantitative scholars such as Michael Schudson, Joshua Meyrowitz, Doris Graber, Gaye Tuchman, and Herbert Gans, as well as those scholars who think of themselves as critical theorists. But it also needs methodologi-

---

[24]Phillip J. Tichenor, George A. Donohue, and Clarice N. Olien, "Mass Communication Research: Evolution of a Structural Model," *Journalism Quarterly* 50 (1973): 419-425; George A. Donohue, Phillip J. Tichenor, and Clarice N. Olien, "Mass Media Functions, Knowledge and Social Control," *Journalism Quarterly* 50 (1973): 652-659.

[25]Pamela J. Shoemaker with Elizabeth Kay Mayfield, "Building a Theory of News Content: A Synthesis of Current Approaches," *Journalism Monographs* 103 (June 1987).

cal rigor. There may be some truth to John Platt's claim that progress in knowledge will come about only through *strong infer-ence*. The difficulty for the field of mass communication theory in the next few years will be to find either a middle path between these two approaches, or a successful blend of them. At this point in its development, the field can benefit from qualitative re-search, from rigorous quantitative hypothesis-testing research, and from many other approaches somewhere in between.

Wilbur Schramm, Definer of a Field

Wilbur Schramm (1907-1987) probably did more to define and establish the field of communication research and theory than any other person. He founded two institutes of communication research (and helped to found a third), wrote several basic textbooks in a field that had none before, and trained a small army of followers who, for the first time, thought of themselves as full-time communication scholars.

Schramm's major intellectual impact was almost single-handedly defining the paradigm widely used for decades in communication research. Along the way, he also contributed more than a few theoretical ideas of his own and helped to discover significant work by others. His contributions were not only in the areas of communication research and communication theory, but also in mass communication and society and in international communication, where he wrote basic texts.

Wilbur Lang Schramm was born August 5, 1907, in Marietta, Ohio. His father, Arch A. Schramm, and mother, Louise Lang, had played duets on the violin and piano while they were courting, and Wilbur absorbed their musical influence and went on to become an accomplished flute player. His father was a school teacher, a prominent attorney, and a judge of the Children's Court. Schramm attended Marietta College, where he was a letter-winning athlete. While there, he began reporting for the Associated Press. He graduated from Marietta College in 1928, and faced a choice of interesting careers: auditioning for John Philip Sousa's band, trying out for the Columbus Red Birds baseball team, or becoming city editor for the Marietta *Daily Times*.[1] Instead, he went to study English and American literature at Harvard. Schramm was influenced greatly by his teachers at Harvard, including particularly English professor Bliss Perry and philosophy professor Alfred North Whitehead. Schramm spoke many years later of the experience of talking with Whitehead in

---

[1]"Question and Answer Session with Wilbur Schramm," Annual Convention of the Association for Education in Journalism, Fort Collins, Colorado, August 21, 1973.

his office.[2] Whitehead had an owl on his bookcase, and the owl would look down at Schramm as if to say "How come I'm so much brighter than you?" And then Whitehead would ask questions like, "Are you sure you've asked that question quite right? Are you sure you've asked it the right way?" And then, "Why did you ask it that way? What's the use of asking it that way?"

Schramm received his master's degree from Harvard in 1930, and then went to the University of Iowa to work for a PhD in American Literature. He roomed with Wallace Stegner, who later would become a Pulitzer Prize-winning novelist. Stegner says Schramm decorated his dresser with pictures of the first flutist in the Boston Symphony and English professor Bliss Perry. Stegner never knew anyone before who put up pictures of his teachers.[3]

Schramm stayed on at Iowa as a faculty member in the English Department. He married Elizabeth Donaldson on August 5, 1934. They had two children, Mary and Michael, both born in Iowa City. Schramm continued to pursue his interest in literature, becoming the founder and first director of the famous Iowa Writers Workshop. From 1941 to 1947, he published a number of short stories—1 appearing in the *Atlantic Monthly* and 13 others in the *Saturday Evening Post.* He received the O. Henry award for short stories in 1942. From 1943 to 1947, he was director of the School of Journalism at Iowa.

In 1947, he went to the University of Illinois to become assistant to the university president and director of the University Press. While there, he founded the Institute of Communications Research and became its first director, and was later the first Dean of Communications at Illinois. The Institute had as its purpose "to apply the methods and disciplines of the social sciences (supported, where necessary, by the fine arts and natural sciences) to the basic problems of press, radio, and pictures; to supply verifiable information in those areas of communications where the hunch, the tradition, the theory and the thumb have too often ruled; and by so doing to contribute to the better understanding of communications and the maximum use of communications for the public good."[4]

In 1955, he left Illinois to become professor of communication at Stanford. There, he founded his second institute, the Institute for Communication Research, again becoming the first director. While still at Stanford, Schramm participated in the planning of the East-West Communication Institute at the University of Hawaii, later established in 1970. In 1973, he retired from Stanford, but only to travel west to become the director of this

---

[2]Ibid.

[3]Wallace E. Stegner, "The Iowa Years," in Daniel Lerner and Lyle M. Nelson (Eds.), *Communication Research—a Half-Century Appraisal* (Honolulu: University Press of Hawaii, 1977), p. 6.

[4]"Illinois Seeks to Reduce Rule of Hunch Decision," *Journalism Class and Lab,* Vol. 5, No. 3 (undated, probably 1948): 2.

third institute. In 1975, he retired as director but became a distinguished center researcher there. Schramm died December 27, 1987, at the age of 80 of a heart attack while watching television at his home in Hawaii.

Schramm's productivity is legendary. He wrote 29 books including his last, *The Story of Human Communication*,[5] which was completed just before his death. Some people have written of his "magic typewriter," and the way pages would come out of that typewriter virtually without need for editing. One graduate student at Stanford in the 1960s remembers seeing Schramm in the men's room of the Institute at an early hour on a Sunday morning and asking if he were working on a paper. Schramm's reply was something like, "A paper, heck! I've got a book-length manuscript to finish this weekend."

Many of Schramm's books became standard texts of the mass communication field, and several of them defined areas of study and teaching that had not existed before, but are now regarded as standard. The book *Mass Communications*, published in 1949,[6] was a collection of readings by psychologists, sociologists, and others. Edited by Schramm, it became the first text in the new field of mass communication science. The year 1954 saw the publication of *The Process and Effects of Mass Communication*,[7] a collection put together at the request of the United States Information Agency. It contained Schramm's famous introductory essay, "How Communication Works." In 1956, there appeared *Four Theories of the Press*, which Schramm wrote with Fred S. Siebert and Theodore Peterson.[8] It was inspired by the work on press freedom and responsibility completed by the Hutchins Commission. The theories developed in the book were normative rather than quantitative, but the volume nevertheless presented a set of standards for evaluating and comparing press performance that was used for many years. The volume *Responsibility in Mass Communication* appeared in 1957.[9] The intellectual ties between this book and the Hutchins Commission are brought out by the fact that the introduction was written by commission member and theologian Reinhold Niebuhr. The book became the standard text in many of the first courses in mass communication and society and helped to give direction to that heretofore amorphous area. *Television in the Lives of Our Children*, written with Jack

---

[5]Wilbur Schramm, *The Story of Human Communication* (New York: Harper & Row, 1988).

[6]Wilbur Schramm (Ed.), *Mass Communications* (Urbana: University of Illinois Press, 1949).

[7]Wilbur Schramm (Ed.), *The Process and Effects of Mass Communication* (Urbana: University of Illinois Press, 1954).

[8]Fred S. Siebert, Theodore Peterson, and Wilbur Schramm, *Four Theories of the Press* (Urbana: University of Illinois Press, 1956).

[9]Wilbur Schramm, *Responsibility in Mass Communication* (New York: Harper & Brothers, 1957).

Lyle and Edwin B. Parker, appeared in 1961.[10] The volume indicates Schramm's ability to pick out significant problems, and often to do so before others. It presented fundamental research on a topic that would preoccupy communication researchers for many years—the effects of television on children. *Mass Media and National Development* was written at the request of Unesco and published in 1964.[11] This book represents still another facet of Schramm and an effort to which he devoted great energy—the attempt to figure out ways that mass communication could help underdeveloped countries to develop more quickly.

What set Schramm apart from others was the fact that he was both a humanist and a scientist. He bridged the two cultures described by C.P. Snow,[12] as scholars are not supposed to be able to do and as few have done. Schramm's interest in science can be traced back directly to psychologist Carl E. Seashore, an Iowa professor who was studying the psychology of music. While an assistant professor of English at Iowa, Schramm began working with Seashore. Schramm was given a year's research leave sponsored by the American Council of Learned Societies, and he spent the year using Seashore's acoustic equipment to study the characteristics of poetry. The results were reported in the volume *Approaches to a Science of English Verse*, which appeared in 1935. Schramm indicates in his foreword that he had become somewhat impatient with the "belles-lettristic approach" to literary studies.[13] He also expresses agreement in the book with Lord Kelvin's famous aphorism: ". . . when you cannot measure it, when you cannot express it in numbers, your knowledge is of a meagre and unsatisfactory kind." In short, it appears that Schramm was led to a scientific approach out of an intense desire for understanding. A similar desire for understanding of *communication* is apparent in his several attempts to write an essay on "How Communication Works," the first in the 1954 edition of *The Process and Effects of Mass Communication* and the second ("The Nature of Communication Between Humans") in the 1971 revised edition.[14] Perhaps no person ever struggled more to understand the deceptively simple act of human communication.

As a teacher, Schramm conveyed an incredible enthusiasm for the study of mass communication. He gave his PhD students

---

[10]Wilbur Schramm, Jack Lyle, and Edwin B. Parker, *Television in the Lives of Our Children* (Stanford, CA: Stanford University Press, 1961).

[11]Wilbur Schramm, *Mass Media and National Development* (Stanford, CA: Stanford University Press, 1964).

[12]C.P. Snow, *The Two Cultures and A Second Look* (Cambridge: Cambridge University Press, 1964).

[13]Wilbur Lang Schramm, *Approaches to a Science of English Verse* (Iowa City: University of Iowa, 1935), p. 5.

[14]Wilbur Schramm and Donald F. Roberts (Eds.), *The Process and Effects of Mass Communication* (rev. ed.) (Urbana: University of Illinois Press, 1971).

the feeling that mass communication research was a calling, and one as important as being a minister or a doctor. In seminars at Stanford, he would frequently speak of "passing on the torch," and it was easy to get the feeling that you were indeed part of an army forging ahead into the dark night of ignorance. Schramm would tell his seminars at Stanford things like this: "It's a great time to be working in this field. If you think of the things to do and the new tools coming up to do it with, this field is going to be quite different in ten years." Much of what Schramm was doing in seminars actually amounted to teaching creative thinking in a research context. For instance, he might tell about watching Nobel Prize-winning physicist William Shockley working with a group of children and the questions he asked to teach them problem-solving. Then he would say something like, "If there's one bit of advice I would give you as I pass on the torch, it would be this: Look through the other door. Look through the other window. Use polarized light. So many things in this field would benefit from some new insights."

Some of the graduate students who passed through these Schramm seminars and went on to make significant contributions to the field of journalism and mass communication were Steven H. Chaffee, George Comstock, Godwin Chu, Wayne Danielson, G. Ray Funkhouser, Nat Katzman, Jack Lyle, John Mayo, Maxwell McCombs, Emile McAnany, Bill Paisley, Edwin B. Parker, Donald Roberts, Lee Ruggels, Phillip Tichenor, and Serena Wade.

Schramm was not only a writer, researcher, and teacher, but also a pioneering developer of curriculum. While at Iowa, he wrote a memorandum describing a new degree—the doctorate in communication. The degree was to be an interdisciplinary one, with supervision by a committee made up of faculty from journalism, sociology, political science, and speech. Also during his Iowa stay, Schramm wrote an article describing the "three skeins" of journalism education—vocational education, general education, and professional education.[15] Schramm put a strong emphasis on professional education, arguing that journalism was just as much a profession as law, medicine, or theology.

In addition to influencing and shaping the field by textbooks and other books, Schramm contributed a number of theoretical ideas to the field of mass communication research. These include his many models, his suggestion of an active audience for the mass media, his explanation of news seeking behavior in terms of various types of rewards, and "the bullet theory," his image for some of the first thinking about mass communication effects.

One of Schramm's major intellectual contributions to communication theory might be characterized as the search for the perfect model. Both the 1954 essay "How Communication Works"

---

[15]Wilbur L. Schramm, "Education for Journalism: Vocational, General, or Professional?" *Journal of General Education* 1 (January, 1947): 90-98.

and the 1971 essay "The Nature of Communication Between Humans" contain a half dozen original diagrams, all attempting to illustrate the process of communication or various aspects of it. And there are probably other Schramm models. One of the models in the 1954 essay shows a mass communication organization broadcasting many identical messages in a figure that looks something like a tuba. Bruce Westley has written that while he and Malcolm MacLean were working on the model now known as the Westley-MacLean model, they heard about "Schramm's tuba" and wondered if it was going to leave them anything to say.[16]

In trying to explain why people read newspapers, Schramm came up with the concepts of *immediate reward*, based on Freud's Pleasure Principle, and *delayed reward*, based on Freud's Reality Principle.[17] This conceptualization has influenced a number of researchers and still serves as a cornerstone for studies of news-seeking behavior.[18] Schramm himself used a modified version of the idea in *Television in the Lives of Our Children* when he wrote of *fantasy-oriented* and *reality-oriented* TV watchers.

One of Schramm's major concerns was discovering the *effects* of mass communication. He originated the phrase "the bullet theory" to describe some of the early thinking about mass communication that attributed very powerful and uniform effects to the mass media. He cited the bullet theory mainly to show that it was inaccurate in light of later communication research. In something of a critique of Schramm, some scholars have recently suggested that no one really ever believed in the bullet theory and that the idea is somewhat of a straw man. But this argument may be overstated. Certainly the formation of the Institute for Propaganda Analysis in this country in the 1930s would indicate that some people had a fear of very powerful effects from the mass media and is just one indication that Schramm's idea had acceptability.

Schramm also anticipated a popular theoretical idea today—the *knowledge gap*—in *The People Look at Educational Television*, a book he published in 1963 with Jack Lyle and Ithiel de Sola Pool.[19] The authors wrote that educational television was not fulfilling the dream of some of its founders—the dream that it would become the school and university of people who had little

---

[16]Bruce H. Westley, "MacLean and I and 'The Model,'" *Journal of Communication Inquiry* (Spring, 1976): 26-35.

[17]Wilbur Schramm, "The Nature of News," *Journalism Quarterly* 26 (1949): 259-269.

[18]Lewis Donohew, Seth Finn, and William G. Christ, "'The Nature of News' Revisited: The Roles of Affect, Schemas, and Cognition," in Lewis Donohew, Howard E. Sypher, and E. Tory Higgins (Eds.), *Communication, Social Cognition and Affect* (Hillsdale, NJ: Lawrence Erlbaum Associates, 1987), pp. 195-218.

[19]Wilbur Schramm, Jack Lyle, and Ithiel de Sola Pool, *The People Look at Educational Television* (Stanford, CA: Stanford University Press, 1963), p. 166.

opportunity for education.

Schramm's work was occasionally criticized, and one of his more prominent critics was Marshall McLuhan. In his *Understanding Media*,[20] McLuhan singled out Schramm, Lyle, and Parker's *Television in the Lives of Our Children* for taking a literary approach to the effects of television and consequently having nothing to report. Schramm was intrigued by McLuhan; he told a class soon after the publication of *Understanding Media* that McLuhan was "one of the most interesting persons on the stage. He keeps saying these things that don't quite mean anything." Schramm did not duck McLuhan's criticism, either; in his revised edition of *The Process and Effects of Mass Communication*, Schramm reprinted Chapter 1 of *Understanding Media*, the very chapter that criticized Schramm's work.

Schramm's greatest contribution to the field probably came not from his individual theoretical ideas, interesting as they are, but from his framing of the key questions concerning communication in a way that defined the field. It is not overstating it to say that Schramm created the dominant paradigm[21] used in communication research for decades. That paradigm had two prongs, and they are succinctly expressed in the title *The Process and Effects of Mass Communication*. Schramm worked extremely hard at understanding and describing the process of mass communication—an effort brought out clearly in the 1954 "How Communication Works" and the 1971 "The Nature of Com-munication Between Humans." The attempt to understand the process of mass communication is also illustrated by the many models Schramm conceived to explain the process. One of the major characteristics of the communication research field has been a plethora of models, and Schramm undoubtedly had an influence on this tendency.

The search for *effects* has been the other prong of the paradigm for communication research that Schramm created. Many of the titles of Schramm books and chapters reflect this concern with effects. The uses and gratifications approach to the study of mass communication has grown up as an alternative to the effects paradigm, but it remains to be seen whether this approach will be as influential or productive.

Another significant role played by Schramm was that of *synthesizer* of research on communication conducted by others. This role may be one of his most important at a time when communication research, like most of the social sciences, is characterized by many discrete studies high in empiricism but low in theory-building. Schramm's attempts at synthesis are particularly evident in the two essays explaining how communication works, but

[20]Marshall McLuhan, *Understanding Media: The Extensions of Man* (New York: McGraw-Hill, 1964), pp. 19-20.

[21]Thomas S. Kuhn, *The Structure of Scientific Revolution*, (2nd ed.) (Chicago: University of Chicago Press, 1972).

may also be found in other works. A volume such as *Learning from Television: What the Research Says*, which Schramm and Godwin C. Chu published in 1967,[22] was an obvious attempt to synthesize a large body of research. Books and articles by Schramm frequently have sections with titles such as "What the Mass Media Can Do" or "The Significance of These Results," indicating his desire to synthesize and demystify diverse research results.

Schramm also contributed to communication theory by discovering the work of others. The best example is his decision, while director of the University of Illinois Press, to publish Claude Shannon's *The Mathematical Theory of Communication*, the basic work describing information theory.[23] Information theory is a mathematical conceptualization which defines information as a reduction in uncertainty and provides a quantitative measure of information. Schramm came across Shannon's essay in the *Bell System Technical Journal* and thought it might be of value to fields outside telephone engineering. Although wanting to publish the work, he was also concerned that nonengineers might have difficulty understanding it. So he asked mathematician Warren Weaver to write a more general explanation of Shannon's theory. The Weaver section appeared second in the published volume under the title "Recent Contributions to the Mathematical Theory of Communication." Schramm said later that the Weaver section really should have appeared first, and in later reprints the University of Illinois Press rearranged the volume that way. Although some recent writers have suggested that information theory did not ultimately add much to our understanding of mass communication,[24] it is undeniable that the ideas of information theory have had impact on many fields, not just mass communication research.[25]

Schramm has been criticized for taking essentially a linear approach to mass communication, with the focus on messages originating from a sender and proceeding more or less intact until they have an intended effect on a receiver. Some researchers have felt that this was a misleading conceptualization that lim-

---

[22]Wilbur Schramm and Godwin C. Chu, *Learning from Television: What the Research Says* (Washington, DC: National Association for Educational Broadcasters, 1967).

[23]Claude E. Shannon and Warren Weaver, *The Mathematical Theory of Communication* (Urbana: University of Illinois Press, 1949).

[24]John Durham Peters, "Institutional Sources of Intellectual Poverty in Communication Research," *Communication Research* 13 (October 1986): 527-559.

[25]For examples, see John Robinson Pierce, *Symbols, Signals, and Noise: The Nature and Process of Communication* (New York: Harper & Brothers, 1961); Wendell R. Garner, *Uncertainty and Structure as Psychological Concepts* (New York: John Wiley and Sons, 1962); and Baruch Lev, *Accounting and Information Theory* (Evanston, IL.: American Accounting Association, 1969).

ited understanding of mass communication for years.[26] But if Schramm started out with this conceptualization, he at least modified it later. The 1971 chapter on "The Nature of Communication Between Humans" put much more emphasis on communication as relationship or sharing.[27] And, in *Television in the Lives of Our Children*, Schramm was one of the first scholars to emphasize the idea of an active audience. He and his co-authors wrote of the child watching television making choices "from a great and shiny cafeteria." This idea anticipated much of the later thinking subsumed under the uses and gratifications approach.

One of Schramm's unusual contributions to mass communication theory was his extensive use of metaphor, clearly a result of his literary background. These metaphors gave his writing a vitality that was often missing from other social science prose. For instance, in *Television and the Test Scores*, Schramm was not afraid to label television as "the thief of time."[28] Schramm's use of metaphor went beyond adding color or vividness to writing, however—many of his theoretical concepts were actually metaphors. Examples include the image of mass communication effects building up like a stalagmite on a cave floor from the 1954 "How Communication Works," the cafeteria image for children using television from *Television in the Lives of Our Children*, the bullet theory and the discussion of the "watchman" function of the press from the 1971 "The Nature of Communication Between Humans," and the description of communication as a "temperature controlling device" in *The Mass Media and National Development*.

One of Schramm's favorite metaphors was to describe communication research itself as an oasis (or a crossroads) where many have passed, but few have tarried. By this, Schramm meant that up to a certain point in time, most of the research on human communication was being conducted by people from other fields, such as psychologists, sociologists, and political scientists. Schramm also frequently gave credit to "four founding fathers" for creating communication research: sociologist Paul Lazarsfeld, political scientist Harold Lasswell, and psychologists Kurt Lewin and Carl Hovland. But it seems clear that it was Schramm who first decided to spend his life in the oasis, studying the process of communication and the institutions that engage in that process. Furthermore, he also was able to inspire dozens of others, who became his doctoral students and then went on to successful careers of their own, to spend some time in that oasis.

---

[26]Brenda Dervin, "Communication Gaps and Inequities," in Brenda Dervin and Melvin J. Voigt (Eds.), *Progress in Communication Sciences*, Vol. 2 (Norwood, NJ: Ablex Publishing Co., 1980), pp. 87-88.

[27]Wilbur Schramm, "The Nature of Communication Between Humans," in Schramm and Roberts, p. 8.

[28]Wilbur Schramm, *Television and the Test Scores* (Princeton, NJ: College Entrance Examination Board, 1977), p. 3.

For these reasons, he is perhaps himself a better candidate than any of the four men whom he named to be the true "founding father" of communication theory.

Malcolm MacLean
and 'the Iowa Experiment'

During his lifetime, Malcolm Shaw MacLean Jr. (1920-1974) was one of the four or five best known quantitative researchers and theorists in the field of journalism. He was a prominent participant in the famous "rump group" sessions held by researchers after the regular meetings of the Association for Education in Journalism when researchers could not get paper presentations scheduled on the regular program. He was a co-creator of one of the most widely-known models of mass communication, the Westley-MacLean model.[1] In addition, he possibly went further than any other journalism educator of his time in attempting to apply communication theory to the teaching of journalism. This effort took place in what has come to be known as "the Iowa experiment"—the attempt to teach journalism through a simulation laboratory rather than through traditional journalism courses.

MacLean's view of theory was not necessarily a conventional one. He criticized other academics for being too concerned with their "semantic differential and cognitive dissonance laboratories."[2] Instead, MacLean had his own theory of communication, which was never fully written out, but which was based on ideas concerning perception and general systems theory. Basically, he viewed perception as a highly subjective and creative act. Under this view, no two people see the world in the same way. The simulation laboratory was designed to bring this fact home, and to let the student discover what kinds of communication could take place in light of this fact.

MacLean was also an inspiring teacher, particularly in a one-on-one situation. Keith Sanders, a doctoral student at Iowa during MacLean's years, has said, "He had a nearly infallible ability to gauge a student's current level of capability and to deal with the

---

[1]Bruce H. Westley and Malcolm S. MacLean, Jr., "A Conceptual Model for Communication Research," *Audio-Visual Communication Review* 3 (Winter 1955): 3-12.

[2]David K. Berlo, "Prologue: Reminiscences of Malcolm MacLean," *Journal of Communication Inquiry* (Spring 1976): 2-10.

student at that level, but always encouraging you to reach a little bit further; to take the step you felt you weren't quite ready to take yet. There was a flip side, however. Once having scaled some barrier, you were never again permitted to slip backward. He left us with the distinct impression that he always expected a bit more of us than we thought was possible."[3]

MacLean was born in St. Paul, Minnesota, on June 28, 1920. His father, later a prominent educator, was an instructor in English at the University of Minnesota at the time Malcolm was born. His father also spent several years working for newspapers, including the Minneapolis *Tribune*, the Laguna Beach (Calif.) *Life*, and the LaSalle (Ill.) *Daily Post*. The senior MacLean returned to the University of Minnesota to become the director of a new venture in higher education called the general college. It was chartered to explore several problems facing the American university, including how to provide students with a general or liberal education in the face of ever-expanding specialized curricula with inevitable fragmentation into multiple courses and rigid sequences. The elder MacLean later became president of Hampton Institute, a black college in Virginia, and worked hard to hire more black faculty members and black administrators. He was both an innovative educator and a humanitarian, and it appears that both of these attributes were transmitted to his son.

The younger MacLean attended Phillips Academy in Andover, Massachusetts. One of his vitas states that he spent several precollege years "reading, traveling, learning photography and studying singing." He spent a freshman year at the University of Minnesota in the academic year of 1939-1940 and a year as a sophomore at the University of New Hampshire in 1940-1941. In 1941, he became a photographer with the National Advisory Committee for Aeronautics at Langley Field, Virginia. From 1942 to 1946 he served as a battalion photographer with the 817th Aviation Engineer Battalion of the United States Army. He was a corporal in the Army of Occupation when it marched north through Italy. In Italy, he met Eleonora Monti, the woman he would marry. In later years, people who had been friends of MacLean at various universities would speak fondly of having dinner with the MacLeans and enjoying Nora's Italian cooking.

After the war, MacLean received his bachelor's and master's degrees from the University of Minnesota. For both degrees, he majored in journalism and minored in psychology. He was also an instructor at that university from 1949 to 1950. In 1950, he followed Ralph Nafziger, who was leaving the University of Minnesota to go to the University of Wisconsin at Madison, and entered the PhD program in mass communication at that university. In 1954, he became the third PhD graduate from the program.

---

[3]Letter from Keith P. Sanders to James W. Tankard, Jr., September 6, 1987.

After finishing his PhD, MacLean became one of the first members of the "Rump Group" of the AEJ, a group of journalism scholars who would stay an extra day after the association's annual convention in order to present and discuss quantitative research papers. The well-known Westley-MacLean model was first presented at the first "rump session" at the University of Colorado in 1955. MacLean remained at the University of Wisconsin as an assistant professor until 1956. It was during this period that he and faculty colleague Bruce H. Westley produced the Westley-MacLean model.

In 1956, MacLean moved to Michigan State University, where he became an associate professor, and, later, a professor. There, he worked with such colleagues as David K. Berlo and Paul Deutschmann. In 1964, he went to the University of Iowa to become the George H. Gallup Professor of Communication Research. He remained at Iowa for the rest of his career.

Keith Sanders recalls bowling with MacLean on the faculty bowling team when both were at Iowa. One night MacLean was bowling badly, as usual, and Sanders asked him what he was trying to do. MacLean explained that he was working on a theory of bowling in which the path of the bowling ball was a vector and strikes were produced by the ball striking the one and three pins at the proper angle. "This is just like factor analysis," MacLean said. "If I can figure out the proper angle of rotation—and then throw the ball there—I should be able to strike every time."[4]

In 1967, MacLean became the director of the School of Journalism. At about the same time, he and such colleagues as Richard Budd began discussing "fundamental changes" in journalism education.[5] The result was "the Iowa experiment," an attempt to introduce an innovative program of journalism education based on open-ended learning rather than technique-oriented training.

MacLean was influenced in his thinking and writing by a number of scholars, particularly those whose work dealt with the personal nature of knowledge or with various approaches to learning. Among his favorites were Jerome Bruner, Abraham Maslow, Michael Polanyi, William Stephenson, and George H. Mead.[6] He also liked Kurt Lewin's aphorism, "There is nothing so practical as a good theory."[7]

MacLean did not write a "master work" presenting his ideas.

---

[4]Ibid.

[5]Malcolm MacLean, "On the Education of Responsible Newsmen." Paper presented at the 23rd Annual Conference of the American Association for Public Opinion Research, Santa Barbara, California, May 8-11, 1968, p. 12.

[6]Jae-won Lee, "Reality, Metaphor and Reporter's Role," *Journal of Communication Inquiry* (Spring 1976): 124-136.

[7]Kurt Lewin, *Field Theory in Social Science: Selected Theoretical Papers* (New York: Harper & Row, 1951), p. 169.

Instead, there are a number of articles presenting various theoretical ideas pertaining to communication theory.

One of his earliest papers is probably his most famous and most widely read—that is the article he co-authored with Bruce Westley titled "A Conceptual Model for Communications Research" and which presents the Westley-MacLean model. Westley has told of how the article came about.[8] One day at the University of Wisconsin, MacLean came down the hall to Westley's office and asked him if he wanted to co-author an article reviewing scholarly work in journalism and mass communication. The article had been requested by Bill Allen, editor of the new journal *Audio-Visual Communication Review*. Westley, who was trying to write a dissertation, agreed somewhat reluctantly to help out. MacLean had started the literature review for the article, but it became quickly apparent to the two authors that they were going to need some kind of organizing principle for the article. They considered existing models, such as Lasswell's Who Says What to Whom model and Shannon's information theory model, but didn't think that either of them did the job. Finally, they thought of a new model based on Theodore Newcomb's A B X model. Westley had studied with Newcomb at the University of Minnesota. Newcomb's model was developed to describe interpersonal communication. In the Newcomb model, the A and the B are two people, and the X is some object they are communicating about. Westley and MacLean changed the A B X model into an A C B X model, with the A and C being two types of communicators that can occur in a mass communication situation. The B role is taken by a receiver or audience. The A role is essentially an advocacy or persuasion role. The C role is essentially a channel or reporting role. Westley and MacLean initially chose the terms *purposive* and *fortuitous* to describe the different types of communication engaged in by the A and C roles. They were criticized for implying with the word *fortuitous* that journalists do not consciously influence what is passed on to readers. They later revised the model to substitute *non-purposive* for *fortuitous*.

By the time the model was fully developed, its description had grown to article length. The co-authors decided to write a two-part series, with the model in the first article and the review of the literature in the second. The two articles were published in *Audio-Visual Communication Review*, and most scholars probably do not even know about the second one, which contained the literature review that started the whole project.

The Westley-MacLean model differs from some of the other popular models of communication in that it includes the "real world" as part of the model. As journalists, Westley and MacLean recognized that communication needs to be about something, and they incorporated that idea into their model. Their model also

---

[8]Bruce H. Westley, "MacLean and I and 'The Model,'" *Journal of Communication Inquiry* (Spring 1976): 25-34.

differs from some earlier models in that it includes, but makes a distinction between, two different types of communication—persuading and informing. It is also a very general model, being applicable to communication at a number of levels—the intrapersonal, or the level of one person perceiving an object; the interpersonal, or the level of two persons communicating; and mass communication, or the level of an organization communicating with a large number of people. Finally, by incorporating both the A and the C roles, the Westley-MacLean model can reflect the tension or conflict that often exists in real-world situations involving communication. For instance, the model can bring out the complexities of communication about an event such as the Three Mile Island nuclear power plant accident. We can think of the realities of the power plant accident as the X's or objects of orientation; the various reporters and members of the news media as the C's; the public relations workers for the power company, the federal regulatory agencies, and the governor's office as various A's; and the members of the public, who are in need of information, as the B's. In this case, the A's and the C's have different goals and are therefore in conflict. The Westley-MacLean model brings out this reality nicely, as few other models of communication do.

The Westley-MacLean model became the starting point for other researchers, including the team of George Donohue, Clarice Olien, and Phillip Tichenor. Their early article "Predicting a Source's Success in Placing News in the Media" took the Westley-MacLean model as a theoretical framework.

Perhaps because of the generality and relevance of the Westley-MacLean model, the article describing it has been widely reprinted. A year or so after the article appeared in *Audio-Visual Communication Review*, Raymond Nixon asked permission to reprint it in *Journalism Quarterly*.[9] This must be one of the few cases of a journal article being deliberately reprinted in another journal. The model is also presented and discussed in many textbooks on mass communication. *Journalism Quarterly* has received more requests to reprint the figures from the Westley-MacLean article than anything else that has appeared in the journal.[10] MacLean used to joke that because of the popularity of the model, the first thing he had to do with new students was convince them that his first name was not Westley.[11]

The Westley-MacLean model received further attention in 1989 when Stephen Lacy of Michigan State University presented a revision of the model at the AEJMC convention.[12] Lacy at-

[9]Bruce H. Westley and Malcolm S. MacLean, Jr., "A Conceptual Model for Communications Research," *Journalism Quarterly* 34 (1957): 31-38.

[10]Telephone interview with Guido Stempel, Sept. 12, 1989.

[11]Berlo, p. 6.

[12]Stephen Lacy, "The Westley-MacLean Model Revisited: An Extension of a Conceptual Model for Communication Research," a paper presented to the Theory and Methodology Division of the Association for Education

tempted to update the model to incorporate new research areas that had developed in the 30 years since the model was first published.

Westley and MacLean worked on other projects together, including an attempt to measure manifest objectivity in radio and television news called "obform analysis." This procedure was described in a mimeographed publication titled "Obform Coding Instructions" and was later used by Donald Shaw as the basis of a measure of objectivity in his study of news bias and the telegraph. Another joint Westley-MacLean project involved comparing Wilson Taylor's Cloze Procedure with Flesch's readability formula in predicting the readership of labor newspapers.

MacLean was also an expert research methodologist, particularly with such complex quantitative methods as Guttman scaling, factor analysis, and Q Methodology. Some of his ideas on factor analysis were presented at an early "rump group" AEJ session and were later printed in *Journalism Quarterly*. His endorsement and use of Q Methodology, a technique primarily associated with William Stephenson, probably helped it to achieve a much wider acceptance in journalism and other communication disciplines.

In another area, MacLean did some theoretical work on editorial games in which editors (or other news selectors) and audiences would "pick" stories. One example of this kind of research is reported in the *Journalism Quarterly* article "Picture Selection: An Editorial Game," by MacLean and Anne Li-an Kao.[13] This kind of research, dealing with how well editors can predict the likes and dislikes of readers, was an early example of coorientation research.

MacLean also contributed to communication theory through his ideas on human perception. These ideas are presented in a paper he wrote with Hans Toch published in 1967, again in *Audio-Visual Communication Review*.[14] Toch and MacLean present a transactional view of perception—one that sees perception as the product of a creative act. The article emphasizes the subjectivity of perception. Toch and MacLean support the subjectivity of perception by citing empirical studies, such as the Hastorf and Cantril study "They Saw A Game."[15] But they also back it up with Zen-like parables, such as Cantril's story of three umpires:

The first umpire said, "Some's balls and some's strikes and I

---

in Journalism and Mass Communication, Washington, DC, August 1989.

[13]Malcolm MacLean and Anne Li-an Kao, "Picture Selection: An Editorial Game, " *Journalism Quarterly* 40 (1963): 230-232.

[14]Hans Toch and Malcolm S. MacLean, Jr., "Perception, Communication and Educational Research: A Transactional View," *Audio-Visual Communication Review* 10 (September-October 1962): 55-77.

[15]Albert H. Hastorf and Hadley Cantril, "They Saw a Game: A Case Study," *Journal of Abnormal and Social Psychology* 49 (1954): 129-134.

calls 'em as they is." The second umpire said, "Some's balls and some's strikes and I calls 'em as I sees 'em." While the third umpire said, "Some's balls and some's strikes but they ain't nothing till I calls 'em."

The transactional view of perception, although borrowed from psychology and not wholly due to MacLean and Toch, has many obvious implications for communication and, particularly, for journalism. One of the goals of the Interdisciplinary Communication Laboratory set up by MacLean and others at the University of Iowa was to give students the *experience* of perceiving and attempting to communicate on the basis of that perception. MacLean distrusted what he called "instant knowledge pills," the passing on of knowledge through lectures and other conventional methods. The simulation laboratory was designed to allow students to learn through experience.

One of MacLean's teaching techniques was what he called "The Eye-Witness Game."[16] Various participants in the game were exposed to the same event, but through different channels. Some were allowed to see the event itself. Some could not see the event but could interview eye-witnesses. Some only received reports from those who did interview eye-witnesses. Finally, all participants were asked to write a short story describing the event. The stories usually turned out to be very different. MacLean would then discuss what had happened, and the group would often reach the conclusion that "there is no clearly true story of the event." MacLean would then go on to ask, "Given this, which might be preferred stories and *why?*"

In playing "The Eye-Witness Game" and in doing other things in the simulation laboratory at the University of Iowa, MacLean was attempting to teach journalism in some new ways. He was attempting to apply communication theory, as others have tried to do, but MacLean believed that knowledge, even theoretical knowledge, needs to come from experience.

This was a radical approach to journalism education. It also did not help MacLean's popularity that he was an outspoken critic of most journalism education. He expressed this criticism freely in a number of position papers, memos, and working papers through the years. He dared to ask whether journalism schools were not turning out too many "hacks."[17] In one of these papers, MacLean presents a "fable" of a young engineering professor named J. Worthington Peabody who becomes the first director of a new School of Automobilism. The school had courses like Fundamentals of Auto Design I, Fundamentals of Auto Design II, Auto

---

[16]Luigi D. Manca, "Seven Notes on MacLean," *Journal of Communication Inquiry* (Spring 1976): 35-60.

[17]Malcolm MacLean, "A Process Concept of Communication Education: A Position Statement for the Educational Policies Committee," Iowa City, School of Journalism, University of Iowa, November 17, 1966, pp. 4-5.

Body Manufacture, Auto Distribution and Sales, and Auto Management. MacLean goes on at length to describe the concern in the field when some schools begin to hire PhD's in "manufacturology" with little or no practical experience instead of the "real pros" from the automobile industry. In the same paper, MacLean suggested that journalism schools should attempt to turn out "heretical, subversive infiltrators." These heretics should be competent in basic communication skills. They should be deeply concerned and thoughtful about the human condition. They should feel keenly their responsibility to their fellow humans. And rather than trying to overthrow the establishment, they should help to make it an establishment that works.

MacLean's strong social concern was also shown in another paper he wrote after the racial disorders and protests in Watts and other locations during the summer of 1967. He wrote, "I see an implied demand that our communicators need to know deeply, empathically, and at the same time to be able to analyze objectively and communicate what it means to be poor among the rich, to be hungry among the well-fed, to be black among the white, to be degraded among the smug, to be sick among the healthy, to be unheard, unheard, unheard . . . in a society noisy with messages."[18]

The new experimental program at Iowa met with considerable opposition—from members of the faculty, from members of the state's press, and even from some state legislators. MacLean himself came under personal attack. In 1971, MacLean was brought before a subcommittee of the Iowa legislature looking into the budgeting of Iowa's three state universities, and was questioned about his salary, the contents of journalism school laboratory publications, the number of secretaries in relation to the number of faculty, and so forth. Soon after this inquiry, the American Council on Education for Journalism took accreditation away from the Iowa program because it no longer offered traditional sequences of journalism courses. MacLean initially announced that the new program would continue on as before, but soon after that he resigned as director of the school.

Although the simulation laboratory was not a success at Iowa, similar programs were later set up at the University of Wis-consin-Milwaukee and Northern Kentucky State College.[19]

MacLean served as president of the International Com-munication Association for the academic year 1972-1973. He held this honor during the same year his program was running into some of its greatest controversy. On February 20, 1974, he died of an apparent heart attack.

MacLean never fully wrote out his theoretical ideas concerning mass communication, which drew upon general systems the-

---

[18]MacLean, "On the Education of Responsible Newsmen," p. 6.

[19]Sharon Murphy, "MacLean and Learning," *Journal of Communication Inquiry* (Spring 1976): 101-107.

ory and transactional perception. Possibly the duties of administering the Iowa program and the excitement of actually applying some of these ideas in the simulation laboratory kept MacLean from fully elaborating his theory on paper. Ironically, his greatest intellectual contribution is likely to be his work on the Westley-MacLean model—one of his earliest pieces of scholarship and an idea that came about originally as an organizing principle for a review of the literature.

Donohue, Olien, and Tichenor and the Structural Approach

George A. Donohue (1924-), Clarice N. Olien (1933-) and Phillip J. Tichenor (1931-) have been involved for nearly 30 years in a program of mass communication research at the University of Minnesota. From the beginning, the program has been aimed at understanding the conditions that lead to increased or decreased *information gain*, particularly but not exclusively concerning science and technology, in society. As part of this effort, they devised the knowledge gap hypothesis, a significant idea that has led to dozens of follow-up studies.

Donohue, Olien, and Tichenor regard the knowledge gap hypothesis as important, but they do not view it as their major contribution. Rather, they regard it as a kind of "bell ringer" that might bring attention to their main contribution—the application of a structural approach to the study of mass communication.[1]

The structural approach that these researchers have taken involves looking at communities and their mass media systems as social structures. The approach makes an important distinction between larger communities, which tend to be pluralistic, and smaller communities, which tend to be less differentiated. There are many important differences between these types of communities, but one of the most important deals with the role of conflict. In large communities, conflict is seen as inevitable and even necessary for system maintenance, whereas in smaller communities conflict is seen more as something to be avoided. Another important aspect of the structural approach concerns groups within the social structure. These groups often differ in status and power, as well as in access to mass communication. This kind of analysis of the social structure of communities and their media systems has many interesting implications for mass communication, and it is to the task of spelling out and investigating these implications that the Minnesota team has devoted

---

[1]Letter from Donohue, Olien, and Tichenor to James W. Tankard, Jr., October 28, 1987.

much of its energy.

George A. Donohue was born October 26, 1924, in Great Neck, New York. He received his BA in 1948 from Washington State University at Pullman. From 1951 to 1953 he was an instructor at that university. In 1953, he moved to the University of Minnesota, where he became an instructor. He remained at Minnesota, becoming assistant professor in 1955, associate professor in 1959, and professor and head of rural sociology in 1962. He received his PhD from Washington State University in 1967.

Clarice N. Olien was born February 26, 1933, in Clarkfield, Minnesota. She received her BS in secondary education from the University of Minnesota in 1955. In 1961 she became an assistant extension specialist in rural sociology at the University of Minnesota. In 1962 she received her MA from that university with a major in sociology and a minor in anthropology, and she also became an instructor in rural sociology at the university. She was promoted in 1970 to assistant professor, in 1973 to associate professor, and in 1979 to professor.

Phillip J. Tichenor was born July 31, 1931, in Sparta, Wisconsin. He received his BS in agricultural journalism from the University of Wisconsin in 1953 and his MS in the same field from the same university in 1956. From 1956 to 1962, he was employed as an instructor and extension information specialist at the Institute of Agriculture, University of Minnesota. In 1962, he became an assistant professor at the University of Minnesota. In 1965, he completed the PhD in mass communication research from Stanford University, with a dissertation that dealt with science communication and knowledge of science. In 1965, he became an associate professor and in 1970 a professor at the University of Minnesota. He holds a joint appointment with the School of Journalism and Mass Communication and Rural Sociology.

Donohue was working as an assistant professor of sociology in 1956 when Tichenor joined the university. Donohue had done a number of studies of social conditions in rural Minnesota, and Tichenor, working as an agricultural journalist for the Institute, had written and distributed press reports to community media based on the studies. They first collaborated (along with two other authors) on a report published in 1959. Donohue and Olien first collaborated (along with another author—not Tichenor) on an article published in 1962.

The three team members who would go on to do many studies together began their first research field work in the early 1960s as a result of their joint interest in the consequences of purposive communication in social change. Purposive communicators include such people as county agricultural agents, school superintendents, religious leaders, and civic group leaders. The researchers designed and launched a study of one particular purposive communicator role—the county agricultural agent. It led to the first publication of the team—the June, 1963, Extension

Series No. 6 "Purposive Communications: A Study of County Agents' Educational Material in Minnesota Newspapers." The report identified the county agent as having a well-established role as a source of news and feature material for newspapers. It indicated that differences in display and other treatment given to extension news varied more according to type of newspaper (daily versus weekly) than to the nature of the event.

Their next research project used the Westley-MacLean model as a conceptual base. The study focused on county extension agents attempting to place information about agriculture in newspapers.[2] These county agents could be viewed as "A"s in the Westley-MacLean model. The goal of the study was to identify the factors that predict a source's success in placing news in the media. The project tested some advice that public relations specialists had drawn from group dynamics literature and gave to purposive communicators—that they should get to know the editor personally, have frequent telephone conversations, have coffee frequently, and take part in social gatherings that editors attend. While some variables taken from the group dynamics model— agreement by editors and sources of news values, for instance— were related to placement of messages in the media, others were not. Furthermore, some variables not at the psychological level, such as the type of community, were useful predictors, pointing to the importance of a less microscopic level of analysis. Additional analysis identified the power status of the editor in the community as an important predictor. These variables began to hint at the importance of social structure—a factor not included in the Westley-MacLean model—in determining which messages were printed and which were not. The Minnesota team began to reconceptualize its research to take into account the importance of social structure.

The importance of conflict as a variable also became apparent. Further research indicated that newspapers in smaller communities were less likely to report conflict. The power status of the editor was identified as another important variable. Having an editor in the power structure was associated with less conflict reporting in small community newspapers, but with more reporting of conflict in large community newspapers.[3] The researchers began to reconceptualize information as something under a high degree of control.

The importance of social structure also showed up in a study of the accuracy of science news.[4] This study showed that the most

---

[2]Tichenor, Olien, and Donohue, "Predicting a Source's Success in Placing News in the Media," *Journalism Quarterly* 44 (1967): 32-42.

[3]Olien, Donohue, and Tichenor, "The Community Editor's Power and the Reporting of Conflict," *Journalism Quarterly* 45 (1968): 243-252.

[4]Tichenor, Olien, Annette Harrison, and Donohue, "Mass Communication Systems and Communication Accuracy in Science News Reporting," *Journalism Quarterly* 47 (1970): 673-683.

powerful predictors of the accuracy of science news were assignment of the story by an editor (as opposed to the reporter originating the story), the scientist's perception of organizational policy for news reporting, the scientist's administrative role, and the scientist's beliefs about newspaper accuracy. Most of these factors are related to a social systems perspective emphasizing control in message production. Variables that dealt more with the individual and less with the social system, such as the reporter's experience in science writing, were not related to the accuracy of science news reporting.

Their empirical findings, then, led Donohue, Olien, and Tichenor to reconceptualize their theory less in terms of individual and group psychology and more in terms of social structure. In doing so, they shifted from a micro-conceptual to a macro-conceptual framework. It identifies media structure, message environment, audience system structure, and social conflict as key factors in information flow. In this approach, some of the important variables to be studied are community structure, mass media input, and the level of social conflict that the issue has generated.

The knowledge gap hypothesis, which was initially stated in an article in *Public Opinion Quarterly* in 1970, emerged from considering social change and the role of communication within that change.[5] It can also be seen as an attempt to relate social system variables—in particular, socioeconomic categories—to mass communication effects, particularly on information level. Tichenor, Donohue, and Olien started with the assumption that in a participative, democratic system, information should flow at a maximum rate to enable all citizens to vote intelligently and express their concerns in a rational manner. This assumption recognizes the idea that possession of information is basic for social power. The researchers also recognized that in any democratic system some groups will be more powerful than others, and that information is a necessary resource for all groups in seeking to improve their power positions. At the same time, it was known that attention to the mass media was highly selective, with persons of higher education more likely to be exposed to public affairs information. Concern about these kinds of disparities showed up in the "Great Society" programs for improving education for the disadvantaged.

This kind of thinking led the research team to question some advice often given by information specialists—that the more information you pour into a system, the more likely you are to reach all groups and thus equalize the distribution of information. They assumed, on the contrary, that stepping up the flow would lead to greater disparities in information. This led them to the hypothesis that the mass media are creating and enlarging a knowledge gap between segments of society. Or, to put it more

---

[5]Letter from Donohue, Olien, and Tichenor to Tankard, October 28, 1987.

formally, "As the infusion of mass media information into a social system increases, segments of the population with higher socioeconomic status tend to acquire this information at a faster rate than the lower status segments, so that the gap in knowledge between these segments tends to increase rather than to decrease."[6]

The term "knowledge gap" was adopted after it was used in some of the early informal discussions of the three researchers about the process of information flow. It also fit with some of the ongoing discussion at the time concerning achievement and opportunity gaps in society.[7]

Some time after the initial paper describing the knowledge gap hypothesis, the research team published two papers attempting to spell out their basic theoretical approach—the structural approach—more fully.[8] These papers took a systems theory approach—looking at society and the communities making up society as either systems or components of systems. In these papers, they identified one of their basic assumptions—that all communication is under some form of human control in the interest of the achievement of objectives and goals. Starting from this assumption, the key questions become: Who controls information, how, for what purpose, and with what social consequences? Information is assumed to be controlled primarily in the interest of system maintenance. The system being maintained may be the media subsystem itself, a source subsystem with which the media have systemic relations, or the social system as a whole. The maintenance function is fulfilled by two sets of processes—the *feedback-control* process and the *distribution-control* process. Feedback-control is used by Donohue, Olien, and Tichenor to refer to a regulatory function performed by the media subsystem for the social system as a whole. Historically, this has been expressed as the "watchdog" function of the press, with the press serving as a "fourth estate" that checks on government. Distribution-control serves a maintenance function through selective dissemination of information, or through selective withholding of information. Censorship is one example of distribution-control. The development of these concepts led the researchers to formulate several propositions, including the following:

The less complex and differentiated the system, the more likely mass media within the system are to confine themselves to the

---

[6]Tichenor, Donohue, and Olien, "Mass Media Flow and Differential Growth in Knowledge," *Public Opinion Quarterly* 34 (1970): 159-170.

[7]Letter from Donohue, Olien, and Tichenor to Tankard, October 28, 1987.

[8]Tichenor, Donohue, and Olien, "Mass Communication Research: Evolution of a Structural Model," *Journalism Quarterly* 50 (1973): 419-425; Donohue, Tichenor, and Olien, "Mass Media Functions, Knowledge and Social Control," *Journalism Quarterly* 50 (1973): 652-659.

distributive aspect of system maintenance.

And, the corollary to that proposition:

The more differentiated and pluralistic the system, the more likely mass media are to perform a feedback-control as well as a distributive function.

A few years after the initial paper describing the knowledge gap was published, the authors went on to refine the hypothesis and investigate it further. Some of their research suggested that under certain conditions, a knowledge gap may be reduced rather than increased as media input increases. One of the important factors that appeared to make a difference was the amount of conflict about a local issue. As the amount of conflict increases, the knowledge gap tends to decline. This gap reduction is more likely to happen when the issue is one that arouses general concern from the community as a whole, and it is more likely to happen in a small, homogeneous community than in a large, pluralistic one.[9]

The researchers have also extended knowledge gap research to differences *between* communities. Most previous knowledge gap research had concentrated on disparities between higher and lower status groups. In a study focusing more on the differences between communities, the investigators looked particularly at the effect on knowledge levels of the "pullback" of metropolitan dailies from smaller surrounding communities.[10] Metro daily newspaper circulation has declined in nonmetropolitan areas, with the biggest declines coming in agricultural counties. Donohue, Tichenor, and Olien found that smaller newspapers within the region pick up some of this circulation, but not all of it. Furthermore, they do not make up for all the lost content. In addition, in the outlying communities, education is more strongly associated with reading the metro paper than with reading the local paper, bringing out another case of differential access to information based on status. The authors label this as a new kind of gap— a "reading gap."

They also have suggested an *attitudinal* hypothesis that is similar in some ways to the knowledge gap hypothesis. This hypothesis states that "the higher the level of perception of conflict regarding an issue in a community, the lower the correlation in that community between socioeconomic status and attitudes toward alternative courses of action."[11] This hypothesis contra-

---

[9]Donohue, Tichenor, and Olien, "Mass Media and the Knowledge Gap: A Hypothesis Reconsidered," *Communication Research* 2 (1975): 3-23.

[10]Donohue, Tichenor, and Olien, "Metro Daily Pullback and Knowledge Gaps: Within and Between Communities," *Communication Research* 13 (1986): 453-471.

[11]Tichenor, Jane M. Rodenkirchen, Olien, and Donohue, "Community

dicts the prevailing wisdom that educating people about certain issues will lead to greater support for certain alternatives, just as the knowledge gap hypothesis contradicted the prevailing wisdom that increased information flow will lead to a widespread increase in knowledge throughout a community.

The knowledge gap hypothesis has generated extensive research by scholars other than Donohue, Olien, and Tichenor. An article published in 1983 that reviewed the knowledge gap literature identified 58 studies of the hypothesis.[12] Many more studies have been done since that time. The knowledge gap hypothesis has particularly attracted the interest of Scandinavian researchers, who seem especially concerned about the role of communication in increasing or decreasing equality in society. A group of Swedish researchers has identified what it calls *communication potential* as a key variable in the occurrence of knowledge gaps. Communication potential is based on three factors: individual characteristics, such as personality traits or ability to speak a language; characteristics dependent on social position, such as income and education; and characteristics of the social structure, including the family or other groups a person belongs to. If there are systematic differences between groups in these three factors, then there will be differences in the acquisition of knowledge, as well as differences in the achievements of various goals.[13]

A number of critics have pointed out that, as originally formulated, the knowledge gap hypothesis was too narrow. Some have suggested that it was too narrow in terms of the conceptualization of effects. Everett Rogers, for instance, has said of the hypothesis: "It should deal with the *attitudinal and overt behavioral effects* of communication as well as just 'knowledge'; thus, I propose calling it the 'communication effects gap' hypothesis."[14]

Jack M. McLeod, Carl R. Bybee, and Jean A. Durall have suggested an alternative concept, the *equivalence of informed political participation*.[15] This concept is a kind of inverse of the knowledge gap, in that it is putting emphasis on the *equivalence*

Issues, Conflict, and Public Affairs Knowledge," in Peter Clarke (Ed.), *New Models for Mass Communication Research* (Beverly Hills, Sage Publications, 1973), pp. 45-79.

[12]Cecilie Gaziano, "The Knowledge Gap: An Analytical Review of Media Effects," *Communication Research* 10 (1983): 447-486.

[13]Anne-Marie Thunberg, Kjell Nowak, Karl Erik Rosengren, and Bengt Sigurd, *Communication and Equity: A Swedish Perspective* (Stockholm: Almqvist & Wiksell International, 1982).

[14]Everett M. Rogers, "Communication and Development: The Passing of the Dominant Paradigm," *Communication Research* 3 (1976): 233.

[15]Jack M. McLeod, Carl R. Bybee, and Jean A. Durall, "Equivalence of Informed Political Participation: The 1976 Presidential Debates as a Source of Influence," in G. Cleveland Wilhoit and Harold de Bock (Eds.), *Mass Communication Review Yearbook* (Vol. 2) (Beverly Hills, CA.: Sage, 1981), pp. 469-493.

of levels of knowledge or other politically-relevant variables across social status categories, rather than the differences or gaps. Furthermore, the type of gap that can occur is given a broader conceptualization. These authors looked at equivalence in terms of five possible effects, including increased knowledge, but also including stimulating involvement, facilitating vote decisions, increasing participation, and strengthening of system values. For each effect, the authors also looked for equivalence of two types—equivalence of exposure and equivalence of predictive strength (benefit from exposure). They found that differences were more likely to occur on the effects variables other than knowledge, providing some empirical support for the idea of broadening the gap hypothesis.

Swedish researcher Lennart Brantgarde also attempted to expand the conceptualization of knowledge gap effects, proposing that they could occur at the levels of information-seeking, knowledge retention, and dissemination of information to others.[16] He found the poorly educated were high in information consumption, but low in retention and dissemination, whereas the well-educated showed the opposite tendency.

Researchers have also suggested that the original formulation of the knowledge gap hypothesis was too narrow in terms of its conceptualization of the causal variable. In the McLeod, Bybee, and Durall article, for instance, differences were looked at not only by comparing social classes (as measured by education) but also by comparing old and young, as well as the politically interested and the politically uninterested. B.K.L. Genova and Bradley S. Greenberg have also argued that interest in public affairs might be a better explanation of public information gain than such socioeconomic factors as education.[17]

James S. Ettema and F. Gerald Kline have provided a restatement of the knowledge gap hypothesis in terms more related to the individual's needs for information:

> As the infusion of mass media information into a social system increases, segments of the population motivated to acquire that information and/or for which that information is functional tend to acquire that information at a faster rate than those not motivated or for which it is not functional, so that the gap in knowledge between these segments tends to increase rather than decrease.[18]

---

[16]Lennart Brantgarde, "The Information Gap and Municipal Politics in Sweden," *Communication Research* 10 (1983): 357-373.

[17]B.K.L. Genova and Bradley S. Greenberg, "Interests in News and the Knowledge Gap," in Wilhoit and Bock, *Mass Communication Review Yearbook*, pp. 494-508.

[18]James S. Ettema and F. Gerald Kline, "Deficits, Differences, and Ceilings: Contingent Conditions for Understanding the Knowledge Gap," *Communication Research* 4 (1977): 188.

Criticism of the knowledge gap hypothesis on more fundamental grounds has come from researcher Brenda Dervin.[19] She
argues that the knowledge gap hypothesis emerged from a research tradition that focused on the purposes of the source. It is
from this perspective that people who do not receive certain information from the mass media are seen as lacking. Dervin calls
this a "blame-the-victim syndrome." She called for a new perspective from which "it is the sources who are seen as lacking, particularly in their responsiveness to the needs of the receivers."[20]

Researcher Cecilie Gaziano has pointed out that although
there is a great deal of research on the knowledge gap that is
essentially based on finding correlations between education and
knowledge, there is little research that has actually looked at or
manipulated mass media coverage of issues as a variable. She has
recommended that panel designs or perhaps even experiments be
used to better pinpoint the role of changing mass media information flow.[21]

One of the strengths of the Minnesota team's approach to
mass communication research has been the care with which it
has engaged in theory-building. Overall, the structural approach
has served as a strong conceptual framework, leading to numerous insights and hypotheses. The researchers have stuck with
this approach through the years after an initial attempt at a social psychological approach, and it has been a well that has not
run dry. From this approach the researchers have systematically
generated hypotheses, which they have then tested, often two or
three at a time, in empirical studies. Over the years, they must
have investigated 40 or 50 of these hypotheses. The 1970 article
that originally presented the knowledge gap hypothesis can be
presented almost as a model of theory-building. If we take Gerald
Hage's *Techniques and Problems of Theory Construction in Sociology*[22] as a guide for what should be included in a theory, for
instance, the 1970 article includes many of the components Hage
advocates. The paper includes the concepts of mass media information, socioeconomic status, and knowledge (*general variable
concepts*); the hypothesis itself (the *theoretical statement*); five
reasons the hypothesis should be expected to be true (the *theoretical rationale*); two operational forms of the hypothesis (the *operational linkage*); and, of course, some data supportive of the hypothesis.

---

[19]Brenda Dervin, "Communication Gaps and Inequities: Moving
Toward a Reconceptualization," in Brenda Dervin and Melvin J. Voigt
(Eds.), *Progress in Communication Sciences* (Vol. 2) (Norwood, NJ: Ablex,
1980), pp. 73-112.

[20]Ibid., p. 81.

[21]Gaziano, pp. 474-475.

[22]Jerald Hage, *Techniques and Problems of Theory Construction in
Sociology* (New York: John Wiley & Sons, 1972).

It appears that the structural approach being used by Donohue, Olien, and Tichenor has the potential to generate many more fruitful hypotheses, in addition to the knowledge gap hypothesis and the others these researchers have tested. After all, the structural approach is dealing with the relationships between the mass media, knowledge, conflict, power, social class, and social inequality—some of the most important concepts in human society.

Steven Chaffee and Jack McLeod: The Wisconsin Collaborators

For many years, the Mass Communication Research Center at the University of Wisconsin has been the site of a major outpouring of research on journalism and mass communication. Much of that output has been the work of two men—Steven H. Chaffee (1935-) and Jack M. McLeod (1930-)—and their students.

A major factor contributing to this flow of research was the ability of Chaffee and McLeod to devise general conceptual models that served as frameworks for research studies. Principal among these models were the Family Communication Pattern model and the coorientation model. In turn, these general models have led to subsequent research in several important areas: political socialization, adolescent media use, and the effects of television violence. Using these models, Chaffee and McLeod and their students were able to generate numerous studies and to appear frequently on the convention program of the Communication Theory and Methodology Division of the Association for Education in Journalism and Mass Communication.

The two men have also played major roles in upgrading research efforts in AEJMC, the major scholarly association in the field of journalism. They were involved in the founding of the Theory and Methodology division in 1965 and helped bring about such innovations as making research papers available to be read before convention sessions and having discussants at sessions. These ideas were initially tried in the Theory and Methodology division and then spread to other divisions.

McLeod was born August 30, 1930, in Chicago. His father was a clerk for the Chicago and Northwestern Railroad. His older brother had a photography business, and Jack was a photographer for his high school newspaper. He began studying journalism at the University of Wisconsin in Madison in 1948, with the intention of becoming a Washington correspondent or a foreign correspondent. During his studies, however, he began to think those goals might be difficult to achieve and that the more realistic result of pursuing a career in journalism was likely to be a reporting job for some small newspaper in Wisconsin.

At about the same time, McLeod became acquainted with Malcolm MacLean, an instructor in the School of Journalism working on a doctorate. MacLean persuaded McLeod to help him build a Guttman scalogram, which was part of MacLean's dissertation. At that time, a Guttman scalogram was an apparatus consisting of plywood boards and balsa wood slats containing BBs. By manipulating the slats, one could analyze questionnaire responses and determine to what extent they formed a Guttman scale. McLeod estimates that not more than a dozen people in the world ever built a scalogram board. As McLeod helped MacLean build this apparatus in MacLean's bedroom, he became excited about the possibilities of doing research to answer important questions about human communication. McLeod picked up from MacLean not only an enthusiasm for communication research, but also a notion that students and faculty members could be colleagues, as well as a sense that research could be used in support of worthwhile social change.[1]

McLeod finished his bachelor's degree in journalism at Wisconsin and stayed on to get a master's degree. His master's thesis was a content analysis and thus involved some use of research techniques. After finishing at Madison, McLeod returned to Chicago to do some survey interviewing. He then went into the Army for a 2-year term. In 1955, he went to the University of Michigan, where he finished a second master's, this time in sociology. He continued his graduate work and finished a PhD in social psychology. At Michigan, McLeod studied with social psychologists Ted Newcomb and Daniel Katz, with sociologist Morris Janowitz, and with statistician Hubert Blalock. His dissertation, "Yielding as a Response to Cognitive Imbalance," was finished in 1962 under Newcomb's guidance.

In 1962, McLeod returned to the University of Wisconsin as an assistant professor in the School of Journalism. He joined such other researchers on the faculty as Bruce Westley and Percy Tannenbaum. McLeod soon took over the job that Tannenbaum had held of chairman of the Mass Communication Research Center, the position he still holds.

Chaffee was born August 21, 1935, in South Gate, California. His father was a postal clerk who went to law school at night while Chaffee was in high school and who eventually became a lawyer. Chaffee started delivering newspapers when he was 9. He also started reading them and reports he had the feeling, "I can do better than that." He attended the University of Redlands, where he majored in history and was editor of the school newspaper for 2 years. After graduating in 1957, he enlisted in the Navy and became the Public Information Officer at the U.S. Naval Station at Long Beach. Upon his discharge from the Navy, he started graduate school in journalism at the University of California at Los Angeles, with the intention of working in journalism to support

---

[1]Telephone interview with Jack M. McLeod, Oct. 7, 1987.

himself while he studied for a PhD in sociology. During a journalism department party early in the first semester, Chaffee was talking to Walter Wilcox, a faculty member who had finished a PhD at Iowa. Chaffee told Wilcox what he was interested in, and Wilcox told him about a new field called mass communication research. On Wilcox's advice, Chaffee enrolled in Jack Lyle's course in mass communication theory. Lyle had just finished a PhD in mass communication research at Stanford.[2]

Chaffee says the first piece of communication research that he got excited about was Schramm, Lyle, and Parker's *Television in the Lives of Our Children*.[3] The book came out while Chaffee was in Lyle's course, and Chaffee reviewed it for the school newspaper. He was impressed that the book reported 11 separate studies, and says it showed him that there was a whole field of mass communication research opening up.[4]

Chaffee finished his MS in journalism at UCLA in 1962 and then began PhD work in communication at Stanford, where Lyle had received his PhD and where Schramm and Parker were on the faculty. There, Chaffee studied with Schramm, Parker, and Nathan Maccoby, but most closely with Richard Carter.

At Stanford, a group gathered for coffee every afternoon at the Tressider Student Union. It typically was made up of Carter, who was an assistant professor, and several graduate students, including Chaffee, Maxwell McCombs, Lee Ruggels, and sometimes Jim Brinton. McCombs and Chaffee talked particularly about the discrepancy they perceived between the research they were studying, which dealt with topics like attitude change, and the field they were interested in, which was journalism. Chaffee and McCombs would also try to clarify what Carter had said in class and how his abstract ideas could be applied to research. Chaffee went on to do his dissertation under Carter's guidance. It was based on Carter's concepts of *salience* and *pertinence* of an attitude object, ideas which he developed as part of his paradigm for understanding communication and affective relations.[5] Chaffee received the PhD in 1965.

In that same year, he moved to the University of Wisconsin to become an assistant professor in the School of Journalism, where he began his highly fruitful collaboration with McLeod. Around 1967, the burden of the school's research efforts were thrust onto McLeod and Chaffee when Westley, Tannenbaum, and Richard Carter all left Wisconsin. It was then that McLeod became chairman of the Mass Communication Research Center.

Chaffee remained at Wisconsin for much of his academic ca-

[2]Telephone interview with Steven H. Chaffee, Oct. 7, 1987.

[3]Wilbur Schramm, Jack Lyle, and Edwin B. Parker, *Television in the Lives of Our Children* (Stanford, CA: Stanford University Press, 1961).

[4]Ibid.

[5]Richard F. Carter, "Communication and Affective Relations," *Journalism Quarterly* 42 (1965): 203-212.

reer until 1981, when he returned to Stanford to become director of the Institute for Communication Research. In the early 1980s, he shuttled back and forth between Wisconsin and Stanford, spending a year or two at one place and a year or two at the other, until 1986 when he settled in at Stanford, where he is now Janet M. Peck Professor of International Communication and chairman of the Department of Communication.

The first joint Chaffee and McLeod research began soon after Chaffee arrived at Madison. It dealt with family communication patterns, or, as it would come to be known, FCP. McLeod's dissertation at the University of Michigan had dealt with the effect of family environment on susceptibility to persuasion. When Chaffee arrived, McLeod and Vernon Stone, also on the journalism faculty, had already begun a research project trying to study the role of family environment in producing the kind of inoculation against attitude change that was being studied by social psychologist William McGuire.[6] Stone had written some questionnaire items to measure family communication patterns. These items became the items used with little change throughout most of the family communication pattern research. Chaffee was to join McLeod in teaching the graduate-undergraduate course in research methods that fall, and they decided to conduct a class survey dealing with family communication. The results of this research were presented in two papers at the Association for Education in Journalism convention in Iowa City the following summer, with H.S. Eswara and Dan Wackman as co-authors. This convention in 1966 was the first AEJ convention at which there was a Theory & Methodology Division. With McLeod serving as paper chair for T&M and with Chaffee helping, these initial T&M paper sessions saw the first use at AEJ of discussants and having papers available before sessions.

Chaffee and McLeod expected to find that the family communication items measured a single dimension—something like "open" and "closed" families. McLeod says he did "an eyeball factor analysis" of the correlations of the items, however, and it looked like there was more than one dimension.[7] Wackman, who was working as a research assistant for McLeod, did a computer factor analysis, and the results confirmed that there were at least two dimensions. One dimension dealt with what the researchers called *socio-orientation*. Families that stress this orientation put an emphasis on maintaining harmonious personal relations, avoiding controversy, and repressing feelings on extrapersonal topics. A second dimension dealt with what the researchers called *concept-orientation*. Families that stress this orientation put an

---

[6]William J. McGuire, "Resistance to Persuasion Conferred by Active and Passive Prior Refutation of the Same and Alternative Counterarguments," *Journal of Abnormal and Social Psychology* 63 (1962): 326-332.

[7]Videotaped interview with Jack M. McLeod, Theory and Methodology Division, AEJMC, 1977.

emphasis on the expression of ideas, exposure to controversy, and encouragement to join in on controversy.

Since the two dimensions were found to be uncorrelated, the researchers were able to create the following four-fold typology of family communication patterns:

Protective. These families stress socio-orientation only. The child is encouraged to get along with others and is prohibited from expressing dissent.

Pluralistic. These families stress concept-orientation only. They encourage children to explore new ideas and make up their own minds.

Laissez faire. These families stress neither type of orientation.

Consensual. These families attempt to stress both orientations. The child is exposed to controversy but is encouraged to develop concepts that are consistent with the parents' ideas.[8]

Family communication patterns, as measured with the four-fold typology, turned out to be good predictors of both parent and child media use habits, as well as a number of other things. For both adolescents and parents, protective families produce heavy television use and low news consumption, whereas pluralistic families produce low television use and heavy news consumption. Members of consensual families tend to be heavy users of all media, whereas members of laissez-faire families tend to be light users of all media. Stone and Chaffee also showed that family communication patterns are related to persuasibility, with people from families high in socio-orientation being more persuasible than people from families low in socio-orientation, and with an expert source leading to enhanced attitude change for persons high in concept-orientation and decreased attitude change for persons low in concept-orientation.[9]

The family communication pattern model also became useful in research Chaffee and McLeod did on television violence, a major topic in mass communication research in the 1970s. At that time, the Surgeon General's Scientific Advisory Committee on Television and Social Behavior was conducting a major investigation of the effects of television violence. Chaffee and McLeod were asked to become involved in the research because some of their surveys dealing with family communication patterns had also contained measures of television watching, including the viewing of television violence. They carried out additional re-

---

[8]Steven H. Chaffee, Jack M. McLeod, and Charles K. Atkin, "Parental Influences on Adolescent Media Use," *American Behavioral Scientist* 14 (January/February 1971): 323-340.

[9]Vernon A. Stone and Steven H. Chaffee, "Family Communication Patterns and Source-Message Orientation," *Journalism Quarterly* 47 (1970): 239-246.

search for the Surgeon General's committee, and found that family communication patterns were related to both aggressive behavior and television violence viewing. Socio-orientation was a rather good predictor of both violence viewing and aggressive behavior. Concept-orientation had a negative association with aggressive behavior. Overall, their research showed a positive correlation between violence viewing and aggressive behavior, and this correlation held up when they controlled for family communication variables.

The family communication pattern typology has been used in numerous other studies, particularly by students of Chaffee and McLeod. Chaffee recommended that students include FCP items in their questionnaires even when studying something else, because it would give them something to fall back on.[10] McLeod, however, has commented that it may not be appropriate to plug FCP items into just any research study. As McLeod once said, "FCP is not an additive that one dumps into your gas tank to get more research mileage."[11]

The second major idea of Chaffee and McLeod—the coorientation model—extended and combined the thinking of the two men's major professors, Carter and Newcomb. Newcomb, with whom McLeod had studied, had developed a symmetry or consistency model dealing with the communication between two people (A and B) about an object of interest to both (X).[12] He postulated a strain toward consistency or symmetry in the attitudes toward X held by A and B. The more A and B are attracted toward one another, the greater will be the strain toward consistency in their attitudes toward X.

Chaffee and McLeod made two modifications of the Newcomb model. The first was to add the idea, taken from the field of person perception (the study of how people perceive other people), that the A-B-X triangle could itself be viewed by both A and B, and that it could be viewed differently by the two. For example, B might have a favorable attitude toward X, but A might misperceive it as being unfavorable. The second modification was to add the idea from Carter that a person does not orient toward a single object in the environment, but toward a discrimination between objects.[13] For any two objects, discriminations might be made on each of the attributes on which they can be compared. Carter introduced the term *salience* to refer to a person's summary evaluation of one object and *pertinence* to refer to a single discrimination between two objects on the basis of a difference in a common attribute.

---

[10]Videotaped interview with Steven H. Chaffee, Theory and Methodology Division, AEJMC, 1977.

[11]Videotaped interview with McLeod, 1977.

[12]Theodore M. Newcomb, "An Approach to the Study of Communicative Acts," *Psychological Review* 60 (November 1953): 393-404.

[13]Carter, pp. 203-204.

Chaffee and McLeod developed a measurement model for research dealing with the basic two-person coorientation situation. This model postulates a number of variables that are useful to look at in communication studies. One is *congruency*, or the similarity between a person's own cognitions and that person's perceptions of the other person's cognitions. A second variable is *accuracy*, or the extent to which one person's estimate of the other's cognitions matches what that person really thinks. A third kind of variable deals with the degree of similarity between the orientations of A and B toward X. This is actually applied in terms of two variables, and this is where the Carter concepts come in. *Agreement* is the extent to which A and B have the same summary evaluations (or *saliences*) for objects. *Understanding* is the extent to which A and B have similar cognitive structures in terms of objects and attributes (or *pertinences*).[14]

The main utility of the coorientation measurement model is that it suggests some new measures for the effects of communication. Chaffee and McLeod have argued that much communication research in the past has been concerned with *agreement* as a dependent variable. Examples of this kind of research would include most of the research on attitude change, influence, and conformity. Chaffee and McLeod argue that agreement is a poor choice for a dependent variable because attitudes and values are based on individual variables and constraints and are unlikely to be changed by communication alone. They suggest that *understanding* might make a better variable for communication studies. Understanding refers to the similarity of orientations toward a number of objects on a number of attributes. It is a more complicated measure, and it has not been used much. It may be a more realistic variable for communication studies, however, because communication might be able to change these more subtle orientations.

Chaffee and McLeod also suggest that *accuracy*, or the similarity between our perception of B's thinking and B's actual thinking, might make an ideal variable for measuring the effects of communication. If we can't expect communication to change people's attitudes, it may be reasonable to expect communication at least to make each person aware of what the other person is thinking. Accuracy has in fact been adopted as a variable by researchers in speech communication studying interpersonal communication.

The coorientation model spurred an extensive body of research—some by Chaffee and McLeod themselves, some by their students, and some by other researchers outside of the Chaffee and McLeod research family.

The coorientation model is essentially a model of communi-

---

[14]Jack M. McLeod and Steven H. Chaffee, "Interpersonal Approaches to Communication Research," *American Behavioral Scientist* 16 (March/April 1973): 469-499.

cation, not a theory. As such, it becomes a useful paradigm for conceptualizing research. It is particularly useful for suggesting a set of variables for use in studies.

One difficulty with the coorientation model, which Chaffee and McLeod acknowledge, is that it basically deals with interpersonal communication. It is not always clear how the coorientation model relates to mass communication. Studies using the coorientation model sometimes don't even deal with mass media variables. In some studies, mass media variables are brought in as possible explanations of differences in coorientation variables, but they almost seem to be brought in as an afterthought. For instance, Stamm, Bowes, and Bowes used the coorientation paradigm to examine how townspeople and students in a university town viewed the police.[15] Reading about students in the local newspaper was introduced as the only media variable, and it was found not to increase the accuracy of perception of one group by the other.

Another coorientation study which did use mass media variables was a study by Clarke of teenagers' information-seeking about popular music.[16] Most coorientation studies have used coorientation variables as dependent variables, but in this study, Clarke used a coorientation variable, congruency, as an independent variable. Clarke found that congruency, or the awareness of other persons thought to like the same musical groups, was a strong predictor of teenage information-seeking about popular music.

A third approach for relating the coorientation model to mass communication is to examine the coorientation of various individuals involved in the mass communication process, including reporters, editors, and readers. For instance, Martin, O'Keefe, and Nayman used the coorientation paradigm to examine perceptions of editors and readers.[17] The study found that editors were more accurate in their perception of readers than readers were in their perception of editors.

Both coorientation and family communication are narrow in scope. They don't address many of the problems of the field of mass communication. But, of course, neither do many other theoretical ideas or conceptualizations in the field of mass communication research. Neither coorientation nor family communication is a hot topic for research the way they were 15-20 years ago.

---

[15]Keith R. Stamm, John E. Bowes, and Barbara J. Bowes, "Generation Gap a Communication Problem? A Coorientational Analysis," *Journalism Quarterly* 50 (1973): 629-637.

[16]Peter Clarke, "Teenagers' Coorientation and Information-Seeking About Pop Music," *American Behavioral Scientist* 16 (March/April 1973): 551-566.

[17]Ralph K. Martin, Garrett J. O'Keefe, and Oguz B. Nayman, "Opinion Agreement and Accuracy Between Editors and Their Readers," *Journalism Quarterly* 49 (1972): 460-468.

Both topics had considerable heuristic value, however, having generated many research studies. Studies using the coorientation model still appear in the literature from time to time.[18]

Many of the ideas of family communication patterns and coorientation were worked out on a blackboard in either Chaffee or McLeod's office, and Chaffee says there was a multiplicative effect, with one idea building on another. Chaffee would say something, and then McLeod would say, "Well, the way I would put that is this." The excitement of these sessions spread to graduate students, who were quick to pick up on the new ideas and try to do research exploring them.[19]

Except for one co-authored paper in 1979, Chaffee and McLeod did not write another paper together after the studies for the Surgeon General's committee in 1971. The two men took leaves of absence from Wisconsin in alternate years, and they became involved in some national committees appointed by the Social Science Research Council to look at mass communication. Chaffee went on leave in the spring of 1972 to study the California presidential election primary. McLeod's leave in 1973 took him to the Centre for Television Research at Leeds, England, where he began collaborating on election studies with Jay Blumler. He continues to work with Blumler today. While Chaffee and McLeod stopped doing co-authored papers, their individual research efforts were often parallel. They sometimes did FCP or coorientation studies with others instead of together. And they often did separate research on the same topic, such as Watergate, the Ford-Carter debates, or young voters and political socialization. Chaffee's recent work has included the *Handbook of Communication Science*, which he co-edited with Charles R. Berger.[20]

One of the major contributions of Chaffee and McLeod has to be the large number of students whom they trained through the Mass Communication Research Center and who have gone on to become successful communication researchers at other institutions. Just in terms of their ideas showing up in Theory and Methodology sessions at the AEJMC convention, or in terms of the number of citations to their work, Chaffee and McLeod have had a significant impact on the field of mass communication research. Beyond that, they have developed two separate research models or approaches that stand on their own as intellectual achievements. Coorientation, in particular, is important because it is part of the movement away from attitudinal variables and

---

[18]Leonard Tipton, Peggy Prichard, and Nate Pickard, "Public Opinion as Collective Coorientation," paper presented at the annual meeting of the Theory and Methodology Division, Association for Education in Journalism and Mass Communication, San Antonio, Texas, August 1-4, 1987.

[19]Telephone interview with Chaffee, Oct. 7, 1987.

[20]Charles R. Berger and Steven H. Chaffee (Eds.), *Handbook of Communication Science* (Newbury Park, CA: Sage, 1987).

toward cognitive variables in communication research. The concepts of *understanding* and *pertinence* from the coorientation model can be seen as precursors of such concepts in recent cognitive psychology as *schemas* and *frames*. As we see increasing attention to such concepts, the Chaffee and McLeod coorientation model may still have a strong role to play in the development of mass communication theory.

Maxwell McCombs, Donald Shaw, and Agenda-Setting

One of the most popular topics of mass communication research in the past 15 years has been the agenda-setting function. Although the notion of agenda-setting may have been around awhile in a vague form, it was first formulated in a precise form and tested by Maxwell E. McCombs (1938-) and Donald L. Shaw (1936-). Their study of the 1968 presidential election was reported in *Public Opinion Quarterly* in 1972.[1] Since then, there have been some 200-300 additional studies of agenda-setting.

McCombs was born December 3, 1938, in Birmingham, Alabama. His father was a supervisor in a steel mill; and his mother, a registrar in an elementary school. McCombs became interested in writing and, while in high school, worked on the school paper and took some journalism classes. He then attended Tulane University, where he received a BA in journalism in 1960. He was editor of the school paper, *The Hullabaloo*, during his senior year. The program at Tulane was a traditional one and did not involve research. At this point, McCombs intended to make a life career in journalism. On the recommendation of Walter Wilcox, one of his professors at Tulane, he went to Stanford to study for an MA. At Stanford, he found that his advisor was to be Chilton R. (Chick) Bush, a professor in the communication department. McCombs has said he was the "victim of a benevolent conspiracy" between Wilcox and Bush.[2] Bush steered McCombs in the direction of research and drew up a first quarter schedule that involved courses in statistics, learning theory, content analysis, and communication theory. In that year at Stanford, McCombs not only completed an MA but also took the equivalent of the first year of the PhD program in mass communication research. He was interested in pursuing the PhD, but Stanford would support

---

[1]Maxwell E. McCombs and Donald L. Shaw, "The Agenda-Setting Function of Mass Media," *Public Opinion Quarterly* 36 (Summer 1972): 176-187.

[2]Videotaped interview with Maxwell E. McCombs, Theory and Methodology Division, AEJMC, 1977.

students past the first year only if they had significant professional experience. So McCombs returned to Louisiana and worked as a reporter for the New Orleans *Times-Picayune* for 2 years.

He returned to Stanford, enrolled in the PhD program, and began working with Richard Carter as his adviser. Carter taught him the importance of a thorough theoretical conceptualization. When Carter moved to Wisconsin, Nathan Maccoby became McCombs' adviser. McCombs also worked as a research assistant to Wilbur Schramm. His dissertation dealt with the effects of television on children's learning. While still working on his dissertation at Stanford, he began traveling once a week to teach in the Department of Journalism at UCLA. He finished the PhD in 1966 and then joined the UCLA faculty fulltime as an assistant professor. A year later, McCombs went to the University of North Carolina. Six years after that, in 1973, McCombs went to Syracuse University to become the John Ben Snow Professor of Research and the director of the Communications Research Center. In 1985, he became the chairman of the Department of Journalism at the University of Texas.

Shaw was born October 27, 1936, in Raleigh, North Carolina. His father held a doctorate in plant pathology and worked as a professor at North Carolina State University and as a researcher for the U.S. Department of Agriculture. Shaw developed an early interest in writing and was influenced by his brother Luther, who was a reporter for the Asheville *Citizen*. Shaw was the co-editor of his high school newspaper at Waynesville High School from 1954 to 1955. He received an AA degree in liberal arts from Mars Hill College in North Carolina in 1957, followed by an AB in journalism from the University of North Carolina in 1959 and an MA in journalism from the same university in 1960. While he was at the University of North Carolina, he worked for the student newspaper, *The Daily Tar Heel*. During his MA work, he minored in history, and he was to follow that up with a lifelong interest in historical research. After graduating, Shaw worked as a reporter for the Asheville *Citizen* and the Asheville *Times*. He then began work on a PhD in Mass Communications at the University of Wisconsin, which he finished in 1966. He continued with his interest in history at Wisconsin and became an advisee of Harold Nelson, a historical researcher on the Wisconsin faculty. At Wisconsin, Shaw also took courses from such quantitative researchers as Jack McLeod and Percy Tannenbaum. His dissertation, which dealt with the impact of the telegraph on the development of objectivity in newspapers, was essentially a content analysis. It was perhaps this willingness to use quantitative methods that made Shaw, although basically a historian, a logical choice to work with McCombs on agenda-setting. After finishing the PhD at Wisconsin, Shaw went as an assistant professor to the University of North Carolina, and that is where he has remained.

The idea of agenda-setting first began to take form when Mc-Combs was at UCLA. He and John Smith, later to become the director of Grassroots Television in Aspen, Colorado, were both assistant professors at UCLA and shared an office in the journalism department. They were in the habit of going out one afternoon a week to relax and talk about research. One afternoon they were talking at the Century Plaza Hotel in Los Angeles, and they began to speculate over why a recent minor scandal in the Johnson administration had not had more impact on the public. They examined the front page of the Los Angeles *Times* for that day and noticed that there were three news stories important enough that any one of them could have been the lead story. One dealt with the results of the British General Election, the second concerned the firing of the controversial director of the Los Angeles poverty program, and the third was the scandal in the Johnson administration. The Los Angeles *Times* gave the local poverty program story the biggest play, followed second by the British election. The Washington scandal received the least play, with only a one-column picture and a small headline. McCombs and Smith discussed the possibility that the relative play given to a story might have an effect on how people reacted to the story. McCombs later formulated this notion into the agenda-setting hypothesis.[3]

McCombs also bought the Bernard Cohen book, *The Press and Foreign Policy*, at the UCLA bookstore. It contains the famous quote used in much of the agenda-setting literature—that the press "may not be successful much of the time in telling its readers what to think, but it is stunningly successful in telling its readers what to think *about*."[4]

When McCombs arrived at North Carolina in the fall of 1967, he was assigned an office near that of Shaw. The two became interested in working on some collaborative research and decided to apply for a small research grant from the National Association of Broadcasters. They proposed a study of the effects of the upcoming presidential election campaign on a small sample of voters in Chapel Hill. The proposal did not mention the term *agenda-setting*. Shaw has said they were trying to get away from overly complex approaches that had become common at the time, particularly in attitude change research. He said they tried to ask the simplest possible question: "If the press talks about it, do people talk about it in the aggregate?"[5] The N.A.B. grant was approved, and some time during the next year the concept of agenda-setting was introduced into the research. Steven H. Chaffee recalls that he talked to McCombs at the 1968 AEJ convention in Lawrence, Kansas, and that McCombs told him that he and Shaw were about to conduct the first empirical test of the agenda-setting hypothe-

---

[3]Ibid.

[4]Bernard C. Cohen, *The Press and Foreign Policy* (Princeton, NJ: Princeton University Press, 1963), p. 13.

[5]Telephone interview with Donald L. Shaw, Oct. 29, 1987.

sis. Chaffee said he had never heard the term *agenda-setting* before, but he knew exactly what McCombs meant from the conversations they used to have at the Tresidder Union while graduate students at Stanford.

The N.A.B. grant study was done with a sample of undecided voters during the presidential election campaign of 1968. McCombs said the choice of undecided voters was deliberate because he and Shaw were trying to maximize the chance of finding an effect. The Chapel Hill test involved comparing the content of the mass media during an election campaign with what voters said were the key issues of the campaign. It was thus unusual in being a study that combined the techniques of content analysis and survey research. The content analysis focused on the local and national newspapers, magazines, and television news broadcasts that were the major sources of political information. The mass media agenda was determined by measuring the attention (in terms of space and time) given to the various campaign issues. The public agenda was determined by interviewing 100 undecided voters about what they thought were the key issues in the campaign. For major news items, the correlation between the media agenda and the public agenda was .967. For minor news items, the correlation was .979. These results indicated a strong correspondence between mass media coverage during the election campaign and the public perception of what issues were most important.

McCombs and Shaw submitted a paper reporting the results of the study to the Theory and Methodology division of AEJ, and it was summarily rejected. McCombs' recollection is that the paper was rejected because it was "insufficiently grounded in theory."[6] Shaw speculates that it was probably rejected because it was "too unorthodox" or it had "too narrow a sample."[7]

The authors considered dropping further publication efforts. Instead, they submitted two articles based on the data to *Public Opinion Quarterly*, one dealing with agenda-setting and the other dealing with the effects of an election campaign on cognitive structure. The editors replied that they liked both articles, but they didn't have room to print them both. They asked the authors to submit only one, or an article combining the two. McCombs and Shaw decided to go with the agenda-setting article, but put a little of the cognitive structure research at the end. *Public Opinion Quarterly* published the article in 1972.

Shaw has said that, as a research team, McCombs' strengths and weaknesses and his own complemented each other. Shaw said that in writing he tended to "push the data pretty hard—perhaps too hard sometimes," whereas McCombs was more methodologically rigorous and more cautious as a writer.

The intellectual roots of agenda-setting go back at least a half century before the 1972 *Public Opinion Quarterly* article. Mc-

---

[6]Interview with Maxwell E. McCombs, Oct. 29, 1987.
[7]Telephone interview with Shaw, Oct. 29, 1987.

Combs and Shaw have traced the general notion back to the thinking of Walter Lippmann, who wrote in 1922 in *Public Opinion* about the mass media giving us the "pictures in our heads" in the area of public affairs. In the original *Public Opinion Quarterly* article, McCombs and Shaw also quoted researchers Kurt Lang and Gladys Engel Lang as coming up with an early statement of the agenda-setting function. Lang and Lang had written in 1959 that the mass media "are constantly presenting objects suggesting what individuals in the mass media should think about, know about, have feelings about."

The original statement of the agenda-setting hypothesis postulated that "the mass media set the agenda for each political campaign, influencing the salience of attitudes toward the political issues."[8] A later restatement emphasizes that the hypothesis is a causal one: "increased salience of a topic or issue in the mass media influences (causes) the salience of that topic or issue among the public."[9]

The correlations from the Chapel Hill study were impressive, but they left open the question of causal direction. Were the media shaping the public's perception of what problems were important, or was the public's ranking of issues by importance influencing the coverage of the media? The Chapel Hill data were not decisive on this issue.

McCombs and Shaw attempted to deal with the question of causal direction in a follow-up study conducted with several other authors and based in Charlotte, North Carolina, during the next presidential election. The results of the Charlotte study were reported in a book devoted to agenda-setting and entitled *The Emergence of American Political Issues: The Agenda-Setting Function of the Press*.[10] The Charlotte study used a panel design, in which interviews were conducted and mass media content were examined at several points in time throughout the campaign. By studying the campaign through time and comparing early and late agendas for the public and the media, the panel technique let the researchers begin to gather evidence about the causal direction. Although this evidence was not as clearcut as the researchers might have liked, it did provide some support for the notion of the media influencing the public agenda rather than the notion of the public influencing the media agenda.

The question of causal direction has remained a key issue in agenda-setting research. Some of the most decisive evidence regarding this question has come from experiments by the research team of Shanto Iyengar, Mark D. Peters, and Donald R. Kinder. In a typical experiment, these researchers manipulated the content

---

[8]McCombs and Shaw, p. 177.

[9]Donald L. Shaw and Maxwell E. McCombs, *The Emergence of American Political Issues: The Agenda-Setting Function of the Press* (St. Paul, MN: West Publishing Co., 1977), p. 12.

[10]Ibid.

of the television news broadcasts that subjects watched for about a week.[11] One group of subjects would see newscasts that had been altered to play up one issue, such as inflation, while another group of subjects would see newscasts altered to play up a different issue, such as defense. The typical results at the end of the week found each group of subjects increasing their importance ranking for the issue they had seen played up and decreasing their importance ranking for the issue they had not seen played up. In this situation, it is clear that the mass media content had an effect on the audience perception of the importance of the issues.

The agenda-setting hypothesis has been extended and refined in some important ways. McCombs and David Weaver, in another phase of the Charlotte study, suggested that the concept of *need for orientation* was an important variable in determining when agenda-setting would take place and when it would not. They proposed a model in which need for orientation is determined by two factors: *relevance of information* and *degree of uncertainty concerning the subject of the message.*[12] They hypothesized that the more individuals feel a need for orientation, the more susceptible they are to the agenda-setting effects of the media. Data from the Charlotte study supported this hypothesis. Recently, McCombs and Weaver have suggested a link between agenda-setting research and uses and gratifications research, with *need for orientation* as a bridging concept.

In another extension of the agenda-setting hypothesis, some researchers have discussed two types of issues—*obtrusive* and *unobtrusive*—and have suggested that agenda-setting takes place mainly with unobtrusive issues. Obtrusive issues are those that affect people directly and those that they do not need the mass media to bring to their attention. An example of such an issue would be inflation. Unobtrusive issues are issues that do not affect people directly and that they would learn about primarily through the media. An example would be pollution, because there are many environmental hazards that people do not experience directly. Harold Gene Zucker carried out a study of television coverage of three obtrusive and three unobtrusive issues and public opinion regarding those issues, and found evidence that agenda-setting occurred mostly with the unobtrusive issues.[13]

Another recent extension of the agenda-setting hypothesis is the notion of *bias by agenda*. Basically, this is the idea that the is-

---

[11]Shanto Iyengar, Mark D. Peters, and Donald R. Kinder, "Experimental Demonstrations of the 'Not-So-Minimal' Consequences of Television News Programs," *American Political Science Review* 76 (December 1982): 848-858.

[12]David H. Weaver, "Political Issues and Voter Need for Orientation," in Shaw and McCombs, *The Emergence of American Political Issues*, pp. 107-119.

[13]Harold Gene Zucker, "The Variable Nature of Mass Media Influence," in Brent D. Ruben (Ed.), *Communication Yearbook 2* (New Brunswick, NJ: Transaction Books, 1978), pp. 225-240.

sues played up by the media might be the issues that are of interest to a particular ideology, such as a liberal ideology or a conservative ideology. For instance, if the media repeatedly ran stories on the plight of migrant workers, the damage to the environment by pollution, and the problem of hunger in America, it might be argued that the media were playing up a liberal agenda. One study of this possible bias by agenda in the television network evening newscasts found some evidence of a liberal bias by agenda from CBS and NBC and a conservative bias by agenda from ABC.[14]

The agenda-setting hypothesis has generated more follow-up studies than most other concepts in the field of mass communication research. A study of the most frequently cited sources in *Journalism Quarterly* articles found the original *Public Opinion Quarterly* article to be one of the most frequently cited pieces of mass communication research.[15]

One of the reasons for the popularity of the agenda-setting idea—with journalism researchers, at least—may be that it deals so squarely with the news function and the concerns of the journalist. The idea of agenda-setting and the approach to research that it created helped journalism researchers to get away from attitude change and other non-journalism related topics that seemed to be bogging down mass communication research.

Another reason for the popularity of agenda-setting research may be that it, along with some other research such as George Gerbner's work on cultivation, effectively revived the effects question in mass communication research. Much communication research up until the early 1960s had minimized the effects of mass communication. Through agenda-setting, it appeared that mass communication might have some significant effects after all.

Another strength of agenda-setting research is that researchers in that area have done a better job than researchers in many areas of mass communication research of following the ideal scientific model. In particular, agenda-setting research has been cumulative, with later studies building on earlier studies, and thereby extending the theory.

If agenda-setting researchers have done such a good job of following an ideal scientific model, the question might be asked whether agenda-setting research has now achieved the status of a theory? Certainly it may come closer than many other research areas. It does at this point have a number of concepts and a number of hypotheses, and there is clear evidence of later research extending and refining earlier research. Perhaps the major drawbacks that keep us from speaking of "the theory of agenda-setting"

---

[14]Michael J. Robinson, "Jesse Helms, Take Stock," *Washington Journalism Review* 7 (April 1985): 14-17.

[15]James W. Tankard, Jr., Tsan-Kuo Chang, and Kuo-Jen Tsang, "Citation Networks as Indicators of Journalism Research Activity," *Journalism Quarterly* 61 (1984): 89-96.

are these:

1. The focus of the hypothesis is somewhat limited. Basically, the hypothesis attempts to explain the effects of news reporting dealing with politics on public perception of the importance of issues. That is only a small portion of all mass communication.

2. The various studies, with their new concepts and refinements, have not been pulled together in an integrated and formal theory. This job probably could be done, but so far it has not.

Critics of agenda-setting have challenged the hypothesis primarily for being too simplistic and too narrow. As originally stated, the agenda-setting hypothesis suggested a relationship between the relative frequency of the news media's coverage of a set of issues and the relative salience of the same set of issues in the public. This approach, which looks for correspondence between issues at the aggregate level, has dominated much of the subsequent agenda-setting research. The approach has been criticized for suggesting a simple "mirror-image" hypothesis about media effects and for not focusing enough on the *process* of agenda-setting.[16] Most of the agenda-setting research tends to consist of cross-sectional studies, or studies at one point in time. If agenda-setting is a process, studies are needed that extend over a period of time. This focus on the aggregate of issues in the media and in the public has also de-emphasized media exposure, a variable that is basic to the agenda-setting process. If agenda-setting is taking place, it should show up for audience members who are high in exposure to the media but not for audience members who are low in exposure to the media. But few agenda-setting studies have even considered the workings of this crucial variable. McCombs himself has pointed out that other designs besides the aggregate design are needed to investigate agenda-setting,[17] but nevertheless many studies still follow the early model.

Other researchers who have criticized agenda-setting—in its original formulation, at least—for being too narrow and simplistic include Lang and Lang, two authors who were cited in the original McCombs and Shaw paper. Taking Watergate as an illustrative example, the Langs have argued that the emergence of an issue is a complex, reciprocal process over time that involves the mass media, prominent public figures, and the public.[18] They

[16]Lutz Erbring, Edie N. Goldenberg, and Arthur H. Miller, "Front-Page News and Real-World Cues: A New Look at Agenda-Setting by the Media," *American Journal of Political Science* 24 (February 1980): 16-49.

[17]Maxwell E. McCombs, "The Agenda-Setting Approach," in Dan D. Nimmo and Keith R. Sanders (Eds.), *Handbook of Political Communication* (Beverly Hills, CA: Sage, 1981), pp. 121-140.

[18]Gladys Engel Lang and Kurt Lang, "Watergate: An Exploration of the Agenda-Building Process," in G. Cleveland Wilhoit and Harold de Bock (Eds.), *Mass Communication Review Yearbook* (Vol. 2) (Beverly Hills, CA: Sage, 1981), pp. 447-468.

have suggested the name *agenda-building* for this more complex process.

There also remain some unanswered questions. Paramount among these is the question of who sets the media agenda? Do the people who work in the media have great power to play up some issues and play down others? Or is this power constrained by reality itself, or by other factors such as professional norms and checks and balances in the practice of journalism? Do certain influential political writers, such as R.W. (Johnny) Apple, Jr., of the New York *Times*,[19] help determine the agenda of other political writers, who in turn influence the public's agenda? What is the role of pseudo-events, of public relations campaigns, or of political organizations and pressure groups in getting certain issues on the agenda? These questions of who sets the media agenda need to be explored further.

Another basic question is how powerful (or how general) is agenda-setting? McCombs himself has warned that the infinite expansion of agenda-setting to all possible circumstances couldn't go on forever. If the media were all-powerful as agenda-setters, he has said, then all the women who watch soap operas should talk to other women about nothing but the whiteness of their laundry, because that is clearly the agenda that is being set in between the soap operas.[20]

---

[19]See Timothy Crouse, *The Boys on the Bus* (New York: Random House, 1973), p. 79, for a description of Apple's influence over other reporters.

[20]Videotaped interview with Maxwell E. McCombs, 1977.

6

The Methodologists

Donald R. Avery
University of Southern Mississippi

The Methodologists

The development of quantitative methods in the study of mass communication is of recent vintage. *Journalism Quarterly*, one of the important scholarly journals devoted to media studies, has published research concerned with methodological subjects for only about 30 years. Such subjects accounted for only 14% of the *Quarterly's* content prior to 1950, and most were content and audience analyses. Less than 2% of material in the *Quarterly* concerned methodology.

The poor state of methodology in early media studies is not surprising because, historically, journalism research methods were borrowed from other disciplines. Only in recent decades has the field been able to claim scholars educated primarily in communication and not in the sister disciplines of sociology, psychology, and political science. Still, the communication graduate student is most apt to hear the names of political scientist Harold Lasswell, sociologist Paul Lazarsfeld, psychologist Kurt Lewin, and a number of others, all trained outside communication.

Yet the study of the mass media goes back more than a century to studies devoted to historical, ethical, and legal aspects of newspapers. Methods changed little as radio and film joined the newspaper as subjects for research. Because newspaper journalism skills were taught in journalism programs, research in these programs tended to follow from that tradition—mostly qualitative—and matured along with journalism education. Modern quantitative research methods had their genesis in the years between the two world wars.

What happened was the result of two prevalent concerns. First, with the advent of radio, there grew a major concern with the propaganda effects of the new medium. Second, the ability of newspapers and radio to deliver persuasive messages became an important issue.

Many believed that the United States had been hood-winked into World War I on the basis of Allied propaganda. Here was an issue ripe for research. Content analysis was obviously the method of choice, for if one wished to know if propaganda were present in the papers, correspondences, utterances, and writings of those in power, that could be determined by analyzing content.

Or at least so it was thought. Out of this perspective grew the so-called "bullet theory" (Lasswell's hypodermic-needle model) in which mass communication persuades a passive audience. The theory, largely discredited by research, has its adherents among the public today.

As has been pointed out elsewhere,[1] Lasswell and other scholars studying propaganda believed that the public had little control over its rationality and, thus, needed to be protected from demogogues and others who would take advantage of human weakness. After all, democracy depended on its adherents being able to discuss issues rationally. It took no great leap to conclude that the public needed protection in light of the perceived influences of propaganda. However, fundamental questions about that influence needed answers. The approach to research methods development used by early researchers to study propaganda (i.e., develop a research technique to address a specific practical problem) continues today. It is often what Lazarsfeld[2] termed administrative research.

Administrative research was designed to study the mass media industry to learn how best to reconcile the needs of journalists, audience, and financial interests, a basically economic issue. In fact, one of his earliest research projects concerned marketing and advertising. Lazarsfeld believed it was possible for everyone to benefit from the media; it was simply a matter of doing enough good research so that needs and interests could be identified. He contrasted such administrative research with critical research, which studied the place of the mass media in the social structure, a basically non-economic concern.[3] The dominant approach to communication research, now as then, is administrative.

With the advent of radio, for the first time in history newspapers had strong competition. The advertiser wishing to get the most return for his dollar demanded to know which of the two media delivered more consumers. Media's desire to convince advertisers provided the impetus for the development of demographic categories and statistical methods for counting consumers. The federal government also became more interested in census information and began to develop more sophisticated survey techniques. In addition, public opinion polling became more prevalent and more in demand.

The rise of Nazi Germany provided a large influx of educated immigrants to the United States, many of whom became crucial

---

[1]Dennis K. Davis and Stanley J. Baran, *Mass Communication and Everyday Life: A Perspective on Theory and Effects* (Belmont, CA: Wadsworth Publishing Company, 1981), p. 26.

[2]Paul F. Lazarsfeld, "Remarks on Administrative and Critical Communications Research," *Studies in the Philosophy of Social Science* 9 (1941): 2-16.

[3]Ibid.

figures in the development of the sciences. Arguably, these new minds, which gravitated to American universities, provided the stimulus for much new mass media research and theory.

However, it was World War II that provided the jumping off point for quantitative mass media research in America. The issues addressed were practical and generally of interest to the military. Hovland's groundbreaking propaganda studies for the U.S. Army have been cited often; Lasswell's work with content analysis for the Library of Congress[4] is the direct source for Berelson's *Content Analysis in Communications Research*; and the methodological work of Stouffer for the U.S. Army is also important as a precursor.[5] One important result of the war-time work was that many researchers who had worked together for the military continued their collaborations after the war.

Changes in American higher education also had enormous impact on the development of mass media research techniques as graduate education in communication began to appear in several universities. Graduate students provided a labor pool for scholars and made possible more extensive kinds of research. Without this change, content analysis with its economies of labor might have remained the predominant research technique. The discovery that large-scale research operations at the university level could attract huge amounts of funds led many administrators to create research centers to conduct sociological and, incidentally, communication research. However, it was not until the early 1940s that a department to focus on mass communication research was first established by a school of journalism, this at the University of Minnesota.

Universities began offering the PhD in mass communication in the years after World War II, and the increased number of scholars produced more and improved quantitative research techniques. The field of study had grown to the point that by 1955 a handful of quantitatively oriented scholars could begin meeting at annual conventions of the Association for Education in Journalism (outside the regular convention program; hence, the reason it became known as the "rump" group) to discuss both mass communication research methodology and theory. It would be another 11 years before the group would be recognized as a legitimate part of AEJ. In 1966 the Theory and Methodology Division of AEJ was established.

Although it is true that quantitative mass communication research has matured over the years and its methodologies become more sophisticated, it has often been a case of scholars using techniques from other disciplines, rather than developing new methods. Not only have modern mass communication researchers tended to borrow from other disciplines, they have also

---

[4]May Katzen, *Mass Communication: Teaching and Studies at Universities* (Paris: Unesco Press, 1975), p. 47.
[5]Ibid.

expanded the methods used by their predecessors. From the methodologies used by early mass communication scholars have grown the primary empirical methodologies of today: content analysis, experiment, field studies, and survey.[6]

Content analysis is an important tool for studying communication content in its myriad forms. Among the many definitions, perhaps the most useful is the one offered by Kerlinger. "Content analysis," he said, "is a method of studying and analyzing communications in a systematic, objective, and quantitative manner to measure variables."[7]

Its use began at least as early as the 1600s when the state church of Sweden ordered a study of hymnals to find ideas that might undermine the church. The method may be as simple as counting the number of stories about religion in a specific newspaper or as complex as attempting to measure the use of symbols in media over decades. Content analysis may be so basic as to require only elementary mathematics or so sophisticated that the statistical methods used may call for computers with megabytes of memory. As a tool, content analysis is simple enough to be easily learned and has broad-based application. However, the technique is not without its critics.

Much of the criticism has grown out of the association of content analysis with journalism. One critic has said that content analysis is only what a reader does with a newspaper, just a bit more complex.[8] This criticism may have been true in the early decades of this century, but certainly is less so today because of the contributions by several of the scholars in this volume. However, a number of other criticisms are not disposed of as easily. First, the method is time-consuming and costly; second, it cannot be used to study effects of content on the audience; third, findings may be merely artifacts of content categories; fourth, findings are difficult to compare because of differences in definitions and content categories among scholars; and fifth, there may not be a large enough sample to reach meaningful conclusions.

Content analysis is one of the research techniques that journalism scholars can generally claim for their own. After all, the method is a natural for mass communication research. It is an

---

[6]See generally Roger D. Wimmer and Joseph R. Dominick, *Mass Media Research* (2nd ed.) (Belmont, CA: Wadsworth Publishing Company, 1983, 1987). The material for the discussion that follows this citation was drawn from several sources, but the Wimmer and Dominick book was the principal source. See also Earl Babbie, *The Practice of Social Research* (5th ed.) (Belmont, CA: Wadsworth Publishing Company, 1973, 1989); Alexis S. Tan, *Mass Communication Theories and Research* (2nd ed.) (New York: John Wiley & Sons, 1981, 1985); and Fred N. Kerlinger, *Foundations of Behavioral Research* (2nd ed.) (New York: Holt, Rinehart & Winston, 1964, 1973).

[7]Kerlinger, p. 525.

[8]Klaus Krippendorff, *Content Analysis: An Introduction to Its Methodology* (Beverly Hills: Sage Publications, 1980), p. 11.

unobtrusive measure; that is, researchers do not intrude into their study in the manner that they do in, say, survey research. Other unobtrusive methods are employed in mass communication research, but content analysis is the most widely used.

The laboratory experiment is also frequently used in mass communication research, particularly by those trained in social science methods. It is the method considered most scientific, but it is one of the methods most apt to raise the hackles of the traditional journalism scholar not trained in the method. The issue raised by scholars who use traditional methods is that those employing social science methods are guilty of several scholarly flaws. Among the issues raised by critics: social scientists let the facts speak for themselves, only trivial questions are susceptible to study by social science methods, aggregates rather than individuals are studied, respondents may not be truthful, there are always exceptions to findings, and scientists cannot make definitive statements regarding their research.

Basically, in an experiment, the researcher takes a group of people, does something to them, and records the result. Experiments permit causation to be assigned because researchers can control and manipulate the research environment. The key concept in experimental research is control. Researchers can control the kinds of variables selected and how they are manipulated; they can control the way subjects are selected; and they can control the laboratory environment. The reason control is so important is that it permits the researcher to exclude rival causative effects. The major criticisms of the laboratory experiment are that it is artificial, subjects are aware they are being manipulated, and it lacks external validity. The means of getting around some of the problems associated with the laboratory experiment is found in its methodological cousin, which we may call field studies.

Among the various types of field studies are field experiments, field observations, focus groups, and case studies, all used to varying degrees by mass communication scholars. Laboratory experiments and field studies are often seen as being at opposite ends of a continuum. The key again is control. In field studies, researchers have less control over the environment and the subjects because the environment is more natural, but subjects may be less influenced by the researcher, at least in field experiments and some field observations. In field observations that use participant observation, there may be considerable influence by the researcher. Also it is quite difficult to control intervening environmental variables in both field experiments and field observations. Focus groups have flexibility, can be conducted quickly, and are generally less expensive than other methods. But there is a downside to focus groups: they depend on a highly trained leader, a stong personality on the panel can skew results, and groups are small and not representative of the population. The major advantages of case studies are that they permit the collection of data from a broad base of information, they can suggest causes of events, and they provide enormous detail. Case studies also are open to criticism. They are not very scientific, the data may be difficult to summarize because of its mass, and it is hard to generalize. One point that differentiates field studies from the other methodologies is that the latter are typically intended to be quantitative, whereas field research usually produces qualitative data.

The survey is probably the best method for obtaining original data to describe a population that is too large to study directly. It is a method of inferring information about a large population from data collected on a small sample. In mass communication research, the survey is used to measure attitudes and opinions. Surveys may be classified as telephone, mail questionnaire, panel, personal interview, and controlled observation. The best examples of surveys are those conducted by Harris, Roper, and Gallup. The survey is used to get at information in the real world— such as sexual behavior, voting preferences, and aggressive behavior—that is not available through other methods. Some of the criticisms surrounding the technique include questions about the depth of information obtainable, problems with sampling error, the intrusive nature of the technique, deception by subjects, and inability of subjects to express themselves.

In addition to the four primary research methodologies, one other empirical method often used by mass communication scholars should be mentioned. Longitudinal research involves the collection of data at more than one point in time. There are three primary types of longitudinal research: panel studies, trend analysis, and cohort analysis. In panel studies, the same sample of subjects is measured over a period of time. In trend studies different subjects are asked the same questions over a period of time. Cohort analysis involves measurements of samples that share significant events, such as birth date. Longitudinal analysis uses all other methods discussed except content analysis.

A final matter should be raised. Perhaps the most important advance in research has not been a methodology but a device. Stated simply, the computer made sophisticated quantitative methods possible. The day of keypunched computer cards and card readers with the enormous labor involved has passed to be replaced with the optical character reader, which can scan a page of data and convert it into language the computer understands. Even the need of mass communication scholars for a so-called mainframe computer (always difficult and expensive to get time on) to do most research is over. The development of microcomputers has placed into the hands of scholars data processing devices that were unheard of a few years ago. A content analysis project that might have required 10,000 computer cards and considerable computer time a decade ago, can now be executed on a personal computer costing $2,000 to $3,000 and at the researcher's own pace. A researcher's bookshelf is as apt to hold a computer journal as *Journalism Quarterly*. The computer has also influenced graduate education. Research projects that might have daunted a student in the 1950s can often be conducted during a single semester today because of the computer. Although fear of the computer has created its own devil for students, mastery of the device may have in fact led more graduate students into a research career. Certainly computers have made quantitative research a little less frightening.

Most of the scholars who have engaged in journalism research have not been concerned with methodological questions. Their research has often been traditional, based less on science than on holistic methods. Along with the six educators who are treated in full biographies in this section, there are others who have been leaders over the years. Quite often they have been better known for their methodological work than other aspects of their research. Most will be remembered by their students and by other scholars who continue to build on the pioneering work they did.

Despite Berelson's gloomy forecast for the state of mass communication research almost three decades ago,[9] the field is alive and well and should continue to grow. The next generation of mass communication scholars is already in place and expanding the methodologies required by that growth. And the scholars are not coming from communication programs alone but from related fields as well. It remains to be seen if, as Schramm suggested,[10] the field is absorbed by other disciplines. If that happens, then in a sense the study of mass communication will have come full circle.

---

[9]Bernard Berelson, "The State of Communication Research," *Public Opinion Quarterly* 23: 1 (1959): 1-15.

[10]Wilbur Schramm, "The Beginnings of Communication Study in the United States," in Dan Nimmo (Ed.), *Communication Yearbook 4* (New Brunswick, NJ: Transaction Books, 1980), pp. 73-82.

Ralph Nafziger
and the Methods Schism

Ralph Otto Nafziger (1896-1973) was one of the founding giants in communication research methods. He was first and foremost a journalism educator, but more than that he inspired others to go beyond the teacher and develop their own identity as scholars. He helped establish journalism and communication programs at both the undergraduate and graduate level in addition to doing trail-breaking communication research. In fact he served journalism education in virtually every capacity possible.

Nafziger is associated less with a specific research method and more with a methodological orientation. He, along with David M. White, is responsible to a large extent for the schism that exists today among communication scholars over quantitative versus qualitative methods. Because theirs was only the second volume on communication research methods (the first had been co-written by Nafziger), decisions made in that book helped shape research traditions in communication. Their decision to exclude historical and legal research methods and to orient the work toward social science methods implied that the latter were more important then traditional qualitative methods. Communication research has not been the same since.

Born in Chicago April 18, 1896, he was the son of Albert and Emmy (Brennemann) Nafziger. He married C. Monona Hamilton June 18, 1932, and they had two children, Ralph Hamilton and James Albert Richmond. He was a veteran of World War I, having served in the infantry in 1918-1919.

Nafziger's education would be suspect among many modern educators because he took all his degrees from the same school, the University of Wisconsin. He received his BA in 1921 but waited some 9 years before going on to graduate education. He was awarded the MA in 1930 and 6 years later the PhD. In the years between receiving his undergraduate degree and beginning his graduate program, he was learning the craft that would make him such an important teacher and scholar.

As is sometimes the case with journalists, Nafziger changed jobs often. He began his journalistic career at North Dakota State

College, where he was an assistant newspaper editor in 1921 and 1922. In 1922 he became editor of the Enderlin (N.D.) *Independent.* After 1 year he moved to the Fargo (N.D.) *Daily Tribune,* where he worked as an editorial writer. During 1924 and 1925 he was a reporter for the Fargo *Forum.* From 1925 until 1928 he was a reporter on the Omaha (Neb.) *World-Herald.* It was the longest period Nafziger held a newspaper job. His professional journalism career ended after he served as editor for the University Press Bureau at the University of Wisconsin from 1928 to 1930.

Following the completion of his MA in 1930, Nafziger began, as an assistant professor of journalism at the University of Wisconsin, his long and distinguished teaching career. He moved to the University of Minnesota in 1935 with a promotion to associate professor. He was promoted to professor in 1937 and became director of the research division of the School of Journalism in 1944, a job he held until 1949. He returned to the University of Wisconsin in 1949 as director of the School of Journalism, where he remained until his retirement in 1966. He was named professor emeritus that year.

Retirement did not mean going fishing for Nafziger. He was an adviser and consultant to the Indian Institute of Mass Communication in New Delhi in 1966-1967. This was not the first time Nafziger had worked away from a regular teaching role at an American university. He was a consultant to the Office Coordinator of Information in Washington, D.C., in 1941. The following year he was chief of the Media Division, Office of Facts and Figures (Office of War Information). He was a press specialist for the State Department in Germany in 1952.

Nafziger was also busy doing seminars and lecturing on journalism and communication subjects. He spent the fall 1957 at the University of Strasbourg lecturing at a UNESCO seminar on journalism research. The following year he served on the board of trustees of the International Center for Journalism. In 1961 he was chairman of the international seminar on journalism education held in Manila. He was director of studies of the Berlin Institute on Mass Communication in Developing Countries in 1964. The same year he was also director of the UNESCO seminar on journalism education held at Nagpur, India. He was a lecturer at the East-West Center, Honolulu, in 1971.

He was widely honored during his life, receiving the major accolades that journalism education has to offer. He was a recipient of the Sigma Delta Chi research award in 1937. In 1970 he received a citation for meritorious service to journalism education. He received two prestigious honors in 1971. The first was the Sigma Delta Chi Distinguished Teaching in Journalism award; and the second is the most important honor a researcher in journalism can receive, the Paul J. Deutschmann award given by the AEJMC.

Nafziger was a member and officer in many organizations devoted to journalism and communication. He was a member of the

American Association of Teachers of Journalism (the forerunner of the AEJMC) and served that body as its president in 1941. He continued in the association after it became AEJ and was elected to a second term as president in 1951. He was also a member of the American Association of Schools and Departments of Journalism (AASDJ). He was chairman of the AASDJ council on research, 1942-1946, a member of its accrediting committee, 1946-1950, and president of the association in 1958.

At the age of 70, when most people would be happy to retire and take it easy, Nafziger took on the job of creating and organizing a central office for AEJMC and became the organization's first executive secretary, a job he held until shortly before his death in 1973. His reports to the membership, later reprinted in *Journalism Quarterly*, were models of efficiency, thoroughness, and organization. His 6 years in the position established the pattern that has been followed by subsequent executive secretaries. Nafziger had enormous impact on the field of journalism through his teaching and organizational leadership.

He had considerable influence through his research efforts as well. Students followed his lead not only in methodologies but in research subjects. One source of Nafziger's influence was the discipline's oldest scholarly journal, *Journalism Quarterly*. Not only did he produce a sizable body of writing for the journal, he served on its editorial board during the years that journalism research was experiencing enormous theoretical and methodological growth. His stint on the board covered the tenure of two of the journal's six editors. In all, Nafziger served for 20 years, 1935-1955. In addition he edited a number of special sections and projects for the journal.

Despite Nafziger's important work in journalism education and research, he has been known as an international communication expert. His first major work, *International News and the Press* (1940), was the first in-depth bibliography of international news. The work was annotated at a time when very little of a bibliographic nature had been done. Perhaps Nagziger's relationship to newspapers produced a blind side, but the book listed works only on newspapers; there was nothing on film, radio, newsreels, and so forth. This blind spot, or at least orientation, remained with him all his life.

Following World War II Nafziger (with Thomas F. Barnhart) published *Red Wing and Its Daily Newspaper*, a study of the effects of the war on a local daily newspaper. The authors found several significant changes in the newspaper between the pre-war years and 1944. There were significant reductions in space devoted to news and to pictures, but the amount of space given to advertising increased. Methodologically, Nafziger created a symbol coding technique to study changes in the newspaper. Not surprisingly, references to war-related names such as Germany, Russia, and Axis increased while references to local and national matters decreased.

Nafziger and Marcus M. Wilkinson co-edited the first text devoted to journalism research methods. A pioneering work, *An Introduction to Journalism Research* was published in 1949 under the auspices of the Council on Research of the Association of Accredited Schools and Departments of Journalism. It was a collection of six essays on various journalism research subjects. The mere fact of the work's publication so late speaks to one of the shortcomings of the field of journalism research, not the least of which was the lack of adequate texts devoted to the subject. By the time of the book's publication, graduate research had spread across the country and certainly was a large enough field that its own methodology was developing. However, there were few studies in journalism research cited or discussed in the book. This lack of research examples at times reduced the chapters to near abstractions.

Clearly the book was only an introduction, as stated in the title, but it was hardly a text designed to teach scholars how to do journalism research. This was a serious shortcoming. To be of any great use the text needed to explore the methodologies in enough depth so that students might use them in their own research. Certainly some of the chapters offered enough depth to be useful, such as the chapters on statistics, and legal research, and perhaps the section on experimental method. But overall the best that can be said is that it was a beginning. Nafziger was one of the first to recognize the need for adequate books on methods. However, the only part of the book he actually wrote himself was the introduction. It is revealing of Nafziger's views toward research.

"Research," he said, "is an inseparable part of the educational process in journalism. . . . There can be no up-to-date teaching unless research continues to expand and sharpen subject matter. There can be no enrichment of subject matter for teaching or practice unless students, including prospective research men, are exposed to research method and the results of research."[1]

The direct descendant of Nafiziger and Wilkerson's book was edited by Nafziger and David M. White. *Introduction to Mass Communications Research*, published in 1958, was a considerable improvement over the earlier work, if somewhat similar in content. Not only was there a new cast writing the chapters, but some of their subjects had changed. Gone were traditional historical and legal research methods. Gone also was the chapter on content analysis. However, there was a chapter on the subject in the book's second edition published in 1963. It was clear, not only from the title, but from the chapter subjects that the book was about social science research methods. It was this orientation that led to the schism between traditional and social science methods found among communication scholars today.

---

[1] Ralph O. Nafiziger and Marcus M. Wilkerson (Eds.), *An Introduction to Journalism Research* (Baton Rouge: Lousiana State University Press, 1949; reprint ed., New York: Greenwood Press, 1968), p.5.

A curious thing happened to the book between the two editions. The first edition can be praised for much that it accomplishes; the second edition can be condemned for its failure to go far enough. The first edition was a considerable improvement over its ancestor because it used mostly research from journalism and communication to demonstrate the techniques discussed, and that research seemed adequate to support the various chapters. However, that same research seemed less than adequate for the second edition, leading one reviewer to suggest that material be borrowed from related disciplines to provide "the obvious, even if hopefully, temporary solution." [2] The major problem with both editions is that if they were truly introductions to their subjects, they were entirely too shallow; if they were intended to be used with supporting materials from outside communication, they were barely needed themselves.

Nafziger was a contributor to many journals including considerable work with *Journalism Quarterly*. His work in that journal included some research with methodological implications. The 1930 study "A Reader-Interest Survey of Madison, Wisconsin" is typical of the attention Nafziger gave his work. He reported on a study of the reading and buying habits of readers of the *Wisconsin State Journal*. The methodology was sophisticated for the period. Nafziger dealt with sampling problems, questionnaire construction, and other methodological concerns. It is interesting to observe Nafziger working through the methodological problems to their solution.

The major difficulty in the *Wisconsin State Journal* study concerned obtaining a valid cross-sectional sample. Nafziger described how to achieve a valid sample. He discussed using economic and social class as a basis for drawing a sample but pointed out that such classifications may be misleading unless they are representative of population proportions. He cited a number of techniques that might provide accurate proportions, such as charting rentals, land values, incomes, occupations, and so forth. He concluded that the best method to determine family income (the basis for drawing a sample) was to be found in state income tax records which were public. Nafziger spent over two pages in the *Wisconsin State Journal* piece working through methodological problems associated with the questionnaire. After pointing out that the writer made no claims regarding the proof that the questionnaire was foolproof, Nafziger discussed response rates, investigator bias, respondent honesty, inter-instrument comparisons, and brevity and simplicity.

Today, much of what Nafziger wrote in the *Wisconsin State Journal* article would not appear in print (nor would it be needed) because modern scholars assume a depth of knowledge not possi-

---

[2]Leonard J. Fein, review of *Introduction to Mass Communications Research*, by Ralph O. Nafziger and David Manning White (Eds.), in *Journalism Quarterly* 41 (1964): 411.

ble 50 years ago. Perhaps, the reader misses something by the presence of shortcuts in today's research. It is a learning experience to follow Nafziger as he develops a piece of research.

Such development is shown in another study by Nafziger, with Malcolm MacLean Jr. and Warren Engstrom. The study, "Useful Tools for Interpreting Newspaper Readership Data," from *Journalism Quarterly*, worked through the many problems encountered in readership studies by looking at two surveys of Minnesota newspapers, and then suggested that such readership figures could be analyzed most effectively through the use of frequency distributions and factor analysis. All in all, the article is a most lucid piece of scholarship.

Nafziger's career spanned some of the most important years in the growth of journalism research methodology from its formative period into its maturity. Through his own work he was responsible for crucial early development, and through his students he will be responsible for development into the next century.

William Stephenson
and Q-Methodology

William Stephenson (1902-1989) was unique among American journalism educators. He was the inventor of a research method. The Q-Method has seen widespread use not only in journalism but in the larger social science research field as well. However, it may not be strictly accurate for journalism to claim Stephenson for its own or for the scholar to claim Q-Methodology for his own.

He was the son of John and Jane Stephenson and was born May 14, 1902, in Durham, England. He married Mary Richardson on Christmas Day, 1929; they had two sons and two daughters. Stephenson brought his family to the United States in 1948 and became a naturalized citizen in 1956.

He was one of the best educated scholars who have conducted research in journalism. He received the BSc, with first class honors, from Durham University in 1923. One year later, he received the MSc and in 1926 the PhD (in physics) also from Durham University. He received a second PhD, this time in psychology, in 1929 from London University. He also received an MA from Corpus Christi College, Oxford University, in 1935.

Stephenson began his teaching career in 1929, serving as a tutor at University College, London. In 1935 he was named assistant director of the Institute of Experimental Psychology at Oxford University. He was reader in experimental psychology and the Institute's director from 1945 until 1948. Upon his arrival in the United States he became a visiting professor of psychology at the University of Chicago, a position he held until 1950. In 1951, he became Walker-Ames professor at the University of Washington and from 1952 until 1955 was a visiting professor at the University of California at Berkeley. He decided to take his skills to private industry in 1955 and was named director of research for Nowland & Co. in New York City. However, after 3 years he was named distinguished research professor of advertising in the University of Missouri School of Journalism. He also served as the John F. Murray professor of journalism at the University of Iowa in 1974 and 1975.

In addition to his position with Nowland & Co., Stephenson

worked extensively with private companies within the communication industry both in the United States and in England. He was a consultant to the British Army from 1943 until 1947 and was a consultant to the U.S. Air Force in 1952.

He lent his expertise to a number of organizations in which he held membership. He was a founding fellow of the Rorschach Forum, a fellow of the British Psychological Society, and a member of the American Psychological Association, the American Statistics Society, the Institute of Management, and Statistics Association.

Stephenson had a varied scholarly career. He was a prolific scholar and writer before coming to the United States. For example, between 1931 and 1935, he published some 14 articles in such scholarly journals as *Nature, British Journal of Psychology, Character and Personality, British Journal of Medical Psychology*, and the *British Journal of Educational Psychology*. He continued to publish throughout his life.

Despite many early publications including his first book, *Testing Schoolchildren* published in 1948, he is best known as the inventor of the Q-Method. Although he was writing about factor analysis and Q-Methodologgy in the early 1930s, his first major exposition of the methodology was in *The Study of Behavior: Q-Technique and Its Methodology*, published in 1953. The book received widespread attention among scholars, and some immediately began employing the technique. Q-factor analysis is really the obverse of R-factor analysis. The Q-Method is particularly useful in communication because, unlike R-factor analysis, which looks at correlations between variables, Q-factor analysis looks at correlations between individuals, communities, and so forth. Although Stephenson is generally given credit for inventing the Q-Method, perhaps it would be more correct to say he developed and named the technique. Burt[1] first wrote about the Q-technique in 1912, although he did not give it that name. Stephenson first discussed Q-analysis in a scholarly journal in 1935.[2]

The Study of Behavior was generally received either as a methodological savior of science or a devil that no one could or needed to understand. One reviewer stated the devil theory's case against the book this way: "Our inference is that [Stephenson's] aims were the following: (a) to challenge much of current methodology in psychology, (b) to explain Q-Methodology and (c) to show by illustration how it can put psychology's house in scientific order, and (d) to demonstrate that theory testing and scientific conclusions are possible on the basis of a single case."[3]

---

[1]C.L. Burt, "The Mental Differences Between the Sexes," *Journal of Experimental Psychology* 1 (1912): 273-284.

[2]William Stephenson, "Correlating Persons Instead of Tests," *Character and Personality* 4 (1935): 17-24.

[3]Quinn McNemar, review of *The Study of Behavior: Q-Technique and*

The reviewer's points are well taken. In *The Study of Behavior*, Stephenson took on virtually the entire contemporary psychology and methodology establishment. Despite having written extensively on factor analysis, he appeared to have grave doubts about the technique (at least in the R-Method). He also raised serious questions about measurement, generalization, and large-scale samples. Indeed, he seemed more interested in attacking those who did not support him than in trying to educate them about his methodology. His statement that he was "in step and all others out"[4] is reflective of his approach regarding many theoretical and methodological issues.

The book attacked other scholars, particularly Burt, for not understanding Stephenson's work. However, in *The Study of Behavior*, as has been the case with much work in Q-Methodology, the writing, organization, and presentation make the book hard to comprehend. This may be the reason that so many have had difficulty understanding, using, and writing about the method.

However contentious *The Study of Behavior* was among psychologists, Stephenson's next book met a better fate among another group of scholars. The publication of *The Play Theory of Mass Communication* in 1967 received immediate attention from communication theorists and researchers. One of the book's major accomplishments was a relatively clear discussion of Q-Methodology, including the theory behind the method and how it might be used in communication. The book provided Stephenson with an opportunity to demonstrate the efficiency of Q-Methodology over very large surveys. He noted that in one study his Q-sort yielded the same conclusions as a survey of thousands of subjects, except he was able to reach his findings using 20 to 30 interviews. He also argued that Q-Methodology reveals attitudes of individuals and not simply aggregates. All-in-all, quite a provocative claim.

"One is tempted," one book reviewer argued, "to dismiss the significance of Q-Methodology as being a creature of its master. It seems to depend too much upon the keenness of the investigator. It is, as Stephenson himself might be tempted to call it, a methodology of 'convergent selectivity,' e.g., a sum of the individualism, the selectivity and the expressiveness of the investigator."[5]

However, one must go beyond the merely methodological to appreciate the importance of what Stephenson did in the book. The concept of play as a vital communication variable was one generally not given credence before Stephenson. The author's theory of play is very broadly based; and the book relates the con-

---

Its Methodology, by William Stephenson, in *Psychological Bulletin* 51 (1954): 527-528.

[4]William Stephenson, *The Study of Behavior: Q-Technique and Its Methodology* (Chicago: University of Chicago Press, 1953), p. 348.

[5]Alex S. Edelstein, review of "The Play Theory of Mass Communication," by Willliam Stephenson, in *Journalism Quarterly* 44 (1967): 565-566.

cept of play to the American character, war, peace, how the public sees events, how leisure time is used, and how people use the media. It was media use that forced communication scholars to sit up and take notice. After all, the play concept was such a simple, but far-reaching, idea. People might use the media because they considered them fun.

"One is a free man in front of a television set, or with a newspaper in one's hand, to a degree not achieved before by man in his long history," said Stephenson.[6] There is a sense of freedom inherent in Stephenson's arguments. Media scholars for so long had been concerned about the passive receiver, about propaganda and its influence on the audience, that they came somewhat late to the thought of free receivers who used the media for their own purposes. Perhaps it was Stephenson's experience with advertising that led him to the conclusion that audiences possess far more freedom of choice than some earlier scholars had generally granted them.

Q-Methodology is particularly useful in looking at Stephenson's play theory. Because the method permits the scholar to get at the attitudes of the individual rather than the aggregate, judgments may be made about how one individual makes communication-related decisions. The television viewer selects a particular program from among all the choices available at a particular moment. That decision is made on the basis of the programs available to fill the time slots, and is not a decision that can be understood on the basis of the average of the sample, Stephenson argued. His arguments have the power of logic, plus, in recent years, a considerable body of research behind them.

As Q-Methodology is a creation of the man, so in many ways is the man something of a creation of the method he invented. His identification with the method prompted (some would say forced) Stephenson to discuss, defend, continually refine, and ultimately use the Q-Method in most of his work in communication.

One of the more interesting and typical pieces of scholarship concerning the Q-Method appeared in *Psychological Bulletin* in 1952, about the time Stephenson was writing *The Study of Behavior*. The journal article has some of the same feeling of defensiveness found in the book and, incidentally, adopts the royal "we" throughout. The posture is immediately apparent from the first sentence: "With the exception of the present author, all who have given some consideration to R and Q techniques have decided that, after all, they are not different in any important respect."[7] It is precisely this point that is argued persuasively by other scholars. It is also a point on which Stephenson did not yield.

It would be misleading, however, to suggest that Stephenson's

---

[6]William Stephenson, *The Play Theory of Mass Communication* (Chicago: University of Chicago Press, 1953).

[7]William Stephenson, "Some Observations on Q-Technique," *Psychological Bulletin* 49 (1952): 483-498.

work during his mature years was devoted only to defending Q-Methodology. He was able to use the method profitably in an array of research efforts. A study published in *Journalism Quarterly* in 1960 is an excellent example of what Stephenson accomplished with the method. He demonstrated how Q-Methodology could be used as an alternative to majority rule among experts judging outstanding photojournalism.[8]

Stephenson reported in 1963 the use of Q-Methodology in a study comparing advertising in 1929 with advertising in 1959.[9] He looked at the theoretical argument that advertising keeps viewers infantile and dependent. The Q-analysis found that there were more infantile mechanisms in full-page advertisements in 1959 than in those advertisements from 30 years earlier. However, he also found that viewers more easily identified with rational approaches and those of a more abstract nature. There were fewer attempts in this research to defend and promote method than were found in some earlier attempts to use Q-Methodology.

In a 1964 *Journalism Quarterly* study Stephenson brought together Q-Methodology and his play theory of communication.[10] The study used a Q-sort of statements from various communication scholars on why people read the newspaper. Stephenson began with 38 such statements that he considered objective. To these he added two subjective statements to the effect that reading the newspaper is enjoyable and an absorbing habit and that it is associated with relaxation and leisure. He argued that reading the newspaper is play and that people read the newspaper because it is pleasurable in the same way that a child's game is pleasurable.

Stephenson was an outspoken critic of the establishment in psychology, particularly when in the defense or promotion of his own ideas. His big idea and the one he needed to defend most was the Q-Method. Whether it was his invention or only his development is beside the point. He was associated with the methodology for so many years it is hard to think of one without thinking of the other.

---

[8]William Stephenson, "Principles of Selection of News Photographs," *Journalism Quarterly* 37 (1960): 61-68.

[9]William Stephenson, "The 'Infantile' vs. the 'Sublime' in Advertising," *Journalism Quarterly* 40 (1963): 181-186.

[10]William Stephenson, "The Ludenic Theory of Newsreading," *Journalism Quarterly* 41 (1964): 367-374.

Bruce Westley, Eclectic Scholar

Bruce H. Westley (1915-1990) will undoubtedly be remembered by communication scholars for what he called a "youthful indiscretion," a general communication model authored over 30 years ago with Malcolm S. MacLean Jr.

Westley and MacLean did not set out to create the general model of communication associated with their names. Their intent had been only to write a review article of the scholarly work that had been done in journalism and mass communication. However, what resulted was much more significant and enduring. It was the first theoretical model designed to account for intrapersonal, interpersonal, and mediated communication. The model explains how one person reacts to his environment, how two persons communicate, and how gatekeepers function within the mass communication environment. The model has been widely cited in the literature.

The dichotomy between interpersonal and mass communication suggested in the model was not new with Westley and MacLean. The traditional view treats the two as separate, a position with which Westley disagrees. He argues that the two are not forces competing for the receiver's attention. "They don't compete at all. The mass media make disturbing inputs while interpersonal communication, on the other hand, has the distinct function of squaring these inputs and helping them be absorbed into the culture."[1]

Although some critics might argue that Westley is merely restating the two-step flow theory in which mass media send information to receivers through opinion leaders, he disagrees. The two-step flow theory, he has explained, is merely one of several approaches that treat interpersonal and mass communication as competing.[2]

Born May 26, 1915, to Dr. Martin D. and Eva Hutchison Westley in Cooperstown, North Dakota, Westley had his hands in

---

[1]Lewis Donohew, "A Mass Communication Pioneer," *Focus* (May 6, 1981) 1-2.
[2]Ibid.

printer's ink by his high school years, serving as editor of the award-winning Cooper High School *Record*. The ink stayed on his hands for the next 23 years as he was more often than not a practicing newspaperman. Strangely, little of Westley's research activity deals directly with newspapers.

As so often is the case with those who work for newspapers, Westley worked on a variety of newssheets. His first job was as, he fondly recalled, a reporter and printer's devil on the tiny LaMoure (N.D.) *Chronicle*. For 4 summers from 1935-1938 he was very nearly the itinerate journalist celebrated in myth as he worked on two North Dakota newspapers, the *Farmer-Globe* and the *News-Times*, in addition to serving as publicist for the Grand Forks State Fair. Over the next four years he was reporter, editor-manager, or news editor on three different newspapers, the *Cavalier County Republican*, the Casselton (N.D.) *Reporter*, and the Providence *Journal and Evening Bulletin* in the Rhode Island capital. Add stints as a part-time copy editor on the Madison *Wisconsin State Journal*, and Westley could be said to have had nearly as much time as a practicing journalist as many who make journalism a career.

While newspapering, Westley earned a PhB in journalism from North Dakota State University in 1938 and an MS in journalism from Columbia University in 1941. The U.S. Army sent him to Harvard University in 1943 to study personal psychology, and he found himself immersed in social psychology rather than journalism. It was that year at Harvard "that really turned me around," he said. "Columbia got me out of North Dakota, and Harvard got me thinking very seriously about more graduate work in behavioral sciences."[3]

The names of his instructors at Harvard read like a who's who of psychology and statistics. Westley studied under internationally famous psychologists Gordon Allport and Kurt Lewin (on the faculty at Massachusetts Institute of Technology but who taught one day each week at Harvard). Lewin was particularly influential in setting a direction for Westley's career. There was also the "funny little man who would jump up and clap his hands in the rat lab when the rats did as they were supposed to."[4] He was a giant of general psychology, O.H. Mowrer. Two others got Westley interested in quantitative methods: Truman Kelly, who had done pioneering work in statistics and was early involved in factor analysis, and the statistician R.B. Cattell.[5]

By the end of World War II Westley's circumstances had changed. He was married with a child (eventually the father of five children) and could no longer afford what daily newspapers could pay. It was his inability to find an acceptable job with a newspaper that led to his first job in teaching, an instructorship

---

[3]Interview with author, July 1986.
[4]Ibid.
[5]Ibid.

at the University of Wisconsin (1946). He chose Wisconsin over another major midwestern university because he believed that Wisconsin was going to be a major producer of research for the field. It was his desire to be a part of that tradition that led him to advanced graduate work at the University of Michigan and circumstances that changed his life and perhaps cost him a doctorate.

Westley's study of social psycholgy (there were few PhD programs in communication at the time) at the University of Michigan put him in contact with major figures in the field. Among those under whom he studied were methodologist Daniel Katz, survey researchers Eleanor Maccoby, Charles Cannell, and Angus Campbell, psychological scaling master Rensis Likert, and social psychologists Roger Brown and Robert Zajonc. However, the greatest influence on Westley at the University of Michigan was social psychologist Theodore Newcomb. There are direct and traceable connections between work Newcomb was doing in microsociology at Michigan and later work done individually by Westley and jointly by Westley and MacLean.

Westley considered himself "fortunate" to have studied among the eminent scholars who taught at Michigan but pointed out with some bitterness that he had difficulty getting a dissertation done after leaving the University of Michigan.[6] That experience made him somewhat unique. In an era that esteems the doctorate so highly, Westley was a man of major reputation who did not hold the terminal degree. At least partially responsible for his failure to obtain the doctorate was his work with the Research Center for Group Dynamics at the University of Michigan.

However, Westley's work with the Center led to a joint authorship of an important publication, *The Dynamics of Planned Change*, with Ronald Lippitt and Jeanne Watson. The book ended up as Westley's substitute for a dissertation. It may have been a worthy substitute for others, if not necessarily for Westley. Willard Spalding's comments in the book's foreword address the volume's importance:

> The significance of such a project is self-evident and its value triplefold. As a theoretical analysis, a comparative study, a commentary on research proceedings and professional training, this is a book of high academic consequence. . . . A worthy and very serviceable contribution, this book crystallizes our thinking on a challenging and important subject and will prove to be a milestone in the evolution of our knowledge of the phenomenon of change.[7]

The book remains an important contribution to the psychol-

---

[6]Ibid.
[7]Ronald Lippitt, Jeanne Watson, and Bruce Westley, *The Dynamics of Planned Change* (New York: Harcourt, Brace and Company, 1958), p. iii.

ogy literature. As important as the early work on change was and despite the wide dissemination of the Westley and MacLean general model of communication, Westley may be best known for a work that is only marginally concerned with research. His 1953 text, *News Editing*, now in its second edition, has been used by thousands of today's professional journalists. Although outdated (many examples in the 1972 edition were out-of-date when the book was written), the text is still a useful guide to copy editing and an excellent commentary on Westley's knowledge of the craft.

The publication for which Westley is best known among graduate students, however, is probably the methods text he co-edited with Guido H. Stempel III. *Research Methods in Mass Communication*, published in 1981, is widely used. The names of the book chapters' authors read like a who's who of communication theory and methodology. Recognizing that no single scholar could be expert in the growing field of communication, the two editors selected several areas where they themselves were expert and then sought the leading scholars to write the chapters in other areas. The book covers so much methodology beyond the usual survey and content analysis, it is doubtful that a basic question can be raised by a student that cannot be answered by the book. But it is more than a methods text. As *Journalism Quarterly's* book reviewer points out, it is a historical document:

> At last, apparently, we [communication scholars] no longer are merely stepchildren of sociology, social psychology, political science and history. Those fields and others still have much to say to us, of course, but our own literature, evidenced in this book, now allows us to engage in a two-way dialogue. Perhaps, at last, we are truly a discipline, not just a loose collectivity of communication interests.[8]

Many would argue with the review's overly optimistic assessment of communication methodology. Certainly it is not a position with which Westley would be comfortable, for there is no claim in the book or elsewhere that any communication methods have grown entirely from the work of communication scholars. All communication methods have been borrowed from other social and natural sciences. In no case does the literature support the assertion that communication has progressed beyond the stepchild phase. And although communication scholars may engage in a two-way dialogue with other sciences, it is often as parent to child, not as equals.

Perhaps the key to the success of the methods text is the editors' touch. They managed to preserve the points of view of the contributors, and that is no small feat. The methods book may do

---

[8]Donald Lewis Shaw, review of *Research Methods in Mass Communication*, by Guido H. Stempel and Bruce H. Westley, *Journalism Quarterly* 58 (1981): 496-497.

for graduate students what the editing book did for undergraduates: train the next generation.

Westley's contributions can be found in a number of significant books and monographs that usually dealt with communication theory and research methods. In addition, he wrote over 30
articles for scholarly journals. The articles were as eclectic as one
is apt to find from a single scholar. They included research into
agenda-setting, social change, information campaigns, media
credibility, newspaper readership (and non-readership), politics,
audience analysis, media effects, and media use.

Westley was a strong contributor to several academic disciplines. He held memberships in the American Psychological Association, American Association for Public Opinion Research,
International Communication Association, American Association for the Advancement of Science, and the AEJMC. Because the
leadership of organizations influences their memberships, Westley can be said to have had considerable impact on AEJMC by
virtue of the positions he held in the organization.

He served as president of AEJMC in 1973-1974 and headed or
chaired several bodies within the association. His influence was
most felt as chairman of the Council on Communication Research, chairman of the Advisory Board, and member of the Executive Committee. He was also head and a founding member of
the Theory and Methodology Division which permitted him to
control to a certain extent the direction of the division. Some
have argued that the division has been unduly controlled by a
small group of scholars who were responsible for the establishment of the division. Perhaps Westley exerted that kind of control
over AEJMC. However, he had even greater impact in another
area, publications.

Westley was the founding editor of *Journalism Monographs*,
serving in that capacity for 16 years (1966-1982). The position
gave him the final decision for perhaps 80% of the pieces that
have been published in *Journalism Monographs*. Here, as well as
in his research, Westley was eclectic in his interests. Only a small
percentage of *Journalism Monographs* articles have concerned
research methods in communication. Westley also served for 11
years (1963-1972) as associate editor of *Journalism Quarterly*.
His impact was probably greater in *Journalism Quarterly* because
of the greater number of short manuscripts (representing the bulk
of formative research in a discipline) he decided upon. He also
served as associate editor of *Communication Yearbook 7* (1983)
and *Communication Yearbook 8* (1984).

In addition to his reputation as a communication scholar, he
was well-known for his work as a teacher. Beginning with his
first job at the University of Wisconsin, he taught continuously
for 35 years (1946-1981). At the University of Wisconsin he was
an instructor (1946-1947), assistant professor (1947-1955), associate professor (1955-1964), and professor (1964-1969). After 22
years at Wisconsin, he moved to the University of Kentucky to be-

come chairman of the department of journalism (1969-1975). After stepping down as chairman, he continued to teach in journalism until his retirement in 1981. He also lectured or performed research activities at a number of other institutions including West Virginia University, Syracuse University, Stanford University, University of Minnesota, University of Michigan, East-West Communication Institute, and the International Center for Higher Education in Journalism for Latin America.

Widely recognized by the discipline, Westley was honored in 1982 for service as editor of *Journalism Monographs*. He received the AEJMC's first Harold L. Nelson Award (for distinguished contributions to the study of mass communication) in 1981. He was awarded the Paul J. Deutschman Award for Contributions to Research in 1985.

Few communication scholars have been as instrumental in the growth of communication theory and methods as Westley. He worked with or knew virtually all of the important scholars in communication and many of the most influential in related disciplines. Perhaps the key to his contribution lies in those related disciplines that he brought to bear on communication problems.

Guido Stempel
and Newspaper Readership

Guido H. Stempel III (1928-) is best-known for his work as editor of *Journalism Quarterly*, journalism's oldest scholarly journal, for his pioneering research in political coverage and newspaper readership, and for his impact on the major organization of the discipline, AEJMC. Content analysis and the survey were his research methods of choice. He was not a pioneer in either content analysis or survey techniques; however, he made profitable use of both.

Born August 13, 1928, Stempel at the age of 23 had both a BA and a MA from Indiana University and had already begun working as a practicing journalist, serving as both reporter and sports editor of the Frankfort (Ind.) *Morning Times*. It was during his senior year at Indiana University that he got his first taste of research, and he was hooked. His first research was a readership study, an interest that has remained with him throughout his career.

That first effort was a study of the readership of the Indiana University *Daily Student*. The findings led Stempel to be wary of what readers *say* they want in a newspaper. The study found that 65% of the respondents said they wanted the *Daily Student* to carry more national and international news yet the readership of the national-international stories in the newspaper was 15% less. "I remember [the early readership study] every time I read another report urging newspapers to run more international news because a survey has shown the readers *say* they want more international news."[1]

Stempel was typical of most undergraduates in that he generally read little about journalism beyond textbooks. However, while working toward his master's degree, he found himself reading a number of criticisms and assessments of journalism that led him to conclude that much of the literature in journalism dealt in untested assumptions and invalid conclusions. Because he believed that scholars knew very little about the content of

---

[1]Stempel letter to author, June 19, 1986.

newspapers, his interest gravitated toward content analysis, a method he believed could answer many of the important questions about newspaper content. It was a natural progression from the questions raised in his mind about newspaper content to doing a content analysis for his master's thesis. Not only did the thesis permit him to use content analysis, it also introduced him to political studies, for the thesis was a content analysis of editorial pages of Indiana dailies in four presidential years.

With his MA in hand, Stempel began the doctoral program at the University of Wisconsin, where a new world of content analysis possibilities opened for him. Of particular importance to Stempel was his introduction to the World War II work of the Harold Lasswell group. It led Stempel to become interested in the methodological questions raised by *The Language of Politics*. In a content analysis seminar, he studied sampling. The result was his first contact with *Journalism Quarterly* and his first publication, "Sampling Size for Classifying Subject Matter in Dailies," published in 1952.

Stempel carried his interest in content analysis into his dissertation, a methodological study of reliability in content analysis, which provided the basis for his second *Journalism Quarterly* piece, "Increasing Reliability in Content Analysis." His continuing interest in reliability is evidenced by his most recent work on the subject, "Reliability of Six Techniques of Content Analysis of Local Coverage," published in *Journalism Quarterly* some 24 years after the first work.

Stempel's interest in content analysis quickly shifted from concern with methods to an interest in applications of the technique. In 1955 a group of researchers proposed a study of the 1956 presidential election to test empirically Adlai Stevenson's 1952 charges of a one-party press. Editors and publishers reacted unfavorably to the proposed study, fearing the research would support the charge, and the researchers dropped the idea. However, Stempel and a colleague at Pennsylvania State University decided to do the study in a limited fashion. A content analysis of 25 Pennsylvania dailies found that in a year when incumbent Dwight Eisenhower won the state easily, newspaper coverage favored him only slightly, but that the pattern did not show bias. Their findings ran counter to traditional wisdom which suggested that American newspapers were generally Republican and thus favored the Republican candidate.

At about the same time as the Pennsylvania study, Stempel became interested in a survey by *Practical English* concerning the question of which were the best newspapers in the country. He concluded that coverage by the so-called prestige press would be important and coverage by those newspapers would reflect the best in American journalism. He studied some 900 issues of the prestige press in 1960, 1964, 1968, 1980, and 1984. These latter studies supported what he had found in the Pennsylvania study.

"Overall," Stempel remarked, "those studies have shown that

coverage of presidential campaigns has been remarkably even. It is evident that at least some of the prestige press papers make a conscious effort to balance coverage. The bias that some politicians still insist is there simply doesn't show up under careful analysis, and other researchers have come to the same conclusions. One candidate may get more coverage than another, but sometimes that is because he is doing more and genuinely making more news. And, the most obvious manifestation of bias—favoring in the news columns the candidate endorsed editorially—simply doesn't show up."[2]

Another significant Stempel contribution using content analysis concerned charges that newspaper content was becoming standardized. Traditional wisdom was that wire services stimulated newspapers to use certain stories by telling editors which stories other newspapers were using on their front page. This criticism focused on the fact that the number of newspapers had declined by the middle 1950s and the number of cities with competing newspapers were few. Stempel's content analysis of six Michigan dailies found little support for standardization or agreement among newspapers. The limited sample did not permit generalization of the findings beyond the newspapers studied, but Stempel concluded, arguably, that critics' claims about standardization were exaggerated.

As late as 1985, a *Journalism Quarterly* article authored by Stempel reported little agreement among various media in the stories they used. Media have similar mixes of subjects (government, politics, diplomacy, war, defense, etc.), leading scholars to assume that the same stories were being selected by different media. Stempel, however, has argued otherwise.

A particularly noteworthy area of Stempel's research has been his series of readership studies looking at newspaper format. During his professional career, newspapers have gone from an eight-column vertical format to a six-column horizontal format and recently to modular formats. The earliest readership study done by Stempel (with William Click) was in 1967. That study, which compared the traditional eight-column format with its modern counterparts, found that readers generally favored the modern format. However, there was some evidence that readers tended to equate the modern format with sensationalism. An expanded study under the auspices of the American Newspaper Publishers Association in 1974 found overwhelming support for the horizontal format. Additional research showed that readers favored modular formats and the use of color.

Another important research arena for Stempel has been the study of the effects of concentration of media ownership. Traditionally, scholars have looked at media ownership in terms of local newspaper competition and pointed out that fewer than 5% of cities with daily newspapers have competing dailies. However,

---

[2]Ibid.

the criticism did not consider broadcast competition. As early as 1967 Stempel did an analysis that showed that most daily newspapers had broadcast competition but that the monopoly medium was radio.

Based on traditional wisdom Stempel had expected to find many cities where there was single ownership of the only newspaper, the only television station, and the only radio station. One of the cities where the traditional view was true was Zanesville, Ohio. Stempel wrote a piece based on his study of the media in Zanesville and two other Ohio cities where there was not single ownership. It was an extensive study that involved public opinion surveys in the three cities and content analysis of the newspapers and the television and radio newscasts. The findings documented that a total monopoly did have an effect. News coverage was less extensive and the stories carried were more similar than in non-monopoly cities. The surveys found that the audience in Zanesville was generally satisfied with what it received from the media. Stempel concluded that the effect of monopoly was not as powerful as critics assumed.

The work for which Stempel is best known among students, if not scholars, is the research methods textbook he and Bruce Westley edited in 1981. The book, *Research Methods in Mass Communication*, was only the third such work devoted to communication research and the first in over 20 years. There have been others since, but the Stempel and Westley book remains the most widely used. Although the editors had intended to write an advanced theory and methodology book, a survey of teachers of methods courses revealed that what was needed was an eclectic text. Although both editors wrote chapters, most of the book was written by people the editors considered experts in the field. What resulted was a book that was much broader than the two earlier works and still remains the most catholic of books in the field.

Stempel's research efforts, which continue with a number of unfinished studies, have been broad. He has published in most major outlets available to communication scholars, including *Journalism Quarterly*, *Newspaper Research Journal*, and *Journal of Communication*, and a host of less prestigious publications.

A scholar may have the most profound impact on an academic discipline through work with the scholarly journals which serve that discipline. To a great extent the editor of a scholarly journal influences the kind of research done in that discipline by the simple expedient of selecting or rejecting manuscripts and by setting policy by which research is selected. If this is so, Stempel has had considerable influence on the direction of research in journalism through his editing of *Journalism Quarterly* from 1972 to 1989. Indeed, he probably has had more impact than most editors since he has been associated with the journal since 1968, when he was named to the Editorial Advisory Board and later an associate editor.

The journal changed considerably during Stempel's years. Not only did it grow larger; it was opened to a greater number of scholars, it was more tightly edited, and, perhaps most important, Stempel says that it is now fully refereed.

When Stempel became editor, the journal was only partly refereed, but he moved quickly to complete the process. "I did so because I thought this was important to [AEJMC] members to have a refereed publication as part of their organization. It would make publication in the *Quarterly* worth more to the individual faculty member."[3] However, Stempel faced opposition to the refereeing process, and some members of AEJMC have argued for a relaxation.

Despite resistance to refereeing, Stempel is convinced that some manuscripts now get published that would not have been in the past, because Stempel's philosophy was to help the scholar improve the manuscript, rather than to flatly reject it. "On some publications, it seems to me the focus of the review process is trying to find a reason to reject. I wanted our goal to be to get the best manuscript possible from the writer and to advise the writer on how to improve it."[4] A high level of polish in a submission was usually required, for Stempel accepted less than 20% of manuscripts in their original form. Overall, he accepted about 40% of submissions.

Perhaps Stempel's most controversial decision as editor involved limiting the text of manuscripts to 14 pages or 4,000 words. Critics argued that the limit was artificial and reduced the quality of submissions and ultimately the quality of the journal. Stempel disagrees, saying the intent of the limit was to permit editors to edit tightly. The limit was exceeded ocassionally when warranted. "We suggest ways to cut [manuscripts] to authors," Stempel said near the end of his *JQ* tenure, "and we edit them down. Some authors have objected, but more have told us that their manuscript is better as a result. I believe by now we have published at lest 250 more articles than we would have been able to had we not instituted this policy."[5]

Despite Stempel's objections, length limitations have had an effect on what kinds of research may be submitted. Favored are those pieces, often quantitative in nature, that can be written short, whereas pieces requiring more length to develop may have no outlet at all. Having the same editor for many years may have had the effect of turning the editor's agenda into the journal's agenda.

In addition to the research and the journal, Stempel has provided leadership in the most important organization in the discipline. He has been involved with AEJMC for over two decades, and his impact has been far-reaching. "I think I had considerable influence on the process of standing committees of AEJMC re-

---

[3]Ibid.
[4]Ibid.
[5]Ibid.

viewing divisions," he concluded. "I became chairman of the Committee on Research at a time when we were all unsure of the process, and there were complaints from some divisions. What I started to do, writing each division a letter of evaluation with specific suggestions, worked and became the norm for the three standing committees (Research, Teaching Standards, and Professional Freedom and Responsibility)."[6]

Through the encouragement of Stempel's committee, the divisions of AEJMC began to pay more attention to research, and several divisions which had never reported research began to do so under the committee's prodding. Stempel estimates that "there are easily three times as many research papers presented at the [annual] convention as there used to be."[7]

Stempel is Distinguished Research Professor in the School of Journalism at Ohio University.

In a career spanning over 30 years, he has had an enormous impact on the field of journalism. His influence on *Journalism Quarterly* will be for felt years. His pioneering work in presidential campaign coverage and his studies of newspaper format added significantly to the literature. His work with AEJMC helped change the nature and influence of that organization.

---

[6]Ibid.
[7]Ibid.

Percy Tannenbaum and the Social Psychology of Communication

Percy Hyman Tannenbaum (1927-), social psychologist, communication educator, theorist, methodologist, and co-developer of the semantic differential, is one of the most prolific scholars in mass communication research, having published in virtually every major journal associated with communication as well as authoring, co-authoring, or editing a number of important books in the field.

He has been an eclectic scholar and a prolific writer, authoring and editing a number of books as well as writing more than 100 articles for scholarly journals around the world. He has performed research in every major area of communication study: intrapersonal, interpersonal, and mass communication. In addition he has studied media effects, psycholinguistics, consistency, and meaning, among other topics. Overall, Tannenbaum must be said to have had his hand in most communication pies.

However, he is best known for a volume written 30 years ago with Charles Osgood and George Suci, *The Measurement of Meaning*. The work, weakly theoretical in nature, was designed primarily as a progress report on a technique to measure meaning, the semantic differential. Bipolar adjectives define a seven point scale on which subjects rate concepts ("mother," "television," etc.). A typical scale might have "good" and "bad" as the opposite adjectives. The ratings on several scales enable the research to construct a picture of the concept as seen by respondents.

The semantic differential was developed over a period of two decades. While the original concept was highly theoretical, the methodology became almost more important than its theoretical undepinnings. As with much research in the 1950s and 1960s, the semantic differential requires the use of factor analysis. So the technique has suffered not only those criticisms directed at it but also those directed at factor analysis. However, *The Measurement of Meaning* is an important work, if only for its partial lucidation of a methodology.

Tannenbaum was born in Montreal, Quebec, Canada, May 31, 1927, the son of Charles and Ronya Tannenbaum. He married

Brocha Kaplan September 16, 1948, and they have two children, Brian and Nili. Although Tannenbaum has lived in the United States for many years, he began his college education in Canada. He was awarded the BSc from McGill University in 1948. It was during this period that he had his only experience as a practicing newspaperman. He was a reporter for the Montreal *Herald* from 1947 until 1950. He moved to the United States and fairly flew through graduate school, receiving an MS in 1951 and a PhD in communication in 1953, both from the University of Illinois.

He began his teaching career as an assistant professor of communication at the University of Michigan in 1953. Returning to the University of Illinois in 1954 he was named a research assistant professor. He remained at Illinois until 1959, when he left to become professor of psychology and journalism and director of the Mass Communication Research Center at the University of Wisconsin. After 8 years he moved to the University of Pennsylvania and became a professor of communication and psychology in 1967. In 1970 he became a professor of public policy and research psychologist at the University of California at Berkeley. He has since been named a professor of the Graduate School of Public Policy and director of the Survey Research Center at the school.

Tannenbaum has lectured, consulted, and advised widely. He has been a visiting professor at the University of Stockholm, University of Zurich, Hebrew University, Stanford University, and the University of Southern California. He was chairman of the Social Science Research Council Seminar of Communication Research in 1957. He was a faculty member of the Salzburg Seminar on American Studies in 1964. He spent 1965-1966 as a fellow of the Center for Advanced Study in Behavorial Sciences. Beginning in 1965 he was a consultant to the National Science Foundation Panel on Social Psychology. He was a consultant to the National Institute of Mental Health and the National Academy of Sciences. In addition to consulting widely with government and industry groups, he has been a stringer for *Time* and a freelance writer for other magazines.

An important work with which Tannenbaum is associated is one of those works that appear to have been written by a committee. *Theories of Cognitive Consistency: A Sourcebook*, published in 1968, had six co-editors/contributors.[1] It was the preparation of this volume that was the reason for Tannenbaum's fellowship to the Center for Advanced Study in the Behavioral Sciences. By any measure the book is a major work. It consists of 84 individual reviews of the various consistency areas, such as dissonance, balance, congruity, and so forth. Tannenbaum made important contributions to the book. Most of what he wrote was theoretical;

---

[1]Robert P. Abelson, Elliot Aronson, William J. McGuire, Theodore M. Newcomb, Milton J. Rosenberg, and Percy H. Tannenbaum, *Theories of Cognitive Consistency: A Sourcebook* (Chicago: Rand McNally, 1968).

but methodological concerns, primarily, the semantic differential, were not far from his mind. His contributions to the book are insightful and significant.

Engaging in a kind of scholarly elitism, social scientists have not found the entertainment function of broadcasting a serious enough matter to warrant much attention. If only for this reason, *The Entertainment Functions of Television*, edited by Tannenbaum, is noteworthy. The eight essays in the book cover a range of subject matter that is certainly useful in promoting empirical research. However, the writers often appear unable to divorce themselves from a bias against television, treating the subject at times as if it is unworthy of attention from serious scholars.

"Too often," argued one reviewer, "the discussions appear to be embedded in the normative Platonic-Presbyterian view that experiencing too much entertainment, unaccompanied by proper lacings of cognitive stuff, actually may pose a hazard to our mental well-being. The acknowledged imbalance that *The Entertainment Functions of Television* reflects deny the reader important insights into a fuller range of considerations to be taken into account in pursuing the matter empirically."[2]

Tannenbaum admits that the volume lacks balance and a theme. And the work is entirely too narrow and superficial, focusing as it does primarily on the somewhat narrow research of its authors, who apparently only wanted to refine their own research agendas without being burdened with new ideas. However, it is important to note that Tannenbaum performed an important service to the field by raising the issues at all.

His 1983 volume, with Leslie J. Kostrich and others, is a study that no doubt needed doing but may be essentially trivial. *Turned-On TV/Turned-Off Voters: Policy Options for Election Projections* is concerned with possible effects on the outcome of elections that the network practice of projecting winners before the polls close may have. The authors accept without challenge the traditional wisdom that attempts at persuasion are just fine before the election but somehow undesirable on election day. Despite the careful review of the literature on the subject, there is little in the way of conclusive evidence that a problem exists. As is sometimes the nature of policy makers, Tannenbaum offers several minor options for dealing with the issue without determining that a problem exists.

Turned-On TV/Turned-Off Voters is a classic case of getting the most out of graduate teaching. By Tannenbaum's own admission the book was put together in a graduate seminar, with students and others contributing mightily to the effort. Tannenbaum does give some credit to the work done by his students but notes ultimately that "I was the principal investigator and, in ef-

---

[2]Harold Mendelsohn, review of *The Entertainment Functions of Television* (Percy H. Tannenbaum) in *Journal of Communication* 32 (1982): 206-208.

fect, the main if not the sole author. I culled all that my associates and seminar students had prepared but in the end the words and positions represented are mine alone. I doubt any of my associates on this project would agree with the bulk of it. It is, accordingly, I and I alone that bear the sole responsibility for any errors of omission or commission contained herein."[3]

Tannenbaum is the author of one of the chapters in Nafziger and White's *Introduction to Mass Communicaitons Research.*[4] The chapter, "Experimental Method in Communication Research," is an important statement regarding how Tannenbaum looks at the world of research. It is a too limiting view for a field of study as broad as communication. However, one should not be surprised to find him supporting the experimental method to the virtual exclusion of other methods. After all, his academic and clinical training in psychology and behavioral studies leaves the experiment as the method of choice. He argues that the experimental method is quantitative, objective, and so forth, and other methods in communication fall short in comparison.

One other piece, written with Bradley S. Greenburg, should be mentioned. The chapter, "Mass Communication," in the *Annual Review of Psychology*[5] is a survey up to 1967 of the literature in mass communication, much of which is experimental. It is a particularly fine piece of scholarship that looks at the various theoretical areas in communication, with some attention to methodological concerns. There is an excellent bibliography, for which the authors thank their graduate students.

Perhaps the best way to gather a picture of what Tannenbaum has accomplished in his research is to look at the large body of scholarly journal publications. Although many scholars in mass communication have been quite catholic in their use of research methods, much of Tannenbaum's research has been experimental, not surprising when one recalls that he was trained as a social psychologist.

A good example of the kind of early experimental work Tannenbaum did was the condensation of his thesis published in *Journalism Quarterly.* He developed an experiment in which college students were exposed to newspaper stories with different headlines to test how the headlines influenced the total impression made by the news story. In a discussion that is masterly in the manner of its qualifications, Tannenbaum, nevertheless, generalizes from the laboratory to the real world to a degree

---

[3]Percy H. Tannenbaum and Leslie J. Kostrich, *Turned-On TV/Turned-Off Voters* (Beverly Hills: Sage Publications, 1983), p.14.

[4]Ralph O. Nafziger and David M. White, *Introduction to Mass Communications Research* (rev. ed.) (Baton Rouge: Louisiana State University Press, 1963), pp. 51-77.

[5]Percy H. Tannenbaum and Bradley S. Greenberg, "Mass Communication" in Paul R Farnsworth (Ed.), *Annual Review of Psychology* (Palo Alto, CA: Annual Reviews, Inc., 1968), pp. 351-386.

hardly supported by the evidence.

Tannenbaum followed up the next year with an experiment designed to discover if radio newscast leads produced results similar to the earlier study. He concluded that they did. However, one could look at the same data and conclude that the most likely effect was confusion. Interestingly, Tannenbaum used this study to mention his next research effort, which looked at the questions of recency versus primacy.

That study, "Effect of Serial Position on Recall of Radio News Stories," tested the importance to recall of sequence of news stories. As is well known today, those items toward the middle of a presentation are apt to be less easily recalled than those at the beginning or toward the end. Two interesting points raised in the study have bearing on Tannenbaum's career. First, in discussing the theoretical aspects of the experiment, he referred to communication as being a specialized area within psychology and argued that any scholar seeking a theory of communication should focus on psychology and related areas. Second, although disclaiming any attempt to give policy advice to radio broadcasters, he offered the advice anyway: repeat news item highlights to increase listener recall.

In 1955 Tannenbaum used the semantic differential to look at the effects of television on information and meaning. The study used a local televised congressional hearing as the vehicle for the experiment. Using the semantic differential, he found that television viewing of the hearings produced a significant difference in the way objects and messages were perceived. He departed from his normal methodology in this study and used a survey for part of the research.

Three journal articles from the early 1960s are of interest because of their study of sensationalism, a subject historically studied using traditional approaches. The studies, all written with other scholars, were experimental in design and used the semantic differential. The first study attempted to determine the dimensions of sensationalism and to develop an index of sensationalism (Sendex)[6] in various messages. The Sendex is basically 12 semantic differential scales used to judge sensationalism in media. The remaining two experiments continue to test the Sendex, with modifications.

Among some of the other experimental research associated with Tannenbaum are studies of typeface connotations and the effects of bylines on changes in attitude, both using the semantic differential; an experimental study looking at the encoding behavior of news photographers; syntactic structure consistency in journalistic style using content analysis; and a study of the language used to communicate scores on sports pages.

Tannenbaum has written on a broader range of subjects than

[6]Percy H. Tannenbaum and Mervin D. Lynch, "Sensationalism: the Concept and Its Measurement," *Journalism Quarterly* 37 (1960): 381-392.

most scholars in the field of mass communication. Written invariably from a background of social psychology, his work has often brought depth and insight to the study of media subjects. Often a theorist, he also has added much to scholars' understanding of methodology, particularly through his use of the semantic differential.

Wayne Danielson
and Computer-Assisted Research

Wayne Allen Danielson (1929-) has spent virtually his entire life as either a student, a teacher, or an administrator. Among his many contributions to the advancement of mass communication in general and methodology in particular, his most important work has been in the use of computers.

For the past quarter-century Danielson has been deeply interested and involved in the use of computers in the publication industry and in the impact of computers on news writing and editing. His work with speech synthesis from newspaper text is a demonstration of that interest. He anticipates that the computer will continue to have an enormous impact on journalism. "I believe that the computer," he wrote in 1979, " will have a profound effect on the distribution of news and knowledge in general in the remainder of this century and in the next."[1]

The son of Author Leroy and Bessie Ann Danielson, he was born December 6, 1929, in Burlington, Iowa. He married the former Beverly Grace Kinsell, March 19, 1955, and is the father of four children.

He was awarded a BA from the University of Iowa in 1952. The following year he received his MA and in 1957 was awarded the PhD in mass communication research, both from Stanford University. It was during his study for the doctorate that he served as a practicing journalist, and even then research was very much on his mind. In 1953-1954 he worked as a reporter and research manager for the San Jose *Mercury-News.*

Danielson has extensive teaching experience. He was acting assistant professor in journalism at Stanford University in 1956-1957. From 1957 until 1959 he was an assistant professor of journalism at the University of Wisconsin. He moved to the University of North Carolina at Chapel Hill in 1959 and was appointed associate professor of journalism. He was promoted to professor in 1963 and was named dean of the School of Journal-

---

[1]Frances Carol Locker (Ed.), *Contemporary Authors* (114 vols.) (Detroit: Gale Research Company, 1979), Vol. 109: pp. 77-80.

ism in 1964, a post he held until 1969. That year he was named dean of the School of Communication at the University of Texas-Austin. He was also appointed professor of journalism and computer science. He stepped down as dean in 1979 but has remained on the journalism faculty. His tenure includes a stint as director of graduate studies.

Danielson has been deeply involved in a number of academic and professional organizations. These memberships give an indication of the breadth of his scholarly interest. He belongs to the International Communications Association, American Sociological Association, American Association for Public Opinion Research, Southern Sociological Society, and the Associated Press Managing Editors Association. He has served as vice-president (1966-1967) and president (1967-1968) of the American Association of Schools and Departments of Journalism. He served on the steering committee of the New Research Center of the American Newspaper Publishers Association (1964-1973). He was a member of the advisory committee of "Seminars for Newsmen" for the Southern Newspaper Publishers Association (1969-1975).

However, the organization membership that offered Danielson the greatest opportunity to exert influence was the Association for Education in Journalism and Mass Communication. He served AEJMC as vice-president in 1969-1970 and as president in 1970-1971. He chaired the publications committee, 1968-1972, and the research committee, 1980-1983. He has served a term on the publications committee. Although not a founding member of the Theory and Methodology Division of AEJMC, he has been a member of the division almost from its beginning and has exercised a large measure of influence over its direction. Each of the positions Danielson held in AEJMC permitted him considerable impact and influence on the organization. Danielson served as editor of *Journalism Abstracts*, 1963-1968 and 1971. From 1964 to 1972 he served on the advisory board of the most influential scholarly publication, *Journalism Quarterly*, although the influence of an advisory board member is limited.

Despite administrative and organizational pressures, Danielson has managed to produce important research and writing. His most important full-length work is *A Computerized Bib-liography of Mass Communication Research, 1944-1964*, co-authored with G. Cleveland Wilhoit. Published by the Magazine Publishers Association in 1967, the volume was compiled to assist magazine executives, among others, to locate mass communication articles in social science journals and contains listings for 2,338 articles. A most useful tool is the KWIC index used in the work. This keyword index makes finding material relatively simple. The bibliography is an important addition to the mass communication literature.

Danielson has also co-authored *Exercises and Tests for Journalists*, with E.L. Callihan and Harold L. Nelson, published in 1961; *Programmed Newspaper Style*, with Blanche Prejean, in

1971; *Programmed Newsstyle,* also with Blanche Prejean, in 1977; and *Only in Chapel Hill,* a photographic essay with Jock Lauterer (Danielson wrote the text) in 1967.

Some of Danielson's most important work, however, has been as contributor to the volumes of other scholars. His chapter, "Content Analysis in Communication Research," in *Introduction to Mass Communication Research* is particularly noteworthy. Although the edition, edited by Ralph O. Nafziger and David M. White, was published in 1963 (originally published in 1958 without the Danielson contribution), Danielson's discussion of content analysis remains the most articulate and useful short discourse on the subject yet written. Many more recent and considerably longer discussions of content analysis are less informative, especially for graduate students.

Because of his interest in computers and computer technology it was not surprising that when Guido H. Stempel III and Bruce H. Westley, co-editors of *Research Methods in Mass Communication,* were casting about for experts to write the chapters, they chose Danielson to write the discussion of data processing. The book, only the third devoted strictly to mass communication research in some 30 years, was published in 1981. However, in what could be considered a classic case of clashing expertise, Stempel, rather than Danielson, wrote the two chapters devoted to content analysis.

From the chapter titled "Data Processing," it is clear that Danielson considers data processing the most important aspect of a research project and the major reason some students fail. "It has been our experience that on the college scene most failures to complete master's theses and doctoral dissertations stem from inadequacies in data processing for the student," argued Danielson. "It is difficult, therefore, to overstate the importance of good data processing, for it is from the proper collection, coding, and analysis of the data that we will find or fail to find the answers to the research questions we have posed."[2] However, in this excellent discussion, Danielson was not so enamored of computers that he forgot that not every research project requires megabytes of computer memory. He showed that paper and pencil calculations still work for some research.

Danielson's research has revealed a wide-ranging interest in different subjects and in the use of various methodologies. An early example of his research expertise is found in the 1956 *Journalism Quarterly* study "Eisenhower's February Decision: A Study of News Impact." The subject of the research was the decision by the president to run for a second term. This work used a multi-method approach. The before-and-after interview panel study was also descriptive and experimental. The purpose was to

---

[2]Wayne A. Danielson, "Data Processing," in Guido H. Stempel III and Bruce H. Westley (Eds.), *Research Methods in Mass Communication* (Englewood Cliffs, NJ: Prentice-Hall, 1981), pp. 105-106.

test the predicted effects of Eisenhower's decision on certain attitudinal variables (survey), to describe how the panel found out about the president's decision (diffusion), and to define the images of several candidates through the use of the semantic differential (experimental). The study showed signs of considerable methodological sophistication for the period.

Contained within the Eisenhower study was an element of information diffusion. In 1960 Danielson (with Paul J. Deutschmann) used a survey to extend the concept to a full diffusion study. This particular study, however, included newspapers, radio, and television. Respondents were asked (among other questions) how they learned about three breaking news stories, and the researchers found support for the diffusion process although differences were noted between the broadcast media and newspapers.

Two studies demonstrate the breadth of Danielson's interest in content analysis. The first was purely methodological, and the second used content analysis. In 1965 Danielson (with James J. Mullen) published work in *Journalism Quarterly* that not only followed his interest in content analysis but also in his growing fascination with computers. The study, "A Basic Space Unit for Newspaper Content Analysis," departed from the traditional content analysis that leads to the researcher sampling all relevant content, an approach that is tedious and time consuming. Danielson and Mullin substituted what they termed the "Basic Space Unit" or BSC. They defined the BSC as "an area one column wide and one-twentieth of a column deep."[3] The researchers have written a computer program for drawing samples based on the BSC that demonstrates that the procedure is most effective. However, the approach has not been widely adopted by others doing content analysis.

The second study published in 1961 looked at press coverage of the 1960 presidential campaign. The analysis (with John B. Adams) involved a comparison of campaign events with how those events were reported in newspapers. A content analysis of a sample of 9 daily newspapers and how they covered 23 presidential campaign events was the basis for determining the completeness of and the amount of coverage made available to the average newspaper reader.

One area of continuing scholarly interest shown by Danielson is readability and particularly the use of computers in studies of the subject. A study published in 1958 (with James E. Brinton) combined Danielson's interest in methodology, computers, and readability. The work, "A Factor Analysis of Language Elements Affecting Readability," was based on earlier work done by others but was not simply a replication. The authors were interested in using factor analysis in identifying fundamental relationships

---

[3]Wayne A. Danielson and James J. Mullen, "A Basic Space Unit for Newspaper Content Analysis," *Journalism Quarterly* 42 (1965): 108-110.

that may provide some of the theoretical bases of readability. It was an important attempt, for it supported previous elements in readability formulae while suggesting new factors.

Perhaps the best work done by Danielson on readability involved the creation of a new readability formula that utilizes better use of computers. The research published in 1963 (with San Dunn Bryan) grew out of problems encountered by the authors in programming the Farr-Jenkins-Paterson revision of the Flesch readability formula.[4] Unlike other formulae, the one created by the authors uses the average number of characters per space and the average number of characters per sentence. The new formulation is equal in predictive power to the Farr-Jenkins-Paterson formula but operates about twice as fast. The following year the two authors used their new formula for research reported in *Journalism Quarterly*. The study, "Readability of Wire Stories in Eight News Categories," showed that the predicted grade-level readability of the Associated Press material was the seventh month of the sixth grade.

In addition to his long and influential career in scholarship, teaching, and administration, Danielson has often been a consultant to news organizations, suggesting applications of computers in research. He continues to work with computers and the creation of data bases, do research, and teach.

---

[4]J.N. Farr, J.J. Jenkins, and D.G. Paterson, "Simplification of the Flesch Reading Ease Formula," *Journal of Applied Psychology* 35 (1951): 333-337.

Glossary of Terms

Absolutism — A belief that the phrase "no law" in the First Amendment means absolute prohibition of any restriction or punishment of freedom of expression.

Academic isolates — Journalism and mass communication professors who read only academic journals and tend to belong only to academic associations.

Access theory — A theory of interpretation of the First Amendment in which "freedom of expression" is defined as the right of each citizen to possess access to forums of expression.

Accuracy — In the coorientation model, the extent to which one person's estimate of the other's cognitions matches what that person really thinks.

Actual malice — A fault burden and the defense in defamation cases, especially when the plaintiffs are public officials or public figures, which is defined in *New York Times v. Sullivan* as a "defamatory falsehood" used "with knowledge that it was false or with reckless disregard of whether it was false or not."

Administrative research — The study of the mass media as an industry to learn how best to reconcile the interests of journalists, audience, and financial interests.

Agenda — A set of issues ranked according to their importance.

Agenda-building — The complex process, involving the mass media, prominent newsmakers, and the public, by which an issue moves up on the public's agenda.

Agenda-setting function — The hypothesis that attention to issues in the mass media increases their salience in the minds of the public.

Agreement — In the coorientation model, the extent to which two people have the same summary evaluations and saliences for objects.

Anti-litter laws — Ordinances of municipalities based on justification that litter is an evil that local government has a right to prevent. The ordinances sometimes have imposed prior restraints of expression.

Antiquarianism — In historical research, the collection of dates, names, facts, and other specifics without explanation.

Authoritarian theory — A theory of freedom of expression, common before the 19th century, coupled to the concept of divine right of monarchies and other totalitarian theories.

Balancers — Individuals who believe the inalienable freedoms of the Bill of Rights are co-existent and must be balanced when one right conflicts with another. No right, including the First Amendment, has inherent ascendancy over another right.

Bias by agenda — The idea that the issues played up by the mass media might be the issues that are of interest to a particular ideology, such as liberal or conservative.

Blackstonian doctrine — A doctrine advanced by Sir William Blackstone, the father of English law, in the 18th century. Liberty of the press, Blackstone wrote, meant that governments could impose "no previous restraints" on expression.

Bullet theory — The idea that mass communication has powerful and uniform effects on audience members. Sometimes called "hypodermic needle" theory.

Classical liberalism — The philosophy of individual freedom and democracy combined with a high sense of personal and public responsibility, associated with the political beliefs of the Enlightenment and the U.S. Constitution.

Cloze Procedure — A method of measuring the readabililty of prose by replacing words in the text with blanks and seeing how well a sample of readers can fill in the blanks.

Commercial speech — Messages communicated via media space or time to promote, sell, or market goods, services, or ideas. The Supreme Court has said that commercial speech must flow freely and non-deceptively.

Common law — Law discovered as a society develops customs and precedents through dispute resolution or court decisions.

Concept-orientation — A family communication style characterized by expression of ideas and exposure to controversy.

Congruency — In the coorientation model, the similarity between a person's own cognitions and that person's perceptions of the other person's cognitions.

Consensual families — Those who attempt to stress both socio-orientation and concept-orientation. The child is exposed to controversy but is encouraged to develop concepts that are consistent with the parents' ideas.

Consensus interpretation — In American history, the explanation that Americans, rather than being divided by ideological and social conflicts, generally have agreed on fundamental beliefs, such as freedom, private property, Constitutional law, and democracy.

Contempt of court — An act designed to obstruct the fair administration of justice or aimed at embarassing or diminishing the dignity of the court. In effect, the judge is the accuser, prosecutor, judge, and jury in the implementation of contempt of court charges.

Content analysis — A technique to describe, analyze, and measure communication content systematically and objectively.

Coorientation — The act of two persons (or other entities) perceiving the same object and each other's perceptions.

Cosmology — Study of — or branch of philosophy dealing with — the origin, design, and structure of the universe.

Critical research — The study of the mass media as cultural texts; also, of the role of the mass media in the social structure.

Critical theory — Approach to the study of mass communication that considers the mass media as cultural texts that record the meaning of experience; sometimes emphasizes control of the mass media as a topic and qualitative rather than quantitative research methods.

Crucial experiment — An experiment that provides evidence for one hypothesis or explanation while simultaneously ruling out an alternative explanation.

Cultivation theory — The hypothesis that heavy television viewing influences audience members' perceptions and values.

Cultural interpretation — See "Sociological interpretation" and

"Symbolic meaning." In history, an explanation emphasizing the interrelationship of the media with the surrounding environment.

Defamation — Falsehood, written or spoken, that injures reputations of persons, small groups, corporations, or products by causing public hatred, contempt, or ridicule of the reputations. Generally, libel is written, and slander is spoken.

Deconstructionism — A philosophical and literary/critical movement that states that what seems to be an event is really a construct of a quasi-linguistic system. One is in a position to undo the construct or to recognize that the construct has already undone itself — with far-reaching implications for thought of every sort. It affords a perspective from which any number of modern movements can be seen as parts of a generalized shift from a logocentric metaphysic of presence to a new recognition of the play of differences among relations.

Democritean materialism — The basic postulate of Greek atomism: Atoms and the void alone are real; the differences between physical objects, including both qualitative differences and what we think of as differences in substance, were all explained in terms of modifications in the shape, arrangement, and position of the atoms.

Developmental interpretation — In media history, an explanation that emphasizes the origin, performance, and progress of practices normally associated with "proper" journalism.

Discovery — A pre-trial right possessed by principals in civil actions in which attorneys for each side may compel the disclosure of facts or evidence.

Due process of law — A Fifth and Fourteenth Amendment guarantee that the inalienable rights of U.S. citizens will not be abridged by a discriminatory judicial process.

Eclectics — Journalism and mass communication professors who read both academic and industry media and tend to belong to both types of associations.

Eidos — The formal content of a culture, encompassing its system of ideas, criteria for interpreting experience, and so on.

Emotional distress — See "Infliction of emotional distress."

Empiricism — The philosophy that knowledge is based on (or must rely on) experience, observation, and/or experiment.

Epistemology — A branch of philosophy that investigates the origin, nature, methods, and limits of human knowledge.

Ethos — The fundamental or distinguishing characteristics, tone, or beliefs of a culture.

Existentialism — A philosophy stressing the individual human being, especially in terms of the subjectivity of experience, freedom of the individual, and uniqueness of situations. It emphasizes man's responsibility for making his own nature as well as the importance of personal freedom, personal decision, and personal commitment.

Experimental method — A technique in which the research environment is manipulated.

Factor analysis — A multivariate statistical method in which independent artificial dimensions called factors are correlated with real-world variables.

Fairness Doctrine — The much-debated broadcast regulation that required between the late 1940s and late 1980s that a licensee guarantee the broadcast of all sides of a controversial issue of public importance.

Family communication patterns — Tendencies of families to communicate in certain ways, measured on the socio-orientation dimension and the concept-orientation dimension.

Field studies — Qualitative observational technique in which research is conducted in a natural environment.

Freedom of Information Act — A federal open records law adopted in 1966 that requires the disclosure of records held by executive branch agencies unless an agency can legitimately claim one of nine exceptions to disclosure.

Functionalism — A philosophy that emphasizes practical utility. See "Utilitarianism."

Gag laws — Laws or rules that impose prior restraints on freedom of expression.

Government in the Sunshine Act — A 1976 law requiring federal executive branch agencies to conduct open meetings unless an agency can claim one of ten exemptions to disclosure.

Guttmann scale — An attitude scale to which people should respond in consistent ways, that is if they disagree with one statement, they should disagree with certain of the other statements.

Hypothesis — A tentative assumption (proposed in social and behavioral sciences as a means of testing its consequences).

Idealism — A theory that ultimate reality lies in a realm transcending phenomena or in individual consciousness or reason.

Industry isolates — Journalism and mass communication professors who read only industry media and belong only to industry associations.

Infliction of emotional distress — Imposition of an emotional trauma on an individual to whom one has an obligation, through negligence that goes beyond the pale of decency.

Information theory — A mathematical conceptualization of information which defines it as a reduction of uncertainty and provides a quantitative measure of it.

Instrumentalism — A philosophy that the truth of an idea is determined by its usefulness. See "Pragmatism" and "Utilitarianism."

Knowledge gap hypothesis — The proposition that as the flow of mass media information into a social system increases, those segments of the population with higher socioeconomic status tend to acquire this information at a faster rate than the lower status segments.

Laissez faire families — Those who stress neither socio-orientation nor concept-orientation.

Legal notices — Statutorily required, paid publication of notices of proposed governmental action.

Legists — Persons who possess special knowledge of the law.

Libel — See "Defamation."

Libertarianism — A philosophy evolving out of 17th-century natural rights theory, which envisioned a self-righting process growing out of liberty of expression in which everyone could discover the truth when all ideas were permitted in the marketplace.

Licensing — A requirement that the communicator have the permission of government to communicate.

Marketplace of ideas — The concept advanced by Milton in *Aeropagitica*: "Who ever knew Truth put to the worse in a free and open encounter?"

Marxian theory (or philosophy) — A doctrine emphasizing materialistic philosophy, class conflict, control of the means of production as of preeminent importance, and the eventual triumph of the proletariat. Its developers, Karl Marx and Friedrich Engels, argued that throughout history the state has been a device for the exploitation of the masses by a dominant class, that class struggle has been the main agency of historical change, and that the capitalist system inevitably will, after the period of the dictatorship of the proletariat, be superseded by a socialist order and a classless society.

Material determinism — A doctrine that change is materially caused.

Material socialism — As opposed to Christian socialism, a philosophy of socialism whose basis is materialism.

Materialism — The philosophy or theory that physical matter is the only reality and that all phenomena are the manifestations or results of matter.

Materialistic metaphysics — A philosophy which presumes that ideas exist *a posteriori* to material existence.

Metaphysics — The branch of philosophy concerned with cosmology and the ultimate grounds of being. It sometimes is thought of as the counterpoint of physical science.

Model — A simplified representation of a complex phenomenon, such as communication, constructed to facilitate understanding.

Natural rights — Rights that are derived from the relationships among human beings; rights that are discoverable through reason and man's innate sense of morality.

Need for orientation — A state of readiness to accept a message determined by the relevance of the information in the message and the degree of uncertainty concerning the subject of the message.

Objectivitism — A system of knowledge that stresses that truth lies only in objective reality as opposed to subjective experience.

Obtrusive issues — Issues that affect people directly and that they do not need the mass media to bring to their attention.

Ontology — The branch of metaphysics that studies the nature of existence or being as such, as distinct from material existence, spiritual existence, etc.

Orientation — See "Need for orientation."

Outliers — Journalism and mass communication professors who read no industry or academic media and tend to belong to no traditional associations.

Panel design — A research approach in which the same sample of survey respondents is interviewed more than once.

Pantheism — A doctrine that equates God with all of nature or specifically with universal forces. It denies God's personality and tends to identify Him with nature.

Paradigm — An example, or model; an approach to research adapted by a number of researchers because of its utility.

Pertinence — An individual's discrimination between two attitude objects on the basis of a difference in a common attribute.

Phenomenology — A system of knowledge which stresses the description of phenomena as they appear to cause perception and without regard to questions of their reality.

Pluralistic families — Those who stress concept-orientation only. They encourage children to explore new ideas and make up their own minds.

Pornography — Works which, when taken as a whole, as defined in *Miller v. California* (1973), include material that is appealing to prurient interests, is patently offensive, and lacks serious literary, artistic, political, or scientific value.

Positivism — The philosophy that valid knowledge can be based only on mathematics, science, and observation. Among its cardinal arguments is the denial of metaphysics.

Pragmatic functionalism — A concern with the ongoing "workability" of society, based on the ideas of John Dewey, George Herbert Mead, Charles Horton Cooley, and others of the "Chicago School" of sociology.

Pragmatism — The philosophy that truth of a proposition is determined by its practical consequences. See "Utilitarianism."

Present-mindedness — In historical study, the error of applying present-day values and ideas to the past.

Primary sources — In historical research, records left by eyewitnesses or individuals close to an event.

Prior restraints — Governmental actions prohibiting acts of communication, typically achieved through injunctions.

Privacy — The right to be left alone. William Prosser delineates violations of privacy into four torts: public disclosure, publication of unprivileged, true, embarrassing information; false light, non-defamatory falsehoods; newsgathering intrusion into private zones without consent; and appropriation, use for purposes of trade without consent of a person's name, likeness, or signature.

Privilege — See "Reporter's privilege."

Progressive interpretation — An ideological explanation of American and media history that favors liberalism and "the people" against conservatism and the elite.

Protective families — Those who stress socio-orientation only. The child is encouraged to get along with others and is protected from expressing dissent.

Q-methodology — A type of data analysis (largely associated with William Stephenson) which groups individuals according to correlations among the rank ordering of test items by those individuals.

Qualitative method — A research method whose findings are analyzed by some means other than mathematical ones.

Quantitative method — A research method whose findings can be measured mathematically.

Reading gap — The tendency in outlying communities for persons higher in education to read the metropolitan daily more than persons lower in education.

Reporters' privilege — The concept that a reporter can protect the identity of anonymous sources because of one or more rationales: the morality of a confidentiality pledge, a state reporters' privilege law, or First Amendment protection. Courts have ruled this right, written into Shield Laws, is conditional.

Retraction statute — A law in some states requiring a plaintiff to request a retraction before filing a defamation suit. Retraction in some states is a partial or complete defense; in others it prevents recovery of some damages. Retractions may complicate libel defenses because they involve admissions of fault.

Right of reply — A concept that an individual who is personally attacked in print or on the air has a legal right to respond. The U.S. Supreme Court has found the concept unconstitutional for print media but constitutional for broadcast media because of the concept of public ownership of the airwaves.

Right to know — A right of the public to be informed of government proceedings, with its roots found by its proponents in natural rights, social contract theory, the U.S. Constitution, and other sources. In contemporary practice the people's right to know is conditional.

R-methodology — A type of data analysis using factor analysis which groups items according to correlations among the rank ordering of those items by individuals. Somtimes, standard "objective" survey questionnaire methods.

Romantic materialism — The assumption that matter, alone real, is evolving in a beneficent manner and that nature is benign to humankind.

Romanticism — A philosophy emphasizing emotion and imagination rather than reason.

Salience — Prominence; an individual's summary evaluation of one attitude object.

Scalogram — The procedure for developing a Guttman scale for measuring attitudes.

Scholasticism — A philosophy, predominant in the Middle Ages, combining Christian dogma with the philosophical system of Aristotle.

Scientism — See "Positivism." Assumes that scientic methods are equally appropriate to all other disciplines, including the humanities and social sciences, as to science.

Secondary sources — In historical research, accounts (such as books and articles by historians) written by individuals who were not eyewitnesses to an event but which are based instead on other people's reports.

Semantic differential — The technique that uses bi-polar adjectives (for example "good"-"bad") to define a multi-point scale on which subjects rate concepts, such as "mother," "television," and so forth.

Semiotics — The study of signs and symbols as they function in language.

Shield laws — See "Reporters' privilege."

Social responsibility theory — The doctrine of liberty of the press in which the media are responsible to the culture, social system, and government in which they operate.

Sociological interpretation — In history, an explanation emphasizing the interrelationship of the media with the surrounding environment.

Socio-orientation — A family communication style characterized by maintaining harmonious personal relations.

Solipsism — A theory that the Self is the only thing that exists or can be proven to exist.

Soviet Communist theory — The liberty of the press doctrine that the communist government knows what is best for the people. Hence, the media are operated and controlled by the government.

Strong inference — An approach to research that stresses multiple working hypotheses and use of testing to eliminate alternative possibilities.

Structural approach — An approach to research that involves looking at communities and their mass media systems as social structures.

Structuralism — Psychology centering on the analysis of the structure or content of conscious mental states by introspective methods. Also, a philosophy that postulates lawful behavior for self-regulating structures.

Sunshine Act — See "Government in the Sunshine Act."

Survey method — The method used to infer information about a large population from data collected on a small sample. In mass communication research, it is used to measure attitudes and opinions.

Symbolic meaning — An interpretation of history that claims that the importance of the media primarily has rested on the "meaning" of the world that the media have presented to audiences.

Teleology — The study of evidence of design in nature; the doctrine of final cause, especially as the design of the universe indicates a Creator.

Telos — The goal; the end of an idea or philosophical system.

Theory — A set of abstract propositions that provide explanation and prediction.

Transactional view of perception — An explanation of perception as residing neiter within the perceiver nor the perceived alone but growing out of the interplay of both.

Tort — An injury or wrong done to a person or property of another for which a civil action may be filed.

Transcendentalism — A philosophy that emphasizes the transcendent (the unknowable) as the ultimate reality or the primacy of the spiritual and/or transcendent over the material and empirical.

Understanding — In the coorientation model, the extent to which two people have similar cognitive structures in terms of objects and attributes (or pertinences).

Unfair competition — A doctrine that protects a newsgathering institution from loss of the value of its news products when they are being used by another newsgatherer without independent investigation and investment of resources.

Unobtrusive issues — Issues that do not affect people directly and that they would learn about primarily through the mass media.

Uses and gratifications approach — Approach to the study of mass communication that emphasizes the active nature of the receiver or audience.

Utilitarianism — The philosophy that the test of truth or right conduct is its usefulness, that virtue is based on utility, and that conduct should be directed toward promoting the greatest happiness of the greatest number of persons.

Watchdog function — The press' role of checking on government.

Weltanschauung — "World view"; a comprehensive conception of the world from a particular standpoint; the philosophy of an individual or a group, especially a race, with an interpretation of world history or civilization.

Index

Absolutism, 193, 203, 220, 222.
ABX model, 236, 252, 273.
Academia
  Journalism profession and, 36.
  Response to journalism education,
  7, 13-14, 16, 25-6.
Access to information, 196, 223-4.
Accuracy, 260-1, 274.
Adams, Charles K., 7.
Adams, John B., 328.
Administrative law, 20.
Administrative research, 290.
Adorno, Theodor, 123.
Advertising, 12, 19, 57, 290, 306.
Agee, Warren, 109.
Agenda building, 286.
Agenda setting, 16, 234, 236, 278ff.
  Criticisms of, 285-6.
Aggression, 273.
Agnew, Spiro, 30, 112.
Agreement, 274.
Algren, Nelson, 30.
Alien and Sedition Acts, 223.
Allen, Bill, 252.
Allen, Eric, 188.
Allen, John, 55.
Allied Daily Newspapers, 21.
Allport, Gordon, 308.
American Association of Schools and
  Departments of Journalism
  (AASDJ), 11, 14, 77, 92, 127, 192,
  298, 326.
American Association of Teachers in
  Journalism (AATJ), 10, 11, 12, 14,
  17, 75, 77, 126, 129, 142, 212, 298.
American Bar Association, 184.
American Council on Education and
  Journalism (ACEJ), 77-8, 256.
American Journalism (Mott), 76, 91,
  93ff, 106.
American Journalism Historians As-
  sociation, 105.
"American Magazines To-Day"
  (Drewry), 144.
American Newspaper Publishers As-
  sociation (ANPA), 14, 36, 109, 182.
American Society of Journalism
  School Administrators (ASJSA),
  45.
American Society of Newspaper Edi-
  tors (ASNE), 196, 199.

Anderson, Don, 205.
Antiquarianism, 69-70.
Anti-trust, 211.
*Approaches to a Science of English
  Verse* (Schramm), 242.
Aquinas, Thomas, 153.
Arnold, Edmund C., 26, 45, 53-8.
  Awards, 56.
  Biography, 54.
  Design concepts, 53, 55-6.
  Education, 54, 55.
  Influence, 53, 55, 57, 58.
  Journalism career, 54-5.
  Public speaker, 57.
  Teaching career, 57.
Arthur, William R., 181, 189, 209.
Asheville *Citizen*, 279.
Asheville *Times*, 279.
Associated Press, 239.
Associated Press Managing Editors
  Association, 18.
Associated Press v. United States,
  211.
Association for Education in Jour-
  nalism and Mass Communication
  (AEJMC), 22, 105, 184, 230, 234,
  268, 271, 276, 281, 291, 297, 317-8.
  Presidents of, 45, 46, 51, 107, 167,
  192, 216, 224, 298, 311, 326.
  "Rump session," 230-1, 249, 251,
  291.
Association for Humanist Sociology,
  84.
Athens *Banner-Herald*, 142.
Atlanta *Constitution*, 142.
Atlanta *Journal*, 142.
Attention to communication, 261.
Attitude change, 232, 271, 323.
Attitudinal hypothesis, 263-4.
Audience, 232, 243, 247, 305.
*Audio-Visual Communication Re-
  view*, 252.
Ault, Phillip, 109.
Authenticity, 165.

B
Bagdikian, Ben, 45.
Bailyn, Bernard, 66, 114.
Balancing, 222-3.
Baltimore Community College, 101.
Baltimore *Home News*, 100.

Baltimore *Suburban Times*, 100.
Bancroft Prize, 93, 96, 114.
Barlow, R.R., 135.
Barnhart, Thomas F., 298.
Barron, Jerome A., 183.
Barth, Karl, 165.
"Basic Space unit for Newspaper Content Analysis" (Danielson, Mullen), 328.
Bay City Junior College, 54.
Beard, Charles A., 64, 110.
Becker, Lee, 19n.
Bellow, Saul, 30.
Bennett, James Gordon, 73, 78, 79, 96, 163.
Benson, Ivan, 181, 189, 209.
Berelson, Bernard, 291, 295.
Berger, Charles R., 276.
Berlo, David K., 251.
Better Journalism For a Better Tomorrow (Drewry), 147.
Bezanson, Randall P., 185.
Bias
    By agenda, 284.
    In news, 315.
    Of print, 168-9.
Bias of Communication, The (Innis), 168.
Bibliography of Law on Journalism, A (Swindler), 207, 208-9.
Big Story (Braestrup), 114.
Black, Hugo, 210.
Black Press, The (Wolseley), 52.
Blake, Henry Ingraham, 73.
Blalock, Hubert, 269.
Bleyer, Willard, 7, 10, 11, 15, 63, 76-82, 83, 85, 99, 134-5, 144, 188, 215, 217, 229.
    Biography, 77.
    Classic liberal, 78.
    Death, 89.
    Democracy, views on, 76, 78, 79.
    Developmental historian, 78-9, 81.
    Education, 77.
    Founder of AATJ, AASDJ, ACEJ, SDX, 77-8.
    Journalism career, 78.
    Masses, views on, 79, 80.
    Offices held, 78.
    Professionalism, views on, 81.
    Progress of journalism, 81.
    Progressive reformer, 80-1.
    Responsibility of press, 77, 78.
    Offices held, 78.
    Progress, views on, 78-9.
    Publications, 77.
    Social scientist, 229.
    Teaching career, 84.
Blumler, Jay, 276.
Bohemian Magazine, 69.
Boston *Globe*, 57.
Boston *News-Letter*, 70.
Boston University, 186.
Bowers, Claude, 64.
Bowes, Barbara J., 275.
Bowes, John E., 275.
Bowles, Samuel II, 80, 81.
Braestrup, Peter, 114.
Brandeis, Louis D., 188, 222.

Brantgarde, Lennart, 265.
Brinton, James E., 328.
Broadcast law, 210, 224.
Brooklyn College, 84.
Broun, Heywood, 137.
Brown and White Style Book (MacDougall), 30.
Brown, Roger, 309.
Brownsville *Daily Telegraph*, 84.
Bruner, Jerome, 251.
Bryan, San Dunn, 329.
Bryn Mawr College, 132.
Buckley, William F., 200.
Budd, Richard, 251.
"Bullet theory," 243, 244, 290.
Bulletin (University of Georgia), 146, 147.
Burger court, 183.
Burke, Edmund, 152.
Burke, Kenneth, 170.
Burt, C.L., 304.
Bush, Chilton, 27, 31, 36-40, 192, 230, 278.
    As scholar, 36.
    Awards, 36.
    Biography, 36.
    Death, 37.
    Education, 36.
    Journalism career, 36.
    Public opinion research, 36.
    Teaching career, 36.
Business, media as, 11, 103, 111, 120, 210.
Butler, Nicholas, 7-8.
Bybee, Carl R., 264, 265.
Bylines, 323.

C
California Monthly, 107.
California State University, 186.
Callihan, E.L., 326.
Calvinism, 214.
Camp, Eugene, 7.
Campaigns (political), 137-8, 281, 282, 314, 328.
Campbell, Angus, 309.
Campbell, John, 70.
Campbell, Laurence, 49, 52.
Camus, Albert, 163.
Cannell, Charles, 309.
Canyon *News*, 215.
Careers in Religious Journalism (Wolseley), 51.
Carey, James, 123, 167-75.
    Biography, 167.
    Education, 167.
    Offices held, 167-8.
    Publications, 168.
    Teaching career, 167.
    Weaknesses as philosopher, 173-5.
Carson, Rachel, 31.
Carter, Richard, 270, 273, 279.
Carter, T. Barton, 186.
Case studies, 294.
Casey, Ralph, 50, 134-41, 217, 230.
    Biography, 134.
    Education, 134.
    Impact on education, 136
    Journalism career, 134.

Optimism, 140-1.
Propaganda, study of, 136ff.
Teaching career, 134-6, 141.
Casselton *Reporter*, 308.
Cattell, R.B., 308.
Cause-effect relationship, 88-9, 282-3.
Cavalier County Republican, 308.
Censorship, 137-8.
Chaffee, Steven, 236, 243, 268-77, 280-1.
Biography, 269.
Education, 269-70.
Teaching career, 270-1.
Chaffee, Zechariah, 217.
Chain journalism, 140.
Change, causes of, 168, 261.
Chicago *Herald-Examiner*, 187.
"Chicago School," 120, 124, 173.
Chicago *Sun*, 30.
Christian Science Monitor, 57, 142.
Chu, Godwin, 243, 246.
Cincinnati *Gazette*, 71.
Circle Magazine, 69.
Circulation, 79, 80, 89, 94.
City University of New York, 84.
Civil liberties, 111.
Civil rights movement, 63.
Civil War, 120.
Clarke, Peter, 275.
Class struggle, 114.
Cleveland, Grover, 71.
Click, William, 315.
Cloze procedure, 254.
Cognition, 123, 232.
Cohen, Bernard, 280.
Cohort analysis, 294.
Cold War, 33.
Colonial press, 95, 101.
Columbia Scholastic Press Association, 143.
Columbia University, 7-8, 29, 92, 100, 142, 180, 195, 198, 199, 231, 308.
Columnists, 137.
"Communication" as journalism, 4.
Communication potential, 264.
Communications Lawyer, 184.
Competition among newspapers, 70, 315-6.
Computerized Bibliography of Mass Communication Research, A (Danielson, Wilhoit), 326.
Computers, 294-5, 325, 328.
Comstock, George, 243.
Concept-orientation, 272, 273.
"Conceptual Model for Communications Research, A" (Westley, MacLean), 252.
Conflict
In history, 113.
Social, 258, 260ff.
Congruency, 274, 275.
Conneaut *News-Herald*, 201, 202.
Consensus interpretation, 113.
Conservatism, 11, 30, 62, 64, 65, 83, 110, 111.
Consistency model, 273.
Constitutional law, 208.
"Contempt of Court and the Press"

(Siebert), 187.
Content analysis, 133, 281, 289, 291, 292-3, 314, 328.
Criticism of, 292.
"Content Analysis in Communication Research" (Danielson), 327.
Content Analysis in Communications Research (Berelson), 291.
Control of communication, 262.
Cooke, Janet, 223.
Cooley, Charles Horton, 120, 121.
Coolidge, Calvin, 93.
Coorientation model, 236, 254, 268, 273-6, 277.
Copyright, 211.
Cornell University, 6-7, 180, 198.
"Corporate journalist," 161ff.
Cosmology, 119.
Council for the Advancement of Science Writing, 43.
"Counter-propagaganda," 139.
Cramberg, Gilbert, 185.
Credibility of newspapers, 35.
Creston *News Advertiser*, 202.
Critical research, 290.
Critical theory, 123, 124-5, 233.
Critical Writing for the Journalist (Wolseley), 52.
Criticism of journalism, 11, 12, 14, 45, 46, 64-5, 74, 155-6.
Criticism of journalism education, 4-5, 6, 8, 12, 35.
Crosman, Ralph L., 181, 189, 209.
Cross, Harold L., 180, 182, 184, 195-200.
Awards, 199.
Biography, 198.
Education, 198.
Journalism career, 198-9.
Love of freedom, 197.
Publications, 199.
Teaching career, 195, 199.
"Crucial experiments," 235.
Crusading, 31, 64.
Crutchfield, George, 57.
Cultivation theory, 236.
Cultural approach, 181ff.
"Cultural Approach to Communication, A" (Carey), 169-71.
Cultural interpretation, 66, 105.
Cultural studies, 123, 124, 125.
"Cultural Values in the Study of Journalism" (Murphy), 128-9, 132.
Curriculum in journalism eduction, 4, 6, 13, 15, 21, 26, 27.
Cycles in history, 104, 105.

D
Daily Newspaper in America, The (Lee), 83, 85ff.
Ideology, 88.
Methodological problems, 89.
Theoretical concept behind, 85-6.
Dana, Charles, 96.
Danielson, Wayne, 224-5, 230, 233, 243, 325-9.
Biography, 325.
Education, 325.
Journalism career, 325.

Offices held, 326.
Publications, 326-7.
Teaching career, 325-6.
Darwin, Charles, 120, 121.
"Data Processing" (Danielson), 327.
Davidson, W. Phillip, 33-4.
Dawn of Daily Newspaper Journalism, The (Murphy), 131.
Day, Benjamin, 62, 79, 163.
Decline of the West (Spengler), 87.
Delta State University, 159.
Democracy, 64, 78, 113, 197, 290.
  Journalism education and, 4, 7, 8, 10, 11.
  Media and, 49, 76, 79, 80, 81, 94, 261.
Dennis, Everette, 184, 217.
Dervin, Brenda, 266.
Design of newspapers, 53, 55-7, 315.
Detroit *News*, 202.
Deutschmann, Paul, 251, 328.
Development of American Journalism (Kobre), 102, 105.
Development of the Colonial Newspaper, The (Kobre), 101.
Developmental interpretation, 62-4, 65, 70ff, 81, 96, 99, 101, 102, 105.
Devol, Kenneth S., 186.
Dewey, John, 120, 121, 168, 169, 173.
Dicken Garcia, Hazel, 221.
Diffusion of information, 328.
Doan, Edward, 12.
Doctoral study, 17, 136.
Donohue, George, 253, 258-67.
  Biography, 259.
  Education, 259.
  Teaching career, 259.
Drake University, 186.
Drewry, John, 13, 142-8.
  Awards, 143.
  Biography, 142.
  Education, 142.
  Journalism career, 142.
  Offices held, 142.
  Optimism of, 146-7
  Publications, 147.
  Teaching career, 142.
Duluth *Herald*, 187.
Durall, Jean A., 264, 265.
Durham University, 302.
Dyer, Edith, 192.
Dynamics, of Planned Change, The (Westley), 309.

E
Economics, 156, 157, 204-5.
Edelstein, Alex, 217.
Editor and Publisher, 14, 17, 69, 195.
Editorial Thinking and Writing (Bush), 39-40.
Education in journalism,
  Academe's response to, 7, 13-4, 16, 25-6.
  Challenges to, 25.
  "Communication" and, 4.
  Criticism of, 4-5, 16, 25-6, 37.
  Critics of press, 15.
  Curriculum, 4, 9, 13, 15, 21, 26, 27.
  Defender of status quo, 12.

Democracy and, 4, 8, 10.
Failures of, 20, 28.
First programs, 3-4, 6-9.
Graduate, 15-6, 291.
Growth of, 10.
History of, 3-4, 6-22.
Ideas from, 5.
Improvement of media and, 5, 81-2.
Improvement of society and, 10, 13, 15, 81.
Influence of, 22.
Journalists' response to, 3, 4, 6, 7, 8, 12, 13, 14, 18, 20, 21, 35, 37, 135.
Liberal arts in, 4, 6, 7, 20, 21, 25, 26, 27, 35, 37, 39, 128, 132, 144.
Newspapers and, 6, 7, 8.
Number of programs, 10.
Number of students, 10.
Professional and career training in, 4, 5, 6, 9, 11, 12, 13, 14, 15, 16, 19, 20, 21, 22, 37.
Role of, 4-5, 10, 21, 22.
Science and, 129-30.
Separation from journalism profession, 45-6.
Skills training, 25, 27, 28.
Social science in, 4, 37, 135, 136, 141.
Teachers, 5, 13, 26.
Theory in, 4, 15, 16, 21.
Undergraduate, 15-6
"Effect of Serial Position on Recall of Radio News Stories" (Tannenbaum), 323.
Effects
  Of media, 169, 172, 242, 245, 261, 274, 279, 323.
  Theories, 122, 169, 231, 233, 237, 244, 284, 285.
Eisenhower, Dwight, 314.
"Eisenhower's February Decision: A Study of News Impact" (Danielson), 327-8.
Eleanor Blum Distinguished Service to Research Award, 107.
Emergence of American Political Issues, The: The Agenda-Setting Function of the Press (Shaw, McCombs), 282.
Emery, Edwin, 65, 99, 105, 106-15, 136.
  Ability as researcher, 113-4, 115.
  Awards, 107.
  Biography, 107.
  Dogmatism of, 113.
  Education, 107.
  Ideology, 107, 110, 112, 114.
  Impact of, 108-9
  Journalism career, 107.
  Offices held, 107.
  Progressive historian, 106-7, 110ff.
  Publications, 107, 109.
  Students of, 106, 108-9.
  Teaching career, 107.
  View of history, 111-2, 115.
Emery, Mary, 107.
Emery, Michael, 109, 113.
Emory University, 149.
Empire and Communications (Innis),

168.
Enderlin *Independent*, 297.
English departments, 143.
Engstrom, Warren, 301.
Enrollment in journalism programs, 19.
Entertainment Functions of Television, The (Tannenbaum), 321.
Environmental reporting, 32.
Equal opportunity, 84.
"Equivalence of informed political participation," 264-5.
Erie *Dispatch*, 202.
Essentialism, 163.
Eswara, H.S., 271.
Ethics, 74, 132-3, 165, 203.
Ettema, James S., 265.
Evanston *News-Index*, 30, 48.
Evolution, 64.
  Theory of, in history, 85-8, 102, 105.
  Theory of, in philosophy, 121.
Existential Journalism (Merrill), 160ff.
Experimental method, 293, 322, 328.
Exploring Journalism (Wolseley), 49.
Exposure to media, 285.

F
"Factor Analysis of Language Elements Affecting Readability, A" (Danielson), 328-9.
Fairness Doctrine, 224.
Families, 236.
Family communication pattern, 268, 271ff.
Fargo *Daily Tribune*, 297.
Fargo *Forum*, 297.
Federal Bureau of Investigation, 32.
Feedback, 262.
Festinger, Leon, 122.
Field studies, 293.
Fifth Amendment, 196.
Filler, Louis, 97.
Fine, Barnett, 14.
First Amendment, 179, 183, 196, 197, 207, 208, 217, 222.
Fishman, Mark, 233.
Flesch, Rudolph, 254, 329.
Florida State University, 101.
Focus groups, 293.
Ford, Edwin, 109.
Ford, Henry, 187.
Foundations of American Journalism (Kobre), 101.
Four Theories of the Press (Siebert, Peterson, Schramm), 191, 193, 241.
Fourier, Charles, 120.
Fourteenth Amendment, 179, 183, 196, 222.
Frames, 277.
Francois, William E., 186.
Frank Luther Mott Research Award, 93.
Frankenmuth *News*, 54, 55.
Frankfort *Morning Times*, 313.
Frankfurt School, 123.
Franklin, Marc A., 186.
Free and Responsible Press, A, 149.

Freedom of information, 182, 198, 223.
Freedom of the press, 84, 86, 88, 89, 94, 112, 155, 189, 216.
  History of, 62, 96, 151, 191.
  Theories of, 193.
Freedom of the Press from Hamilton to the Warren Court (Nelson), 221-2.
Freedom of the Press in England 1476-1776 (Siebert), 188, 191, 192-3.
Freud, Sigmund, 244.
Friendly, Fred W., 185, 188.
Fuller, Larry, 18n.
Function of media, 155, 156.
Functional Newspaper Design (Arnold), 53, 55.
Functionalism, 121, 123.
Funkhouser, G. Ray, 243.
Futurism, 124.

G
Gannett Center for Media Studies, 168.
Gans, Herbert, 233, 235, 237.
Garrison, William Lloyd, 120.
Gatekeeping, 16.
Gaziano, Cecilie, 266.
Genova, B.K.L., 265.
Gerald, J. Edward, 180, 181, 182, 185, 201, 214-9, 220, 225.
  Awards, 216.
  Biography, 214.
  Education, 214, 215.
  Journalism career, 215.
  Offices held, 216.
  Pedagogy, 217.
  Publications, 215-6.
  Teaching career, 215.
Gerbner, George, 236, 284.
Germany, 290-1.
Ghiglione, Loren, 17n.
Gillmor, Donald A., 183, 184, 185, 217.
Gitlow v. New York, 179, 181, 222.
Godkin, E.L., 6, 72, 79ff.
Gouldner, Alvin, 170.
Government in the Sunshine Act, 198.
Graber, Doris, 237.
Graduate education, 15-6, 291.
Gratification, 232, 245, 247, 283.
Gray, Richard, 217.
Great Depression, 11, 12, 42.
Great Plains, 214.
Greeley, Horace, 72-3, 79ff, 96, 120, 163.
Greenberg, Bradley S., 265, 322.
Griffith v. Georgia, 210.
Grimes, Frank, 214.
Guide Publications, 100.
Guttman scalogram, 269.

H
Habermas, Jurgen, 123.
Hage, Jerald, 233, 266.
Hale, William G., 181, 189, 209.
Hamilton, Alexander, 111.
Hammond, Charles, 71.

Handbook of Communication Science (Chaffee, Berger), 276.
Harding, Warren G., 93.
Harold L. Nelson Award, 312.
Harrington, H.F., 48.
Hart, Hornell, 132.
Harvard University, 239, 240, 308.
Hastings *Tribune*, 208.
Headlines, 322.
Hearst, William Randolph, 79, 111.
Hegel, Georg, 152.
Heisenberg, Werner, 122.
Higbie, Charles, 50.
High school journalism, 57, 58.
"High Tech and Higher Ed" (Carey), 173.
Higher Ground for Journalism (Drewry), 147.
Historians, 61-115.
  Critics of conservatism, 64-5.
  Defenders of press, 61, 66, 67, 74.
  Ideology of, 62, 63-5, 86, 88, 107, 110, 112, 114.
  Influence of, 66.
  Present-mindedness, 65, 68, 69, 86.
  Professional perspective of, 63, 95.
  Propagandists, 66.
  Relationship to journalism, 61.
  Sociologists as, 66, 86-7, 102-4.
  Weaknesses, 65-7.
History
  Cultural interpretation, 66.
  Developmental interpretation, 62-4, 96, 99.
  Freedom of the press, 62, 64.
  Ideological, 65, 86, 88.
  Methodology, 86-7, 89, 99-100, 104, 296, 299.
  Of ideas, 150.
  Of news, 61-2.
  Progress and, 64, 70, 81, 95.
  Progressive interpretation, 64-5, 88, 106, 110ff.
  Purpose of, 67.
  "Symbolic meaning" interpretation, 66.
  Textbooks, 63, 65.
  Value of, 129.
History of American Journalism (Lee), 68, 69ff, 76.
History of American Magazines, A (Mott), 92-3, 96.
History of the American Newspaper Publishers Association (Emery), 107, 109.
Hitler, Adolph, 149, 165.
Hixson, Richard F., 185.
Hoaxes (MacDougall), 34.
Hochberger, Simon, 19.
Holmes, Oliver Wendell Jr., 188.
Holsinger, Ralph L., 186.
Hoover, Herbert, 93-4.
Hosokawa, Bill, 20.
Hough, George III, 192.
Housman, Robert, 17n.
Hovland, Carl, 122, 229, 231, 232, 236, 247, 291.
"How Communication Works" (Schramm), 241, 242, 243-4, 245,

247.
Hudson, Frederic, 62, 63.
Hudson, Robert, 108.
Hume, David, 151.
Humphrey, Hubert, 110.
Hutchins Commission, 149, 193, 204, 218, 241.
Hyde, Grant, 76.
"Hypodermic needle" theory, 122, 290.
Hypotheses, 122.

I
Ickes, Harold, 11, 64.
Ideas, 156.
Ideological Origins of the American Revolution, The (Bailyn), 114.
Ideology, 63-4, 65, 86, 88, 107, 110, 112, 114, 156, 160.
Imperative of Freedom, The (Merrill), 162, 164.
Improvement of society, 78.
"Increasing Reliability in Content Analysis" (Stempel), 314.
Indiana University, 186, 216, 313.
Individualism, 150, 152, 160-1, 214.
Individuals, role of in history, 85, 102.
Industrial Revolution, 150.
Industrialism, 121.
"'Infantile' vs. the 'Sublime' in Advertising, The" (Stephenson), 306.
Inference, 235.
Influence of media, 79, 145, 157, 282-3.
Information diffusion/flow/gain, 258, 262, 328.
Information theory, 246, 252.
Ink on Paper (Arnold), 57.
Innis, Harold, 124, 168, 169, 171, 173.
Innovation, 28.
Inoculation theory, 237.
Instruction Manual for Law of the Press (Thayer), 202.
Instrumentalism, 121.
International News and the Press (Nafziger), 298.
"International Protection of Rights in News" (Siebert), 191.
Interpersonal communication, 252, 253, 275, 307.
Interpretations of Journalism (Mott, Casey), 138-9.
Interpretative Reporting (MacDougall), 28, 29, 30-2, 49.
  Criticism of, 31.
Interpreting the Church Through Press and Radio (Wolseley), 51.
Intrapersonal communication, 253.
Introduction to Journalism, An (Murphy), 127, 131.
Introduction to Journalism Research, An (Nafziger, Wilkinson), 299.
Introduction to Mass Communication (Emery, Ault, Agee), 110, 112.
Introduction to Mass Communication Research (Nafziger, White), 299-300, 322, 327.
Iowa State University, 186, 201, 221.
Iowa Writers Workshop, 240.

"Is Journalism a Profession?" (Drewry), 144.
Issues, obtrusive and unobtrusive, 283.
Iyengar, Shanto, 282.

J
James, William, 121.
Janowitz, Morris, 269.
Jefferson, Thomas, 94, 95, 111.
Jehovah's Witnesses, 218.
Jensen, Jay, 149-58.
  Biography, 149.
  Education, 149.
  Journalism career, 149.
  Liberalism, 150ff.
  Teaching career, 149.
  Weaknesses of, 157-8.
"Jim dash," 56.
"John Dunlap's 'Packet' And Its Competitors" (Murphy), 131.
John Peter Zenger Award, 199.
Johns Hopkins University, 100.
Johnson, E. Marion, 135.
Johnson, Joseph French, 7.
Jones, Robert L., 136.
Journal of Journalism History, 105.
Journalism Abstracts, 326.
Journalism History Guidebook (Kobre), 105.
Journalism in the United States (Hudson), 62.
Journalism IS Communications (Drewry), 146.
Journalism Monographs, 311.
Journalism Quarterly, 92, 108, 126, 298, 311, 313, 316-7.
Journalistic Escalation (Drewry), 147.
Journalists, response to journalism education, 3, 4, 8, 12, 13, 14, 18, 20, 21, 135.
Journalist's Bookshelf, The (Wolseley), 50.
"Journalists: Born or Made?" (Camp), 7.
Judge, 69.

K
Kansas City *Star*, 57.
Kansas City *Times*, 57.
Kansas State University, 42.
Kao, Anne Li-an, 254.
Kappa Tau Alpha, 92, 127.
  Research award, 93, 188, 192, 199.
Katz, Daniel, 269, 309.
Katzman, Nat, 243.
Kelly, Truman, 308.
Kerlinger, Fred N., 292.
Kielbowicz, Richard, 108-9.
Kinder, Donald R., 282.
Kingsbury, Susan M., 132.
Klapper, Joseph, 152.-3.
Knowledge-gap hypothesis, 236, 244-5, 258, 261ff.
  Criticism of, 264-6.
Kobre, Sidney, 99-105.
  Advocate of press, 105.
  Awards, 105.
Biography, 100.
Developmental historian, 99, 102.
Education, 100.
Journalism career, 100.
Pedagogy, 105.
Present-mindedness, 105.
Publications, 100.
Sociological approach, 102-4.
Teaching career, 101.
Weaknesses as historian, 99-100, 104.
Kostrich, Leslie J., 321.
Krieghbaum, Hillier, 26.
  Axioms of, 41.
  Biography, 42, 44.
  Education, 42, 43.
  Interest in science, 43-4, 45.
  Journalism career, 42, 43.
  Offices held, 43, 45.
  Publications, 43, 45.
  Teaching career, 42-3, 44.
Kuhn, Thomas, 122, 171.

L
Labor, 111.
Lacy, Stephen, 253-4.
Lafferty, John J., 3.
Laissez-faire, 119.
LaMoure *Chronicle*, 308.
Land grant colleges, 14.
Lang, Gladys Engel, 282, 285-6.
Lang, Kurt, 21, 282, 285-6.
Lansing *State Journal*, 55.
Lasswell, Harold, 123, 140, 229, 247, 252, 289, 290, 291, 314.
Lauterer, Jock, 327.
Law of Mass Communications, The (Nelson, Teeter), 183, 220, 222-4.
Law of Newspapers, The (Arthur, Crossman), 189, 209.
Law of the Press, The (Hale, Benson), 189, 209.
Law of the Press (Fisher and Strahan), 209.
Lawhorne, Clifton O., 185.
Lazarsfeld, Paul, 229, 231, 232, 236, 247, 289.
Learning from Television: What the Research Says (Schramm, Chu), 246.
Lee, Alfred McClung, 65, 66, 83-90, 100, 102.
  Awards, 84.
  Biography, 83-4.
  Education, 84.
  Evolutionary theory of, 85-7.
  Ideology, 83, 86, 88.
  Journalism career, 84.
  Progressive historian, 88.
  Sociologist, 83.
  Teaching career, 84.
  Weaknesses as historian, 86-9.
Lee, James Melvin, 63, 68-75, 76, 81, 83, 85.
  Antiquarianism, 69-70.
  Author of first history textbook, 68, 69.
  Biography, 69.
  Death, 75.

Defender of professional journal-ists, 74.
Developmental historian, 70, 71.
Education, 69, 75.
Journalism career, 69.
Offices held, 75.
Present-mindedness, 68, 69, 70.
Professional views, 71.
Publications, 75.
Teaching career, 69.
Lee, Robert E., 3, 120.
Legal Control of the Press (Thayer), 180, 182, 201, 202-4, 209, 210, 220.
Legal research methods, 296, 299.
Legal studies, 179-225.
Lehigh University, 30.
Leonard, Richard, 18n.
Leslie's Magazine, 69.
Levy, Leonard, 66, 221-2.
Lewin, Kurt, 236, 247, 251, 289, 308.
Libel, 183, 210-1, 223.
Liberal arts
  In journalism education, 4, 6, 7, 20, 21, 25, 26, 27, 39, 128, 132, 144.
  Journalism as, 143.
Liberalism, 110, 111, 112, 113, 150ff.
Liberalism, Democracy and the Mass Media (Jensen), 150ff.
Libertarianism, 162-3, 184, 187, 193.
Licensing, 218.
Likert, Rensis, 309.
Lincoln, Abraham, 72.
Lincoln *State Journal*, 208.
Lindley, William, 135.
Linguistic dominance, 174.
Linotype News, 55.
Lippitt, Ronald, 309.
Lippmann, Walter, 137, 153, 282.
Literature, 143.
Litter law, 210.
London University, 302.
Longitudinal research, 294.
Loomis, William W., 181, 189.
Los Angeles *Times*, 280.
Louisiana State University, 159.
Louisville *Courier-Journal*, 57.
Louisville *Times*, 57.
Lowell *Sun*, 57.
Loyola University, 180, 202.
"Ludenic Theory of Newsreading, The" (Stephenson), 306.
Lyle, Jack, 241-2, 243, 270.
Lyman, R.L., 144.

M

MacArthur, Douglas, 149.
Maccoby, Eleanor, 309.
Maccoby, Nathan, 270, 279.
MacDougall, Curtis D., 28, 29-35, 48, 230.
  Biography, 29-30.
  Critic of conservatism, 30.
  Criticism of, 31.
  Death, 35.
  Education, 29.
  Influence of, 32.
  Journalism career, 29-30.
  "New journalism," 30, 31.
  Politics of, 30, 32, 33, 34.

Publications, 30, 33, 35.
Reporter responsibility, 30.
Students of, 32.
Teaching career, 32.
View of education, 35.
Writing style, 34.
MacLean, Malcolm, 231, 233, 249-57, 269, 301, 307, 309.
  Biography, 250.
  Education, 250.
  ICA president, 256.
  Journalism career, 250.
  Methodologist, 254.
  Pedagogy, 255-6.
  Social concern, 256.
  Teaching career, 250-1.
  View of theory, 249.
Madison *Democrat*, 126.
Madison, James, 196.
Magazine journalism, 96, 144.
Magazine World, The (Wolseley), 49-50.
Main Currents in the History of American Journalism (Bleyer), 76, 77.
Malice, 211, 222.
"Man as Symbol Maker" (Jensen), 153-4.
Mann, Thomas, 165.
Marietta College, 239.
Marquette University, 126.
Mars Hill College, 279.
Martin, Ralph K., 275.
Marxism, 112, 120, 124, 150, 157, 173, 174.
Maslow, Abraham, 251.
"Mass Communication" (Tannen-baum), 322.
Mass Communication Law: Cases and Comments (Gillmor, Barron), 183.
Mass Communications (Schramm), 230, 241.
Mass Media and Modern Society (Jensen), 153-4.
Mass Media and National Develop-ment (Schramm), 242, 247.
Masses, 78, 79, 80.
Materialism, 120, 123.
Mathematical Theory of Communi-cation, The (Shannon), 246.
Mayfield, Elizabeth Kay, 237.
Mayo, John.
McAnany, Emile, 243.
McCarthyism, 35.
McCombs, Maxwell, 243, 270, 278-86.
  Biography, 278.
  Education, 278-9.
  Journalism career, 279.
  Teaching career, 279.
McCormick, Robert, 13, 180, 181, 187, 188.
McCoy, Bruce, 135.
McGill University, 320.
McGuire, William, 237, 271.
McLeod, Jack, 236, 264, 265, 268-77, 279.
  Biography, 268.
  Education, 268-9.
  Teaching career, 269.

McLuhan, Marshall, 124, 169, 174, 235, 245.
Mead, George Herbert, 120, 121, 251.
Measurement of Meaning, The (Tannenbaum), 319.
"Measuring the Ethics of American Newspapers" (Murphy), 132-3.
Media Law Reporter, 184.
Media review boards, 45.
Mencken, H.L., 144.
Merganthaler Linotype Co., 55.
Merrill, John, 159-66, 167.
  And individualism, 160ff.
  Biography, 159.
  Education, 159.
  Existential philosophy, 160ff.
  Journalism career, 159.
  Teaching career, 159.
  Weaknesses as philosopher, 163-6.
Merrill, Samuel, 181, 209.
Metaphysics, 120, 156-7.
Methodology, 289ff.
Meyrowitz, Joshua, 237.
Miami University, 126.
Michigan Press Association, 55.
Michigan State University, 55, 192, 251.
Mills, C. Wright, 155, 171.
Milton, John, 137, 151, 184.
Milwaukee *Sentinel*, 77.
Minneapolis *Journal*, 42.
Missouri Press Association, 7, 8-9, 12-3, 216.
Models of communication, 231-2, 236, 243-4, 245, 252-3, 268, 273-6.
Modern American Journalism (Kobre), 101.
Modern Newspaper Design (Arnold), 53, 55-6.
Mondale, Walter, 110.
Monopoly, 120.
Montreal *Herald*, 320.
Moss, Rep. John E., 223.
Mott, Frank Luther, 63, 76, 91-8, 99, 106, 138.
  Awards, 91, 92-3, 96.
  Biography, 92.
  Chronicler, 96.
  Defender of press, 93-4.
  Democracy, views on, 94.
  Developmental historian, 94ff.
  Education, 92.
  Journalism career, 92.
  Journalistic standards, 94-5.
  Narrow perspective, 97.
  Offices held, 92.
  Present-mindedness, 95, 97.
  Publications, 92-3, 94.
  Rank as historian, 96.
  Teaching career, 92.
  Weaknesses, 96-7.
Movable type, 172.
Mowrer, O.H., 308.
Muckraking, 31, 121.
Mullen, James J., 328.
Mullins, Edward, 15n.
Multivariate analysis, 235.
Murphy, Lawrence W., 126-33, 143, 146.

  Biography, 126.
  Defender of journalism education, 128.
  Education, 126.
  Historian, 131-2.
  Journalism career, 126.
  Offices held, 126-7.
  Publications, 127, 131.
  Teaching career, 126.
Mussolini, Benito, 149.
"Myth-making," 138-9.

N
Nader, Ralph, 31.
Nafziger, Ralph, 135, 230, 250, 296-301.
  Awards, 297.
  Biography, 296.
  Creator of methods schism, 296, 299-300.
  Education, 296.
  Journalism career, 296-7.
  Offices held, 298.
  Teaching career, 297.
  Views on research, 299.
Nagpur University, 51.
National Association of Science Writers, 43.
National Commission on the Causes and Prevention of Violence," 155.
National Conference of Editorial Writers, 35.
National Council for Research in Journalism, 78, 92.
National Council on Education for Journalism, 78, 127.
Natt, Ted M., 21.
Natural law, 151.
"Nature of Communication Between Humans, The" (Schramm), 242, 244, 245, 247.
Nayman, Oguz B., 275.
Near, J.M., 187.
Near v. Minnesota, 179, 180, 181, 187, 188, 210, 218.
Nelson, Harold L., 181, 182, 183, 185, 217, 220-5, 279, 326.
  Awards, 222, 224, 225.
  Balancer, 222-3.
  Biography, 220.
  Education, 220.
  Journalism career, 221.
  Libertarian, 220, 222.
  Offices held, 224.
  Publications, 221.
  Teaching career, 221.
Nelson, William Rockhill, 81.
Neo-liberalism, 152ff.
Neo-scholasticism, 153.
Nevins, Allan, 66.
New Deal, 182.
New Horizons in Journalism (Drewry), 145.
New Jersey Press Association, 13.
"New journalism," 30, 31.
New Left interpretation, 113.
New Orleans *Times Picayune*, 13, 279.
New York *Evening Post*, 195.
New York *Herald*, 62, 73, 134.

New York *Herald Tribune*, 180, 195, 198-9.
New York *Sun*, 62, 95.
New York *Times*, 73, 111.
New York Times v. Sullivan, 211.
New York *Tribune*, 72, 120.
New York University, 6, 44, 68, 69, 84.
New York *World*, 71.
Newark *Star Eagle*, 100.
Newcomb, Theodore, 236, 252, 269, 273, 309.
News, 94.
    Coverage, 73, 314-5.
    History of, 61, 62, 70, 71, 73, 78.
News content, theory of, 237.
News Editing (Westley), 310.
News Media and the Law, 184.
News Research Center, 36.
News Research for Better Newspapers (Bush), 37.
News-seeking, 244.
News values, 232-3.
Newspaper Business Management (Thayer), 204.
Newspaper Law (Loomis), 189.
Newspaper Reporting of Public Affairs (Bush), 37-9.
Newspapers, social role of, 145.
Newton, Isaac, 152, 153.
Niebuhr, Reinhold, 241.
Ninth Amendment, 196.
Nixon, Raymond, 253.
Nixon, Richard, 44, 224.
Nixon v. U.S., 198.
Noelle-Neumann, Elizabeth, 122, 123.
North Dakota State University, 297, 308.
Northern Kentucky State College, 256.
Northwestern State College, 159.
Northwestern University, 13, 29, 33, 35, 42, 48, 50-1, 126, 192, 201.

O
Oberlin College, 201.
Obform analysis, 254.
"Objective Theory of the Press, The" (Jensen), 154-5.
Objectivity, 31, 254, 279.
Obscenity, 183, 211.
Ochs, Adolph, 79, 80, 111.
Odell, S. Jack, 159-60.
Ohio University, 318.
O'Keefe, Garrett J., 275.
Olien, Clarice, 253, 258-67.
    Biography, 259.
    Education, 259.
    Teaching career, 259.
Olson, Kenneth, 11.
Omaha *World-Herald*, 297.
Oneonta *Star*, 69.
Open meetings and records, 197, 198.
Oral cultures, 168.
Oral tradition, 169.
Orientation, need for, 283.
"Origins of the Radical Discourse on Cultural Studies in the United States" (Carey), 171.
Osgood, Charles, 231, 319.

Outing Magazine, 69.
Overbeck, Wayne, 186.
Ownership of media, 233, 315-6.
Oxford University, 302.

P
Packard, Vance, 31.
Paisley, Bill, 243.
Pamphlets of the American Revolution (Bailyn), 114.
Panel studies, 294, 327.
Park, Robert, 120, 121, 173, 229.
Parker, Edwin B., 242, 243, 270.
Parrington, Vernon L., 64, 110.
Partisanship, 71, 72.
Party press, 71, 72, 95.
Paterson, James, 209.
Patterson, Joseph Medill, 13, 89.
Paul J. Deutschmann Award, 224, 297, 312.
Payne, George Henry, 85.
Peabody Awards, 142.
Pedagogy, 32, 189-90, 202, 217, 242-3, 267-8.
Pember, Don R., 185.
Pennsylvania State University, 167, 314.
Penny press, 62, 63, 71, 95-6, 131.
People Look at Educational Television, The (Schramm, Lyle, de Sola Pool), 244-5.
People's Right to Know, The (Cross), 196, 199, 200, 210, 223.
Perception, 249, 254, 255.
Perry, Bliss, 239.
Persuasion, 16, 271.
Pertinence, 270, 273, 277.
Peters, Mark D., 282.
Peterson, Paul, 19n.
Peterson, Theodore, 49-50, 153, 191, 241.
Pfaff, Daniel W., 217.
Philadelphia *North American*, 48.
Philadelphia *Times*, 7.
Philosophy, 119ff.
Philosophy and Journalism (Merrill), 159-60.
Photojournalism, 306, 323.
"Picture Selection: An Editorial Game" (MacLean, Kao), 254.
Platt, John, 235, 238.
Play Theory of Mass Communication, The (Stephenson), 304-5.
Polanyi, Michael, 123, 173.
Political independence, 71, 72, 94.
Political parties, 137-8.
Pope, James S., 196, 199.
Positivism, 122, 123.
Pragmatism, 120, 121, 160, 173.
"Predicting a Source's Success in Placing News in the Media" (Donohue, Olien, Tichenor), 253.
Prejean, Blanche, 326-7.
Present-mindedness, 63, 65, 68, 69, 70, 86, 95, 97, 105.
Presidential campaigns, 137-8, 281, 282, 314-5, 328.
Presidents (U.S.), 93-4.
Press and America, The (Emery), 105,

106, 107, 109, 111ff.
Press and Foreign Policy, The (Cohen), 280.
Press and the Constitution, 1931-1947, The (Gerald), 216, 217-8.
Press Congress of the World, 94.
Press in the Contemporary Scene, The (Casey), 139.
Press in Perspective, The (Casey), 140.
Pressures on the Press (Krieghbaum), 44-5.
Prestige press, 314-5.
Primacy, 323.
Primary sources, 89, 96, 114, 131.
"Principles and Standards of Education for Journalism," 11.
Principles of Publicity (Casey), 137.
"Principles of Selection of News Photographs" (Stephenson), 306.
Print cultures. See "Visual cultures."
Printing, 3, 7.
Prior restraint, 179, 188, 210, 224.
Privacy, 203-4, 209, 211, 222.
Privilege, 223.
Problems of Law in Journalism (Swindler), 182, 209-11, 220.
Process and Effects of Mass Communication (Schramm), 230, 231, 241, 242, 245.
"Professional and Nonprofessional Teaching of Journalism" (Murphy), 129.
Professional training, in journalism education, 4, 5, 6.
Professionalization of journalism, 78, 81, 96, 144, 145, 219.
Profit motive, 11-2, 65, 83, 86, 88.
Profitable Newspaper Advertising (Arnold), 57.
Progress, 64, 70, 78, 95, 97, 105, 121, 122, 146, 157.
Progressive interpretation, 64, 88, 106, 110ff.
Progressive reform, 80-1.
Propaganda, 16, 84, 136ff, 289, 290, 291.
Propaganda, Communication, and Public Opinion (Casey), 140.
Property rights, 190-1.
Providence *Journal*, 308.
Psychology, 323.
Public Nuisance Law, 187.
Public meetings and records, 197, 198.
Public opinion, 34, 36, 79.
"Public principle," 223.
Public relations, 19, 121, 140.
Publicity, 137.
"Publisher of perish," 18-9.
Publisher's Auxiliary, 55.
Pulitzer, Joseph, 7-8, 10, 11, 15, 79ff, 96.
Pulitzer Prize, 91, 92, 96, 114, 123.
Pullen, Rick D., 186.
Purpose of media, 64.
"Purposive Communications: A Study of County Agents' Educational Material" (Donohue, Olien, Tichenor), 259-60.

Q-R
Q-Methodology, 123, 254, 302ff.
Criticism of, 303.
Qualitative research, 123, 235.
Quantitative research, 123, 132-3, 289ff.
Quiett, Glenn C., 137.
Radio, 289, 290, 323, 328.
Raymond, Henry, 72, 73, 163.
Readability, 254, 328-9.
"Readability of Wire Stories in Eight News Categories" (Danielson), 329.
"Reader-Interest Survey of Madison, Wisconsin, A" (Nafziger), 300-1.
Readership, 37, 313.
Reading gap, 263.
Reading *Herald-Telegram*, 48.
Reading *Times*, 42.
Reagan, Ronald, 111, 112, 224.
Reality, 170.
Recency, 323.
Red Wing and Its Daily Newspaper (Nafziger), 298-9.
Reed, Sen. James, 187.
Reform, 80, 81.
Reid, Whitelaw, 6, 7.
Relativism, 156.
"Reliability of Six Techniques of Content Analysis of Local Coverage" (Stempel), 314.
Religion, 157.
Religious journalism, 51.
Reporters, 30.
Reporters Committee of Freedom of the Press, 184.
Reporting, 73, 128.
Research
Administrative, 290.
Applied, 18.
Case studies, 294.
Computers in, 294-5.
Content analysis, 289, 292-3.
Critical, 290.
Criticism of, 292, 294.
Divisions of, 16.
Emphasis on, 18, 130, 135-6.
Experiment, 293.
Field studies, 293.
Focus groups, 293-4.
Historical, 66-7, 86-7, 89, 101, 104, 113, 299.
Journalists' response to, 18, 135.
Legal, 184, 217, 296, 299.
Methods, 289ff.
Methodological orthodoxy, 234-5.
Problems in, 18, 66-7.
Public opinion, 36.
Qualitative-quantitative schism, 123, 234, 296ff.
Quantitative, 289, 291, 294.
Social science, 296, 299-300.
Survey methods, 294.
Research Methods in Mass Communication (Westley, Stempel), 310, 316, 327.
Responsibility
Of Individual, 78.
Of press, 77, 149.

Social, 149, 156, 163-4, 193.
Responsibility in Mass Communication (Schramm), 241.
Retraction, 203.
Revolution, American, 114.
Revolutionary press, 95.
Reward theories, 244.
R-factor analysis, 303, 305.
Rhetorical theory, 40.
Right to know, 195ff.
Rights and Privileges of the Press, The (Siebert), 181-2, 189, 209.
Ripon College, 29.
Ritual view of communication, 169, 171, 172, 174.
Rivers, William, 45, 153.
Roberts, Donald, 243.
Roberts, Nancy, 108.
Rogers, Everett, 264.
Rohrer, Daniel M., 185.
Romanticism, 151.
Roosevelt, Franklin, 94.
Rousseau, Jean-Jacques, 151.
Rucker, Bryce, 45.
Ruggles, Lee, 243, 270.
Rutgers University, 13.

S
Saginaw *News*, 55.
Salaries, 20-21.
Sales of books, 105.
Salience, 270, 273-4.
Salisbury, Harrison, 42.
Sampling, 300.
"Sampling Size for Classifying Subject Matter in Dailies" (Stempel), 314.
San Francisco *Examiner*, 107.
San Jose *Mercury-News*, 325.
Sanders, Keith, 249, 251.
Sartre, Jean Paul, 163.
Saturday Evening Post v. Butts, 211.
Schemas, 277.
"School of Journalism, The" (Reid), 6.
"Schools of Journalism, Past and Future" (Murphy), 130.
Schramm, Wilbur, 36, 45, 191, 229, 230, 231, 232, 236-7, 239-48, 270.
    Biography, 239.
    Criticisms of, 244, 245, 246-7.
    Death, 241.
    Education, 239-40.
    "Father" of communication theory, 247-8.
    Journalism career, 239.
    Pedagogy, 242-3.
    Publications, 241.
    Synthesizer of theories, 245-6.
    Teaching career, 240-1.
    Theoretical ideas, 243-4.
    Use of metaphor, 247.
Schudson, Michael, 66, 237.
Schuneman, R. Smith, 109.
Schuylkill *News*, 48.
Schuylkill Seminary, 48.
Schwartz, James W., 225.
Schwartz, Thomas, 184.
Science, 124, 132, 156.
    Journalism as, 129, 132.

Science and the Mass Media (Krieghbaum), 43-4.
Science journalism, 43, 44-5.
Science news, 260-1.
Scientific method, 231.
Scientism, 156.
Scripps, E.W., 96.
Scripps-Howard, 137.
Seashore, Carl E., 242.
Seattle *Post-Intelligencer*, 134.
Secondary sources, 89, 101, 114.
Secrecy, 195ff, 222.
Seldes, George, 64.
Self, 152-3, 160.
Semantic differential, 319, 323, 328.
Sendex, 323.
Sensationalism, 79, 80, 323.
Shannon, Claude, 246, 252.
Sharkey, Joseph E., 131.
Shaw, Donald, 225, 254, 278-86.
    Biography, 279.
    Education, 279.
    Journalism career, 279.
    Teaching career, 279.
Sheffield *Times*, 149.
Shield laws, 211, 223.
Shoemaker, Pamela J., 237.
Sidis v. F-R Publishing, 209.
Sidney Kobre Award, 105.
Siebert, Fredrick, 180, 181, 182, 184, 185, 187-94, 203, 209, 217, 219, 220, 222, 225, 230, 241.
    Awards, 188, 192.
    Biography, 187.
    Education, 187, 188.
    Journalism career, 187.
    Legal philosophy, 189.
    Offices held, 192.
    Pedagogy, 189-90.
    Publications, 191-2.
    Teaching career, 188, 192.
Sigma Delta Chi, 36, 84, 199, 202, 205, 297.
    Research award, 93, 107, 202, 216, 222, 297.
Simpson College, 92.
Smith, Adam, 119, 163.
Smith, Brainard, 7.
Smith, Bruce, 140.
Smith, Henry Ladd, 107.
Smith, John, 280.
Smythe, Ted Curtis, 108.
Snow, C.P., 242.
Social forces, 85.
Social Responsibility of the Press, The (Gerald), 218-9.
Social responsibility theory, 149, 156.
Social science, 229, 230, 240.
    In journalism education, 4, 37, 131-2, 135, 136, 141.
    Research methods, 299-300.
Social structure, 258, 260ff.
Socialism, 111, 114.
Society for the Study of Social Problems, 84.
Society, nature of, 150-1.
Society of Professional Journalists. See "Sigma Delta Chi."

Sociology, 83, 86-7, 102-4.
Socio-orientation, 271, 273.
Soloski, John, 185.
"Some Notes on the Course in Law of
   the Press" (Siebert), 190.
"Some Observations on Q-Technique"
   (Stephenson), 305.
South Bend *News-Times*, 42.
Southern Illinois University, 186.
Southern Newspaper Publishers As-
   sociation, 13.
Space-binding media, 168, 172, 173.
Spalding, Willard, 309.
Spencer, Dale, 186.
Spengler, Oswald, 87.
Sport Writing of Today (Murphy, 127,
   131.
Sports journalism, 324.
Springfield *Republican*, 202.
St. Louis *Post-Dispatch*, 208.
St. Louis *Star-Times*, 30, 208, 215.
Stamm, Keith R., 275.
Standardization of news, 315.
Stanford University, 31, 36, 153, 232,
   240, 259, 270, 278, 279, 312, 320,
   325.
Stars and Stripes, 54-5.
Steffens, Lincoln, 31.
Steigleman, Walter A., 186.
Stempel, Guido, 313-8.
   Biography, 313.
   Education, 313-4.
   Journalism career, 313.
Stephens, E.W., 8.
Stephens, W.W., 12-3.
Stephenson, William, 123, 251, 254,
   302-6.
   Biography, 302.
   Education, 302.
   Publications, 303.
   Teaching career, 302.
Stevens, John D., 185.
Stevenson, Adlai, 314.
Stone, Vernon, 271.
Story of Human Communication, The
   (Schramm), 241.
Strong inference, 235, 238.
Structural approach, 236, 258ff.
Students
   And professors, 32, 106, 108-9, 115,
      205, 217, 243, 322.
   Numbers of, 19.
   Shortcomings, 20.
*Study of Behavior, The: Q-Technique
   and Its Methodology* (Stephenson),
   303-4.
Subjectivity, 123.
Suci, George, 319.
Sumner, W.G., 88, 89.
Sunday newspapers, 89.
Superstition and the Press
   (MacDougall), 34.
Supreme Court, U.S., 179, 182, 183,
   218, 222, 223.
Survey research, 294, 328.
Swindler, William F., 180, 181, 182,
   185, 189, 201, 202, 207-13.
   Biography, 207.
   Education, 207, 212.

Journalism career, 208.
Offices held, 212.
Publications, 208, 212.
Teaching career, 207-8.
"Symbolic meaning," 66.
Symbolism, 170, 172.
Syntax, 323.
Syracuse University, 51, 52, 57, 186,
   312.
Systems theory, 262.

T
Tannenbaum, Percy, 231, 269, 270,
   279, 319-24.
   Biography, 319-20.
   Education, 320.
   Teaching career, 320.
Taylor, Wilson, 131, 254.
Teachers, 26.
   As journalists, 5.
   As scholars, 5, 15, 22, 36.
   Defenders of press, 15, 22, 46, 61,
      67, 74-5, 93-4.
   Ideology, 63.
   Professional perspectives of, 63,
      94-5.
   Qualifications of, 13-4, 15, 17, 35,
      143.
   Versatility of, 5.
   Weaknesses of, 5.
*Techniques and Problems of Theory
   Construction in Sociology* (Hage),
   233, 266.
Technology, 103, 122, 124, 157, 172,
   173, 174, 190-1.
Teeter, Dwight, 183, 185, 186, 220,
   225.
Television, 232, 234, 242, 272-3, 279,
   321, 323, 328.
Television and Test Scores
   (Schramm), 247.
*Television in the Lives of Our Chil-
   dren* (Schramm, Lyle, Parker), 232,
   241-2, 244, 245, 247, 270.
Telos, 165.
"Ten Tests of a News Story" (Murphy),
   127-8, 131.
Terkel, Studs, 30.
Texas, 214, 215.
Texas A&M University, 159.
Texas Tech University, 221.
Textbooks, 29.
   History, 63, 64, 65, 66, 68, 69-70, 76,
      106.
   Introduction to mass communica-
      tion, 49.
   Research methods, 299.
Thayer, Frank B., 180, 181, 182, 185,
   201-6, 209, 211.
   Awards, 202.
   Biography, 201.
   Education, 201, 202.
   Journalism career, 202.
   Offices held, 202.
   Publications, 206.
   Showmanship, 205.
   Students of, 205.
   Teaching career, 201, 202.
Theology, 119.

Theories of Cognitive Consistency: A Sourcebook (Tannenbaum), 320-1.
Theory, 229ff.
  Agenda setting as, 284-5.
  Audience, 232.
  Critical, 233.
  Definition of, 229.
  Effects, 231.
  Elements of, 233.
  Funding for, 233-4.
  In history, 85, 87-8, 90.
  In journalism curriculum, 4, 15, 16, 21.
  Models, 231-2.
  Needs, 237-8.
  Of news value, 232-3.
  Systems, 262.
  Two-step flow, 307.
  Weaknesses of, 233-6.
"They Saw a Game" (Hostorf, Cantril), 254.
Tichenor, Phillip, 243, 253, 258-67.
  Biography, 259.
  Education, 259.
  Teaching career, 259.
Time-binding media, 168.
Time Inc., 221.
Tipton *Advertiser*, 92.
Toch, Hans, 254.
Tort law, 210.
Tradition, 103.
Trager, Robert, 186.
Transactional view of perception, 254-5.
Transcendentalism, 120, 163.
Transmission view of communication, 169, 170, 172.
Trend studies, 294.
Truman, Harry, 94.
Truth, 122.
Tuchman, Gaye, 233, 237.
Tucker, Willis, 49.
Tulane University, 13, 278.
Turned-On TV/Turned-Off Voters (Tannenbaum, Kostrich), 321-2.
Turner, Frederick Jackson, 64, 110.
Two Rivers *Chronicle*, 29.
Two-step flow theory, 307.
Typography, 57, 323.

U
"Uncertainty Principle," 122.
Understanding, 274, 277.
Understanding Public Opinion (MacDougall), 33-4.
United Press, 30, 42, 107.
University College (Dublin), 167.
University of Arizona, 199.
University of California, Berkeley, 107, 110, 221, 302, 320.
University of California, Los Angeles, 269, 279.
University of Chicago, 92, 302.
University of Colorado, 33, 251.
University of Georgia, 13, 142, 146, 147.
University of Hawaii, 240.
University of Idaho, 207-8.
University of Illinois, 9-10, 17, 123,

126, 149, 153, 167, 180, 187, 188, 192, 240, 320.
University of Iowa, 17, 92, 159, 167, 230, 240, 249, 251ff, 302m 325.
University of Kansas, 84, 201.
University of Kentucky, 312.
University of Maine, 199.
University of Michigan, 84, 269, 271, 309, 312, 320.
University of Minnesota, 16, 17, 107, 108, 135, 136, 141, 181, 185, 215, 220, 250, 252, 258, 259, 291, 297, 312.
University of Missouri, 8-9, 10, 12-3, 15, 17, 92, 159, 180, 185, 199, 207, 215, 223, 302.
University of Montana, 134.
University of Nebraska, 208, 212.
University of New Hampshire, 250.
University of North Carolina, 279, 325.
University of North Dakota, 126, 131.
University of Oregon, 44, 134, 188.
University of Pennsylvania, 6-7, 320.
University of Pittsburgh, 84.
University of Redlands, 269.
University of Rhode Island, 167.
University of South Carolina, 221.
University of Southern California, 320.
University of Texas, 215, 216, 279, 326.
University of Utah, 216.
University of Washington, 21, 108, 134, 302.
University of Wisconsin, 7, 10, 17, 29, 30, 36, 42, 77, 126, 134, 135, 141, 180, 185, 187, 188, 201, 202, 205, 221, 230, 250, 251, 252, 268, 269, 270, 279, 296, 297, 309, 311-2, 314, 320, 325.
University of Wisconsin-Milwaukee, 256.
Urbanism, 121.
"Useful Tools for Interpreting Newspaper Readership Data" (Nafziger, MacLean, Engstrom), 301.
Utilitarianism, 119.

V-W
Values, 160.
Vietnam, 63, 111, 114.
"Vietnam: A Television History," 112.
Villard, Oswald, 11, 64.
Violence, 155, 232, 234, 272-3.
Virginia Commonwealth University, 57.
Virginia Gazette, 3.
Visual cultures, 168.
Wackman, Dan, 271.
Wade, Serena, 243.
Waldrop, Gayle, 209.
Wallace, Henry, 33.
Warren court, 183, 222.
Washington and Lee University, 3, 13, 75.
Washington *Post*, 123, 223.
Washington State University, 201, 259.

Washington University, 180, 207.
Watchdog function, 262.
Watergate, 63.
Watson, Jeanne, 309.
Watterson, Henry, 6.
Wayne State University, 84.
Weaver, David, 283.
Weaver, Warren, 246.
Wells, Thomas B., 144.
Weltanschauung, 150, 151, 153.
Wesleyan University, 69.
West Texas State University, 180, 214.
West Virginia University, 312.
Westley, Bruce, 131, 233, 251, 252, 269, 270, 307-12, 316.
    Awards, 312.
    Biography, 307-8.
    Education, 308.
    Journalism career, 308.
    Offices held, 311.
    Teaching career, 308-9, 310-1.
Westley-MacLean model, 231-2, 236, 244, 249, 251, 252-3, 260, 310.
What Cheer *Patriot*, 92.
Whipple, Leon, 69.
White, Andrew, 6-7.
White, David M., 296, 299.
White, Horace, 8.
Whitehead, Alfred North, 153, 157, 239-40.
Wiggins, J.R., 196.
Wilcox, Walter, 192, 270, 278.
Wilhoit, G. Cleveland, 326.
Wilkinson, Marcus M., 299.
Will, Allen Sinclair, 144.
William and Mary College, 212.
Williams, Ben Ames, 144.
Williams, Raymond, 171, 173, 174.
Williams, Walter, 9, 12-3, 215.
Wilson, Albert Frederick, 69.
Wilson, Woodrow, 93.
Wisconsin State Journal, 300, 308.
Wolseley, Roland, 26, 47-52.
    Biography, 47-8.
    Education, 48.
    Journalism career, 48.
    Offices held, 51.
    Pacifism, 47, 50.
    Publications, 52.
    Religion, 47, 51.
    Teaching career, 51.
Woodland *Record,* 149.
World War I, 289.
World War II, 16, 54-5, 94, 140, 141, 149, 291, 298.
Wright, Jay B., 186.
Writing for the Religious Market (Wolseley), 51-2.

X-Y-Z
Yale University, 84, 231.
Yellow journalism, 7, 209.
Yellow Press and Gilded Age Journalism, The (Kobre), 101.
Young, Alfred, 221.
Zajonc, Robert, 309.
Zanesville, Ohio, 316.
Zucker, Harold Gene, 283.

For Product Safety Concerns and Information please contact our EU
representative GPSR@taylorandfrancis.com Taylor & Francis Verlag GmbH,
Kaufingerstraße 24, 80331 München, Germany

Printed and bound by CPI Group (UK) Ltd, Croydon, CR0 4YY

01/05/2025

01858376-0001